$\mathcal{A}$ VISITOR'S GUIDE
to the Colonial & Revolutionary

South.

A VISITOR'S GUIDE
to the Colonial & Revolutionary

INTERESTING SITES TO VISIT
Lodging ❋ Dining ❋ Things to Do

Includes

Virginia, North Carolina, South Carolina, Georgia,
Florida, Alabama, Louisiana, Mississippi,
Tennessee, Kentucky, and Washington, D.C.

Patricia & Robert Foulke

The Countryman Press
Woodstock, Vermont

ISBN 978-0-88150-690-7

Book design by Joseph Kantorski
Composition by Eugenie S. Delaney
Cover photograph of Historic Jamestown © Pat & Chuck Blackley
Maps by Paul Woodward, © The Countryman Press
Interior photographs by the authors unless otherwise specified

"Chowning's Tavern Brunswick Stew" and "Syllabubs" recipes on p. 41 reprinted from *The Williamsburg Cookbook,* published by the Colonial Williamsburg Foundation. Reprinted with permission. "Tomato Cobbler" recipe on p. 52 reprinted with permission of The Mount Vernon Inn, Mount Vernon, VA. "Mitchie Tavern Corn Bread" recipe on p. 73 reprinted from *A Taste of the 18th Century* by permission of the Mitchie Tavern, Charlottesville, VA. "Everlasting Syllabub" recipe on p. 106 excerpted from *The Governor's Table, Two Centuries of Cookery at Tryon Palace,* by permission of Tryon Palace Historic Sites and Gardens, New Bern, NC. "She-Crab Soup," "Benne (Sesame) Seed Wafers," and "Frogmore Stew" recipes on p. 145 reprinted by permission of the Charleston Area CVB, www.charlestoncvb.com, Charleston SC. "Louisiana Seafood Gumbo" recipe on p. 239 reprinted by permission of Chef Patrick Mould, Louisiana Culinary Enterprises Inc., www.louisianaschoolofcooking.com, Lafayette, LA. "Galatoire's Shrimp Rémoulade" recipe on p. 247 from *Galatoire's Cookbook,* reprinted by permission of Galatoire's, New Orleans, LA. "Crawfish Chowder from Monmouth Plantation" recipe on p. 258 reprinted by permission from Monmouth Plantation, Natchez, MS. "Shaker Lemon Pie" recipe on p. 301 reprinted by permission of the Inn at Shaker Village, Pleasant Hill, Harrodsburg, KY.

Published by The Countryman Press, PO Box 748, Woodstock, VT 05091
Distributed by W. W. Norton & Company, Inc., 500 Fifth Avenue, New York, NY 10110

Printed in the United States of America

10 9 8 7 6 5 4 3 2 1

Contents

Introduction

This book, *A Visitor's Guide to the Colonial & Revolutionary South,* is the third of three related guides, completing the Eastern seaboard series begun with the previously published *Visitor's Guide to Colonial & Revolutionary New England* and *Visitor's Guide to Colonial & Revolutionary Mid-Atlantic America.* Each can be enjoyed and used by travelers independently, but there are many links between them. As new settlers arrived from Europe and those already here moved from colony to colony, they spread along the eastern coast and began to move across the mountains into the Ohio country and both up from the Gulf Coast and down the Mississippi Valley into the interior South. Overcoming obstacles in culture and economic interests, they eventually combined to fight the Revolutionary War and create the Constitution that firmly united them.

People who travel walk through human history, whether they are conscious of it or not. In this book we hope to enhance the pleasure of your travel along the eastern seaboard of the United States by developing and refining a sense of place. Heightened awareness of what happened where we walk now and of whose footsteps preceded ours satisfies not only curiosity but also a natural longing to be connected with our surroundings.

Those who profess to live only in the present—a persistent myth in American popular culture—forget how disturbed they are when revisiting childhood sites that have changed almost beyond recognition. Constructing the past, and often idealizing it in the process, creates an orientation in time that is inseparable from the sense of place that defines who we are, both individually and collectively. Just as we rewrite our own internal autobiographies year by year, each generation recasts the past in its own molds.

Colonial and Revolutionary history is a kaleidoscope of movement and change, but it is clearly tied to many places that still remain. Rediscovering those places and expanding their meaning is the aim of this book and its predecessors. They are not designed for committed antiquarians or for those who reduce the past to a prologue of the present. They are designed for travelers with a persistent curiosity, those who like to build contexts around what they see.

This book explores colonial and Revolutionary sites, forts, government buildings, churches, inns, houses, historic districts, museums and living history museums, as well as reenactments and festivals throughout the ten southern states and

Washington, D.C. The time span begins in the 1500s with Spanish and French exploration and settlement and extends into the early 1800s as Spain, France, Britain, and the newborn United States struggled to control the South.

Our series on colonial and Revolutionary America combines the features of travel guides and historical narratives to re-create the conditions and ambience of colonial life for travelers and armchair travelers alike. As avid travelers of both sorts ourselves, we hope to bring you a vivid sense of place, time, and character whether you go on the road or stay at home.

Some of the stories are about historical figures you may already know, and others may tickle your fancy. You may enjoy reliving trips already taken, or you may be considering a new venture and want specific information on potential activities and sites within various regions.

A time line at the beginning of each chapter sets the stage for your personal orientation. An introduction describes the founding and development of each colony. Then the focus shifts to places that can still be seen by visitors who want to walk into their heritage to understand it better. Throughout the remainder of each chapter the focus remains on specific places, linking each town and building or site with the events that occurred there. In some cases we may mention the dates of early settlement in a village even if there is little or nothing left to see except the topography. In other cases the process of expanding and modernizing buildings has left a remnant of a colonial home or inn intact after 200 years or more of addition and change. Those with observant eyes may be able to reconstruct what a place might have looked like in the colonial era and get some sense of how its inhabitants lived.

We emphasize both memorializing important political and military events and the underlying context in which they occurred, so the book includes material on the social and cultural history of everyday life—architecture, clothing, food, transportation, occupations, religious practices, customs, folklore, and the like. Some early groups of colonists left Europe and endured the hardships of living in the wilderness of the New World to attain religious freedom and maintain their own cultures. Sometimes those cultures were challenged by later immigrants who eventually managed to deprive them of the vote. In other cases the colonists were constrained by proprietors interested in the profit of the company that financed their start in the New World, as evidenced in the early history of Virginia and Carolina.

Thus the idea of a quintessential colonial America is itself more a convenience for historians than a reality. In fact there were many disparate settlements that gradually and often reluctantly banded together for limited common purposes. Since the southern colonies were quite diverse in national origin, topography, and economic activity, with peoples drawn from different ethnic, regional, and religious traditions in Europe, the story has to be retold for each within the larger framework of American expansion. The process of their amalgamation lasted through the Revolution and beyond, eliciting much controversy and sometimes bumptious behavior. Regionalism, by no means dead today, persisted throughout the colonial and Revolutionary eras and blocked many attempts at cooperation among the colonies. Incompatible economic and social systems, especially those based on slaveholding in many parts of the southern colonies, had to be bridged by compromise in creating and adopting the Constitution. The ultimate failure of those compromises led to the Civil War.

Also, many early European attempts to establish colonies in America were dismal failures, often because the entrepreneurs and adventurers who came were bent on exploiting the new land. Those with money to invest in shares were not used to hard work and often ill equipped for the rigors of living in the wilderness. Some of these marginal ventures in the South, especially those based on profits from the fur trade, were evanescent, while others suffered instability through the interference of European powers. Unlike colonies in New England or the Mid-Atlantic, control of Florida and Louisiana bounced back and forth between Spain, France, and England. Among the settlements that survived and prospered, some were abandoned later as economic or political conditions changed. Permanence, order, and stability were envisioned in royal land grants but seldom achieved in the proprietary charters given to some southern colonies.

One of the destabilizing forces was the constant flow in and out of colonies. People uprooted from their European homelands to escape religious persecution, political suppression, or the devastation of wars continued to migrate within and between the colonies, searching for better land or other opportunities. Many moved on simply to find a new place with topography reminiscent of their native regions, whether flat land, rolling hills, mountains, or river valleys.

The cultural diversity that we prize today also fragmented American experience. Succeeding waves of immigrants—English Puritans, French Huguenots, Spanish Catholics, German Mennonites, Moravians, and Lutherans, Welsh Quakers, Scotch-Irish Presbyterians—clung together in enclaves united by religious principles, ethnic origins, language, and folk traditions. They maintained their identity through forms of worship and customs from home, precious objects from the past, Christmas or festival decorations, and clothing worn on special occasions.

Colonial America, then, is no single fabric but a patchwork quilt of many pieces, each with its own distinctive character and design. As you explore its many wonderful places, keep an eye out for change, instability, transience, variety, and anomaly, and be prepared for surprises. During our research for this book, most of the generalizations we had harbored from American history courses were shattered, to be replaced by sharper images and a keener sense of the many stories that are never fully or conclusively told. When you discard preconceptions and look closely at the places you visit, you too will begin rewriting colonial history in your own mind.

Trip Planning

We have grouped places you may want to visit geographically rather than chronologically, since you will be traveling in literal space and imaginative time. Each colony has its unique character, and we have tried to emulate that in the order of presentation.

Sometimes we choose to begin with the earliest settlement, branching out in various directions to follow people as they moved to new locations; in other cases we are more strictly geographical, moving from the sea inland or along the coast, according to patterns of migration.

In no case do we survey the whole state that developed from the original colony, for several reasons. Among them, the most important is the limited transportation available to settlers. Water was the primary means of movement, especially along larger navigable rivers like the Potomac, Rappahannock, York, Cape Fear, Savannah, St. Johns, Alabama, Mississippi, Ohio, and Tennessee.

Settlement clung to these waterways throughout most of the 17th and early 18th century and slowly moved to other inland areas with the development of roads during the 18th century. Even so, only small portions of the southern colonies had been settled before 1760.

Although the colonial settlements of particular interest are listed within their current states and grouped geographically, we cannot pretend to establish travel patterns that will match each reader's interests and timetable. Some may want to spend a week along the Potomac and Rappahannock, while others will shoot through a string of cities in the same time. Therefore we do not suggest stock itineraries that "cover" the colonial high points in any region, though any reader so inclined could construct one from this book. Most people will want to browse through a region without a rigid schedule, pausing to enjoy the unexpected glimpses of daily life two or three centuries ago.

The Internet can provide you with valuable information if you separate out the advertorials luring people to specific sites or places. Some Web sites of regional and town tourist authorities are very helpful, and links may provide more detail. Yet guidebooks like this one are the most efficient starting place for objective and informed descriptions of the places you may want to visit, with follow-up on the Web to check seasons and opening hours of sites, special exhibits and events, and other current information. Because many historic sites are staffed by volunteers, their hours and seasons are subject to frequent change. It is always wise to call ahead or check the Web site while planning your trip.

For the latest updates contact the state tourist offices or local convention and visitors bureaus that offer detailed maps of towns and regions, guides to historic sites, locations for outdoor recreation, and lists of accommodations and restaurants. Such offices also have calendars of festivals and special events that you may want to work into your travel plans. We list some of the traditional festivals, but their dates change, and some are not held every year, so it is always wise to check before making your plans. For your convenience, we list addresses, telephone numbers, and Web sites (when available) of state, regional, and town tourist offices.

Accommodations and Restaurants

In a country where plentiful wood was the primary building material, restricting suggestions for lodging and food to establishments housed in authentic colonial-era structures makes little sense, since most of these buildings have rotted away or burned down—you would be out in the cold and hungry in many regions of historic interest.

But you can find wonderful accommodations from former eras for an overnight stay if you are not too fussy about the date the structure was first built. This policy makes sense for another reason: Many inns and houses grew with the trade or the family as addition upon addition formed an elongated T at the back of the original square or rectangular structure. Those who restore such buildings have to decide which era will set the pattern. Architectural purists may reject the additions that kept the house alive and full of people, but social historians understand such processes of growth and adaptation. Discriminating travelers usually find colonial, Georgian, Federal, or Victorian lodgings preferable to larger but less interesting modern hotel and motel rooms, so we list the former, but seldom the latter, unless there is a special reason to do so.

Restaurants present another problem not so easily resolved. Only a handful of inns have survived from the colonial era, and most of them serve a mélange of contemporary cuisines with a few colonial specialties. Others listed are located in authentic historic buildings or have succeeded in recreating the ambience of former eras. Although we have at some time enjoyed a meal in the restaurants we list, in no case can we guarantee the current quality of the food. Menus change by the season and the year, and good chefs are notoriously peripatetic.

We do not pretend to be comprehensive in our suggestions for a pleasant place to spend the night or eat a good meal. We like the establishments we list but know there are many others of equal quality that we have not yet discovered. For your convenience, we list the phone numbers and Web sites of recommended inns, B&Bs, and restaurants so you can make reservations and get current information.

Acknowledgments

In the research for this volume, which involved many months of reading, as well as extended travel to colonial and Revolutionary sites in the South, we found ourselves mentally rewriting and extending the history parceled out to us in high school and college. Raised closer to the Canadian border than the Gulf of Mexico, and longtime residents of New England and New York, we had much to learn about the volatile settlement and resettlement of the South under different flags, as well as the course of the crucial southern campaign in the closing years of the Revolution. Again, as in researching our previous volumes on New England and the Mid-Atlantic in this series, we began to fully appreciate the fragility of the American cause during that war and the remarkable bravery and persistence of those who pursued independence against heavy odds. These are stories that need to be told and retold, not only in books but in visits to the historical sites that bring them alive.

We are grateful for the many persons who helped us plan our travels, provided maps, arranged appointments, and suggested places to visit that we had not yet discovered. They include directors and staffs of local and regional visitor bureaus and chambers of commerce, media specialists in state tourist authorities, public-relations representatives and guides at historic sites, and a host of others who went out of their way to give us information and lead us to important places in their communities. In a final burst of research to revisit places we knew and see others for the first time, we embarked on a monthlong trip of five thousand miles. In many memorable ways, we rediscovered the reality of southern hospitality, which in our minds deserves its legendary fame.

We also thank Kermit Hummel, editorial director of the Countryman Press, for his interest in publishing this series of heritage tourism volumes on the colonial and Revolutionary eras—New England, the Middle Atlantic states, and the South. Managing editor Jennifer Thompson has demonstrated both understanding of the complexity of the subjects and patience as the texts developed. And we especially thank editor Glenn Novak for his meticulous attention to detail, knowledge of history, and substantive contributions to the text. Throughout the series he has been skeptical of questionable generalizations, persistent in helping us solve historical puzzles, and a willing collaborator wherever we missed something important. Never before in thirty years of working with editors have we had such a pleasant and productive experience.

Virginia

Historical Introduction
to the
Virginia Colony

Three English ships, the *Susan Constant,* under Christopher Newport, the *Godspeed,* under Bartholomew Gosnold, and the *Discovery,* under Captain Sicklemore (alias Ratcliffe), left Blackwall docks on the River Thames in December 1606 and headed out to sea. After a four-month voyage via the Canary Islands and the West Indies, they coasted into Chesapeake Bay late in April 1607. Captain Newport, as the leader of the group, and 143 men had arrived to settle in the New World. The ships were heavily laden with food, ale, wine, muskets, gunpowder, farm equipment, and tools for building houses.

Their arrival to found a colony was not unprecedented. English voyagers—Drake, Hawkins, Cavendish, Frobisher—had been exploring coastal waters of the new continent ever since John Cabot had first planted a flag in Newfoundland more than a century earlier. During the latter years of the Elizabethan Age, London merchants became increasingly interested in discovering and exploiting the resources of the land. Spanish control of American colonies rich in gold whetted England's appetite for colonization, and the defeat of the Spanish Armada in 1588 made overseas adventures seem more possible. A decade earlier Sir Humphrey Gilbert's attempt to settle Newfoundland had failed, based on the false premise that, at nearly the same latitude, its climate would resemble England's. When Queen Elizabeth granted Sir Walter Raleigh a patent to found a colony named for her in 1585, his two attempts to establish it on Roanoke Island also failed, leading to the mysterious "lost colony." But the definition of "Virginia" at that time was vast and vague, stretching from what is now Maine to North Carolina.

Statue of Thomas Jefferson in the Jefferson Hotel in Richmond

In October 2007 we visited Otley Hall, in Suffolk, England, where Bartholomew Gosnold, as the "prime mover" of the Jamestown voyage (according to George Percy writing in 1608), had used his family connections to promote the enterprise. His wife's cousin, Sir Thomas Smythe, who had made a fortune in London and who became treasurer of the First Virginia Company, organized the funding. Gosnold used Otley Hall, seat of his uncle, to interview the 104 settlers and 55 crew, including John Smith of Norfolk. (Smith was a tenant farmer's son from Lincolnshire who had been promoted to captain for his valor in battles on the Continent.)

Gosnold's role in 1606 was also based on his previous voyage. He had already led a colonizing expedition to what was then northern Virginia, pioneering the fast direct route (forty-nine days), in 1602 as captain of the *Concord*. He had rounded the tip of Cape Cod and named it, as well as naming Martha's Vineyard for his daughter, who had died at age two. The twenty settlers had tried to establish a trading post on the Elizabeth Islands but decided to return home with the ship, discouraged by lack of food and Indian hostility. Both from this experience and his work in organizing the expedition, Gosnold was the expected choice for command, but shortly before sailing, company politics led to the appointment of Christopher Newport as admiral of the fleet.

Saga of the Jamestown Settlement

Jamestown would become the first permanent English settlement in the New World, but its survival was in doubt throughout its first years and sporadically afterward. The first problem was site selection. When the colonists reached the Virginia coast on April 26, they reassembled the shallop that Gosnold had brought in pieces in the hold of the *Godspeed* and landed on both Chesapeake capes, naming them Henry and Charles.

After exploring the lower bay, the fleet sailed up the James River (naming it for their king), to scout for sites far enough from the sea to give them time to fend off any Spanish raids, as their instructions from the company advised. On May 13 they decided to settle on a peninsula roughly two miles long and a mile wide,

---

VIRGINIA *Time Line*

1553	**1585**	**1587**	**1606**
The London Company of Merchant Adventurers of England for the Discovery of Lands Unknown is organized	Queen Elizabeth knights Walter Raleigh and makes him governor of the new territory named Virginia	Raleigh sends an expedition to settle in the Chesapeake, but it does not get beyond Roanoke Island	King James I grants a charter to the Virginia Company for colonization

---

partly because deep water there allowed the ships to be brought to the riverbank for unloading.

In other respects there were severe disadvantages to the site. The water was brackish, with no freshwater springs, and the colonists had to cope with surrounding mosquito-infested swamps in a hot, humid climate. The site was very near a deserted Paspaheg Indian settlement, in the middle of the powerful Algonquian-speaking confederacy ruled by a chief named Powhatan. Problems with the Indians developed early. They chose to attack the fort when Newport had taken a party of men upriver, and were dispersed only when Gosnold fired a cannon on the *Godspeed*. In spite of these difficulties, the colonists managed to build a stockade and later added fifteen houses, a church, and a storehouse inside. Jamestown was born.

When they were safely established within the fort in late June, and the Indians had offered peace, Captain Newport sailed for England. Yet Jamestown's survival, like that of the earlier, abandoned Popham and Roanoke colonies, remained in question. The colonists suffered from lack of potable water, sickness, and worms in their grain. Luckily the Indians saved them from starvation with supplies of corn, bread, meat, and fish. A severe drought, described in recent climate studies as the worst in 800 years, added to their lack of food, since their Indian providers were also suffering from shortages. Famine and swamp fever carried off thirteen settlers in August, and by the middle of September forty-six had died. One of the survivors, George Percy, wrote, "There were never Englishmen left in a foreigne countrey in such miserie as wee were in this new discovered Virginia."

Among the victims was Bartholomew Gosnold, who died in Jamestown on August 22. Conflicts among the councilors appointed by the Virginia Company, as well as uncertain and changing leadership, exacerbated the colonists' problems throughout the remainder of 1607. Many of the original colonists were gentlemen who had not worked with their hands. They needed farmers, laborers, and skilled artisans, men who knew how to plant crops and build houses as well as hunt and fish. When Captain Newport returned with more supplies and additional colonists at the beginning of January, only thirty-eight of the original settlers had survived. And half of the newcomers were gentlemen—more mouths to

1607	**1608**	**1609**	**1612**
The *Susan Constant, Godspeed,* and *Discovery* land at what will become Jamestown	By his own report, Captain John Smith is captured by Powhatan and saved by Pocahontas; fire destroys the fort; Smith explores Chesapeake Bay and tidewater rivers	The "starving time" begins, leaving only 60 of 490 Jamestown settlers alive	John Rolfe introduces West Indian tobacco to Virginia

feed with dwindling food. A few days later the fort burned, destroying ammunition and provisions in the storehouse.

The successive difficulties of the summer and fall had propelled Captain John Smith into an informal leadership role. Self-confident and outspoken, on the voyage out he was in trouble with the future first president of the colony, Edward Maria Wingfield, for not showing proper respect to his betters. When Wingfield assumed his office in Jamestown, he insisted that Smith be removed as a councilor. When Wingfield was replaced and removed from the council during the summer, Smith's position improved. He was restored to the council and became supply master for the colony in the fall, negotiating with the Indians for food. According to his own report, he was taken prisoner during one of these supply expeditions, brought before Powhatan, and condemned to death, only to be saved by Pocahontas. Thus was born the legend that many historians doubt, because Smith was prone to exaggerate his own adventures in print. Some believe that the death threat was an adoption ceremony designed to test his mettle. No matter what the exact details of this encounter were, Smith had gained the respect of Powhatan, and that eased relations with the Indians as long as Smith remained in Jamestown.

After the calamitous fire, Smith began supervising the rebuilding of Jamestown. He was not reticent in using his strong will to turn any malingerers into productive workers. During the spring and summer he led two long voyages, using the shallop (an open boat about thirty feet long that could be sailed or rowed) to explore and map Chesapeake Bay and the tidewater rivers of Virginia. When he returned from the second voyage in September 1608, he became president of the colony. He introduced a "no work, no food" policy and insisted on discipline among the settlers. The results included twenty more dwellings and a blockhouse built, a sweet water well dug, and the manufacture of pitch, tar, soap, and glass begun.

After Smith was severely injured by burning gunpowder in mid-September, he sailed back to England in October for treatment.

After Smith left, the colony endured its worst trial, the "starving time." Without Smith's energy and resourcefulness, the colonists were ill prepared to deal with the renewed hostility of the surrounding Indians that his departure brought. One of them wrote, "Now we all found the losse of Captaine Smith, yea his greatest

VIRGINIA *Time Line*

1614	1619	1622	1624	1625
John Rolfe and Pocahontas marry; Indian attacks cease	A Dutch ship sells twenty Africans to the colonists	Opechancanough attacks on Good Friday, killing a third of the colonists	The Virginia Company loses its charter and is dissolved	King Charles I proclaims Virginia a royal colony

maligners could now curse his losse." When John Ratcliffe led a party of colonists to get food from Powhatan, thirty-four of them were killed, and Ratcliffe was tortured to death. The colonists had come to depend on the Indians for food, as well as on provisions from England, and both stopped during that winter of misery.

When they wandered beyond the bounds of the colony in search of food, they risked being killed by Indians and often were. Before the winter was over, they took to eating their domestic animals, pets, and rodents. By spring the colony had been nearly annihilated: Only 60 of the nearly 500 settlers Smith had left in the fall survived. When the first two vessels arrived in May, William Strachey saw a colony in shambles: "Viewing the Fort, we found the pallisadoes torne downe, the ports open, the gates from off the hinges, the emptie houses (which owners death had taken from them) rent up and burnt, rather than the dwellers would step into the woods a stones cast off from them, to fetch other firewood . . ."

These two small ships, appropriately named *Patience* and *Deliverance,* had been built from the remains of the *Sea Venture,* wrecked in Bermuda by a hurricane. On board was Sir Thomas Gates with news of a revised charter for the colony and stronger powers for the governor. By early June he and the remaining councilors concluded that intransigent Indians and the prospect of further starvation demanded abandonment of the colony. As the defeated colonists sailed down the river, news reached them that a fleet was in the offing with 150 more settlers and a new governor, Thomas West, Lord De La Warr, on board.

They turned back to Jamestown, and two days later the governor arrived to take charge of the colony. Although De La Warr repaired the fort and sent off ships for other sources of food, Jamestown's travails would not end for another year. Sickness and Indian troubles persisted, reducing the settlers to fewer than 150 again, and the governor's own illness led him to return to England. Not until two relief expeditions led by Gates and Sir Thomas Dale arrived in the spring and summer of 1611 did the ordeal begin to end. As two experienced military officers with a mandate to impose discipline on the settlers, Gates as governor and Dale as marshal laid down and enforced strict rules, built the new town of Henrico farther upriver, retaliated against Indians who attacked, burning their villages, and encouraged colonists to grow some of their own food. After four years of

1628	**1633**	**1644**	**1676**	**1693**
The General Assembly is authorized and meets	The General Assembly establishes Middle Plantation (later Williamsburg)	Opechancanough instigates a second massacre, killing between 300 and 500 colonists	Nathaniel Bacon leads rebellion and burns Jamestown	College of William and Mary receives charter

extremely troubled existence, it appeared that Jamestown might last as the first English colony in North America.

Enter Tobacco

Through these difficult early years the colony had repeatedly disappointed its London investors when ships returned with nothing but cargoes of timber products. They had anticipated a profit on their investments within two years and more than once considered abandoning the colony. Instead they reorganized the Virginia Company three times, in 1609, 1612, and 1618, and established a lottery to help defray operating expenses. Short of persistent illusions—the discovery of gold or a northwest passage—a cash crop was needed.

In the colony, John Rolfe began experimenting with tobacco in 1612 because he knew its use was fashionable in England. Finding the local plant used by Indians too bitter, he imported Orinoco leaf tobacco from the West Indies and began cultivating it. Encouraged by Gates and Dale, two years later he succeeded in adapting it to the Virginia climate. When he sent four barrels of cured leaf to England, a labor-intensive industry that would both sustain and plague Virginia was born. Although the Virginia Company was not at first enthusiastic about tobacco—King James hated it—it led its investors to create dividends in land rather than cash. America's first land boom was on, both among colonists already on site and potential emigrants. Unintended consequences lay down the road as a single-crop economy gained ground. Immediately it diverted colonists from growing their own food, and later renewed conflict with Indians as colonists hungry for land pushed into Indian hunting grounds. Ultimately it had enormous consequences in depleting the soil and creating a plantation economy dependent on slaves.

As well as becoming the first American entrepreneur by promoting tobacco,

VIRGINIA *Time Line*

1699	1700	1763	1772	1776
The capital of Virginia moves from Jamestown to Williamsburg	Assembly meets at the College of William and Mary	The Treaty of Paris ends the Seven Years War (French and Indian War)	Virginia forms a Committee of Correspondence with other colonies	Patrick Henry becomes the first governor of the Commonwealth of Virginia

John Rolfe performed another great service to the colony. On April 5, 1614, he married Powhatan's daughter Pocahontas, creating a truce that was dubbed "the peace of Pocahontas." She had come into English hands as a hostage in 1613 when Samuel Argall lured her onto his ship to force Powhatan to return prisoners and stolen guns. Put in the care of Governor Dale, she was educated at a parsonage in Henrico and baptized as Rebecca. Rolfe, a widower who had been involved in her education, wrote the governor for permission to marry her. Dale approved, and when he returned to England in 1616 he took Rolfe and Pocahontas with him in what today we would call a shrewd public relations move.

England had lionized American Indians before, and as a princess Pocahontas was entertained by important people and presented to the queen at court. As Rolfe and Pocahontas were waiting to sail back to Virginia in 1617, she died of consumption in Gravesend. Their little son, Thomas Rolfe, became ill on the voyage from Gravesend to Plymouth and was left in England with Sir Lewis Stukeley. As a young man Thomas returned to Virginia.

Tobacco exports to England grew from a trickle in 1614 to nearly 50,000 pounds three years later and gradually became a common currency in the colony. When 1,216 emigrants left England for Virginia during 1619, among them 90 young women seeking marriage, the company required the men who became their husbands to pay for their passage—in tobacco. The emigrants also included 666 persons headed for the private plantations that burgeoned with need for land to grow tobacco. That year also marked the arrival of twenty Africans, captured during a war with the Portuguese; although their status in Virginia is not clear, they probably became indentured servants.

The new governor, Sir George Yeardley, announced the most important event of the year, the more liberal charter that relaxed the autocratic rule and military discipline of the previous seven years to give the colonists a role in their own governance. The first General Assembly, convened on July 19 in the Jamestown church, included the governor, six councilors, and twenty-two burgesses representing the four public plantations and seven private ones. This first institution for self governance in America had limited powers but endured and became a model for colonial administration.

1780	**1781**	**1788**	**1789**
Capital moved from Williamsburg to Richmond	Benedict Arnold raids and burns Richmond; General Cornwallis surrenders to General Washington at Yorktown	Virginia becomes the tenth state to ratify the Constitution	George Washington inaugurated as the first president of the United States

After Powhatan's death in 1618, there was no immediate change in the colony's relations with the Indians. Chief Opechancanough replaced Powhatan as the head of the confederation and did not openly threaten the colonists. When the new governor, Sir Francis Wyatt, arrived in 1621, he ratified the peace with Opechancanough, who averred that the sky "should sooner fall than it dissolve." The settlers had gradually relaxed their vigilance as the peace of Pocahontas continued though the years, going about their work unarmed and inviting Indians into their homes for trade and meals.

But the new chief harbored a conviction: Powhatan's fear that the colonists would rob the natives of their land was happening before his eyes. He bided his time for an opportune moment to drive the intruders out, and secretly organized the tribes along the whole range of settlements for a surprise attack. It came to all the colonists at eight o'clock on Good Friday morning, March 22, 1622, when Opechancanough thought they would be preoccupied. They were, and it proved a fatal massacre, as Indians who had the run of the settlements brutally killed 347 men, women, and children wherever they were, including the homes that had welcomed them.

The aftermath of the attack was also devastating, as isolated settlements were abandoned and survivors moved toward the center of the colony. Living in constant fear of more attacks, the settlers did not have time to plant adequate tobacco or corn. Then, to add to the troubles, plague and famine arrived, killing between 500 and 600 settlers in the year following the attack. Between 1619 and 1623, emigrants had been sent in droves to populate the colony, some of whom died during long voyages on overcrowded ships. Those who arrived did not have better prospects of survival, since the death rate during those same years reached 75 percent of the population. Retaliatory attacks created casualties on both sides, and the truce that had created some prosperity in Jamestown vanished. Now either the Indians or the colonists would have to be driven from the land.

When the news reached London, the Virginia Company began to totter. Leadership of the stockholders had passed from Sir Thomas Smythe to Sir Edwin Sandys in 1619, but neither the returns nor the conditions on site had improved significantly. There was no way of accommodating the waves of immigrants, and the sickness they brought spread to others. Detailed company instructions often failed to understand the situation and wasted the limited healthy manpower available. The industries the company proposed, like glass-making and shipbuilding, either failed or never got properly started, and the rewards of planting tobacco crowded out other crops. Rivalries within the company produced public charges and countercharges. Out of patience with affairs in such disorder, King James I ordered his attorney general to sue the company in the Court of the King's Bench in 1623, and the court revoked the company's charter. James died before the commission appointed to consider reorganization had reported. King Charles I proclaimed Virginia a royal colony in 1625.

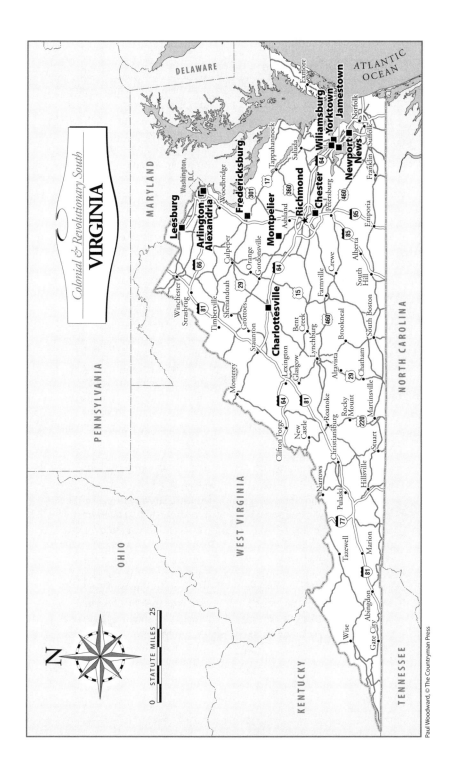

Colonial & Revolutionary South

VIRGINIA

Paul Woodward, © The Countryman Press

SMITH'S *Explorations*

✺ On June 2, 1608, Captain John Smith left Jamestown with fourteen colonists in the shallop to explore Chesapeake Bay. He entered the rivers on the lower Eastern Shore (now part of Virginia) and explored the islands of Tangier Sound, crossed over to the western shore at Calvert Cliffs, and sailed as far north as the Sassafras River. Returning south, he spent a number of days exploring the Potomac to its head of navigation. Remembering company instructions to keep looking for the elusive northwest passage to the Indies and gold, any great river was tempting, and he made an overland hike to visit a mine. At the mouth of the Rappahannock, he was stung by a stingray at the point that still bears that name and returned to Jamestown to heal on July 21.

There he found the governance of the colony in chaos, with a rebellion in progress against the second president, John Ratcliffe. After putting his friend Matthew Scrivener in charge, Smith resumed his voyage three days later with twelve men and reached the head of Chesapeake Bay and met Susquehannok chiefs near Havre de Grace. Coming back down the bay, he explored the Sassafras and Patuxent Rivers and spent most of his time going up the Rappahannock to its head before taking a closer look at the lower James. He reached Jamestown on September 7.

In three months the explorers had sailed and rowed more than 1,700 miles in an open boat, suffering the extended calms and vicious squalls that summer brings to the bay. They met various Indian cultures on every hand in lands settled and used by a large native population. Sometimes they were received for friendly parleys, sometimes openly attacked, and sometimes ambushed. Smith made observations and sketches that were used in his 1612 map, the first extensive and valuable survey of the bay. Remarkably, Smith persevered in these voyages in spite of the fragile and turbulent conditions within the colony.

To commemorate the 400th anniversary of this accomplishment, Sultana Projects of Chestertown, Maryland, built an approximate replica of Smith's shallop from what is known of such vessels of four centuries ago. In the summer of 2007, Captain Ian Bystrom led a crew of twelve volunteers through a 121-day, 1,500-mile voyage to the places Smith had visited. You can follow where they went on www.johnsmith400.org. In addition, there is now a Captain John Smith Trail along the York and James Rivers from Newport News to Richmond. Both motorists and boaters can follow the trail. Maps are available from www.johnsmithtrail.org, as well as from Virginia Welcome Centers.

The Royal Colony and Bacon's Rebellion

One surprising effect of Virginia's new status as a royal colony was benign neglect. Apart from a few periods of active interference, Virginia was left to itself under the hands of royal governors who regarded their role as a tour of duty rather than a career. The General Assembly continued to convene on occasion, even though it was not authorized by the king to meet until 1628 nor even formally exist until 1639. Charles had other preoccupations as the English Civil War approached yet retained the loyalty of many key figures in Virginia. Governor William Berkeley, unlike his predecessors, remained in Virginia for thirty-five years, and both he and the General Assembly denounced the king's execution in 1649.

When Cromwell's Parliament sent a fleet to subdue the recalcitrant colonial leaders in 1652, Berkeley had to surrender and retire to his country estate. The General Assembly was put in charge of governing the colony, with little interference from Cromwell's Commonwealth. Still, the Restoration of the Stuarts in 1660 was celebrated in Virginia, and King Charles II responded by naming it his "Old Dominion" and putting its emblem on his coat of arms.

Soon, however, colonists were to suffer another wave of interference from London as the Crown garnered more control of exports. Tobacco prices had fallen during the previous decade, and they were now to plummet further by additional restrictions on free markets. Under the Navigation Acts, tobacco had to be shipped in colonial or English vessels and sold in England at prices set by London merchants. As a result small and even medium-size plantations became marginal, and large ones slowly began to turn to slave labor to remain profitable. Though outnumbered by indentured servants, the slave population is estimated to have jumped from 300 in 1642 to some 2,000 in 1670.

In spite of the mismanagement and bad press that had brought the founding company down in 1624, Virginia continued to attract more immigrants through the next half century. Many of them were bent on acquiring the higher status and modest wealth that owning even small parcels of land brought, even if they had to serve as indentured servants for seven years before they were able to pursue that goal. At first those who came as freemen built small houses and worked their own land, but soon they felt the need for more labor to cultivate tobacco. If they paid the expenses of importing indentured workers to the colony, they could anticipate patents for additional land. Thus, among the effects of the focus on tobacco were both a continued supply of immigrants and the dispersion of colonists in plantations along the great tidewater rivers and their tributaries. The town centers for trade and manufacturing that the Virginia Company had envisioned never materialized, and the growing population remained largely rural.

This scattering made settlers especially vulnerable to Indian attack, and the next occurred on April 18, 1644, again orchestrated by Opechancanough as the last gasp of the old chief's resolve to drive the intruders out of his land. Although some 500 more men, women, and children were killed, more than in his 1622 attack, it proved less effective because the colony was much larger and therefore more difficult to destroy. Governor Berkeley mounted retaliatory attacks on the Indians, burning their villages, and eventually captured Opechancanough, intending to send him to England, until an irate soldier shot him in the back.

Governor Berkeley, now an old man himself, was not nearly so successful in dealing with Bacon's revolt, a traumatic rebellion that emerged from Indian attacks on the frontier in 1675 and 1676. That frontier had been moving westward to the falls where tidewater navigation on the great rivers stopped. Disputes with individual planters led some of the surrounding tribes to make retaliatory attacks, and planters on the edges of the colony were especially vulnerable. They resented what they saw as inattention to their problems by Governor Berkeley and the large planters safely ensconced downriver. The latter had gained power and authority through holding offices in the counties, the House of Burgesses, and the Governor's Council, and were regarded as an elite oligarchy by those on the fringe.

In April of 1676 a group of dissident planters gathered across the river from Nathaniel Bacon's plantation. Bacon, along with William Byrd, a neighboring planter who had lost three men to an Indian attack, rowed over to investigate. Greeted by a group shouting his name, Bacon succumbed to their wishes and became their leader. Bacon had come to Virginia only two years earlier but had bought a plantation and gained great influence quickly as a cousin by marriage to the governor, who had appointed the young Cambridge graduate to his council.

Berkeley had reason to regret his appointment throughout the rest of that year, as events began to spiral out of control. Bacon and his supporters demanded permission to actively raid and kill Indian tribes suspected of attacking the plantations. Berkeley refused, and in May declared Bacon a rebel, but backed off and pardoned him after he was captured in early June. That same month a newly elected Assembly passed "Bacon's Laws," and after its adjournment Bacon reappeared, backed by 500 militiamen, demanding a commission to attack the Indians. Berkeley bridled and resisted, even rushing out of the statehouse to bare his breast before the militia so they could shoot him. No one fired. Eventually, persuaded by his council, Berkeley granted the commission.

A month later, in July, Berkeley again declared Bacon a rebel. By then the conflict was more between Berkeley and his upstart young cousin than against the Indians, although Bacon went hunting them when he wasn't busy occupying or besieging the capital. That melodrama ended in September, when Bacon's forces occupied and burned Jamestown. In October, they took to plundering loyalist plantations. But the tide turned when Bacon died suddenly and unexpectedly, and by January 1677 Governor Berkeley was back in power, capturing, trying, and executing Bacon's principal associates. In May, after Colonel Herbert Jeffrey had arrived and taken over the governorship, Berkeley sailed for England.

The rebellion had a number of consequences, some of them doleful for Virginians. No longer would they be able to run their own affairs so freely. In later centuries Bacon was portrayed as a folk hero fighting for liberty a century before the Revolution, but some historians have seen his movement as a continuation of the colonists' greed to possess land that by treaties belonged to Indians. Ironically, this turmoil and destruction that began on the frontier pushed Jamestown into decline, and the capital was moved to Williamsburg a year after the statehouse burned in 1698.

An Aristocracy of Self-Made Planters

After the discord of the rebellion, Virginia continued to have difficulties with Indian raids, while low tobacco prices and growing efforts by the Crown to contain the independent spirit of the General Assembly created discontent among the colonists. But that discontent, mostly directed against royal governors, rarely reached troubling proportions during the first half of the 18th century, as long as the plantation economy prospered, the population grew, and land became available for new settlements in the Piedmont and Shenandoah Valley.

The task of restricting the power of the General Assembly and making it comply with instructions from the Crown or Parliament fell to successive governors (an authority often relegated to lieutenant governors while the governors themselves were on leave in England). During the last decades of the 17th century and the first of the 18th, the combination of restrictions from the Navigation Acts and the low price of tobacco made the planters who dominated the assembly uneasy. Governors like Edmund Andros, Francis Nicholson, and Alexander Spotswood, among others, were unable to persuade the assembly to surrender much of its power to regulate colonial affairs. As was the case in Massachusetts, men who had learned the skills of self government were not eager to give them up.

During this same era, the planters themselves had evolved into what is sometimes called a bourgeois aristocracy, based on the opportunistic effort of self-made men rather than inherited titles or land. Tracts of land that could grow tobacco were indeed its base, gradually augmented by marriages that increased a family's holdings. In some ways it became a replica of English country society, where landowners who controlled local government reaped the benefits of work by tenant farmers.

But there were important differences. By 1715 approximately one-quarter of the population consisted of slaves, who were replacing the inflow of indentured servants that had sustained the plantations in earlier years. On smaller plantations, owners and slaves often worked the fields together, and owning slaves was more important for status than class prerogatives. Many of the founders of Virginia's great families came as middle-class emigrants from merchant families in England, and as the generations passed, some of their descendants became the founding fathers of the new nation. By that time inherited land and slaves sustained the most powerful families.

In Virginia, as in other colonies, much of the growing prosperity in the 18th century depended on acquiring and developing more land. By the turn of the century, movement into the Piedmont had begun, and in 1701 French Huguenots settled around what would become Richmond. In succeeding decades Germans,

Swiss, Alsatians, and many Scotch-Irish moved down the Shenandoah Valley. In the second quarter of the century, under Governor William Gooch, more liberal land policies required that only one settler be established per thousand acres. Established wealthy families in the Tidewater once again became entrepreneurs by speculating in western lands, and some built new estates there.

At the midpoint of the century, the Ohio Company (1749) and the Greenbrier Company (1751) received charters and land grants of 100,000 acres. Virginians made their first moves across the Alleghenies into what is now West Virginia and Ohio, but the French and Indian War from 1754 to 1763, followed by the Indian uprising known as Pontiac's Rebellion, played havoc with the colony's westward expansion, and no settlements beyond the Alleghenies were secure.

Seeds of Rebellion

Back in Williamsburg, the political accommodation that had kept relationships between the governor and assembly stable began to unravel through a series of acts by both the Crown and Parliament. Some of these acts affected segments of the population, others virtually everyone. In response to Pontiac's Rebellion in 1763–64, King George III prohibited further settlement in Indian territory west of the Alleghenies, cutting off an expansion that Virginia land companies had already started.

When Parliament imposed the Stamp Tax in 1765 to help defray the cost of the French and Indian War, the response was vigorous, led by Patrick Henry. His speech in the House of Burgesses was interrupted with shouts of "Treason!" after the words "Caesar had his Brutus, Charles the First, his Cromwell, and George III . . ." but according to some reports, Henry resumed "George III may profit by their example." Ignoring Henry's impertinence, the General Assembly resolved that it had the "only and sole exclusive Right and Power to lay Taxes."

In the aftermath, Virginians, like citizens of other colonies, refused to buy stamps, and the Act was repealed a year later, but Parliament restated its right to make laws for the colonies. In 1767, when the Townshend Acts imposed new taxes on a variety of imported articles, Williamsburg became a hotbed of revolt. The General Assembly declared that taxation without representation was unconstitutional and began an unofficial boycott of English goods. Through these disputes Virginians had established connections with Massachusetts and other New England colonies. In 1772 patriots in Rhode Island attacked and burned the revenue schooner *Gaspee,* which had been harassing their shipping. When the news that the British intended to transport and try suspects in England reached Virginia, the House of Burgesses created a committee of correspondence to keep in touch with other colonies.

In the years immediately preceding hostilities, Virginians continued to take the initiative in organizing the colonies against what they regarded as unwarranted parliamentary intrusions in American affairs. When Parliament closed the port of Boston and passed the other Intolerable Acts in response to the Boston Tea Party, the House of Burgesses sent money and supplies to Massachusetts and urged the convening of the first Continental Congress in 1774.

The next year militias were organized, and at the same time that British troops marched on Lexington and Concord, Governor Dunmore tried to remove arms and powder from the magazine in Williamsburg to a British warship. As militias converged on the capital, Dunmore fled to Norfolk, where he used naval forces to raid plantations until he was driven off. In June of 1776, before the Declaration of Independence had been drafted, a revolutionary convention adopted a constitution and chose Patrick Henry as the first governor of the Commonwealth of Virginia.

Virginia's Leadership Role

Although no further military action of importance occurred on Virginia soil until the grand finale of the war at Yorktown in 1781, Virginia troops were engaged in all major campaigns and supplied many key officers in addition to the Continental Army's commanding general. Not only the oldest and most populous of the colonies, but also loaded with experienced legislators at the heart of the revolutionary movement, Virginia assumed leadership roles that were sometimes crucial to success. They succeeded in finding common ground with colonists in Massachusetts, although the two colonies' cultures and economic interests were quite diverse. The autocratic acts, often blunders, of a remote Parliament united New England merchants and shipowners with Tidewater planters, and that combination was a central force in the success of the Revolution and the creation of a new nation.

Regions *to* Explore

TIDEWATER
ALONG THE POTOMAC
CENTRAL VIRGINIA

TIDEWATER

As European settlers approached the roadless wilderness of North America, the efficient movement of people and goods depended on waterways. Thus early settlements clustered around natural harbors deep enough for heavily laden ships, around sheltered bays, sounds and estuaries, and especially along navigable rivers reaching into the interior. Tidewater Virginia's broad and deep rivers—the Potomac, Rappahannock, York, and James—were ideal sites for plantations, with access to the sea yet far enough upstream to be less vulnerable to attacks from enemies and pirates. As later towns developed at the fall line, the rivers also provided a way to reach the edge of the developing Piedmont region.

HISTORICAL TRIANGLE

Colonial National Historical Park (757-898-3400, 757-898-2410, 757-898-2409; www.nps.gov/colo or www.historicjamestowne.org), Box 210, Yorktown, VA 23690. This sprawling park encompasses the land on the peninsula between the James and York Rivers. Nowhere else in the country are so much colonial heritage and activity packed into such small space. The beautiful Colonial Parkway links Jamestown Island and Yorktown Battlefield, both within the park; just outside, between them, lies Colonial Williamsburg.

At the western end of the parkway you can visit Historic Jamestowne and Jamestown Settlement, a living history museum. At the eastern end you can drive through Yorktown Battlefield and walk through Yorktown, as well as Yorktown Victory Center, another living history museum. Between them you will drive 23 miles, diving under Williamsburg and stopping to read historical roadside markers along the way. This scenic road offers views of the James and York Rivers and Virginia woodlands that were once plantations.

JAMESTOWN

Jamestown's future declined after the statehouse burned and Williamsburg became the capital in 1699. No modern town exists today, but Historic Jamestowne (National Park Service) stands on the original 1607 site and includes many archaeological remains. Within its bounds you can walk through the original townsite, visit the Archaearium displaying excavated artifacts from the settlers, walk to the reconstructed glassworks, and drive to marked sites around the island.

Just outside the entrance to Historic Jamestowne stands Jamestown Settlement (Commonwealth of Virginia), a living history museum established in 1957 to celebrate Jamestown's 350th anniversary and recently expanded to celebrate the 400th. The large new theater and gallery offer a film and many exhibits, and the grounds lead to reconstructions of a Powhatan Indian Village, the James Fort, and, at the riverfront, replicas of the three ships that reached the settlement in 1607.

HISTORICAL SITES and MUSEUMS
Historic Jamestowne Visitor Center and Archaearium (757-229-1733, 757-898-2410; www.historicjamestowne.org or www.nps.gov/colo), 1367 Colonial Pkwy., Jamestown, VA 23081. Open daily. Located on the western end of the Colonial Parkway, a new building offers an immersion theater and exhibits. The Archaearium houses more than a million artifacts recovered from the area, a number of which are on display.

Recent finds include an English helmet discovered in 1994 buried 2 feet underground. Elliott Jordan, the conservator with the Association for the Preservation of Virginia Antiquities, worked with a team of archaeologists to excavate what looked like rust-colored soil, wrap it in paper towels, and cover it with plaster. It was taken up looking like "a big ball of dirt." Jordan tipped it on its side and carefully scraped dirt from the inside. He lined the inside with strips of fiberglass cloth to form a support for the helmet, and it was taken to Williamsburg Community Hospital, where a CAT scan was performed. The helmet was corroded but intact, so conservators used a scalpel to chip off the soil, then coated it with a clear resin. Historians think that helmets, a cannon, guns, and armor were buried to keep them away from Indians in 1610.

Earlier discoveries include a 1608 glass-making house and the 1639 brick church tower. Archaeological excavations remain in progress. A human skeleton has been found, as well as swords, armor, jewelry, ceramics, and coins.

Take a short walk from the visitor center across the footbridge into the original town site. A Tercentenary Monument stands where it was placed in 1907 for the 300th anniversary of Jamestown. Nearby, the statue of Pocahontas reminds us of how her marriage to John Rolfe improved relations between the Indians and the English.

The Old Church Tower has been standing since the 17th century. A memorial church was built in 1907 over the foundations of the 1639 brick church. Close to the river stands the statue of Captain John Smith, who controlled the colonists with this threat: "He who will not work, will not eat." The Memorial Cross marks 300 shallow graves of the colonists who died during the "starving time." Walk south along the river into NewTowne, which dates from 1621. The foundations of homes are traced with white bricks.

A 5-mile loop drive wanders through marshes and pine forests of Jamestown Island south of the settlement. It is inhabited by bald eagles, blue herons, ospreys, and white-tailed deer.

Jamestown Settlement (1-888-593-4682, 757-253-4838; www.historyisfun .org), P.O. Box 1607, Williamsburg, VA 23187-1607, located next to Jamestown Island, is a re-creation of the original settlement under the auspices of the Jamestown-Yorktown Foundation, an educational branch of the Virginia state government.

THE *Mysterious* "JAMESTOWN CAPTAIN"

William Kelso, the chief archaeologist for the Jamestown Rediscovery project, has written about the discovery of the original 1607 fort of Jamestown, on a site near the James River. Kelso also discovered the remains of a mysterious "Jamestown Captain," who may be Bartholomew Gosnold. Archaeological evidence tips the scale toward the view that this skeleton is indeed that of Gosnold, who died at age 36, after being in Jamestown only three months. A decorative captain's leading staff was inside the coffin, indicating that he was considered someone of importance.

As part of the process of determining the identity of the skeleton, a DNA sample was removed from what were thought to be the remains of Gosnold's sister, Elizabeth Gosnold Tilney. The Church of England gave permission for this procedure; Tilney had been interred beneath the floor of All Saints Church in Shelley, England. The DNA samples did not match. However, the location of Tilney's coffin was not completely clear, and also it is difficult to use dental analysis in aging studies. So the Advisory Panel on the Archaeology of Christian Burials in England has not ruled out the possibility that there would be a match with Elizabeth Tilney. The Smithsonian National Museum of Natural History is also involved in analyzing Tilney's sample, but results are not known at this time. So the mystery continues.

Open daily. Head for the museum galleries to see the film *Witness 1607: A Nation Takes Root*. You will learn about the 1607 voyage, the first Jamestown settlers and their relationship with the Powhatan Indians, the first Africans to arrive, the leadership of John Smith, and the story of Pocahontas. The museum contains three sections: the English Gallery, the Powhatan Indian Gallery, and the Jamestown Gallery.

Remnants of the settlement on display include weapons such as a 16th-century Iberian matchlock, a helmet, Spanish coins, a "bleeding bowl," mortar and pestle, coffin handles, wine bottles, and Captain John Smith's original map. The king and queen of England gave a ceramic jug to Pocahontas when she was presented at court on January 6, 1617, and it too is on display.

Then head down to the riverfront to visit replicas of the three ships that brought the colonists to Jamestown, the *Susan Constant*, the *Godspeed*, and the *Discovery*. The ship replicas are usually moored at the dock and open to visitors. Climb on board and see the space allotted to passengers and to cargo. Can you imagine what it must have been like to spend months in such cramped quarters during a voyage to the New World? Demonstrations include unfurling sails, changing the watch, posting colors, and steering the ship. A sailor will tell you about his life on board. Ask about the navigational instruments, like the astrolabe, which measures latitude, and other sailing techniques used on that voyage.

Inside the nearby James Fort you will find thatched houses and important public buildings like the church and the storehouse. Interpreters dressed in colonial costume go about their daily tasks cooking, working on their houses, repairing weapons, and participating in military drills. Many of the settlers had little knowledge of farming, and after their wounded leader, Captain John Smith, sailed back to England in 1609, a "starving time" took many lives. The survivors had almost given up hope of relief when more settlers arrived from England with supplies. By 1619 a government structure was in place, and Jamestown remained its center until destruction from the Bacon Rebellion of 1676, combined with the burning of the statehouse in 1698, led to the removal of the government to Williamsburg.

A re-created Powhatan Village offers you the chance to see how the Indians lived, prepared food, made tools and weapons, and prepared for war. Each longhouse, made of bent poles covered with woven mats, could accommodate from 6 to 20 people. Interpreters are there to make tools and weapons from bone and stone, prepare food, and repair their homes. Some of their Tidewater Indian pipes and arrowheads are on display in the museum.

YORKTOWN

Yorktown, at the other end of Colonial Parkway, is a short drive from Jamestown but a leap of more than a century and a half in time to a place where you can trace the sequence of events leading up to American victory in the Revolution. You'll find three venues to explore. The Yorktown Victory Center (Commonwealth of Virginia) is a living history museum, linked to the one at Jamestown. Yorktown Battlefield (National Park Service) has two self-guided driving tours that take you to the major sites of the siege. In between lies the town itself, with some of the historic houses that remained standing after the battle now open to the public, and others in private hands.

HISTORICAL SITES and MUSEUMS

The Yorktown Victory Center (888-593-4682, 757-847-3156; www .historyisfun.org), Route 1020 and Colonial Pkwy., Yorktown, VA 23690, is the place to start for an orientation to the area. Open daily. A time line takes visitors through four phases of the struggle: treaty, taxes, tea, and troops. You'll find out more about the 1763 Treaty of Paris, which vastly increased British holdings in North America, the odious tax acts, the Boston Tea Party, the First Continental Congress, and the culminating Battle of Yorktown, which ended in the surrender of a British army in 1781 and signaled the end of the Revolution. A film, *The Road to Yorktown,* graphically portrays these and other key events.

Exhibits change, so new ones may be in place by the time you visit. When we were there, "At the Water's Edge: The Towns of York and Gloucester" drew a social

You may be in the Jamestown Settlement when they are building a barn or making a canoe, using colonial techniques and tools. Powhatan Indians made dugout canoes from the early 1600s in coastal Virginia, and you can see how interpreters painstakingly hollow out an 18-foot tulip poplar log. Captain John Smith described the methods: "These [boats] they [Powhatan Indians] make of one tree by turning and scratching away the coles with stons and shels till they have made it in forme of a Trough." Some Indian canoes were as long as 40 to 50 feet.

and economic portrait of the towns most involved in the last important battle of the Revolution. Learn about life on board a ship in the "Yorktown's Sunken Fleet" display, based on artifacts taken from the *Betsy*, a British merchant ship sunk during the siege of Yorktown.

The exhibit "Witnesses to Revolution" shows how the conflict affected six persons—an African American patriot named Jehu Grant; a Loyalist, Jacob Ellegood; a Quaker pacifist, Elizabeth Drinker; two Continental Army soldiers; and the wife of a Virginia plantation owner, Frances Bland Tucker. Information was gathered from their personal diaries and correspondence.

Outside, in a re-created Continental Army encampment, interpreters help you imagine the daily life of those in the camp. Soldiers' tents, two officers' tents, a weapons tent, and a cooking center have been re-created. You may be there for a military drill, a demonstration of musket loading and firing, or camp cooking. A typical 1780s farm is represented by the outline of a house and a separate kitchen. Herbs and vegetables grow in the garden, as well as corn and tobacco in a nearby field.

THE SIEGE OF YORKTOWN

In 1780 and 1781 General Charles Cornwallis pursued the strategy of subduing American opposition in the southern colonies. As he tried to extend British control of Georgia northward through the Carolinas, he was effectively harassed but never decisively defeated by General Nathanael Greene's smaller forces. Cornwallis thought that by moving his army into Virginia he could solidify British control in the South. When Sir Henry Clinton ordered him to create a naval base in the lower Chesapeake area, he selected Yorktown for the base and moved his army there in August 1781.

Meanwhile French forces began heading in the same direction to assist the Continental Army. A French fleet under Admiral de Grasse arrived in time to blockade the mouth of the Chesapeake, which prevented Cornwallis from either receiving help or escaping by sea. After de Grasse defeated a British fleet under Admiral Graves at the Battle of the Capes, the French admiral de Barras was able to deliver siege guns to the attacking armies.

The Marquis de Lafayette, who had been tracking Cornwallis, awaited reinforcements in Williamsburg. Washington postponed a planned attack on New York and, joined by a French force under General Rochambeau, headed south on a rapid overland march to embark on transports down the Chesapeake. By the end of September American and French forces numbering 17,000 men had assembled in Williamsburg, twice the 8,300 remaining to Cornwallis after the extended and difficult campaign through the Carolinas.

De Grasse kept his blockade in place, and the allied armies marched down the peninsula to encircle Yorktown, cutting off escape for Cornwallis. They prepared for a siege and began bombarding the British garrison. Overrunning the outlying British redoubts, they set up a closer, second siege line that would soon effectively destroy the enemy garrison.

At this point, after suffering nine days of bombardment and with no chance of victory or avenue for escape, Cornwallis asked for a cease-fire to talk about surrender. The next day, October 19, 1781, he surrendered his army. This was the last major battle of the American Revolution, and the victory led to independence for the United States. Yet no one was sure of that result at the time, and Washington moved the Continental Army back to the Hudson, where it remained within striking distance of occupied New York City for two years. Not until the Treaty of Paris, in September 1783, did the war finally end.

Yorktown Battlefield: The visitor center (National Park Service) overlooking the battlefield offers a film on the siege and a number of exhibits. It's the starting point for two self-guided driving tours around the battlefield and the encampment area that will reconstruct in your imagination the events of October 19, 1781. The 7-mile Battlefield Tour includes the British inner defense line and hornwork, the Grand French Battery, the second allied siege line, British redoubts 9 and 10, the Moore House where surrender terms were negotiated, and the Surrender Field. The 9-mile Allied Encampment Tour begins at the American artillery park, then goes to Washington's headquarters, the French cemetery, the French artillery park, through the French encampment loop, and ends at the British redoubt.

Historic Yorktown (757-890-3300; www.yorkcounty.gov/tourism), 301 Main St. Wandering around Historic Yorktown takes you by a spate of interesting historic buildings. (You can pick up a brochure on a self-guided walking tour at the battlefield visitor center.) On Main Street the Dudley Digges House was home to a lawyer who served as council member for Virginia during the Revolution. The 1692 Thomas Sessions House is the oldest house in Yorktown. On Nelson Street stand the Captain John Ballard House and the Edmund Smith House. Back on Main Street is the "Scotch Tom" Nelson House, a Georgian mansion that was also home to his grandson, Thomas Nelson Jr., who signed the Declaration of Independence. This house, with cannonballs still in its side, is occasionally opened by the Park Service.

In the next block you'll pass the Pate House, the Customhouse, the Somerwell House, a reconstructed medical shop, and the Swan Tavern, which is now an antiques shop. Grace Church on Church Street is noted for the grave of Thomas Nelson Jr. in the churchyard. For more information on which houses are open, and when, call the National Park Service at 757-898-3400.

If you would like a glimpse of the more peaceful pursuits of this maritime town, visit the **Watermen's Museum** (757-887-2641), 309 Water St. Open daily except Mon. There you can get an overview of the work on the bay that helped sustain the Tidewater region through the colonial era and far beyond. The museum has a variety of displays inside and offers hands-on activities outside.

WILLIAMSBURG

When you have finished exploring Jamestown and Yorktown, the towns where the settlement of America began and the Revolution ended, head back to the middle of the peninsula on Colonial Parkway for a visit to the most extensive re-creation of colonial life in America.

HISTORICAL SITES *and* MUSEUMS

You'll want to spend at least a day at **Colonial Williamsburg** (800-HISTORY, 757-229-1000; www.colonialwilliamsburg.com), 102 Information Center Dr., Williamsburg, VA (P.O. Box 1776, Williamsburg, VA 23187). Open daily. The city began inauspiciously as a branch of the Jamestown settlement in 1633, then called Middle Plantation. By the time the capital of the Virginia colony moved to Middle Plantation from Jamestown in 1699, its name had been changed to Williamsburg to honor King William III. It remained the capital for the next 81 years, until 1780, during the Revolution, when the capital was moved to Richmond.

Step back in time two centuries as you walk the streets of colonial days in the footsteps of those who helped develop our nation. We suggest that you first head for the Colonial Williamsburg Visitor Center, which is well marked as you come into town. A film, *Williamsburg—The Story of a Patriot,* provides orientation for your visit. Leave your car in the parking lot and take a shuttle bus to the Historic Area. Duke of Gloucester Street is the Main Street of Williamsburg, running for a mile between the Capitol and the College of William and Mary. You can immerse yourself in the 18th century by simply wandering into buildings along this street and adjoining streets.

Who are the watermen? During the days of William the Conqueror, along the River Thames in England, men who were smugglers were given privileges in return for providing ships and men to the king. They were called watermen. Coastal fishermen and bargemen on the Thames still use the term, and in Virginia it is still used for fishermen on Chesapeake Bay.

You'll have more fun—and learn more—if you start a conversation with anyone in costume, as we did on several of our visits. You have to be a bit of an actor yourself to get the full value and

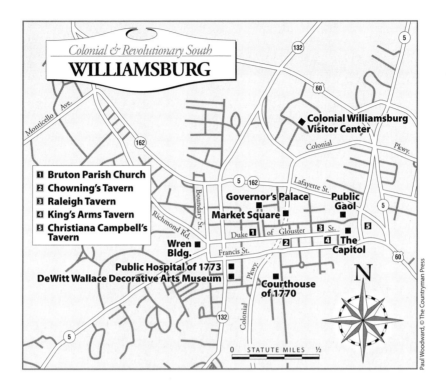

Colonial & Revolutionary South
WILLIAMSBURG

1 Bruton Parish Church
2 Chowning's Tavern
3 Raleigh Tavern
4 King's Arms Tavern
5 Christiana Campbell's Tavern

Colonial Williamsburg Visitor Center

Governor's Palace
Market Square
Public Gaol
Wren Bldg.
The Capitol
Public Hospital of 1773
DeWitt Wallace Decorative Arts Museum
Courthouse of 1770

N

0   STATUTE MILES   ½

Paul Woodward, © The Countryman Press

pleasure of the time warp, speaking to costumed interpreters about events in their experience. They're stuck in the 1770s, and you have to go back there, too.

Across the street in the **King's Arms Tavern,** everyone is encouraged to exchange 18th-century news and views with the proprietress, the widow Jane Vobe. This was the place to keep up to date on what was happening in the colonial world. Jane assured us that she doesn't gossip but just tells what she hears—after all, one has to watch one's tongue or be put in the pillory.

Cocking her ear, she wondered who might be listening, but added that as long as you can hear slaves, you know they're working and not snooping. She told the male half of this writing team that he should really shave off his beard when he has time because men with hair on their faces either have something to hide or are pirates. Men who want to stay in her 14-room inn pay 7½ pence for two-to-a-bed comfort. Meal costs can't exceed 1 shilling—dinner is served at two of the clock, supper at nine of the clock, with the same food brought back redecorated. It pays to appear the first time food is served.

Having gotten into an 18th-century mood with two colorful characters, we headed for the Capitol. As we stood by the green seats in the House of Burgesses we could almost hear George Washington explaining a bill that had to do with hogs. It seems that they had been taking a bath in the drinking water, and he

thought they should be fenced in so people could drink clean water. Legislation had to be sent to the king in England, so an answer could be expected in a few years.

More seriously, Washington explained the Virginia Resolves against the Townshend Acts, passed in this chamber in 1769. Four years earlier Patrick Henry had delivered his notorious "Caesar-Brutus" speech here and proposed a response to the Stamp Act. The Council Chamber, housing the smaller and more powerful group that advised the governor, has a turkey-work carpet on the table. The portrait of Queen Anne hanging here reminds us of her personal tragedy; she had 17 children, all of whom died in infancy except the Prince of Gloucester, who lived to 11. The General Court was the place where pirates were sentenced to be "turned off" or hanged, and other malefactors punished. People could be pardoned the first time, but a T (theft) or M (murder) was burned into the palm of the hand near the thumb to make a second offense unmistakable. No plea bargaining here!

One of our favorite buildings is the **Governor's Palace,** which housed seven royal governors and also the first two governors of the Commonwealth of Virginia, Patrick Henry and Thomas Jefferson. In 1780 the residence of the governor was moved to Richmond. The building was used as a hospital after the battle of Yorktown, but later in 1781 it burned completely.

Today visitors see a carefully researched replica of the original building. You will enter through the hall decorated with guns, swords, pistols, and muskets arranged in patterns, but access wasn't so easy in colonial days. Back then the butler, from his office to the left of the door, managed the visits of those who wished to see the governor. By their clothing and posture, he was able to screen the less important visitors, who waited in the hall, the more important, who were escorted into the parlor on the right, and the most important, who walked upstairs.

When you go upstairs you'll walk through several bedrooms with period furnishings. Don't miss the set of fashion prints—one for each month of the year. In the ballroom, the governor sat at the "preferred" end along with portraits of King George III and Queen Charlotte; when visitors bowed to him they were also bowing to the king and queen.

Market Square is a green open park halfway between the Capitol and the

Stop to chat with interpreters in costume who are eager to talk with you about their crafts. Max, in the Milliner's Shop, told us about the fans that George Washington ordered there. The milliner had the latest styles in clothing and was considered a fashion consultant as she stitched new gowns for balls, changed the trim with the times, and suggested wearing "heart breakers" (corkscrew curls).

A shop on Duke of Gloucester Street in Colonial Williamsburg

We had a conversation with Governor John Murray, the fourth Earl of Dunmore, who asked, "Who be you?"

"Edward Foulke. I came to this country in 1698, replied descendant Robert Foulke, impersonating his ancestor.

Dunmore peered at him and said, "You must be as old as Methuselah!"

Edward Foulke agreed: "I've lost count."

College of William and Mary. In the early days, carts and wagons creaked in with produce from farms. Vendors offered their wares to housewives intent on finding the freshest and choicest produce for their kitchens. The colonial militia mustered on the training field in Market Square. Every free, white, able-bodied man, age 16 to 60, who was a British subject was in the Williamsburg Militia Company. Besides marching, the men conducted foot races, wrestling matches, and other competitions for prizes. The field is still used for British and Patriot encampments.

Bruton Parish Church (757-229-2891), near Palace Green, dates from 1712, when it replaced the previous church on the site. Candlelit concerts and tours are held there. Nearby, the **Courthouse** of 1770 is the place to go for a performance of a courtroom drama of the era. Costumed guides make the experience come alive.

The **Public Hospital**, at the southeast corner of Francis and Henry Streets, was in operation from 1773 to 1885. Rooms display conditions for the mentally ill, including a 1773 cell with a pallet on the floor over a lump of straw, a blanket, and chamber pot—similar to a prison. The window was barred, and patients were chained to the wall. By 1845 conditions had improved and each patient lived in a small apartment with bed, table, chair, and plaster walls. During this age of "moral management" patients were encouraged to spend time doing something—playing the violin, spinning, or playing cards, for example. The "custodial care" era lasted from 1862 to 1885. Patients were subjected to physical restraints but entertained with picnics and tea parties.

The **DeWitt Wallace Decorative Arts Gallery** is accessible by walking through the hospital and downstairs. Collections include musical instruments, silver, pewter, ceramics, clocks, globes, furniture, paintings, costumes, and textiles. Our favorites from the colonial era are an Aesop's fable candlestick, "The Tiger and the Fox" from 1765, a Greybeard face jug from 1645, a turquoise tea urn from 1770, brass pipe tampers from 1650, and crewel wool needlework from 1750.

Some holdings go beyond the decorative, like the Charles Willson Peale portraits of Washington and George III and a copy of the 1755 map that was used in establishing the territories of the United States at the end of the Revolution.

The **Abby Aldrich Rockefeller Folk Art Center** opened after renovation and expansion in May 1992. Abby Aldrich Rockefeller began collecting folk art in the 1920s. Today the collection includes shop signs, weather vanes, carousel figures, portraits, furniture, chests, quilts, sewing implements, mariners' tools, and toys.

We enjoyed the clown tobacconist sign from 1868, a group of weather vanes, a lion carousel figure, a monkey inkwell, a calico cat from 1900–20, a 1907–15 mechanical pump on three levels, and a 1795 Pennsylvania Dutch Easter rabbit, to name a few. Contact Colonial Williamsburg (800-HISTORY) for more information about programs in the center.

At the opposite end of Duke of Gloucester Street from the Capitol stands the Wren Building of the **College of William and Mary**. It is so called not because it can be attributed to Christopher Wren himself but because it resembles his work in elegant simplicity, balanced proportions, and other elements of style. The restored building, which claims to be the oldest college building in the colonies, looks as it did in 1716. The college was founded in 1693 to train clergymen on this side of the Atlantic, and it played a key role in educating distinguished Virginians throughout the 18th century. Phi Beta Kappa, then a secret society for intellectual discussion and fellowship, was founded in the Raleigh Tavern in 1776—a favorite retreat of students, politicians, and gamblers.

There are many places to have lunch or dinner in colonial ambience scattered throughout the properties of Colonial Williamsburg. On their menus you will

---

 To whet your appetite for dishes from the colonial period, you can try some of these recipes at home:

Chowning's Tavern Brunswick Stew

2 chickens	2 cups okra, cut
2 cups lima beans	2 cans corn
2 large sliced onions	4 cups fresh or 2 cans tomatoes
3 medium potatoes, diced	salt, pepper, sugar to taste

Simmer cut-up chicken in 3 quarts of water for a thin stew, or 2 quarts for a thick stew, until meat can easily be removed from the bones, about 2¼ hours. Add the raw vegetables to the broth and simmer, uncovered, until the beans and potatoes are tender. Stir occasionally. Add the chicken and seasonings. Flavor improves if it is left to stand overnight and is reheated the next day.

(RECIPE FROM COLONIAL WILLIAMSBURG)

Syllabubs

1½ cups whipping cream	½ cup white wine
rind and juice of 2 lemons	¼ cup sherry
½ cup sugar	whipping cream (optional)

Whip together the following ingredients in this order: whipping cream, lemon rind, sugar, lemon juice, white wine, and sherry. Whisk the mixture 3–5 minutes, keeping in mind that too much whipping will turn it to butter. Pour into parfait glasses and refrigerate overnight. If desired, pile whipped cream on top of each glass before serving. *Makes 6–8 syllabubs.*

(RECIPE FROM COLONIAL WILLIAMSBURG)

find many authentic colonial favorites, including soups, stews, seafoods, and syllabubs. As you wander through the historic district, look at the day's menus at the Williamsburg Inn, the King's Arms Tavern, Chowning's Tavern, Mrs. Campbell's Tavern, Shields Tavern, and the Williamsburg Lodge. Or, if you would rather use your fingers than your feet for the same information, call 804-229-2141.

If you want to spend a "Christmas Away" from home, consider Williamsburg. Some families bring all ages, presents, and a Christmas tree to spend the holiday in a colonial atmosphere. Events are planned all day and into the evening; everyone has a good time.

And to complete your immersion in the 18th century, there's a rare opportunity to spend the night in authentic colonial lodgings in Williamsburg—rare because almost everywhere else they have been burned, wrecked, or altered almost beyond recognition during centuries of growth and change. If you'd like to stay in authentic digs (we did and loved it!), contact Colonial Williamsburg Hotels and ask what's available.

LODGING

Colonial Williamsburg properties include a wide variety of lodgings, ranging from the spartan and simple to the luxurious and elegant. Some are in historic buildings, others are not. The properties include the Williamsburg Inn, Providence Hall, Colonial Houses & Taverns, Williamsburg Lodge, Williamsburg Woodlands, and the Governor's Inn. All are within the Historic Area, or just outside it, and some are right on Duke of Gloucester Street. For detailed information and reservations call 800-HISTORY.

KINGSMILL RESORT

1010 Kingsmill Rd., Williamsburg, VA 23185
800-832-5665, 757-253-1703;
www.kingsmill.com
The resort is located south of town on 3,000 acres along the James River. Kingsmill is a residential community within itself, built on land owned by Richard Kingsmill in 1736.

RESTAURANTS

CHOWNING'S TAVERN

106 E. Duke of Gloucester St.
757-220-7012
Historic tavern and summer garden. Pub food and southern specialties.

CHRISTIANA CAMPBELL'S TAVERN

120 E. Waller St.
757-220-7015
Tavern with roving balladeers and costumed staff.

KING'S ARMS TAVERN

416 E. Duke of Gloucester St.
757-220-7744
A reconstruction of the original tavern from 1772.

THE REGENCY DINING ROOM

136 E. Francis St., in the Williamsburg Inn
Fine dining in a beautiful setting.

EVENTS

Many events are held around the year. Please visit www.historyisfun.org.

INFORMATION

COLONIAL WILLIAMSBURG
102 Information Center Dr., P.O. Box
1776, Williamsburg, VA 23185
800-HISTORY, 757-229-1000
www.colonialwilliamsburg.com

**WILLIAMSBURG AREA CONVENTION
& VISITORS BUREAU**
421 N. Boundary St., P.O. Box 3585,
Williamsburg, VA 23187
800-368-6511, 757-253-0192
www.visitwilliamsburg.com

HISTORIC JAMESTOWNE
1367 Colonial Pkwy., Williamsburg, VA
23185
757-229-1733
www.historicjamestowne.org

JAMESTOWN SETTLEMENT
P.O. Box 1607, Williamsburg, VA 23187
888-593-4682, 757-253-4838
www.historyisfun.org

YORKTOWN VICTORY CENTER
P.O. Box 1607, Williamsburg, VA 23187
888-593-4682, 757-253-4838
www.historyisfun.org

NEWPORT NEWS

Did you know that Newport News got its name as the Jamestown settlers, eager to leave, saw Captain Christopher Newport with his ship of supplies from England? This was "good news" for the discouraged settlers. Newport went back and forth across the ocean from 1607 to 1619, bringing people, equipment, and hope to the struggling colony.

HISTORICAL SITES and MUSEUMS

Matthew Jones House (757-878-5381; www.newport-news.org), Taylor Ave. and Harrison Rd., Newport News, VA 23603, on the Fort Eustis Army Base. Open June–Aug., weekends. The main part of the house dates from ca. 1727 and was built for Matthew Jones. The glazed-header Flemish bond brickwork is stunning. It is now an architectural museum house featuring three historic periods and is located on Mulberry Island.

Mariners' Museum (800-581-7245, 757-596-2222; www.marinersmuseum .org), 100 Museum Dr. Open daily. This museum is one of the largest international maritime museums in the world. Its collections chart the culture of the sea as well as its conquest by man. From the Age of Exploration we can see a model of the *Niña* from the 1400s and Captain John Smith's map of the Chesapeake Bay. Voyages of the 15th through 18th centuries were possible because of developments in shipbuilding, ocean navigation, and cartography. The gallery includes ship models, rare books, illustrations, maps, and navigational instruments.

A favorite jewel in the collection is the Crabtree Collection of Miniature Ships. Artist/carver August F. Crabtree meticulously carved miniature ships that document the evolution of the sailing ship. It is hard to imagine that he carved so many exquisite boats. They range from a primitive raft to a Venetian galley complete with 359 figures.

REMEMBER *the* MONITOR

❄ It's also beyond our time period, but it would be a shame for you to miss the USS *Monitor* Center, the most recent and important exhibit that opened in March of 2007. After the 1973 discovery of the wreckage of this breakthrough warship, which sank off Cape Hatteras in a storm, the *Monitor* became the first national marine sanctuary two years later. Continuing deterioration of the wreck led to a partnership between NOAA, the Navy, the Mariners' Museum, and many other institutions to salvage and preserve parts of the ship that would otherwise disappear. The results are in this new center, where you can walk on a full-scale replica of the Civil War ironclad that revolutionized naval warfare, see artifacts including the gun turret, and experience a wealth of interactive exhibits.

Although it's beyond our time period, we can't resist telling you about the *Titanic* exhibit, a familiar story poignantly told with the artifacts of daily life from both passengers and crew. There's a silk scarf from Madeline Astor, a bathrobe used to wrap a baby, White Star Line china, a dressing table drawer, and life vests.

INFORMATION

NEWPORT NEWS TOURISM DEVELOPMENT OFFICE
700 Town Center Dr., Suite 320, Newport News, VA 23606
888-493-7386, 757-926-1400
www.newport-news.org.

NEWPORT NEWS VISITOR CENTER
13560 Jefferson Ave., Newport News, VA 23606
888-493-7386, 757-886-7777
www.newport-news.org

ALONG THE POTOMAC

The widest and longest of the Tidewater rivers, the Potomac enticed early explorers searching for the elusive northwest passage through the continent to the riches of Asia. On his first voyage in 1608, Captain John Smith explored the river all the way to the fall line not far upstream from present-day Washington, D.C. Later during the colonial era, the Potomac was lined with plantations, including George Washington's Mount Vernon, and became a major water route from interior lands to world markets.

ARLINGTON

Arlington, named for the estate originally purchased by George Washington's step-son and built by his grand-stepson, was included in the ten-square-mile federal district that Washington ordered surveyed in 1791, formally established as the District of Columbia ten years later. But as economic competition with George-town and Washington began to trouble neighboring Alexandria's merchants, they sought funds to build a canal from Richmond and voted for retrocession to the Commonwealth of Virginia in 1846.

HISTORICAL SITES *and* MUSEUMS
Arlington National Cemetery (703-607-8000; www.arlingtoncemetery.org), Arlington, VA 22211. Open daily. Secretary of War Edwin M. Stanton designated it as a military cemetery on June 15, 1864. More than 300,000 veterans are buried here, including some reinterred from the American Revolution, most of them in Section l, and the War of 1812. Pierre-Charles L'Enfant, who designed the layout of Washington, D.C., was reinterred on the slope in front of the Custis-Lee Mansion. The L'Enfant Monument marking his grave was made of white marble with six marble posts supporting a top slab. The Tomb of the Unknowns is made from Yule marble quarried in Colorado. Three unknown servicemen are buried there. The U.S. Army guards the Tomb of the Unknowns 24 hours a day.

 Arlington House, Custis-Lee Mansion (703-235-1530; www.arlington cemetery.org/historical_information/arlington house or www.nps.gov/arho), off Sherman Dr. Open daily. George Washington Parke Custis, son of John Parke Custis, who was a child of Martha Washington by her first marriage and a ward of George Washington, built the house as a memorial to George Washington. Designed by British architect George Hadfield, the mansion begun in 1802 was not completed for 16 years. George Washington Parke Custis and his wife, Mary Lee Fitzhugh, lived in the house until their deaths in 1857 and 1853, respectively. Custis's only child, Mary Anna Randolph Custis, married Robert E. Lee in 1831.

 The house continued to figure prominently in American history beyond the Federal era. When Robert E. Lee's father-in-law died in 1857, Lee came back to Arlington; his wife, Mary Anna, had the right to inhabit and control the house for her lifetime. Lee found the house in disrepair, and by 1859 he had brought the property back into good shape. He and Mary Anna lived there until 1861. When Virginia ratified an alliance with the Confederacy and seceded from the Union, Lee resigned his commission in the army to serve for Virginia. The federal government seized the property, on the grounds that the taxes had not been paid in person by the owner.

 In the interior of Arlington House, about a third of the 3,000 pieces were owned by the Lees and the Custis family. Among the paintings is a large one depicting George Washington at the Battle of Monmouth. It was painted by George Washington Parke Custis.

The Robert E. Lee Museum is in a white building adjacent to the house. Exhibits include an overview of his life, paintings of family members, and a family tree. Objects that were his include a mess kit, a key to the family tomb, and a pistol presented to him when he was at West Point.

Of special interest is the tomb of Pierre-Charles L'Enfant in front of the house, facing the city he designed. His plan for Washington is carved into the face of the tomb.

ALEXANDRIA

Sixteen miles upstream from Mount Vernon, Alexandria was founded by Scottish merchants in 1749. They named it after John Alexander, who had bought the land in 1669 for "six thousand pounds of Tobacco and Cask." George Washington helped survey the land when he was seventeen years old. Later Washington kept a residence in town, but his original home at 508 Cameron Street, built in 1765, no longer stands. The building on the site now is a privately owned replica. Washington was heavily involved in the communal affairs of Alexandria. He had a pew in Christ Church, organized the Friendship Fire Company, and served as Master of the Masonic Lodge.

The city had become one of the main seaports and trading centers of Virginia by the time of the Revolution. Slaves were sold in the market, yet there were also several free black communities in Alexandria. Blacks were known and valued as skilled artisans.

HISTORICAL SITES *and* MUSEUMS

Today, in spite of the suburban development around the center of Alexandria, visitors can still soak up the ambience of colonial days as they walk the streets of Old Town. (Parking is tight in the center of the Old Town, so the best plan is to stash your car in a parking lot or visit Ramsay House, where you can get a free 24-hour parking proclamation and then find one of the specially marked "tourist" meters that allow you to stay all day.)

> An inscription on a tombstone in the Christ Church churchyard reads:
> "In memory of Sarah the wife
> of John Wrenn who died
> August 13, 1792,
> aged 28 years.
> All you who come to
> my grave to see
> As I am now you soon will be
> Prepare and turn to God in time
> For I was taken in my prime."

Begin your tour at **Ramsay House** (703-838-4200; www.thefunsideofthe potomac.com), 221 King St. Open daily. The house also serves as the visitor center. You can watch a video on colonial Alexandria, pick up brochures to help plan sightseeing, and begin guided walking tours, which are excellent.

Before you begin a walking tour, though, take a few minutes to look around Ramsay House. William Ram-

Carlyle House in Alexandria

say and his wife, Anne, had eight children in this original house, which has been moved from another location. The gambrel roof is similar to those used on other colonial homes between 1675 and 1725. Ramsay was a good friend of George Washington, who walked in Ramsay's funeral procession.

Carlyle House (703-549-2997; www.carlylehouse.org), 121 N. Fairfax St., dates from 1752. Open Tue.–Sun. John Carlyle journeyed from Scotland in 1741 and became a successful tobacco merchant in Alexandria. During the French and Indian War, General Edward Braddock had his headquarters in the Carlyle House, where he held a crucial conference. He invited five colonial governors to meet with him, ostensibly to coerce them into raising money for their own defense in the war. They refused, and he sent a letter to London demanding that the colonists be taxed, setting in motion a long train of parliamentary measures that eventually led to the Revolution. **Market Square**, in front of City Hall, was a parade ground for colonial troops under Braddock's command. Braddock was later defeated near Fort Duquesne and died in that battle.

Turn left on Cameron Street, then onto Royal Street, and you'll come to the 1770 **Gadsby's Tavern Museum** (703-838-4242; www.gadsbystavern.org), 134 N. Royal St., where you can have an authentic colonial meal and tour the museum. Open Apr.–Oct. daily; Nov.–Mar., Wed.–Sun. George Washington was a frequent visitor, and the annual Birthnight Ball took place in an elegant ballroom upstairs every year while he lived; it is reenacted to this day. The museum features a tap-room where the main meal of the day was served. It had board games such as backgammon, and men met there to talk politics and smoke clay pipes. Upstairs you'll find a variety of inn bedrooms, some communal and sparse, others private and comfortably furnished. One sleeping room contains linen sacks filled with straw and a bedstead with a rope frame. Only men slept up there; no lady of quality would think of sleeping elsewhere than with friends or the local clergyman. Any man arriving after the beds were filled had to sleep on the floor. Perhaps fewer bedbugs were encountered on the floor than in bed!

The museum at Gadsby's Tavern offers a display on 18th-century money. A comment by Nicholas Cresswell in 1774 states: "It appears to me that there is a scarcity of cash amongst the people of all ranks here. They game high, spend freely, and dress exceedingly gay, but I observe they seldome show any money, it is all Tobacco Notes."

Continue along Cameron Street to **Christ Church** (703-549-1450; www.historicchristchurch.org), 118 N. Washington St. Open daily. Begun in 1767 and finished in 1773, the church had galleries added in 1787 and the tower in 1820. George Washington's pew is marked with a silver tablet, also that of Robert E. Lee. Washington's pew, number 60, cost 36 pounds and 10 shillings. Don't miss the cut-glass chandelier.

Turn right onto Washington Street to the **Lee-Fendall House** (703-548-1789; www.leefendallhouse.org), 614 Oronoco St. Open Tue.–Sun. "Light Horse Harry" Lee, father of General Robert E. Lee, bought several lots and sold one to his cousin Philip Fendall. He built his mansion in 1785. There Light Horse Harry worked on his farewell address from Alexandrians to George Washington as the latter left to become our first president. About 35 members of the Lee family lived in the house from 1785 to 1903, and many Lee possessions remain there.

Take Prince Street to Fairfax to see the **Stabler-Leadbeater Museum and Apothecary Shop** (703-838-3852; www.apothecarymuseum.org), 105–107 S. Fairfax St. Open Apr.–Oct. daily; Nov.–Mar., Wed.–Sun. George Washington and Robert E. Lee were among the patrons of the store. One record states: "Mrs. Washington desires Mr. Stabler will send by the bearer a quart bottle of his best Castor Oil and the bill for it."

LODGING

MORRISON HOUSE
116 S. Alfred St., Alexandria, VA 22314
703-838-8000;
www.morrisonhouse.com
The Federal-style house is patterned after an 18th-century manor house. It is conveniently located in Old Town so you can walk to see the historic sites. "The Story of Literature," one of the special programs at the Morrison House, is featured, with the library housing books on the history of Alexandria, including George Washington. Once a month the hotel offers book signings and readings.

RESTAURANTS

BILBO BAGGINS RESTAURANT
208 Queen St.
703-683-0300; www.bilbobaggins.net
There are three tavern rooms in three row houses. Ten microbrews and 35 wines are offered.

GADSBY'S TAVERN RESTAURANT
138 N. Royal St.
703-548-1288; www.gadsbystavern restaurant.org
The cuisine is early American in this 18th-century tavern. A strolling minstrel is there for your pleasure.

GERANIO RISTORANTE
722 King St.
703-548-0088; www.geranio.net
The restaurant serves modern Italian cuisine with influences from France and America.

MORRISON HOUSE GRILLE
116 S. Alfred St.
703-838-8000;
www.morrisonhouse.com
The menu offers wild game and fish, free-range fowl, and tender meats.

EVENTS

February: George Washington's Birthday Ball, 703-838-4242
December: Parade of Lights Holiday Boat Parade, 703-838-5005

INFORMATION

ALEXANDRIA CONVENTION & VISITORS ASSOCIATION
221 King St., Alexandria, VA 22314
800-388-9119, 703-838-4200
www.visitalexandriava.com

MOUNT VERNON

Perhaps the single most important historical home in America, Mount Vernon is but a short, scenic drive down the Virginia shore of the Potomac from the nation's capital.

HISTORICAL SITES *and* MUSEUMS
Mount Vernon (703-780-2000; www.mountvernon.org), 3200 Mount Vernon Memorial Hwy., Mount Vernon, VA 22121 (P.O. Box 110). Open daily. The mansion rises from an emerald-green lawn above the Potomac River, symbolizing a perfect melding of gracious living and political responsibility in our first presidency, but it was built there for economic rather than aesthetic reasons. The Potomac, like the Hudson and the Delaware, was a great river leading inland, and as such its value for shipping produce and for general commerce was inestimable.

John Washington, George's great-grandfather, patented the Mount Vernon homesite in 1674. Augustine Washington, George's father, inherited the tobacco plantation of 2,300 acres in 1726, and in 1732 George was born there. When Augustine Washington died in 1743, George's elder half-brother, Lawrence, inherited Mount Vernon.

George Washington eventually inherited the plantation from Lawrence in 1761 and then wrote, "No estate in United America is more pleasantly situated than this. It lies in a high, dry and healthy Country 300 miles by water from the

On the lawn at Mount Vernon

Sea . . . on one of the finest Rivers in the world . . ." In spite of this admiration for his own estate, he was not able to live there for years at a time during the French and Indian War, the Revolution, and an eight-year presidency. But when he was in residence at Mount Vernon, he studied the newest crop technology assiduously and was successful as a planter.

After George's marriage to Martha Dandridge Custis, widow of Daniel Parke Custis, he wrote, "I am now, I believe, fixed at this Seat with an agreeable Consort for Life and hope to find more happiness in retirement than I ever experienced amidst a wide and bustling World." No such luck.

While visiting colonial inns and houses along the eastern seaboard doing research for this book, we were astounded at the number he had actually slept in— rather than the home he loved—and the jocular phrase took on new poignancy. Luckily, Martha Washington spent eight winters with him during his northern encampments. He resigned his commission in 1783 and hoped to spend his remaining life at Mount Vernon. In 1789 he became president for the next eight years, which kept him away from home much of the time. When he finally did retire, he had only two and one-half years left at his beloved Mount Vernon before he died.

The mansion is a familiar sight to most Americans because photographs of its facade, enlarged by Washington with a long columned piazza and other features in Palladian style, have appeared incessantly. He first added onto the smaller house he had inherited before his marriage to Martha, and made other additions in later years. When he was at home, Washington was personally involved in designing, supervising construction, and decorating and furnishing the additions.

Although we had visited Mount Vernon a number of times over the years, our research on the three books in this series of historical guides renewed and deepened our respect and affection for the man who gave up much of his life to establish our country. It was a pleasure to visit his home again and to enjoy the new additions to the site.

Park your car in the large parking lot and walk up to the Donald W. Reynolds Museum and Education Center. You will enjoy a multimedia experience that tells the story in great detail. Twenty-three galleries and theaters are offered to enhance your visit. Take in the 20-minute film that explores "the home to all of us" as it moves all over the estate. We see George Washington approaching wounded men with "I need to see the men," then to a dying man, "Your family will be proud." We watch as he meets Martha for the first time, when he says, "I knew your late husband." Seven months later they were married. We hear an Indian whoop in the woods and see how young Washington grasped command from a mortally wounded General Braddock. Don't forget Christmas night 1776, when he cautioned, "Move quickly, men" as they crossed the Delaware River by boat. In 1783 he resigned his commission—at once a voluntary surrender of personal power and a needed symbolic act for a new democracy—and rode home to Mount Vernon. He would do it again at the end of his second term as president.

Don't miss the authentic one-twelfth-scale replica of the mansion, Mount Vernon in Miniature, in the Ford Orientation Center.

Next you will need to wait in line for the mansion tour. Although we are not patient waiters, we passed the time chatting with others in line and watching children playing on the green.

The Large Dining Room was the last addition to the house. Two shades of verdigris green are used in the decoration, including a wallpaper border. The striking Palladian window has satin and dimity hangings. Vases on the mantel came from England and were made about 1770 in the Worcester factory. Four large oil paintings include views of the Great Falls and the Potomac River at Harpers Ferry by George Beck. River scenes were by William Winstanley in 1793.

The passage, or central hall, contains a key to the Bastille, a gift from General Lafayette in 1790. He wrote: "Give me leave, my dear general, to present you with a picture of the Bastille, just as it looked a few days after I ordered its demolition, with the main key of the fortress of despotism."

The west parlor also has an elaborate fireplace and mantel, with the Washington coat of arms on the top; James Sharples painted the portraits of George and Martha Washington that hang there. Upstairs George Washington's bedroom contains his unusually wide bed, in which he died in 1799; the Windsor armchair next to the bed was in that position when he died.

Mount Vernon Tomato Cobbler

¼ cup olive oil	2¼ cups dry biscuit mix
24 plum or 18 beefsteak tomatoes, halved and seeded	1 tsp dried oregano
	1 tsp dried parsley
salt and pepper	½ cup milk

Brush baking sheets with oil. Put tomatoes face down, brush lightly with oil, season and bake at 350 degrees for 45 minutes, turning once. Chop coarsely and divide between 6 12 oz. soufflé cups. Combine biscuit mix and herbs, then add milk, stirring until just moist. Do not overmix. Divide dough into 6 portions, dust with flour and lightly form into patties. Top tomatoes with biscuits and hold in refrigerator. Bake at 350 degrees, until biscuits are golden and tomatoes bubble, about 15 minutes. *Serves 6.*

Outside on the grounds you can explore the "dependencies." The kitchen, where a staff of two cooks and two waiters produced sumptuous meals, now houses a collection of utensils and cooking gear. According to one writer, "The dinner was very good, a small roasted pigg, boiled leg of lamb, roasted fowls, beef, peas, lettuce, cucumbers, artichokes, puddings, tarts. We were desired to call for what drinks we chose." Other buildings include the smokehouse, greenhouse, icehouse, storehouse, coach house, and slave quarters. A museum has been added to house the large collection of Washington artifacts.

The gardens and greenhouse include four separate gardens filled with annuals and perennials of the period. A botanical garden was used to test new and exotic plants. The fruit garden was where Washington experimented with grapes, overgrown and neglected during the Revolution. He then used it as a nursery with grains and vegetables. An orchard was fenced to keep out livestock and deer.

George and Martha Washington are buried in the family vault. He directed that "the family Vault at Mount Vernon requiring repairs, and being improperly situated besides, I desire that a new one of Brick and upon a larger Scale, may be built at the foot of what is commonly called the Vineyard Inclosure—on the ground which is marked out—in which my remains, with those of my deceased relatives (now in the old Vault) and such others of my family as may chuse to be entombed there, may be deposited."

George Washington's Gristmill and Distillery (703-780-2000; www.mountvernon.org), 5514 Mount Vernon Memorial Hwy., Mount Vernon, VA 22309. Open daily. Washington replaced tobacco with wheat and built a large stone gristmill in 1771. Washington's Scottish farm manager James Anderson and his son John encouraged him to build a whiskey distillery adjacent to the gristmill.

The Andersons began distilling in 1797. They had five copper pot stills, and it was the largest whiskey distillery in the country in the 18th century. It operated until 1802, when Lawrence Lewis inherited it and leased the property. The distillery burned in 1814. Archaeologists excavated and found the stone foundation, the location for the five stills and boiler, drains, and objects such as broken plates, teacups, and drinking glasses. The reconstructed gristmill first opened in 1932 and the distillery in 2007, after extensive archaeological research.

RESTAURANTS

MOUNT VERNON INN
3200 Old Mount Vernon Memorial Hwy.
Mount Vernon, VA 22121
703-780-0011
This is a popular and convenient place to have lunch, right on the plantation grounds.

> ✺ Because music played such an important role in the social life at Mount Vernon, you will see a number of musical instruments in the "little parlor." George Washington gave "one very good Spinit" to his stepdaughter, Patsy Custis, and her brother received a violin and "a fine German flute." Nelly Custis was given a harpsichord in 1793, straight from London.

LEESBURG

Located near the upper reaches of the Potomac, Leesburg sat on the route both southwestward down the Shenandoah Valley and northwestward into Pennsylvania and Ohio. It was an outfitting post for Virginia troops during the French and Indian War, and George Washington had a headquarters here. After the Revolution it served as an emergency archive for the precious documents of the new nation. During the War of 1812 the Declaration of Independence, Constitution, and other important papers were stored in the cellar vault of a nearby mansion when the city of Washington went up in flames under British attack.

Many historic buildings still stand in an attractive and hospitable town that has no artificial trappings designed to attract tourists. The surrounding countryside in Loudoun County is beautiful with rolling hills, old mills, plantation mansions, restaurants, and B&Bs housed in buildings from the colonial era.

HISTORICAL SITES and MUSEUMS
The Loudoun County Museum (703 777-7427; www.loudonmuseum.org), 16 Loudoun St. SW, Leesburg, VA 20175, has a video that provides orientation for a visit to Leesburg and the area. Open daily except Tue. Powhatan Indians, who liked river valleys, lived here for many years and left behind arrowheads and pottery now on display in the museum.

King Charles I granted the land to seven of his faithful followers in 1649, but when the monarchy ended and Cromwell took over, they were not able to claim their land. By 1660, when Charles II had reclaimed the throne, new grants were

The Loudoun County Museum Annex used for special events and programs in Leesburg.

issued. But the land was slow to be settled, perhaps because of fears raised by raiding Iroquois from the north and west. Then the Treaty of Albany in 1722 ordained that the Indians would not come east of the Blue Ridge or south of the Potomac without permission.

By 1757 Thomas Lord Fairfax had surveyed Leesburg, and 70 half-acre lots were plotted. George Washington had been hired at the age of 17, in 1749, to survey land in the area. Silversmiths, blacksmiths, and traders kept the town's tavern busy. Stephen Donaldson was the first silversmith in Leesburg; he built a log building in 1763 that is now the gift shop next to the Loudoun Museum. By 1760 the town that had been "Georgetown" was renamed Leesburg, for Thomas Lee.

Local farmers provided food for George Washington's Continental Army. The area supplied clothing and wagons, as well as sent men to the war. Two generations later, during the Civil War, General Robert E. Lee's men were fed and housed in Leesburg after the Second Battle of Manassas.

The best way to get a sense of Leesburg's heritage is on foot. "A Walk around Leesburg" is available in the museum shop; visitors can stroll around a six-block area to get a feeling for the rich historical background of the city. At 29 W. Market St. is a Federal-style stone house that at one point served as a girls' school. In 1825 the Revolutionary War hero the Marquis de Lafayette visited Leesburg, and the girls performed a dance for him on the courthouse lawn.

The **Laurel Brigade**, 20 W. Market St., is the site of an "ordinary." The long section at the rear of the building was probably built as a ballroom to entertain Lafayette in 1825. Dr. Jacob Coutsman lived next door at 19 E. Market St., and he was the first doctor to reside in Leesburg; the deed was filed in 1758. His office was located at 23 E. Market St., a building that has interesting Flemish-bond brickwork with arches over the openings.

The **Patterson House**, a 1759 Georgian house with a colonial-revival porch at 4 E. Loudoun St., is one of the oldest houses in Leesburg. John and Fleming Patterson came from Scotland to settle here. Hessian soldiers imprisoned in the house drew caricatures on the walls of Washington, Patrick Henry, and other Revolutionary War leaders. It became Captain Henry McCabe's Ordinary in the late 1770s. George Washington enjoyed a dinner of jowls and greens here, prepared by a Mrs. McGill, and Lafayette was toasted by the mayor of the town in 1825 on the front steps.

The **Courthouse** (703-777-0270; www.loudoun.gov), dating from 1757, is located on the corner of King and Market Streets. The bell in the cupola tolled the news of the Boston Tea Party with its very first peals. In 1774 Loudoun freeholders created the Loudoun Resolves protesting the Stamp Act, which were taken to Philadelphia for the Continental Congress in September 1774.

There are a number of interesting houses on Cornwall Street.

The **Gray-Benedict-Harrison** home dates from 1759. The Flemish bond front combines Georgian and Federal styles. John Janney lived at 10 E. Cornwall St. in a house built in 1780. Reverend John Littlejohn lived at 11 W. Cornwall St. During the War of 1812 the Declaration of Independence and the Constitution were taken by wagon to this home just before the British burned

George Carter inherited the problems of his many sisters and was expected to solve them. One of his nieces wrote: "You're the man of the family and there is simply no one else to whom I can apply. Mama says the crops are bad, and there'll be no gowns for the new season. I just can't face life like this."

Washington. Then they were transferred to a cellar vault in Rokeby House in the nearby countryside.

Sir Peter Halkett had his headquarters in the **Stone House**, at 24 W. Loudoun St., before Braddock's disastrous 1755 Battle of Monongahela, and this is the probable site of Washington's headquarters during the French and Indian War.

Oatlands (703-777-3174; www.oat lands.org), 20850 Oatlands Plantation Lane. Open daily Apr.–Dec. Although the mansion dates from 1804, the original owner of the site, Robert Carter, bought the land in 1728. He was the grandson of King Carter, once the wealthiest man in Virginia. George Carter, born in 1777, continued to add to his Georgian red-brick house with plasterwork in the front hall, plus wings and a portico. He married at age 59 and had four children.

The gardens at Oatlands include ornamental statuary and a collection of rare specimen trees.

LODGING

NORRIS HOUSE INN
108 Loudoun St. SW, Leesburg, VA 20175-2909
800-644-1806, 703-777-1806;
www.norrishouse.com
The inn, in the historic district, dates from 1760 and offers bed-and-breakfast accommodations. The Norris brothers were noted as excellent craftsmen. A new conservatory adds appeal to this house in a garden. Six guest rooms.

RESTAURANTS

EIFFEL TOWER CAFÉ
107 Loudoun St. SW
703-777-5142
The owners came from France and offer French cuisine in the dining rooms and on a patio.

LIGHTFOOT RESTAURANT
11 North King St.
703-771-2233

The restaurant is open for lunch and dinner.

TUSCARORA MILL
203 Harrison St.
703-771-9300
This restaurant, nicknamed "Tuskie's," is in a restored 19th-century grain mill. Open for lunch and dinner.

EVENTS

October: All Leesburg turns out for its annual October Court Days. Colonial-dressed interpreters walk through the crowds, getting everyone involved in conversations of the day. Visitors will see Thomas Jefferson, George Washington, and the town crier strolling the streets. During the mid-1700s circuit judges traveled from town to town, and by the late 1700s they held "court days" on specific days in each county. Local people looked upon these days as a time to "make merrie" and enjoy the gossip about various court cases. Now the same traditions prevail, and there are colonial dances, musketry practice, and historical reenactments. The Bluemont Concert Series presents wonderful music. Craftspeople come from all over the Mid-Atlantic region to display and sell their wares. For more information call the Loudoun County Visitors Center at 703-771-2617 or 800-752-6118.

INFORMATION

LOUDOUN CONVENTION & VISITORS ASSOCIATION
2220 Catoctin Circle SE, Leesburg, VA 20175
800-752-6118, 703-771-2170

CENTRAL VIRGINIA

In a colony where the growing economy was powered by tobacco and the extensive plantations needed to grow it, there was little impetus for the establishment of major towns. Those that did begin to flourish were often located at the fall line of rivers, where they could become trading centers looking both downstream into the Tidewater and upstream into the Piedmont. Thus it is no surprise that Virginia's two major towns of the colonial era, Fredericksburg and Richmond, were located at the falls of the Rappahannock and the James Rivers, respectively.

FREDERICKSBURG

Long ago the Indians used the area at the falls of the Rappahannock River for fishing and hunting. Today fishermen come when the shad and herring are running in the spring.

The town dates from 1728, when it was a frontier river port.

In 1713 a deposit of iron ore had been found near the Rapidan River, west of present-day Fredericksburg. Alexander Spotswood, who had arrived as lieutenant governor of Viriginia in 1710, established a town at the site after he had created the architectural plans for Williamsburg. He developed an iron mining operation and imported German ironworkers to his town, which he called Germanna. By 1728 more than 160 ironworkers were on the job. Spotswood also built a mansion for himself on a bluff overlooking the river outside of town and moved his family into it.

Spotswood also built wharves on the Rappahannock River that were used by the tobacco industry. Because of disputes with him, the assembly chose another site for a port—where the town of Fredericksburg is now. The town was named for Crown Prince Frederick, the son of George II (Frederick did not live long enough to become king). The streets were named for Frederick's family—George, Caroline, Sophia, Princess Anne, Hanover, Charlotte, William, and Amelia.

In 1730 Fredericksburg had become the official receiving and shipping center for the tobacco grown in Spotsylvania County and the west.

George Washington lived in Fredericksburg from the age of 6 to 16, on the family farm, Ferry Farm. In 1774 he moved his mother into a house in Fredericksburg and sold Ferry Farm.

HISTORICAL SITES and MUSEUMS

Kenmore Plantation & Gardens (540-373-3381; www.kenmore.org), 1201 Washington Ave., Fredericksburg, VA 22401. Open daily Mar.–Dec. Fielding Lewis arrived from Gloucester County in 1747 with his wife, Catherine Washington, a first cousin of George Washington. Catherine died in 1750, and Lewis then married and built this home for his wife, Betty, the sister of George Washington. He was a successful businessman, and his storehouse held supplies for George Washington during the French and Indian War and also for Mount Vernon.

Kenmore is noted for its decorative plasterwork. Lewis's "stucco man" was lent to do the ceiling in Washington's dining room at Mount Vernon.

After Lewis died in 1781, Betty managed the estate with her stepson, John, until she moved to another farm in 1796. Samuel Gordon bought the house and named it Kenmore. You can watch a DVD on the history of Kenmore in the visitor center. Don't miss seeing Betty's traveling trunk, which was made from a tree trunk.

When we visited in May 2007, the house was being renovated; it will be refurnished gradually. We had a tour of the house and were stunned by the exquisite plasterwork. Research into the paint colors and wallpaper will provide an authentic restoration.

Mary Washington House (800-678-4748, 540-373-1776; www.apva.org/apva/mary_washington_house.php), 1200 Charles St. Open daily. In 1772 George Washington bought this home for his mother. Mary married Augustine Washington in 1731, and George was born in 1732. After Augustine died in 1743, Mary raised her children in their home, Ferry Farm (see below). Look in her bedroom to see her "best dressing glass," which she willed to George. In 1789 George visited her to receive her blessing before his inauguration as our first president. She died the same year and was buried at Meditation Rock on the Lewis estate.

Upon finding a once-beautiful cherry tree whose bark was badly stripped, young Washington's father asked him who had done it. The boy replied "I cannot tell a lie, Pa; you know I can't tell a lie. I did cut it with my hatchet." This legend was almost certainly invented by Parson Weems and continues to live because people want to believe it.

Rising Sun Tavern (540-373-1494; search rising sun tavern), 1304 Caroline St. Open daily. Charles Washington built his home in 1760, and it later became a tavern, called the Golden Eagle. It was said to be the only "proper" tavern in town. Look in the taproom for the collection of pewter plates. Today "tavern

The gardens at Kenmore Plantation in Fredericksburg

wenches" will tell you about the "two-fisted drinkers" and those who "drank like a fish."

Ferry Farm (540-370-0732; www.ferryfarm.org), 268 Kings Hwy. Open Mar.–Dec. George Washington lived at this site from age 6 to 16. The visitor center has exhibits including "George Washington: Boy before Legend," which includes a genealogy of the Washington family. Archaeologists are trying to find the original farm buildings and houses from Washington's era; artifacts found include wig curlers, a copper thimble, a shoe buckle, a knee buckle, clay marbles, a fork and spoon, a teapot, and glass beads. The legends that embellish Washington's boyhood—the cherry tree and throwing a silver dollar across the river—relate to this farm, but almost nothing is known about his life there or his relationship with his father.

LODGING

KENMORE INN
1200 Princess Anne St., Fredericksburg, VA 22401
540-371-7622; www.kenmoreinn.com
This 1793 building is in the historic district. Colonel John Lewis bought the land in 1742 and brought his first bride, Catherine, here in 1747. Nine guest rooms.

LITTLEPAGE INN
15701 Monrovia Rd., Mineral, VA 23117
800-248-1803, 540-854-9861; www.littlepage.com
General Lewis Littlepage was in the diplomatic service in Poland. He willed money to his younger half-brother, Waller Holladay, who purchased plantation land on Prospect Hill in 1805. By 1811 the manor house was built, and it has passed down into the sixth generation of the Holladay family. Guest rooms are available in the main house or in a guest house. Nine guest rooms.

RICHARD JOHNSTON INN
711 Caroline St., Fredericksburg, VA 22401
877-557-0770, 540-899-7606; www.therichardjohnstoninn.com
John Taylow, an architect who built many of the homes in the area, built his home in 1770, and it became the home of the mayor of Fredericksburg, Richard Johnson, in the 1800s.

RESTAURANTS

BISTRO BETHEM
309 William St.
540-371-9999
The walls are covered with artwork that changes periodically. The chef offers American cuisine with a southern touch.

CLAIBORNE'S
200 Lafayette Blvd.
540-371-7080
The restaurant is in the restored train station dating from the early 1900s. Historic prints line the walls.

KENMORE INN
1200 Princess Anne St.
540-371-7622
Offers fine dining and meals in an English pub. The wine cellar is well known.

EVENTS

February: Presidents Day, 540-373-1569

INFORMATION

FREDERICKSBURG VISITOR CENTER
706 Caroline St.
Fredericksburg, VA 22401
800-678-4748, 540-373-1776

RICHMOND

English explorers led by Captain Christopher Newport and Captain John Smith from Jamestown arrived in 1607 and planted a cross on an island. Smith bought land from Chief Powhatan in 1609 and founded "Nonesuch," which was soon abandoned.

South of present-day Richmond, Sir Thomas Dale led 350 settlers in 1611 to a site called Henricus. (The London Company had instructed Dale to find a better location than Jamestown.) This was the second English settlement in America. For a time Pocahontas lived here, in the home of the Reverend Alexander Whitaker, called Rock Hall. She had converted to Christianity and then married John Rolfe. Their marriage calmed tensions between her people and the English. Fort Charles rose at the falls of the James River in 1645.

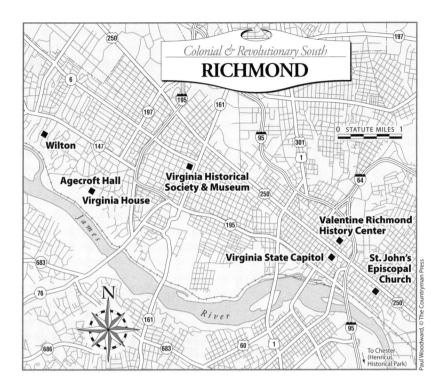

Colonial & Revolutionary South
RICHMOND

Paul Woodward, © The Countryman Press

In 1737 Colonel William Byrd designed, as a mill site and trading center, the city that would become Richmond. Byrd wrote that this land at the fall line of the James River was "naturally intended for marts, where the traffic of the outer inhabitants must center." A disaster took place in 1771 when a 40-foot wave of water came down the James River and demolished houses and tobacco warehouses.

Patrick Henry delivered his famous "Give me liberty or give me death" speech here in 1775, in St. John's Church. Delegates voted to train militia units for the war, with only 5 of the 125 delegates opposing the move.

In April 1780 the state capital was moved here from Williamsburg, to gain safety from the British and also to provide a more central location. Nevertheless, in 1781 Benedict Arnold, now a British general, burned Richmond; Governor Thomas Jefferson was forced to flee the city. In 1786 Jefferson's Statute for Religious Freedom, which he had drafted in 1779, was enacted into Virginia law with the help of James Madison. Jefferson and Charles-Louis Clérisseau designed the state capitol building.

HISTORICAL SITES *and* MUSEUMS

St. John's Church (804-648-5015; www.historicstjohnschurch.org), 2401 Broad St. Open daily. This National Historic Landmark is the oldest wooden church in Virginia. In the spring of 1775 over 100 Virginians met here, including George

Washington, Thomas Jefferson, Richard Henry Lee, and Patrick Henry, who delivered his famous oration: "Give me liberty or give me death."

Tours of the church include the graveyard, where prominent citizens are buried. They include George Wythe, the first Virginian to sign the Declaration of Independence, and Elizabeth Arnold Poe, the mother of Edgar Allan Poe. (See the events section below for information on the reenactments of the Second Virginia Convention of March 1775. You will see living history interpreters and professional actors portray 10 of the founding fathers. Patrick Henry delivers his oration as a climax.)

Virginia Historical Society (804-358-4901; www.vahistorical.org), 428 North Blvd. Open daily. Many treasures from the past are on exhibit in this extensive museum. Its centerpiece is "The Story of Virginia, an American Experience," in the Robins Center for Virginia History. You can trace back 16,000 years into prehistoric times. The collection includes a 17th-century dugout canoe; an original

Agecroft Hall and gardens: a little bit of old England in Richmond

Conestoga wagon, along with information on John Keger, a wheelwright and wagon maker born in 1775; an 1820s smokehouse and kitchen; and a Richmond streetcar, to name a few. A tavern mug dating from about 1720 is said to have been used to drink a toast to Lord Cornwallis's surrender at Yorktown.

The "Coming Americans" section has a wealth of information on the founding fathers. Don't miss the life mask of George Washington painted by Jean Leon Gerome Ferris. Women in the Revolution includes a display on Dolley Madison and Martha Washington.

When we visited, the museum had a large special exhibit on Pocahontas. Always fascinated by Pocahontas, we enjoy the legend about her courageous act to save John Smith from execution. Myth or not, it is a moving tale. She did in fact marry another Englishman, John Rolfe, and they were able to restore good relations between her people and the settlers.

One of the exhibits that has people bending over and walking around it is the miniature plantation house, Wilton. The Marquis de Lafayette used Wilton for his headquarters during the Revolution, and George Washington stayed there in 1775. Thomas Jefferson visited the house. Mildred Grinstead visited the real Wilton, recorded information with a camera and note pad, and then built a reproduction in miniature. This 64-by-44-inch brick model is built to a scale of one inch to one foot. It contains furniture of the period between 1750 and 1775. There are nine petit point rugs on the floors, and the miniature Simon Willard tall case clock works. It is not to be missed!

When the home was about to be dismantled because it was designated for an industrial site, the Virginia Society of the Colonial Dames of America raised money and moved it brick by brick from Worlds End on the James River to Richmond. (See information below on Wilton House.)

Virginia House (804-353-4251; www.vahistorical.org), 4301 Sulgrave Rd. Open daily. This house is owned and operated by the Virginia Historical Society. It was once the 12th-century Priory of St. Sepulchre in England. Before it was to be demolished, Virginia and Alexander Weddell bought the house, disassembled it and shipped it to Virginia, and reconstructed it in 1928 on a hill overlooking the James River. The collections inside are treasures acquired by the Weddells, who traveled widely. He was ambassador to Argentina and Spain. The gardens were created by Charles Gillette; Virginia Weddell took 20 years to complete her 8 acres of gardens. In the spring visitors are greeted by daffodils and tulips, and then daylilies, wildflowers, roses, iris, lotus, hollies, magnolias, and jasmine appear throughout the year.

Agecroft Hall, located next door, was rescued from Lancashire, England, by Thomas Williams. He had it dismantled, crated, and shipped to Windsor Farms, where the reconstruction took two years and cost $250,000. It served as a family home. Agecroft Hall opened as a museum in 1969. The house is furnished with English and Continental pieces from the Tudor and early Stuart periods (1485–1649).

The great hall was used for special occasions such as Twelfth Night feasts. A Mortlake tapestry, "The Wolf Hunt," hangs on the fireplace wall. The arms and armor are displayed here. Don't miss seeing the original owner's family coat-of-arms in stained glass.

The great parlor was used by the family and contains a 16th-century inlaid gaming table, musical instruments, and books. The 1610 lantern clock has only the hour hand. Upstairs, the sleeping chambers have beds with coverlets and curtains. Carved bedsteads include lions' heads, acanthus leaves, and mythical figures. One room has a rare17th-century painted bedstead.

The Tudor kitchen is new and was patterned from an inventory. The timbers, some of them retrieved after a hurricane, were distressed to look old. The kitchen pieces were sent from England.

Outside, the sunken garden is like the pond garden at Hampton Court Palace in England. Other gardens include the knot garden, fragrance garden, and herb garden.

Virginia State Capitol (804-698-1788; www.virginiacapitol.gov), Capitol Square at Ninth and Grace Sts. Open Mon.–Fri. Thomas Jefferson designed the original Capitol, and it was in use by 1788. Wings were added later, and renovations were completed in 2007, including an underground extension with the entrance on Bank Street. The Rotunda is handsome with its white and black checks on the floor and its collection of sculptures. George Washington stands in the center. He was sculpted by Jean-Antoine Houdon, who visited Mount Vernon, took body measurements, and made sketches. Houdon even made a life mask by oiling Washington's face and covering it with plaster. The statue stands 2 feet, 2 inches. A Carrara marble bust of the Marquis de Lafayette was also created by Houdon. Busts of other Virginia-born presidents who succeeded Washington are in niches around the room.

The Old Hall of the House of Delegates is the largest room in the building. Delegates were seated in rows around the Speaker's chair. In 1791 the House voted here to ratify the Bill of Rights. In this same room in 1807 Aaron Burr was acquitted of treason. Community events and church services were also held here. Today it is a museum, filled with many historical objects. The statue of General Robert E. Lee is on the site where he stood in 1861 when he accepted command of the military forces of the Commonwealth of Virginia.

The Old Senate Chamber has two paintings depicting major historical events. *The Arrival of the First Permanent English Settlers off Jamestown Island, May 13, 1607* was painted by Griffith Baily Coale. *Storming of a British Redoubt at Yorktown by American Troops* depicts the 1781 attack leading to the surrender of British and Hessian troops during the last large-scale battle of the Revolutionary War.

Outside, **Capitol Square** is landscaped with fountains. There's a Bell Tower, an equestrian monument of General George Washington, and a bronze statue of Edgar Allan Poe.

Valentine Richmond History Center (804-649-0711; www.richmond

The Virginia State Capitol

historycenter.com), 1015 E. Clay St., Richmond, VA 23219. Open Tue.–Sun. John Wickham was born in 1763, married in 1791, and had two children before his wife died. He then married Elizabeth McClurg, the daughter of the second mayor of Richmond. They had 17 children. He was part of the legal team that defended Aaron Burr against charges of treason.

His home was designed by Alexander Parris beginning in 1812 and finished in 1815. After Wickham died in 1839, Mann S. Valentine II bought the home. He had a variety of collections on archaeological and ethnographic materials. They were first displayed in the Wickham House, then in three adjacent row houses, and now in the museum. The Wickham House has an elliptical stairway that is supported by hidden iron bars extending from the wall into the treads of the stairs. Neoclassical murals are among the few surviving wall paintings of this time in America. Classical scenes in the parlor from John Flaxman's 1805 drawings for *The Iliad* are especially remarkable.

Wilton (804-282-5936; www.wiltonhousemuseum.org), 215 S. Wilton Rd. Open Tue.–Sun. William Randolph III built his home in 1753, and it was completed in 1759. Originally it stood on the north bank of the James River, east of Richmond. When it was in danger of demolition, the Virginia Society of the Colonial Dames of America raised money and moved it to its present site. Inside, the wide hall was used for dances as well as a reception area. The Hepplewhite tall-case clock was made by Simon Willard in 1795.

Every room in the house is decorated with furnishings of the period. The silver collection is magnificent and includes a French neoclassical epergne on the Hepplewhite dining table. One of the coffeepots was made of silver in London in

Construction on Wilton mansion began in 1753.

1768. The top has a little monkey in Chinese costume. All rooms are paneled, and the fireplaces are marble.

The Randolph portraits displayed are copies of the originals in the Virginia Historical Society. The antique map collection includes one showing the original location of Wilton. The master bedroom has a stairway leading up to the nursery, a very useful feature, since the Randolphs had eight children.

Henricus Historical Park (804-706-1340; www.henricus.org.), 251 Henricus Park Rd. Open Tue.–Sun. This park is a re-creation of the second successful English settlement in the New World. Sir Thomas Dale established Henricus in 1611. Historical documentation describes the site as "convenient, strong, healthie and a sweete seate to plant a new Towne in." Reconstruction is taking place, and so far there is a watch tower, bake house, gardens, and part of a palisade to explore. Interpreters wear period clothing as they go about their daily life in the town.

LODGING

THE JEFFERSON
101 W. Franklin St., Richmond, VA 23220
866-247-2276, 804-788-8000;
www.jeffersonhotel.com
The hotel dates from 1895; it was inspired by the Villa Medici in Florence, Italy. A statue of Thomas Jefferson was created by E. V. Valentine. The stained-glass skylights are stunning, along with the grand staircase. There are 262 guest rooms.

THE BERKELEY HOTEL
1200 E. Cary St., Richmond, VA 23219
888-780-4422, 804-780-1300;
www.BerkeleyHotel.com
This hotel is located in the historic Shockoe Slip area. Fifty-five guest rooms.

RESTAURANTS

BISTRO TWENTY SEVEN
27 W. Broad St.
804-780-0086; www.bistrotwenty seven.com
This restaurant has floor-to-ceiling windows and 20-foot ceilings. It also has an open kitchen so you can see what's cooking. The cuisine is billed as "around the world."

JULEP'S NEW SOUTHERN CUISINE
1721 E. Franklin St.
804-377-3968; www.juleps.net
Julep's is in one of the oldest commercial buildings in Shockoe Slip. Walk up the spiral staircase and you'll see the original 1817 beams. The cuisine is creative, and fried green tomatoes are a specialty.

TARRANT'S CAFÉ
One W. Broad St.
804-225-0035
This popular café dates from 1873. The menu offers seafood and light entrées.

EVENTS

March: "Give me liberty or give me death" reenactment, St. John's Church, 804-648-5015
November: Holiday Family Open House, Wilton House, 804-282-5936
September: Publick Days at Henricus Historical Park, 804-706-1340

INFORMATION

RICHMOND METROPOLITAN CONVENTION & VISITORS BUREAU
401 N. 3rd St., Richmond, VA 23219
800-RICHMOND, 804-782-2777
www.visit.richmondva.com

The term "Renaissance man" suggests an almost inconceivable intellectual power and multiplicity of talents that we associate with Michelangelo and Leonardo da Vinci. Although we sometimes pay lip service to the ideal of being able to do many things well, the explosion of knowledge and hyperspecialization of our world make the possibility hard to believe in, whether we're talking about what it takes to be a nuclear physicist or a professional tennis star.

Yet just two centuries ago the plantation owners and merchants who played the central role in founding our government were indeed men for all seasons, not only soldiers and statesmen but simultaneously farmers, businessmen, architects, scientists, and scholars. Thomas Jefferson represents a whole class of Virginians who demonstrated their capacities and vigor by playing many roles well.

Today there are a number of historic homes and estates to visit near Charlottesville, a small town in Jefferson's time but now numbering 45,000 residents. Monticello is just off I-64 exit 121, perched on a hill beyond the edge of the city below. The plantation still retains the air of a bucolic retreat for a man who needed relief from the hurly-burly of colonial and early Federal politics. Nearby is Ash Lawn–Highland, home of James Monroe, the fourth Virginian to serve as president of the new nation. Charlottesville's centerpiece remains the University of Virginia, which Jefferson designed and founded in 1819.

HISTORICAL SITES and MUSEUMS
Monticello (434-984-9822; www.monticello.org), 931 Thomas Jefferson Pkwy., Charlottesville, VA 22902. Open daily. This is the remarkable house Jefferson built on a hill above Charlottesville, overlooking the university he designed and founded.

In 1993 a special exhibition of Jefferson's possessions commemorated his 250th birthday. Works of art and artifacts that were auctioned off by his daughter, Martha Randolph, to pay debts after his death in 1826 returned to the house. Pieces were on loan from 50 public and private collections around the world.

Things may not make the man, but in Jefferson's case they often tell the tale of his taste, his accomplishments, and his amazing intellectual versatility. They include his famous revolving Windsor chair, the mahogany lap desk on which he wrote the Declaration of Independence, and many portraits, including those of George Washington, the Marquis de Lafayette, and John Adams. Also, a footed silver goblet made by a Parisian silversmith based on Jefferson's drawing, a bronze bell given to Sally Hemings, a household slave, by Martha Jefferson, and Windsor chairs based on his specifications. After a tour of his amazing house, which anticipates many of the innovations in recent home architecture, you'll think of him as the Frank Lloyd Wright of the 18th century. And it's all done in rooms of modest proportions.

Jefferson inherited 500 acres and slaves when he was just 21 years old. He started to build Monticello at the age of 26 and supervised its construction after making detailed drawings. He chose a formal classical design based on the work of the 16th-century Italian architect Andrea Palladio, whose influence pervaded the building of plantation mansions in Virginia. The house had a purpose beyond architectural elegance: Jefferson married Martha Skelton three years later. She bore him six children and died in 1782.

Jefferson attended the College of William and Mary, practiced law, and entered public life at an early age. In 1776 he was chosen to draft the Declaration of Independence. He served as governor of Virginia from 1779 to 1781, and in 1784, after the Revolution had ended, went to France, where he succeeded Benjamin Franklin as minister representing the young nation. In 1790 he became secretary of state under George Washington. Jefferson was elected president of the United States in 1800 and held the office from 1801 to 1809.

Jefferson authorized the crucial purchase of the Louisiana Territory in 1803 and supported exploration of the West by the Lewis and Clark expedition. In 1815

Thomas Jefferson's Monticello

✳ In one of the most sym-
bolic coincidences in
American history, both John
Adams and Thomas Jefferson
died on July 4, 1826. They had
been fellow patriots and friends
before and during the Revolution, bitter political enemies
during the tumultuous 1790s,
and finally reconciled corre-
spondents during their later
years.

he sold his personal library to the Library of Congress, to replace the national library that had been burned by the British during the War of 1812. After a life of incredible accomplishment, Jefferson died at the age of 83 in 1826.

The best place to start comprehending those accomplishments is the Thomas Jefferson Visitor Center, on Route 20 off Interstate 64. There you can view several fine films, including *Thomas Jefferson at Monticello* and *Thomas Jefferson: The Pursuit of Liberty*, as well as collect sightseeing and lodging information. The center also sells a discounted combination ticket for Monticello, Michie Tavern, and Ash Lawn–Highland. (See below for details of sites.) All three historic sites are open daily, apart from a few major holidays, but times vary seasonally. Call 804-293-6789 for more information.

Today visitors to Monticello can view the home in small groups. The entrance hall was the "museum of civilization," which contained Jefferson's collection of Native American and natural history pieces. Visitors used to wait in this room, where they could view his collections. Pieces from his collection include a buffalo robe that depicts a battle, a tobacco pouch of otter skin from the Sauk-Fox, a Crow cradle, and an eagle bone whistle. Jefferson's seven-day calendar clock has markers on the wall for the days of the week; to record them, cannon balls move up and down on a rope, disappearing into a hole in the floor.

The south square room was an extension of his library. The "book room" once contained his 7,000 books before he sold them to the Library of Congress. Books on the shelves now exhibit the same titles. His study contains the revolving chair, a Windsor bench, a revolving-top table, a telescope, and globes.

An alcove containing his bed connects the south square room with his two-story bedroom, a marvelous anticipation of lofts. A skylight provides light, and several oval openings provide air into his closet, which is really on the second floor but accessible from the ground level. A black marble obelisk clock is mounted at the foot of his bed.

Jefferson was always up at first light, and the first thing he did was wash his feet in cold water, which he said kept him from getting sick.

The family gathered most of the time in the parlor to talk, engage in games, play the harpsichord, and entertain friends. Portraits on the walls include those of Magellan, Columbus, Walter Raleigh, and Lafayette.

The dining room, stretching up two stories with a skylight, also contains dumbwaiters designed to bring up wine from the cellar. Because the room is in the coldest corner of the house, windows and doors both have double glass. Look for a

An interior at Ash Lawn–Highland, the home of President James Monroe

revolving serving door with shelves. Servants on the outside put food on the shelves, while those on the inside removed them to serve the table.

An all-weather passageway leads under the house to access the kitchen, smokehouse, cook's quarters, stables, and ice house. Just beyond is Mulberry Row, which has buildings for weaving, nail making, a utility shed, and dwellings for slaves and carpentry. The flower gardens contain 20 oval-shaped beds planted with a variety of flowers. Some of the species came from Europe, some are woodland flowers, others were curiosities. A "roundabout" flower border winds around a curving walk that Jefferson planned in 1807.

Ash Lawn–Highland (434-293-9539; www.ashlawnhighland.org), 1000 James Monroe Pkwy., Charlottesville, VA 22902. Open daily. The home of President James Monroe is located 2½ miles beyond Monticello on VA 795. Monroe

Have you heard of an 18th-century polygraph? Jefferson anticipated carbon paper and photocopiers by two centuries with his most unusual, two-pen, letter-duplicating device. A wooden frame holds two pens, which write in tandem on two sheets of paper—accounting for the duplicates in Jefferson's correspondence.

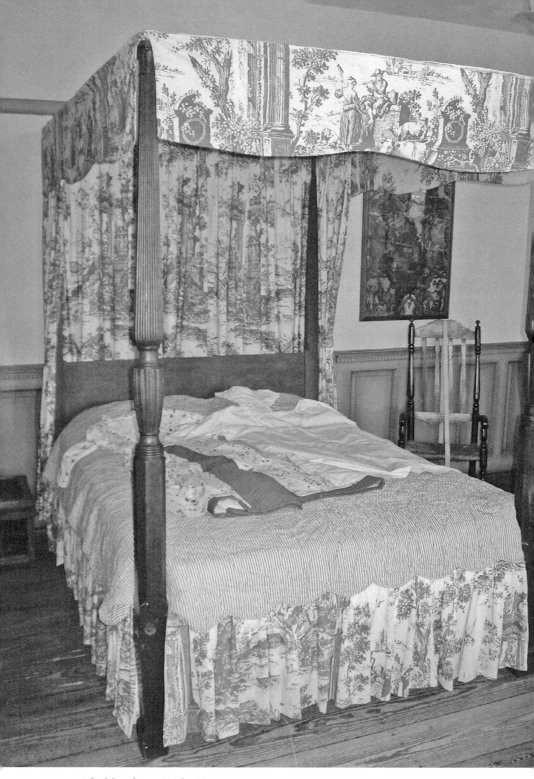

A bedchamber at Michie Tavern

and Jefferson were friends, and Jefferson chose the house site for Monroe, later sending his gardeners over to begin planting orchards. By November 1799 Monroe and his wife, Elizabeth, moved into their new plantation home. Portraits include one of his daughter, Eliza. Many Monroe possessions are still in the house.

Unfortunately, Monroe ran into debt because of his incredible public service and had to sell Ash Lawn–Highland instead of retiring there. He had held more major offices than any other president, including being a U.S. senator, minister to England, minister to Spain and to France, governor of Virginia, secretary of state, and secretary of war. He was president from 1817 to 1825.

In 1974 Jay Winston Johns gave Ash Lawn–Highland to the College of William and Mary, Monroe's alma mater. The college completed a major restoration to coincide with the 200th anniversary of Monroe's purchase of the house as well as the 300th anniversary of the founding of William and Mary.

On the other side of Monticello, on the way to Charlottesville, stands **Michie Tavern** (434-977-1234; www.michietavern.com), 683 Thomas Jefferson Pkwy., Charlottesville, VA 22902. Open daily. It is one of the oldest homesteads in Virginia. William Michie, a Scotsman whose father had come to Virginia as an indentured servant, opened his home as an "ordinary"—a tavern and eating house—to travelers on the stagecoach route in 1784. It was moved to its present location in 1927. The Tavern Museum offers a glimpse into life of that era with the ballroom, keeping hall, parlors, and a wine cellar. Take a tour, and when you get upstairs your guide may invite you to learn a 17th-century dance—great fun!

Visitors can have lunch in the Ordinary, which offers typical 18th-century Virginia cuisine daily. A general store carries Virginia wines, specialty foods, and gifts.

Years after designing his own house and completing his eminent political career, Jefferson laid out an elaborate plan for the **University of Virginia** (434-924-7969; www.virginia.edu), parking at Emmet St. and Ivy Rd. The Rotunda was to resemble the Pantheon in Rome, and in the early years of the university it served as library and classroom together. Pavilions extend from either side of the

 The following recipe is on the "Bill of Fare" at the Ordinary:

Michie Tavern Corn Bread

2 cups self-rising white stone-ground cornmeal	¼ cup milk
½ cup sugar	2 eggs
	½ cup canola oil

Sift together cornmeal and sugar in a bowl. Add milk, eggs, and oil. Stir with a wooden spoon just until all ingredients are wet and smooth. Bake in a greased 8-inch square pan in preheated oven at 425 degrees for 15–20 minutes. Cut into squares and serve.

Rotunda; professors lived in the pavilions, and students lived in 54 rooms in between the pavilions. The Jeffersonian "academical village" has been considerably expanded over the years, but its design influenced most of the major universities on the East Coast, so it is not inappropriate that a statue of Thomas Jefferson by Karl Bitter stands on the grounds. Perhaps we should remember the architect as much as the politician.

The **Pavilion Gardens** are divided into East Pavilion and West Pavilion. Each garden is numbered and has a different design. They are pleasant as a place to study and also designed to be an object of study. Jefferson felt that "such a plan would afford the quiet retirement so friendly to study." Professors planned and cared for some of the gardens; others contained buildings that served utilitarian functions such as quarters for servants and sheds for animals. Thus the liberal and practical arts existed in cooperative union—an ideal at least a century ahead of its time.

There is no doubt that Jefferson was a remarkable man, as his house, gardens, inventions, books, scientific instruments, and the University of Virginia campus visibly demonstrate. Yet we must remind ourselves that he was not so much one of a kind as preeminent in a whole class of individuals whose houses and libraries represent a comparable range of interests. Through a combination of circumstances—classical education, leisure, opportunities for political leadership, and genuine interest in agriculture—a class of American Renaissance men was born who could, and did, do it all.

MONTPELIER STATION

Some twenty miles northeast of Charlottesville, about halfway to Culpeper, lies the impressive family seat of yet another of the founding fathers—and the Father of the U.S. Constitution.

HISTORICAL SITES *and* MUSEUMS

Montpelier (540-672-2728; www.montpelier.org), 11407 Constitution Hwy., Montpelier Station, VA 22957 (mailing address: P.O. Box 911, Orange, VA 22960). Open daily. Montpelier, President James Madison's lifelong home, is undergoing a $23 million restoration, which will be completed in 2008.

The visitor center offers an orientation in the theater. The Treasures of Montpelier are displayed in the Joe and Marge Grills Gallery. Adjacent to the visitor center, the duPont Gallery pays tribute to the other historic Montpelier family, that of William and Annie duPont, who owned and lived on the property for most of the 20th century.

James Madison, our fourth president, is known as the Father of the Constitution and architect of the Bill of Rights. His wife, Dolley Madison, the "nation's first First Lady," was revered and loved for her commitment to the young nation. She was known for her political salons and hospitality.

Thomas Jefferson's Poplar Forest (434-525-1806; www.poplarforest.org),

1548 Bateman Bridge Rd., Forest, VA 24551 (mail: P.O. Box 419, Forest, VA 24551). Open daily except Tue. Poplar Forest, outside Lynchburg, was a private retreat where Jefferson came to rest, rekindle his creativity, and enjoy private time with his family. It was also a working plantation. He wrote, "I write to you from a place 90 miles from Monticello, near the New London of this state, which I visit three or four times a year, & stay from a fortnight to a month at a time. I have fixed myself comfortably, keep some books here, bring others occasionally, am in the solitude of a hermit, and quite at leisure to attend to my absent friends."

Jefferson kept his library of 700 books in the parlor. Visitors are welcome to sit in a reproduction of a Windsor chair and a siesta chair with its low-slung back. His bedroom accommodated a 6-foot-long bed, which meant that that the 6-foot-2 Jefferson slept propped up, a practice customary at the time. A lunette window lighted the stairwell at the west end of the room. The dining room is topped with a 16-foot-long skylight.

During restoration, the pine boards from the 1840s were replaced with floors of polished oak. The 14 hearths and fireplaces were restored. The design of the house provided for the exterior walls to form a perfect equal-sided octagon. Inside, the space is divided into four elongated hexagons surrounding a central square, which is lit from above with a skylight.

LODGING

BOAR'S HEAD INN
200 Ednam Dr., Charlottesville, VA 22903
800-476-1988; www.boarsheadinn.com
A boar's head was used on the signs of taverns and public houses in Elizabethan England as a symbol of hospitality. The inn is on the site of Terrell's Ordinary, which dated from the 1730s. A gristmill was dismantled and reconstructed on the present site. The original fieldstones and timbers are still in place. There are 171 guest rooms.

THE INN AT MONTICELLO
1188 Scottsville Rd., Charlottesville, VA 22902
877-RELAX-VA, 434-979-3593
This historic B&B dates from 1850, when it began life as a farmhouse. Five guest rooms.

PROSPECT HILL PLANTATION INN
2887 Poindexter Rd., Charlottesville, VA 22906
800-277-0844; www.prospecthill.com
The manor house dates from 1732, with outbuildings from the 1840s to the 1920s. Thirteen guest rooms.

SILVER THATCH INN
3001 Hollymead Dr., Charlottesville, VA 22911
800-261-0720, 434-978-4686; www.silverthatchinn.com
The inn dates to 1780, when Hessian soldiers captured at the Battle of Saratoga and marched to Charlottesville built a log cabin. Seven guest rooms.

RESTAURANTS

MICHIE TAVERN
683 Thomas Jefferson Pkwy.
434-977-1234
The Ordinary offers typical 18th-century cuisine.

OLD MILL ROOM
Boar's Head Inn
200 Ednam Dr.
The hand-hewn timbers of the gristmill lend atmosphere to this restaurant. The menu offers a wide range of dishes, including the special chef's "Hot Pot," which changes daily.

EVENTS

January: First Night Virginia, 434-293-6789
May: Ash Lawn–Highland Virginia Wine Festivel, 434-293-9539
July: Monticello Independence Day, 434-984-9822
November: Governor Jefferson's Thanks-giving Festival, 434-293-6789

Current Information

VIRGINIA DIVISION OF TOURISM
901 E. Byrd St.
Richmond, VA 23219
804-545-5500, 800-VISIT-VA
www.virginia.org

North Carolina

Historical Introduction *to the* North Carolina Colony

We sometimes think of North Carolina as a state on a tilt—rising into the Great Smoky and Blue Ridge Mountains at its western edge and dipping into the great sounds of Albemarle and Pamlico along its eastern fringe. In between lie the rolling hills of the elevated Piedmont. The barrier islands stretch along the northern coast in a narrow sand spit, then bend southwesterly and continue with few breaks to the South Carolina border. At the turning point, Cape Hatteras marks some of the most dangerous waters in world oceans, notorious among seamen for shifting shoals, strong currents, and fierce gales.

Europeans first explored North Carolina for possible settlement and two other elusive goals—the long-sought northwest passage to the Orient, and gold. Navigation along the uncharted coast of a new continent was uncertain at best—and especially so nearly two centuries before there was an accurate method of determining longitude. Leading a French expedition, Giovanni da Verrazano sailed along the coast from Cape Fear to Albemarle Sound in 1524 and mistook the great sounds for the Pacific Ocean because he saw no land behind them. The following year Lucas Vázquez de Ayllón explored the region between the Cape Fear and Santee Rivers, and in 1526 he brought 500 settlers back with him from Spanish Hispaniola. In an often-told story of unanticipated difficulties experienced by early colonists, they lost one ship with its supplies and more colonists to disease in a swampy site, probably in South Carolina; the remnant returned to Santo Domingo before the year was out. In 1539–40 Hernando De Soto reached the Cherokees in the mountains and spent a month there looking for gold before turning westward for further exploration. Jealous of Spain's control of ocean routes

Overleaf: Cupola House in Edenton dates to 1725

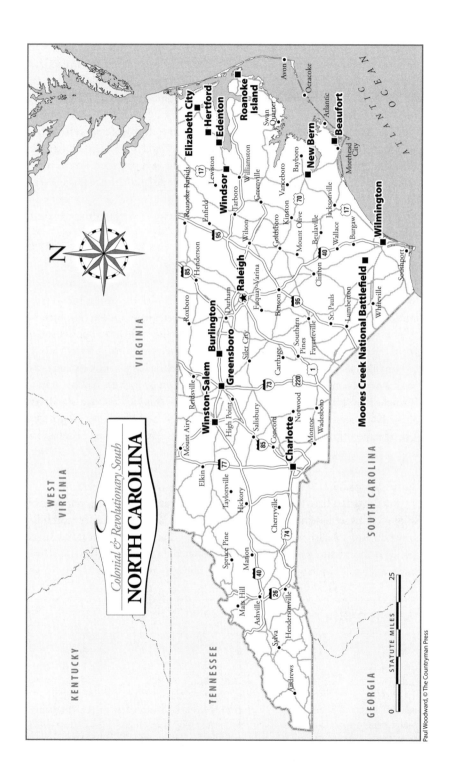

Colonial & Revolutionary South

NORTH CAROLINA

KENTUCKY

WEST VIRGINIA

VIRGINIA

TENNESSEE

SOUTH CAROLINA

GEORGIA

ATLANTIC OCEAN

Elizabeth City
Hertford
Edenton
Roanoke Island
Avon
Ocracoke
Atlantic
Beaufort
Swan Quarter
Morehead City
New Bern
Bayboro
Vanceboro
Williamston
Greenville
Tarboro
Lewiston
Windsor
Windsor
Roanoke Rapids
Enfield
Wilson
Goldsboro
Kinston
Mount Olive
Beulaville
Jacksonville
Wallace
Burgaw
Wilmington
Southport
Clinton
St. Pauls
Lumberton
Whiteville
Moores Creek National Battlefield
Wadesboro
Monroe
Charlotte
Concord
Norwood
Salisbury
High Point
Mount Airy
Reidsville
Winston-Salem
Greensboro
Burlington
Durham
Raleigh
Henderson
Roxboro
Fuquay-Varina
Benson
Siler City
Carthage
Southern Pines
Fayetteville
Elkin
Taylorsville
Hickory
Cherryville
Marion
Spruce Pine
Mars Hill
Asheville
Hendersonville
Sylva
Andrews

17
95
85
70
17
40
1
73
220
77
40
26
74

N

STATUTE MILES
0   25

Paul Woodward, © The Countryman Press

and lucrative American colonies, Queen Elizabeth I authorized an exploring expedition led by Sir Humphrey Gilbert in 1578 that discovered little. Five years later Gilbert was lost at sea while returning to England from another failed attempt to establish a northern colony, and his charter passed on to his younger half brother, Sir Walter Raleigh.

The coastal tidewater plains around Pamlico and Albermarle Sounds contain more water than land. These shallow sounds lie behind barrier beaches that protect them from the ocean, but from colonial days onward provided limited access to deep-draft ships through narrow inlets. Yet the fertile land surrounding the sheltered sounds and their tributary rivers invited early settlement in plantations. So it is not surprising that the first sustained British attempt to establish a permanent colony occurred here.

The "Lost Colony"

The legendary "Lost Colony" was Raleigh's third and final colonizing venture on Roanoke Island. Ironically, all of them had set forth with the strongest and most influential backing. In 1584 Raleigh received a charter from Queen Elizabeth "to inhabit and possess . . . all remote and heathen lands not in actual possession of any Christian Prince." He organized a series of voyages from 1584 to 1587 to accomplish this end. In 1584 Raleigh sent out an exploring expedition that reported back favorably on both the land and the crops grown by friendly Indians around Roanoke Island. The next year he sent a fleet of seven ships to Roanoke Island with Sir Richard Grenville in command and Ralph Lane and others as backup. This second expedition brought 300 soldiers and many other men to establish the colony, including explorer Thomas Cavendish, scientist Thomas Harriot, artist John White, and Manteo and Wanchese, two natives brought back to England by the first expedition.

Intended as a base both for exploring the region and for harassing Spanish shipping, this settlement proved unsuitable for the latter purpose. Oregon Inlet, now near Roanoke Island, had not opened up at that time, and the fleet entered Pamilico Sound through distant Ocracoke Inlet with great difficulty. The *Tiger*, a ship loaned to Raleigh by Queen Elizabeth, ran aground, lost much of her cargo,

---

NORTH CAROLINA *Time Line*

1524	1585	1587	1590
Giovanni da Verrazano explores the coastal area between Cape Fear River and Kitty Hawk	Sir Walter Raleigh establishes a colony on Roanoke Island	Governor John White brings more colonists, then returns to England for supplies; Virginia Dare becomes the first English child christened on American soil	After many delays Governor White returns to find an abandoned settlement

and had to be beached for repairs. The colony did send out a number of exploring expeditions during a year spent on Roanoke Island, including one under Ralph Lane to the Chesapeake that encountered hostile Indians preparing to attack them. The expected ship with needed supplies had not arrived by the early summer of 1586, but Sir Francis Drake did come to leave prisoners on his way back from attacking Spanish settlements in the West Indies. He offered to take most of the colonists back to England, an offer that they ultimately accepted after a hurricane damaged their ships and destroyed one. The delayed supply ship did arrive within a week after they had sailed with Drake, shortly followed by Grenville with more ships and men. Not finding the colonists, Grenville left a tiny contingent of men, probably about fifteen, and ample supplies, then sailed home with the remainder. With better luck on timing, Roanoke might have become the first permanent British settlement in North America.

Raleigh was not deterred from his objective by these misfortunes. He proposed and organized yet a third expedition, with plans to establish a settlement on a more accessible deepwater harbor. It was organized on a civilian basis, with John White as governor of 120 colonists, including some women and children. The original plan had called for settling in tidewater Virginia, at the lower end of Chesapeake Bay, after a brief stop on Roanoke Island to pick up the men left there. That plan also went awry when the ship reached the island in late July of 1587. In a prelude to the "lost" colony, nothing was found but a skeleton near the damaged fort, and natives reported that an Indian attack had driven away the others. Unaccountably, Simon Fernandez, the pilot who had been on the previous two voyages, chose to drop off all the colonists and leave them on the island. It is impossible to know how much his haste to be rid of the colonists was driven by the urge to capture treasure ships on the way back to Spain from the West Indies—a desire shared by all British privateers in these waters, no matter what other business had brought them there. In an era of no communication with captains at sea, many went their own way with relative impunity.

As the ships were gathering wood and water for the return voyage, White and the colonists were put ashore to fend for themselves. They began to repair the damaged houses and assess their situation. It was too late to plant crops, and although

1655	**1663**	**1705**	**1710**	**1711**
Virginian Nathaniel Batts becomes the first permanent settler on Albemarle Sound	King Charles II grants to eight lords proprietor land stretching from Virginia to Florida	Bath established as the first town in the northern counties of Carolina	Swiss colonists settle New Bern	Tuscarora War begins with a massacre of settlers

Manteo was christened and made Lord of Roanoke according to Raleigh's instructions, there were few prospects of food from Indians. Someone needed to return to England with the ships to arrange for more supplies, and Governor White was chosen as the man with the greatest influence. He sailed in late August, sadly leaving behind his daughter and newborn granddaughter, Virginia Dare, the first English child christened in America. After a difficult return voyage, White reached England in late November. The timing could not have been worse. Alarms of an imminent Spanish invasion had put England in the throes of commandeering ships to oppose the expected armada. Apart from the abortive dispatch of two small vessels in April of 1588, both of which returned in May, Raleigh's many attempts to get supply ships under way failed. Not until August of 1590 did White, alone and without supplies, manage to return to his colony. He found that Roanoke had vanished mysteriously. And no one still knows for sure what happened to the colonists between 1587 and 1590.

Eighty-nine men, seventeen women, and eleven children were last seen there on August 27, 1587. Three years later, upon his return, White "saw a great smoke rise in the Ile Roanoke neere the place where I left our Colony in the yeere 1587, which smoake put us in good hope that some of the Colony were there expecting my returne out of England." The smoke may have been an Indian fire, but the place was empty, and there were no traces of the settlers he had brought to the new land. Near the fort White's party found the letters CRO carved on a tree, which seemed to be a sign left for them. The settlers had agreed to carve a cross if they fled in distress; none was found. The party walked inland to the site of the settlement and found chests broken open, books lying under the shrubs, and a message carved on a post: CROATOAN (the Indian word for Hatteras). Perhaps remnants of the colony might be there, the land where their Indian friend, Manteo, had been born. However, the fierce gales that batter the Cape Hatteras region kept White from landing to find out, and he eventually gave up, assuming that further search would yield nothing about the fate of the colonists.

Later reports from natives suggest a number of possibilities. One sees the colonists caught by accident in a war between invading tribes from the south and defending local Indians. Another, reported by William Strachey, resident and his-

NORTH CAROLINA *Time Line*

1712	1718	1722	1770	1771
North Carolina and South Carolina formally separated	Blackbeard the pirate killed off Ocracoke Inlet	Edenton incorporated	Tryon Palace built as North Carolina's first colonial capital	Backcountry farmers (Regulators) battle royal governor's troops in Alamance County

torian of the Jamestown colony, tells of priests who advised Powhatan that a new nation in the Chesapeake region would destroy his own confederation, whereupon he ordered the slaughter of the colonists among other Indians. Yet a third, investigated by John Smith, traces reports that a small remnant survived in the realm of one of Powhatan's enemies along the Chowan River (modern Edenton), but his emissary could find nothing but a report that they were dead. The full story of the colonists' fate may never be known.

More Settlers and More Troubles

By the 1650s colonists from Virginia had settled on Albemarle Sound. Nathaniel Batts built a two-room house at the western end of the sound in 1653. He traded with the Indians, and gradually more settlers came to join him. In 1663 King Charles II rewarded eight prominent men who had helped him regain the crown, naming them lords proprietor of Carolina at their request. The generous land grant stretched from the southern shore of Albemarle Sound to what is now the Georgia-Florida state line. However, the proprietors also wanted the "Southern Plantation" located on the northern side of the sound and in 1665 received that additional territory. Four years later the proprietors set up Fundamental Constitutions to govern their holdings on feudal principles but gradually realized that the settlers would not tolerate total control. So a split form of territorial management evolved, with the governor and council responding to the proprietors' instructions, and an elected assembly representing the people's wishes and demands.

Nevertheless, troubles were brewing. In a harbinger of much later events, Culpepper's Rebellion broke out in Albermarle in 1677. A newly appointed deputy governor and customs collector, Thomas Miller, insisted on enforcing onerous provisions of the Navigation Acts that required payment of duty on shipments between colonial ports as well as those sent to England. For lack of deepwater ports, tobacco planters around Albermarle Sound also had to ship through Virginia and pay what they thought excessive fees for the privilege. So many of them took to smuggling in smaller, shallow-draft New England ships that also bypassed English ports and reached Scotland, Ireland, and continental ports directly. When one of those ships, under the command of Captain Zachariah Gillam, arrived,

1774	**1775**	**1776**	**1780**
Women join in Edenton tea party protest	Citizens from Mecklenburg County write a declaration of independence	North Carolina militia defeats Loyalists at Moore's Creek; in April, in the Halifax Resolves, the colony becomes the first to declare independence	Patriots rout a group of Loyalists at Ramsour's Mill

Miller arrested him for nonpayment of previous duties and confronted one of his passengers, George Durant, a major exporter. Then the crew of the vessel confined Miller, and as word spread, John Culpepper, leader of an armed band, and others joined together to take charge of Albermarle. At a public meeting they elected a new assembly, which in turn appointed a speaker, a council, and a court to try Miller. As the trial began, the appointed governor, Thomas Eastchurch, reached Virginia but died before he could get to North Carolina. The popularly elected government restored order in Albermarle, collected customs duties, and even imposed new taxes to reimburse the proprietors for lost revenues. Miller escaped and fled to England, and the proprietors apologized for his illegal actions as deputy governor, especially attempts to disenfranchise and arrest those who opposed him. Then the proprietors appointed one of their own number, Seth Sothel, as the new governor.

A sea voyage during this era brought with it great risks, and the odds turned against Sothel. Captured by pirates, he spent five years imprisoned in North Africa before escaping and making his way to Carolina in 1683. During that interval, local men filled the void as acting governors. When Sothel arrived and took office, he proved to be the worst governor in the colony's short history—repressive, corrupt, and criminally acquisitive. In 1689 he was tried by the assembly, found guilty, banned from the colony for a year and declared ineligible for any office. When a new governor arrived to replace him, and John Gibbs led another abortive rebellion, the proprietors reverted to deputy governors for the northern counties under the governor in Charles Town in the south, beginning the de facto process of separating the two parts of Carolina that would not be formalized until 1712. This arrangement worked well, until another round of restrictions aroused the Quaker community.

With increasing settlement and the liberty of conscience granted by the proprietors, the Quaker community in Carolina had been growing. At the beginning of the 18th century, however, the assembly began to change its policy, with laws establishing the Anglican Church. They created parishes and declared the ecclesiastical laws of England in force, which required taking oaths for all officeholders. Quakers refused to do so—not without cause, since many of them had left

NORTH CAROLINA *Time Line*

1780	**1781**	**1789**
Lord Cornwallis occupies Charlotte	General Nathanael Greene and Cornwallis battle at Guilford Courthouse	North Carolina becomes the twelfth state

prosperous farms in England and Wales for that very reason. When deputy governor Robert Daniel insisted on enforcing the requirement, Quakers' seats in the assembly were vacated. Their complaint to the governor in Charles Town was heard, and Daniel was replaced by Thomas Cary, who nevertheless insisted on the same compliance. Appeals to London removed Cary and shifted responsibility to William Glover, the president of the council, as acting governor in 1707, but he also refused to admit Quakers without an oath. Factional politics followed, with Cary seizing control and remaining in charge until the proprietors appointed Edward Hyde the new deputy governor. Hyde had to resort to a contingent of soldiers from Virginia to displace Cary.

Indian Troubles

With all this disagreement among the settlers, the Tuscarora Indians took the opportunity to retaliate against the whites who had made increasing incursions on their hunting grounds. The Indians had also been cheated by hard-nosed traders and treated with contempt by some of the new settlers pouring into their land, sometimes sealing off Indian villages from waterways. Tuscarora resentment was highest south of Albermarle, in the midcoast region around the Pamlico and Neuse Rivers, and it peaked after 400 Swiss settlers arrived in 1710 to settle New Bern. Gathering support from neighboring tribes, the Tuscarora attacked at dawn on September 22, 1711. They ravaged the center of the colony for three days, slaughtering most of the men, women, and children. Ironically, New Bern alone—the precipitating cause of the war—was spared in the initial attack. Its founding leader, Baron Graffenried, captured earlier, had agreed not to make war on the tribe in return for his release and the safety of the town. In the face of a common enemy during the Tuscarora War, the squabbling colonists came to their senses and cooperated, Quakers and Anglicans alike. But the war devastated their territory, leaving them with burned houses and barns, slaughtered cattle, and no crops. Seeking help, Governor Hyde first turned to Virginia, where Lieutenant Governor Spotswood threw the return of land north of Albermarle Sound into the bargain, then to Charles Town, where Governor Robert Gibbes and the assembly provided both money and troops. Ultimately it took two military expeditions, led by Colonel John Barnwell and Colonel James Moore and made up largely of friendly tribes, to defeat the Tuscarora and sign a peace treaty in 1713.

A Haven for Pirates

At the same time, the next disaster had been brewing, this time from the sea. The pirates who had been tossed out of the West Indies by the British infested the North Carolina coast, more than a hundred of them, according to some estimates. The remote Outer Banks and the coves and creeks around the mouth of the Cape Fear River provided ideal hiding places for their ships and easy access to the open sea for raids on passing merchantmen. Past collusion with smugglers that enabled the coastal population to evade duties made pirates with contraband to dispose of not entirely unacceptable. As early as 1685 the proprietors warned residents not to "knowingly entertaine, conceale, trade or hold any correspondence by Letter or otherwise with any . . . Pyrates." Yet Blackbeard (Edward Teach), who eventually located in Bath (then the seat of government for the colony) with a pardon from Governor Eden, claimed welcome in the homes of residents. Piracy flourished in North Carolina from 1689 to 1718, claiming goods and some lives from coastal shipping.

Before they were driven out, the Caribbean had been the scene of action for the most notorious pirates. Teach served in merchant ships and a privateer during Queen Anne's War (1703–13) before he turned to piracy, a pattern common to many seamen at the end of wars. He quickly gained and promoted his reputation as the most ferocious pirate on the seas. His beard almost covered his face, and he wore a red coat with two swords hanging, as well as pistols and knives. Those who gave up, and relinquished their money, weapons, and rum, were allowed to depart. But he might maroon the crew and burn the ship if they resisted too much. Paired with pirate Benjamin Hornigold, he captured the French merchantman *Concorde* in 1717, and when Hornigold accepted amnesty and retired, Blackbeard added more armament and renamed his ship *Queen Anne's Revenge*. He was joined by Stede Bonnet, a landowner who had left his plantation and respectable life in Barbados to sail as a pirate in a ship he had purchased, the *Revenge*. By the time Blackbeard left for the Carolinas in the spring of 1718, he had captured two more vessels and assembled a crew of 300 pirates.

Although North Carolina seemed powerless to end the scourge of piracy along its coast, both South Carolina and Virginia proved effective. What had been sporadic harassment of shipping became a disaster when Blackbeard's pirate force blockaded the port of Charles Town for a week in May 1718. A week later his flagship was stranded—perhaps deliberately—and lost at Beaufort Inlet, along with a smaller sloop; Blackbeard fled with his loot to Bath, North Carolina, where he took advantage of an offered pardon. Meanwhile, Bonnet regained control of his *Revenge* (which Blackbeard had commandeered), renamed her *Royal James,* and resumed taking a heavy toll on South Carolina shipping. In response, Governor Robert Johnson commissioned Colonel William Rhett to hunt him down. After a five-hour battle at the mouth of the Cape Fear River, Bonnet was captured in October, tried, and hanged on December 10, 1718. Forty-nine other pirates were hanged in Charles Town in November and December of that year. Meanwhile Blackbeard continued operating out of Bath in violation of his amnesty, and Virginia's Governor

The Scots in Cumberland County could not tolerate the naming of their county for William, Duke of Cumberland, who had killed wounded Scots lying on the Culloden battlefield, so they thought of a small revenge. The flower the English called Sweet William, in his honor, they took to calling "Stinking Billy."

Spotswood sent Lieutenant Robert Maynard of the Royal Navy to find him. Maynard succeeded and killed Blackbeard at Ocracoke Inlet on November 22, 1718, then sailed back to Bath with Blackbeard's head in the rigging to confront residents involved in his activities.

Regional Conflicts

With the end of the Tuscarora War and widespread piracy, things calmed down a bit. Edenton was incorporated in 1722 and soon became the center of government. More settlers arrived from Virginia, Maryland, and Pennsylvania—especially second- and third-generation descendants of the original colonists—because good land was available, and immigrants from Britain funneled through Virginia's deepwater ports. Some of these new colonists settled along the lower Cape Fear River, while others headed for the backcountry. In 1732 a group arrived from the Scottish Highlands and moved up the Cape Fear River into land that became Cumberland County. After the Battle of Culloden in 1746, Parliament made life very difficult for the Scots, so even more fled to North Carolina, where they were welcomed. Another distinct group was the Scotch-Irish, those who had moved from Scotland to Ireland and now were encouraged by the Crown to go to America. Welsh families moved down from Pennsylvania and Delaware to settle in the lower Cape Fear valley, sandwiched between the English and the Scots. And many German Protestant groups—Lutherans, German Reformed, Moravians—came to settle, mostly in the western Piedmont. Just after midcentury they began to spill over into the valleys beyond the Blue Ridge Mountains.

As the center of population moved south and the backcountry filled up, strains developed, first between the interests of those in the north and south, then between east and west. Tensions were exacerbated after the Crown bought out seven of the eight proprietors and North Carolina became a royal colony in 1729. With that change came an emphasis on increased control of colonial affairs, including regulation by the Board of Trade and more authority for the governor and council, less for the assembly. Defending the rights of the assembly preoccupied its elected members, and influence in it was important to the older counties in the north, which elected five members each, as compared to new counties in the south, allotted only two or three. When Governor Garbriel Johnston called the assembly to meet in Wilmington in 1746, bad weather kept northern members away, and the simmering controversy was settled by those present: Each county would be represented by two members, and the capital would be moved to New Bern. In response, Albermarle members refused to attend the assembly for seven years.

More serious problems split east and west after the increasing number of counties in the backcountry threatened to give them control of the assembly. To prevent that, counties in the east were divided to counterbalance those created in the west. The assembly also appointed many key officials like sheriffs and judges in western counties. Settlers resented both the influence of these officials and fees they thought excessive, as well as the requirement that fees had to be paid in cash, which was scarce. Their resentments coalesced around the conviction that they could run their own affairs better, and they met in public to form a group called the Regulators, advertising their principles to gain more adherents. Construction of the elaborate Tryon Palace in New Bern had begun in 1767, exacerbating their unrest, and they established a formal organization the next year. After appealing to the assembly several times for redress of their grievances, members of the group succumbed to the mob spirit in Hillsborough—filling the courtroom, attacking the judge and other officials, rioting through the town. In response the assembly passed a riot act, and Governor William Tryon headed for Hillsborough with 1,400 militiamen. Camped at Great Alamance Creek, he was met by about 2,000 Regulators and ordered them to lay down their arms before he would talk. After an hour, the militia began firing and the battle began, with dead and wounded on both sides. The less disciplined Regulators scattered and later formally capitulated or headed west for Tennessee. Twelve leaders were tried for treason, and six were hanged.

Kindling the Revolution

At the brink of the Revolution, North Carolina leapt ahead, in spite of a firm contingent of Loyalists within its population. The assembly had been battling for local control for nearly a century, first against the feudal model of the proprietors, then against the dictates of the Crown imposed through governors and the council. Their statement in the early 1770s could not be more clearly expressed: "Appointed by the people to watch over their rights and privileges, and to guard them from every encroachment of a private and public nature, it becomes our duty and will be our constant endeavor to preserve them secure and inviolate to the present age, and to transmit them unimpaired to posterity." With such an affirmation of its role, it is not surprising that the assembly led the way through the tangle of events that preceded the Revolution.

As demonstrated in earlier responses to the Stamp Act, this position did represent the will of the people, especially in the lower Cape Fear valley. There opposition to the importation or use of stamped paper was vigorous. Crowds demonstrated in Brunswick, surrounded the residence of Governor Tryon, compelled the resignation of officials charged with collecting stamp duties, and boarded the naval vessel that had impounded several incoming ships, to force their release. When Tryon closed a session of the assembly that had adopted a nonimportation agreement in 1767, almost all its members continued meeting in a convention to establish its details.

Another sign of popular will occurred when Josiah Martin, the governor who succeeded Tryon, refused to convene the assembly in time for it to select delegates to the first Continental Congress in 1774. In response, assembly speaker John Harvey called a mass meeting in Wilmington and proposed a provincial congress, which met in New Bern in August with thirty out of thirty-five counties represented. That congress, the first of five, denounced the Intolerable Acts passed by

Parliament to punish Boston, selected three delegates to the Continental Congress, and pledged to support its recommendations. In October the women of Edenton provided another indication of patriotic sentiment by staging their own "tea party," which was caricatured in England.

When Governor Martin called the assembly to meet in New Bern in April 1775, Speaker Harvey arranged for the second provincial congress to meet in the same place the day before. The two groups virtually merged, with Harvey in charge of both and much the same membership; delegates to the congress were invited to sit in on the deliberations of the assembly. When the assembly approved the actions of the Continental Congress, Martin dissolved it. Later, news of Lexington and Concord and Parliament's declaration that the colonies were in a state of rebellion reached North Carolina. Martin retreated to Fort Johnston and then to a Royal Navy sloop when a large group of minutemen approached the fort to talk to him. But he had already put in motion a plan to regain control of the colony by arming Loyalist Highland Scots, who had sworn an oath never to fight against Britain when they emigrated to North Carolina, and recruiting free blacks and slaves serving on British ships. Meanwhile the third Provincial Congress, purposely convened at Hillsborough in the heart of Regulator country, took advantage of the governor's absence to form a provisional government. When Martin received support for his plan from London and the promise of regular troops led by Generals Clinton and Cornwallis in January, he began assembling Highland troops under General Donald MacDonald. Not waiting for support from British regulars, Martin ordered this army to begin marching toward Wilmington in mid-February.

The North Carolina militia forces under Colonel James Moore's overall command prepared to stop them at Moore's Creek Bridge 18 miles above Wilmington. They arrived at Moore's Creek the night before the Highlanders and hauled away the planks from the bridge, leaving just the runners underneath, which they greased. After marching all night the Highlanders reached the bridge before dawn on a misty morning and launched an immediate attack. With drums and bagpipes playing, they charged across on slippery runners, facing heavy fire from concealed riflemen and two devastating cannons ("Old Mother Covington and her daughter") loaded with swan shot, an early form of shrapnel. In the first few minutes of this short battle, many were shot and others fell off the runners and drowned. Although they outnumbered the Patriots, the Highlanders scattered. Colonel Moore arrived shortly after the battle at the bridge and pursued them, capturing guns, rifles, stores, wagons, and 850 prisoners. This brief battle, just as important for the South as "the shot heard round the world" had been for New England, secured North Carolina from further Loyalist uprisings and deferred British invasion until late in the war.

The success of the Patriots also stirred renewed patriotic fervor. North Carolina became the first colony to vote for independence, on April 12, 1776. The fourth Provincial Congress was held in Halifax, and 83 delegates adopted the

Halifax Resolves. The document begins by pointing out "the usurpations and violences attempted and committed by the King and Parliament of Britain against America" and ends with a resolution: "That the delegates for this Colony in the Continental Congress be impowered to concur with the delegates of the other Colonies in declaring Independency, and forming foreign alliances, reserving to this Colony the sole and exclusive right of forming a Constitution and laws for this Colony, and of appointing delegates from time to time . . . to meet the delegates of the other Colonies for such purposes as shall be hereafter pointed out." This was the first official action for independence by a colony, and it was also directed to collaboration with other colonies. Virginia became the next colony to provide a recommendation for independence, and both were laid before the Continental Congress on May 27, followed by Richard Henry Lee's motion for independence on June 7 and the subsequent drafting of the Declaration of Independence. In December of 1776 Richard Caswell became the first governor of the state of North Carolina, and the first constitution was adopted.

The Southern Campaign

The British southern campaign began in December 1778 when lack of success in the middle Atlantic colonies and the expectation of strong Loyalist support in South brought regular forces under the command of Lord Cornwallis to Georgia. They easily took Savannah, then Charleston the following May, and overwhelmed the defending army under General Horatio Gates at Camden. But shortly after Cornwallis reached the North Carolina border in his campaign to secure the South for the Crown, a segment of his army suffered a stunning defeat in the hill country of western South Carolina at Kings Mountain. Shortly afterward, in December 1780, General Nathanael Greene replaced Gates as commander of American forces, and then, in January, General Daniel Morgan roundly defeated a hated and feared opponent at Cowpens, where British colonel Banastre Tarleton lost 900

KEY *Revolutionary War Dates in* **NORTH CAROLINA**

 February 27, 1776: Loyalist Scots defeated by the North Carolina militia at Moore's Creek Bridge.

September 19, 1776: Cherokees attack Colonel Williamson's Patriots in the Black Hole Gorge south of Franklin. The Patriots manage to clear the pass.

September 26, 1780: Lt. Col. Davie, along with 150 American soldiers, attack Tarleton's Legion at Charlotte, but reinforcements drive them away.

March 15, 1781: The armies of General Greene and Lord Cornwallis meet at Guilford Courthouse. Although the British claim victory, they lose 28 percent of their army.

November 18, 1781: British evacuate occupied Wilmington.

men. Greene's war of attrition had started, and he lured Cornwallis into pursuing him across the Piedmont to just beyond the Virginia border before doubling back to meet him at Guilford Courthouse in a major battle on March 15, 1781.

Greene had harassed Cornwallis for months, and he very cleverly chose the

> In 1917 the Guilford Courthouse site was named the first national park in the country to commemorate a Revolutionary War battle.

site west of Guilford Courthouse for a direct confrontation. He put the North Carolina militia behind a fence with their backs to the woods. Another Patriot line of Virginia militia was placed on a rise in the woods. A third American line of Continental soldiers was placed behind the militias on a hill near the courthouse. Although his troops were tired and badly supplied, Cornwallis was eager to defeat Greene before he got to Virginia for reinforcements and also before more of his own dwindling troops deserted. The British advanced through the first two lines, receiving disastrous casualties, with the Americans falling back by a preset plan. By then they had reformed behind the third line at the courthouse. When American cavalry disrupted his lines, Cornwallis fired grapeshot into the melee, hitting some of his own men as well. Greene saw his cannon captured and ordered a strategic retreat. Cornwallis thought he had won the battle because his men were still holding the field, but the cost of his victory was enormous. With more than a quarter of his men casualties, he returned to Wilmington to consider his options. Ultimately he decided to abandon any further attempts to subdue all North Carolina and marched through to Petersburg, Richmond, and finally Yorktown.

Regions *to* Explore

THE OUTER BANKS
THE GREAT SOUNDS AND THE COAST
THE PIEDMONT

THE OUTER BANKS

This 150-mile stretch of narrow sand islands surrounded by shifting bars and beset by ferocious gales has been notorious among seaman for centuries. Reaching the protected sounds behind them through inlets sometimes filled with confused breaking seas has never been easy. The Outer Banks have been dubbed the "Graveyard of the Atlantic" because more than 650 ships have been wrecked there.

Another hazard in the early 18th century was the presence of pirates, including Edward Teach, better known as Blackbeard. Teach was born in Bristol, England. His career as a pirate began during Queen Anne's War, when he was a privateer sailing out of Jamaica to attack French merchant ships. When the war was over in 1713 he crewed for a pirate in the Bahamas who captured the French slaver *Concorde,* in 1717. He became captain of the vessel and renamed it *Queen Anne's Revenge.* At one point his pirate force numbered 300 men on four ships. The waters off the Carolinas offered plenty of prizes among the coastal shipping, and the Outer Banks provided many places for Blackbeard to hide from both colonial and British authorities. Two of his favorite haunts were at Ocracoke inlet and Bath, then the capital of North Carolina. In November 1718 he was tricked into battle by Lieutenant Robert Maynard on a British sloop, off Ocracoke. It was reported that Blackbeard continued fighting even after being shot, stabbed, and slashed across the throat before he died. His head was hung in the rigging as Maynard sailed into Bath.

ROANOKE ISLAND

Located between the Croatan and Roanoke Sounds, Roanoke Island is 11 miles long and 2 miles wide. A series of colonial attempts at settlement took place on the northern part of the island. Manteo was named for one of two Algonquian Indians who sailed to England with the first expedition and later returned home.

HISTORICAL SITES *and* MUSEUMS
Every summer *The Lost Colony* is presented on stage in **Manteo** on Roanoke Island (800-488-5012, 252-473-3414; www.thelostcolony.org), 1409 National Park Dr., Manteo, NC 27954. Open daily year-round. For over 400 years historians have struggled with a mystery that has never been solved. Queen Elizabeth had granted a patent to discover territory in the New World to Sir Walter Raleigh in 1584. This drama deals with the fate of 117 men, women, and children ready to begin a new life in the New World three years later.

The story has fascinated theatergoers for over 60 years. Pulitzer Prize–winning playwright Paul Green wrote the script, and Porter Van Zandt directed and produced the play. This stunning song, dance, and drama spectacle takes place on summer nights at Waterside Theatre.

Theater on Manteo emerged long before the current production. During the early 1900s local actors staged "pageant dramas" depicting their English heritage. In 1921 Mabel Evans Jones wrote a script and played the leading role of Eleanor Dare, mother of the first English child born on Roanoke Island. Virginia Dare's 350th birthday coincided with opening night on July 4, 1937. During World War II German U-boats glided along the coast, making a blackout of four years necessary. A fire in 1947 and Hurricane Donna in 1960 were momentary setbacks, but the show went on.

Once desolate and deserted, Roanoke Island is now chock-full of interest for visitors. In addition to the play, there are replicas of a ship, a fort, and elaborate gardens to visit.

Roanoke Island Festival Park (252-475-1500, 252-475-1506; www.roanoke island.com), Roanoke Island Festival Park, 1 Festival Park, Manteo, NC 27954. Open daily. The centerpiece of the 25-acre island park is a beautiful representation (not a replica, because no records exist from this fleet) of one of the seven English ships from the Roanoke voyage of 1585. She was designed using research of 16th-century sailing ships. The ***Elizabeth II*** was built to commemorate the 400th anniversary of colonizing activity in America. This 69-foot, square-rigged vessel with three masts is similar to those used in Sir Walter Raleigh's day.

In the visitor center you'll get strong visual impressions of life on board from "A Roanoke Voyage." On board the ship, interpreters in period costume explain their methods of handling sails and navigating. If you've never gone below decks in ships of this era before, you will be amazed at the cramped quarters both passengers and crew had to endure on Atlantic voyages that could last as long as two or three months.

At the Settlement Site you'll see 16th-century blacksmithing and woodworking in process. The Roanoke Adventure Museum offers all kinds of interactive exhibits to try. Don't miss the talking pirate. And there's a film, *The Legend of Two*

The Elizabeth II, *at Roanoke Island Festival Park*

Path, to show you how the Native Americans felt when the English colonists arrived.

The **Fort Raleigh National Historic Site** (252-473-5772; www.nps.gov/fora), 1401 National Park Dr., Manteo. Open daily. The historic site is on the north end of Roanoke Island and has displays, a film, and interpretive programs. It includes a reconstruction of the small earthen fort and sites of some houses from the settlement. Archaeologists found artifacts to establish the location of the fort, built in the shape of a square, with pointed bastions on two sides and an octagonal bastion on another. Restored in the early 1950s, the fort was reconstructed in the same way the original 1585 fort was built, by digging out the moat and tossing the dirt inward to form a parapet. The Elizabethan Room, with original oak paneling and stone fireplace from a 16th-century house, is in the visitor center.

The Thomas Harriot Nature Trail takes walkers through the woods between Roanoke Sound and the houses once built outside the fort.

The **Elizabethan Gardens** (252-473-3234; www.elizabethangardens.org), 1411 National Park Dr., Manteo. Open daily. The gardens, which adjoin the Fort Raleigh National Historic Site, were created by the Garden Club of North Carolina in 1951. Luckily, club members heard about some statuary that was being removed from the Greenwood Estate of John Hay Whitney, ambassador to the Court of St. James's. Although Whitney was thinking of giving the statuary to the Metropolitan Museum in New York, he changed its destination to the Garden Club. The set of statuary includes an Italian fountain and pool with balustrade, wellhead, sundial, bird baths, stone steps, and benches.

The gardens opened on August 18, 1960, the 373rd anniversary of the birth of Virginia Dare. Massive iron gates from the French Embassy in Washington open through a wall of old handmade bricks. The Gate House is patterned after a 16th-century orangery. The walls are hung with an oil portrait of Queen Elizabeth I, a 1663 map of Devonshire, the coats of arms of Queen Elizabeth I and Sir Walter Raleigh, and a roster of the men and women from the Lost Colony.

As you walk through gardens heady with the scent of herbs and flowers, you'll come upon marble statues, like the one of Virginia Dare. Sculpted in 1859, the statue was shipwrecked off the coast of Spain and spent two years on the ocean floor. Today she stands in a beautiful garden, holding a fish net draped around her waist with a heron by her side. Indian legends tell that she grew up with Indians and that her spirit now bounds around Roanoke Island in the shape of a white doe.

Thomas Harriot, a noted scientist on the 1585–86 expedition, wrote a book on "the new found land" in 1588. It described the inhabitants, sources of food and ale, and marketable commodities. Among the latter he mentioned what would become the economic engine of the future: "There is an herb which is sowed a part by itself & is called by the inhabitants Uppowoc . . . . The Spaniardes generally call it Tobacco."

The Elizabethan Gardens, adjoining the Fort Raleigh National Historic Site

LODGING

ELIZABETHAN INN
814 Hwy. 64, Manteo, NC 27954
252-473-2101; fax: 252-473-6688;
ww.elizabethaninn.com
The inn has both an indoor competition-size pool with fitness center and an outdoor pool, plus 78 guest rooms.

THE BURRUS HOUSE INN
509 S. Hwy. 64, Manteo, NC 27954
252-475-1636;
www.burrushouseinn.com
Oceanfront bed-and-breakfast with separate living and bedroom areas. Eight suites.

CAMERON HOUSE INN
300 Budleigh St., Manteo, NC 27954
800-279-8178, 252-473-6596;
www.cameronhouseinn.com
Located in the old town in a restored 1919 bungalow. Seven guest rooms.

TRANQUIL HOUSE INN
405 Queen Elizabeth Ave., Manteo, NC 27954
800-458-7069, 252-473-1404;
www.tranquilinn.com
Located on the waterfront, the inn offers canopied beds and mini-suites. Twenty-five guest rooms.

THE WHITE DOE INN
319 Sir Walter Raleigh St., Manteo, NC 27954
800-473-6091, 252-473-9851;
www.whitedoeinn.com
The 1910 Queen Anne–style home is furnished with antiques. Eight guest rooms.

RESTAURANTS

1587 RESTAURANT IN THE TRANQUIL HOUSE INN
405 Queen Elizabeth Ave.
252-473-1487
Regional American cuisine.

BIG AL'S SODA FOUNTAIN & GRILL
716 S. Virginia Dare Trail
252-473-5570
A 1950s theme offers blue-plate specials, a jukebox, and a soda fountain.

DARRELL'S RESTAURANT
521 Virginia Dare Trail
252-473-5366
A drive-in 40 years ago, this is now a family restaurant offering seafood, beef, and chicken.

WATERFRONT TRELLIS
207 Queen Elizabeth Ave.
252-473-1727

Located right on the waterfront with panoramic views. Sunday brunch.

EVENTS

August: Virginia Dare Faire, Fort Raleigh Site, 252-473-3414

INFORMATION

OUTER BANKS VISITORS BUREAU
One Visitors Center Circle
Manteo, NC 27954
877-629-4386; www.outerbanks.org

THE GREAT SOUNDS AND THE COAST

In the great sounds—Albermarle and Pamlico—water and land merge imperceptibly along shores largely unmarked by distinguishing features. You don't fully appreciate their magnitude until you sail across vast stretches out of sight of land. But in an era when water was the principal highway, these great sounds led colonists to establish settlements on many subsidiary bays and rivers between the Virginia border and Cape Lookout. From Beaufort southward to the Cape Fear River and beyond to the South Carolina border, the barrier islands continue but hug the coast, providing both shelter and easier access to the open ocean.

ELIZABETH CITY

As early as 1757 Daniel Trueblood built a gristmill on Charles Creek, which flows into the Pasquotank River, an arm of Albemarle Sound. By 1764 an inspection station for colonial produce was in place at "the narrows." In 1793 construction began on the Dismal Swamp Canal, the oldest canal still in operation in the country. It connected the Pasquotank River via the Elizabeth River to Chesapeake Bay.

Also that year, North Carolina chartered a community at the narrows which was called Redding. The town commissioners acquired the Narrows Plantation from Adam and Elizabeth Tooley in 1794. The name was then Elizabethtown and finally changed to Elizabeth City in 1801, perhaps for Elizabeth Tooley. Elizabeth City has a historic district for you to stroll through.

HISTORICAL SITES *and* MUSEUMS
Museum of the Albemarle (252-335-1453; www.museumofthealbemarle.com), 501 S. Water St. Open Tue.–Sun. The exhibits trace the history and traditions of

the area beginning with the Native Americans, the English, and African colonists and continuing up to today. The maritime history of the Albemarle area begins with a 1750 dugout canoe. An exhibit on the Dismal Swamp brings out the story of the slaves who hid there. This museum is a branch of the North Carolina Museum of History. The focus is on the general history of the 13 counties in northeastern North Carolina, the area first settled by the English.

LODGING

CULPEPPER INN
609 W. Main St., Elizabeth City, NC 27909
252-335-9235; www.culpepperinn.com
Located in the historic district in a 1930s brick colonial-revival manor house built by William and Alice Culpepper. There's a screen porch and a fish pond. Four guest rooms.

THE POND HOUSE INN
915 Rivershore Rd., Elizabeth City, NC 27909
252-335-9834, fax: 252-335-9934; www.thepondhouseinn.com
Located on the Pasquotank River with views from every room. Four guest rooms.

RESTAURANTS

WEST END STATION RESTAURANT
109 S. Hughes Blvd.
252-335-2006
Located in a restored train station and on the National Register of Historic Places. Check their house specialties.

INFORMATION

ELIZABETH CITY CHAMBER OF COMMERCE
502 E. Ehringhaus St.
Elizabeth City, NC 27909

HERTFORD

Hertford is a sleepy river town steeped in history. A winding road follows the river with cypress trees draped in Spanish moss. Victorian and Georgian homes stand along the way. The town, which is on the National Register of Historic Places, dates to the late 1600s and was incorporated in 1758.

HISTORICAL SITES *and* MUSEUMS

The 1730 **Newbold-White House** (252-426-7567; www.newboldwhitehouse .com), 151 Newbold White Rd., Hertford, NC 27944. Open Mar.–Nov., daily except Mon. This is the oldest brick house in North Carolina. Abraham Sanders, a Quaker, bought the land in 1726. The brickwork is Flemish bond design on the upper part of the house and English bond on the lower; the leaded casement windows have diamond-shaped panes. Inside, the original fireplace has niches in the ends to keep food warm. Closets were a sign of wealth in the 1600s because they were taxed as rooms, and this house has them. The "hall" was the room where the family lived—cooking, eating, weaving, spinning, and playing. Because there were no public meetinghouses, the same room served as a meeting hall for the General Assembly and court sessions.

Periaugen an 18th-century sailing vessel (252-426-7567; www.newbold whitehouse.com), Hertford Municipal Park, Grubb St. This replica is a double-masted 30-foot boat. It is the only known example of the most common colonial workboat from this period.

EVENTS

October: Newbold-White House & Periaugen Ghost Walk, 252-426-7567

EDENTON

Over 400 years of American history play a slow waltz in the bucolic region surrounding historic Albemarle Sound. Edenton is a good place to begin a leisurely survey of this beautiful country—a place the colonists claimed as their choice, as the name suggests. It's still a lovely spot to call home, and local inhabitants are so comfortable they don't bother to lock their doors. We were told that Edenton has 30 churches but only a few bars or cocktail lounges.

HISTORICAL SITES *and* MUSEUMS

Begin your exploration of town at the **Historic Edenton Visitor Center** (252-482-2637; www.edenton.nchistoricsites.org), 108 N. Broad St., Edenton, NC 27932. Open daily. You can watch a 14-minute audio-visual program and then take a guided walking tour of the historic district. Fronting Albemarle Sound and filled with clapboard colonial houses, this section of town suggests what Edenton might have looked like before any tourists came. Historic Edenton Trolley Tours are also available from the visitor center; a number of the following sites are on the tour.

Your first stop is **St. Paul's Church**, West Church Street, where colonists came with conflict in their hearts between loyalty to the Crown and desire for freedom. After being raised in the Church of England, the settlers found this dichotomy disturbing. The parish was organized under the first Vestry Act in 1701, making

---

A group of women in town felt strongly enough to meet and sign this resolution on October 25, 1774: "The Provincial Deputies of North Carolina having resolved not to drink any more tea, nor wear any more British cloth, &c. many ladies of this Province have determined to give a memorable proof of their patriotism, and have accordingly entered into the following honourable and spirited association. I send it to you to shew your fair countrywomen, how zealously and faithfully American Ladies follow the laudable example of their husbands, and what opposition your Ministers may expect to receive from a people thus firmly united against them."

Along the waterfront in historic Edenton

it the oldest charter in North Carolina, and its building, begun in 1736, is the second-oldest in the state. Narrow pews were designed to keep parishioners "aware and awake." The ladies used foot warmers, and the doors on the pews kept some of the heat inside. The solid brass Flemish chandelier is 500 years old.

We walked on to hear a story about the 1725 **Cupola House**, 408 S. Broad St., that demonstrates Edenton's community spirit. In 1918 a group of citizens saved the house when the owner could no longer afford to live there. She had, in fact, sold the woodwork of the lower hall and two downstairs rooms to the Brooklyn Museum of Fine Arts. The Cupola House Association gave her a small house that she could afford to live in when they took over Cupola House for historic preservation. The oldest house in town, Cupola House was constructed by shipbuilders and is thought to be the finest wooden Jacobean-type house south of Connecticut. Francis Corbin, an agent for Lord Granville, the last of the lords proprietor, probably added Georgian interior woodwork between 1756 and 1758. In 1777 Dr. Samuel Dickinson bought the house. His wife, then Elizabeth P. Ormond, was one of the signers of the famous tea party resolutions, proving that politics was not entirely a male domain, even in colonial times.

Inside the Cupola House visitors will see fireplace mantels made of wood painted to look like marble. A portrait of Penelope Barker hangs in the dining room. This sharp marriage entrepreneur had several husbands, cleverly selling the house to her next husband and banking the money. Upstairs there is a dress belonging to Mrs. Dickinson, a three-sided baby crib pushed up against the parents' bed, a French potty chair, and a daybed used for naps. The guest room shows signs of a "ghost" who sits on the bed after it has been made and creates a depression. We also enjoyed seeing a collection of toys, including a tea set, dolls, cradles, and valentines.

Walk down to the water's edge for a view of the **Barker House**, 505 S. Broad St., which was probably built for Penelope and Thomas Barker around 1782. Penelope was the spokeswoman for the Edenton tea party ladies.

You'll see a teapot sitting on a post on the town green and a tablet on the 1767 Courthouse as reminders of the tea party resolution. It was sent to England and published, generating a spate of not entirely complimentary cartoons. London, of course, was outraged at this effrontery, and the *London Times* printed a caricature depicting meddlesome women. The house is now the home of the Edenton Historical Commission.

Benjamin Franklin, Silas Deane, and Charles Lee, American commissioners in Paris, purchased in 1777 the cannons that now sit on the **Town Green**. Forty more were also brought to Edenton in 1778. All of them were eventually pushed into the bay so that the British would not capture them.

The **Court House,** E. King St., dates from 1718. Restorers from Colonial Williamsburg came here to measure it as a model for one of their buildings that lacked documentation, and archaeological digs still continue on its grounds. In early colonial days a circuit judge came here to represent the Crown every few weeks, bringing with him a scarce item—news. During his attendance people wandered in and out, fighting, shouting "he's guilty," and transforming court day into one of public amusement.

The **Iredell House** dates from 1773, when Joseph Whedbee, a silversmith, built the older section of the present structure. He sold it to James Iredell, deputy collector for the Port of Roanoke. Iredell married Hannah Johnston, the sister of the future governor, Samuel Johnston. The parlor contains his portrait, and this

By good luck we were in Edenton on the day the North Carolina Bill of Rights was brought by special guard for display in the Court House. It was in the process of traveling all over the state during 2007. This original was lost during the Civil War when a Union soldier took it to his home in Ohio and later sold it. An antiques dealer subsequently bought it and then tried to sell it to the National Constitution Center in Philadelphia, but the FBI used an undercover operation and the document arrived back in North Carolina for the first time in almost 140 years. The Bill of Rights will be preserved at the North Carolina State Archives in Raleigh after its tour.

was the room where dancing was held, followed by a dinner at midnight.

Portraits of James and Frances Iredell hang in the breakfast room, and the dining room has displays of china and silver. Upstairs, the master bedroom is decorated with a kitten's-ear spread, and you can see a lock box for private papers, quill pens, a horsehide bucket filled with sand for fireplace sparks, a bed warmer, and a foot warmer to take to church.

 **Did you know** how the term "cut the light" originated? If you visit the Iredell House you'll see a scissors with a cup to cut wicks—hence the term.

LODGING

CAPTAIN'S QUARTERS INN
202 W. Queen St., Edenton, NC 27932
800-482-8945, 252-482-8945;
www.captainsquartersinn.com
The colonial-revival home dates from 1907. Each room has a different sailing theme. A wine-and-dine package is offered. Eight guest rooms.

GRANVILLE QUEEN INN
108 S. Granville St., Edenton, NC 27932
252-482-5296;
www.granvillequeen.com
The 1907 southern inn with tall pillars is located in the historic district. It is furnished with antiques. Nine guest rooms.

LORDS PROPRIETOR'S INN
300 N. Broad St., Edenton, NC 27932
252-482-3641; www.lordsprope
denton.com
The inn is in a complex of three restored homes in the historic district. Each has a parlor with a fireplace; breakfasts are served in the Whedbee House overlooking a patio filled with dogwood trees. There are 60 guest rooms.

TRESTLE HOUSE INN
632 Soundside Rd., Edenton, NC 27932
800-645-8466, 252-482-2282, fax: 252-482-7003; www.trestlehouseinn.com
A B&B surrounded on three sides by water on a wildlife refuge. Large redwood beams were milled from railroad trestle timbers for the house. Five guest rooms.

RESTAURANTS

ACOUSTIC COFFEE
302 S. Broad St.
Coffees, gingerbread, cookies, cakes, fresh pastry. Music Friday evening.

CHERO'S MARKET CAFÉ
112 W. Water St.
Daily specials. Sunday brunch.

THAT FANCY CAFÉ
701-C N. Broadway St.
252-482-1909
Daily specials. "Food to suit every fancy."

WATERMAN'S GRILLE
427 S. Broad St.
252-482-7733
Casual seafood restaurant open for dinner.

EVENTS

April: Every other year on odd years Historic Edenton organizes a Pilgrimage of Edenton and the countryside. Visitors have the chance to tour private homes; 252-482-2637.
July: July 4 Celebration on the waterfront, 252-482-2637
December: Christmas Candlelight Tour of private homes, 252-482-2637

INFORMATION

CHOWAN COUNTY TOURISM
Box 245, Edenton, NC 27932
800-775-0111; www.visitedenton.com

A number of 18th- and 19th-century plantations survive in the region around Albemarle Sound. Most houses and plantations around the great sounds of North Carolina are not as large or architecturally pretentious as some in Virginia, South Carolina, and Louisiana, but they are off the beaten track and fun to visit. Perhaps they give northerners a better feel for lives tied in various ways to land rather than cities.

HISTORICAL SITES *and* MUSEUMS

Hope Plantation (252-794-3140; www.albemarle-nc.com/hope), 132 Hope House Rd., Windsor, NC 27983 Open daily. The house was built for Governor David Stone and represents a prosperous era in Tidewater North Carolina. Stone was an early proponent of Jeffersonian Republicanism, and his home reminded us of Jefferson's Monticello. Like Jefferson, Stone was a wealthy man, yet he died at 48 without a will, so his house and goods were sold at public auction.

Fortunately, an inventory was kept, so the restored house could be furnished with similar pieces. The parlor, where Mrs. Stone entertained guests and served tea, is furnished as it would have been in the Federal era. A portrait of Governor Stone hangs in this room. Striking cobalt blue crystal graces the dining room table. The little girls' room contains a dolls' bed and dolls; the children ate there until they were old enough for more formal meals in the dining room. The master bedroom contains an apothecary chest, chess set, a red Wedgwood vase, and some of Mrs. Stone's handwork. The library, with 1,400 books, was said to house the largest private collection in North Carolina at that time. Stone was a precocious scholar; he attended Princeton at age 14 and graduated at 16 in the 1780s.

On the same property stands the 1763 **King-Bazemore House**. William King, a Bertie County planter and cooper, built the house. The initials of William and Elizabeth King are carved with the date on a brick outside. The bricks are laid in Flemish-bond style, and most of the window glass is original. The gambrel roof was constructed to gain space and outwit the king's tax collector; the large room below it was classified as an attic and thereby taxed at a lower rate. Reverend Stephen Bazemore bought the house in 1840. The house was moved to its present location in 1979 to form a historic complex.

When we visited the Bazemore House, we were lucky enough to meet one of its most recent occupants. Bunny Ward Mizelle had lived in this house with her family until she went away to college, and her husband proposed to her within its walls. For her it is no relic of the distant past, but home.

Mrs. Mizelle's grandaddy bought the house, then her father took the deed. After her parents died the house was sold to the family of a first cousin, Adelaide and Henry Bazemore. Mizelle told us that her mother was tempted by an offer of $1,000 for the paneling in one room but turned it down, realizing the historical

Hope Plantation in Windsor

significance of the house as a whole. It is one of two left in North Carolina with brick ends and a gambrel roof.

Inside, furniture was arranged around the walls and pulled out for use when needed. The cupboards contain pewter, blue and white china, and finger vases to hold flowers. Upstairs, the bedrooms housed seven children. The girls' room has a picture of the last King daughter born in the house. The wash room up there is equipped with a little pan for washing. One young visitor recently asked the guide, "How did they get the water up here?" "How did the girls get their bodies into that little pan?" The master bedroom contains the second-oldest-known bedstead of its kind east of the Mississippi, dating from 1710.

LODGING

INN AT GRAYS LANDING
401 S. King St., Windsor, NC 27983
877-794-3501, 252-794-2255, fax: 252-794-2254; www.grayslanding.com
This Georgian home dates from 1790. Five guest rooms.

EVENTS

February: Celebration of African American History, 252-794-3140

NEW BERN

On the Neuse River leading into Pamlico Sound, New Bern, named after Bern, Switzerland, was settled in 1710 by Swiss and German colonists. Queen Anne had granted land to their leader, Baron Christopher de Graffenried. Originally the town was laid out in the shape of a cross, but the Tuscarora Indian raids destroyed that plan and demoralized the colonists, many of whom returned to Europe.

William Tryon, from Surrey, England, came to North Carolina in 1764 as lieutenant governor of the province. He was assistant to the royal governor, Arthur Dobbs. Dobbs died and Tryon became governor in 1765. There was no fixed capital for the provincial government, and sessions were held in New Bern, Wilmington, and Bath. Tryon decided that New Bern should become the capital. A new building went up, and Tryon moved into the "palace" in June 1770.

Taxes levied added to the resentment of the citizens. Backcountry settlers, predominantly Scotch-Irish Presbyterians, thought the distant palace was too luxurious, a final insult in their list of grievances that included the dominance of the lowland east in the assembly's representation, control of appointments for sheriffs and judges in western counties, and the charging of excessive fees by these officials. A year after construction of the palace had begun, the westerners formally organized as "Regulators" to manage their own affairs. However, after a riot in Hillsborough (just north of modern Chapel Hill) and further provocations as they threatened New Bern, Governor Tryon's militia subdued them at the Battle of Alamance in 1771.

The first Provincial Congress of North Carolina met at Tryon Palace in August 1774. It was the first in America to be called and held in defiance of British orders. In January 1777 Governor Richard Caswell and other officials were inaugurated under the first constitution of the independent state of North Carolina. In April 1791 George Washington was entertained at a banquet and ball in Tryon Palace. (Part of the building was destroyed in a fire in 1798 but has been reconstructed on its original foundation.)

HISTORICAL SITES *and* MUSEUMS
Tryon Palace (800-767-1560, 252-514-4900; 610 Pollock St., New Bern, NC 28562 (mailing: Box 1007, New Bern, NC 28563). Open daily. As you walk up the path you will notice the perfect symmetry of this handsome redbrick palace, with gate, chimneys, and windows all perfectly aligned. Walk around the green lawn, where sometimes interpreters play games with children, and up the steps into the house. The entrance hall has four statues in niches, representing the four continents. The library contains 400 first editions in bookcases.

The Council Chamber is also a ballroom, with red silk damask draperies and two cut-glass chandeliers. Portraits of George I, George III, and Queen Charlotte hang on the walls. Ladies retired to the parlor after dinner, where screens protected them from the fire in the hearth. Teacups are laid out for tea. The walnut spinet

The Tryon Palace in New Bern

was made in 1720 in London. The dining room table is set for a special event, with a mirrored centerpiece, hedgehog cake, cream puffs, gelatin, seafood mousse tarts, and mandarin oranges.

Although the furnishings are not original with the house, they are antiques from the period. Upstairs, Margaret Tryon's bedroom has a four-poster bed and a collection of doll beds. Her writing desk with quill pen is still there. Also upstairs, the servants' quarters are extensive to house the large number the mansion required.

The cook in the kitchen entertained us with good humor as she baked breads, pumpkin pies, and Swiss chard. The gardens overlooking the Trent River are lovely.

John Wright Stanly House (800-767-1560, 252-514-4900; www.tryon palace.org), 307 George St., dates from 1783. President George Washington spent two nights in the house and proclaimed it to be "exceeding good lodgings." Stanly's ships were active seizing British ships to help the Patriot cause during the Revolution.

Everlasting Syllabub

4 lemons, thinly peeled and the juice strained
1/4 cup sugar
1/2 cup white wine or sherry
1 1/3 cup heavy cream
3 tbsp brandy
1/4 tsp grated nutmeg

The day before the syllabub is to be made, put the lemon peel and juice in a bowl with the wine and brandy and leave overnight. Next day, strain the wine and lemon mixture into a large bowl. Add the sugar and stir until it is dissolved. Pour in the cream, stirring all the time. Add the nutmeg and whisk the mixture until it thickens and will hold a soft peak on the whisk.

FROM *THE GOVERNOR'S TABLE, TWO CENTURIES OF COOKERY AT TRYON PALACE.*

LODGING

THE AERIE B&B
509 Pollock St., New Bern, NC 28562
800-849-5553, 252-636-5553, fax: 252-514-2157; www.aerieinn.com
This Street-Ward residence in the historic district dates from 1882. Seven guest rooms.

HOWARD HOUSE
207 Pollock St., New Bern, NC 28560
800-705-5261, 252-514-6709;
www.howardhousebnb.com
The house dates from 1890 and is on the National Register of Historic Places. Six guest rooms.

MEADOWS INN
212 Pollock St., New Bern, NC 28560
877-551-1776, 252-634-1776
This antebellum home dates from 1847 and has been a B&B since 1980. Eight guest rooms.

RESTAURANTS

CAPTAIN RATTY'S SEAFOOD AND STEAKHOUSE
202 Middle St.
252-633-2088
Seafood is a specialty and includes catfish, oysters, shrimp, scallops, and crab.

THE COW CAFÉ
319 Middle St.
252-672-9269
The decor is black and white cow design, and they offer "moolishious" dishes as well as homemade ice cream.

EVENTS

April: Spring Historic Homes & Gardens Tour, 800-437-5767
July: Declaration of Independence read on Independence Day, 800-437-5767
December: Tryon Palace Holiday & Candlelight Tours, 800-767-1560, 252-514-4900

INFORMATION

NEW BERN CONVENTION & VISITORS CENTER
203 S. Front St., New Bern, NC 28563
800-437-5767, 252-637-9400

BEAUFORT

Beaufort was the home of the Coree Indians, then of French Huguenots, and was settled by the British in 1709. Robert Turner laid out the town in 1713 and named it after his friend Henry Somerset, Duke of Beaufort. It is the third-oldest town in the state.

At the southern end of the Outer Banks, on what is now called the Crystal Coast, Beaufort was isolated and thereby protected, so the historic district—Beaufort National Register Historic District—remains almost intact. As a fishing village it was called "Fish Town." A Fisherman's Monument commemorates mariners in town. Sea captains remembered the double-porch style of the West Indies and the Bahamas when they built their homes. The rooflines form a steep pitch at the ridge, which breaks to cover the full-length porches. Notice the up-and-down pattern of the picket fences, which is characteristic of Beaufort.

HISTORICAL SITES *and* MUSEUMS

Beaufort Historic Site (800-575-7483, 252-728-5225; 130 Block Turner St., Beaufort, NC 28516. Open Mon.–Sat. This walking town offers many historic sites to visit, so pick up a map in the visitor center. We chose to begin in the **Samuel Leffers One Room Cottage**, dating from 1765. It originally stood on the corner of Live Oak and Front Streets. When the building was moved in 1981, the earlier room was separated from the main cottage in order to travel through the narrow streets.

Leffers was a schoolmaster, surveyor, church vestryman, fisherman, and hunter who lived in the cottage until he married. The cottage was enlarged for his growing family of five children. This type of house was called a "story and a jump," or a one-and-a-half-story house.

The oldest piece of furniture is the spice cabinet from ca. 1675. The cupboard is interesting in that it has a thin top shelf called a "deed shelf," which held family documents and records.

Upstairs the rope bed has a coverlet of linsey-woolsey. The sewing sampler represents the skills a young girl had to master as she learned to hem, fell a seam, draw threads, and hemstitch, gather, make buttonholes, do herringbone stitch, darn, tuck, and monogram.

The **Hammock House** is the oldest in town, dating from 1709. It stands on a hill and was used as a navigation mark on early maps. Blackbeard stayed there when he was in port. There are reports of ghosts in the house, including one of the wives of Blackbeard, and Richard Russell, who was pushed down the stairs by a slave and broke his neck.

> Pigs needed the fences to stay at home. Any found outside the fence could be taken by the finder—but half had to be given to the church warden to feed the hungry.

By the hearth in the Leffers cottage in Beaufort

The **Old Burying Ground** was deeded to the town in 1731 by Nathaniel Taylor and contains graves from the Revolutionary War. Many of the graves face east because those buried wanted to face the sun when they rose on Judgment Day.

Sarah Gibbs died in 1792 and is buried beside her first husband, Jacob Shepard. He went to sea one day and did not return and was presumed dead. Sarah married Nathaniel Gibbs, but when the shipwrecked Jacob returned, the two men agreed that Sarah would stay with Gibbs in life but must spend eternity at the side of Jacob Shepard.

An English family arrived in Beaufort with an infant daughter. Later in life, she wanted to see her homeland, and her father took her to London. The daughter died on the return voyage, and because her father had promised her mother to bring her home, he bought a barrel of rum from the captain and put her body in it. She was buried in Beaufort.

The Carteret County Courthouse dates from 1796 and was the third courthouse in Beaufort. Samuel Leffers served as the court clerk for a few years there. Inside, a bar separates the court officials from the audience. Three justices were required for each session of court, and they sat in three chairs at the back. A green cloth covered the tables so they could write with a quill pen. The jury sat on benches along the side walls.

North Carolina Maritime Museum (252-728-7317; www.ah.dcr.state.nc.us/sections/maritime), 315 Front St. Open daily. This museum offers displays on maritime history as well as coastal plant and animal life. One of the highlights is a collection of artifacts from the 18th-century shipwreck near Beaufort Inlet believed to be the *Queen Anne's Revenge*, the flagship of Blackbeard's fleet. Mysteries still surround the circumstances of that wreck, which occurred just a week after the fleet had successfully blockaded Charles Town, South Carolina, and captured a number of prizes in the spring of 1718.

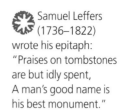 Samuel Leffers (1736–1822) wrote his epitaph: "Praises on tombstones are but idly spent, A man's good name is his best monument."

In the fall of that year, as described earlier in this chapter, Blackbeard's last, fatal fight occurred during a battle with the Royal Navy ships sent to hunt for him at Ocracoke. His head was hung in the rigging and taken back to Virginia to be mounted at the entrance to Port Hampton, along with two other hanged pirates, as a warning to all pirates.

LODGING

PECAN TREE INN
116 Queen St., Beaufort, NC 28516
800-728-7871, 252-728-6733;
www.pecantree.com
In the heart of the Beaufort historic district, the inn is a half block from the waterfront and has three porches and a lovely flower and herb garden. Seven guest rooms.

RESTAURANTS

BLUE MOON BISTRO
119 Queen St.
252-728-5800
The cuisine is innovative, with a nice presentation of garnishes. Ginger-carrot soup is a specialty. The wine list is extensive.

SHARPIES GRILL & BAR
521 Front St.
252-838-0101
Entrées include beef, fish, crab, lamb, and pork.

EVENTS

June: Old Homes & Gardens Tour, 800-575-7483, 252-728-5225

INFORMATION

BEAUFORT HISTORIC SITE
130 Turner St.,Beaufort, NC 28516
800-575-7483, 252-728-5225

WILMINGTON

By 1665 settlement had begun in the Cape Fear River valley. Wilmington was founded in 1730 at the junction of two branches of the Cape Fear. It was an ideal site for what would become a major city, with easy access both to a wide swath of inland terrain and to the Atlantic through Corncake Inlet, some 25 miles downstream. Wilmington soon became a center of political action as well as commerce. The peripatetic assembly often met there before a fixed capital was established at New Bern in 1770. The city became a hotbed of rebellion before and during the Revolution. In November 1765 a Stamp Act protest took place at the courthouse (which stood at that time on the northeast corner of Front and Market Streets), forcing the royal stamp act officer to resign. After the Battle of Guilford Courthouse in 1781, Lord Cornwallis used the city as a base for his army before setting off for Virginia.

HISTORICAL SITES *and* MUSEUMS

Burgwin-Wright House (910-762-0570; www.geocities.com), 224 Market St., Wilmington, NC 28401. Open Tue.–Sat. This Georgian-style town house dates from 1770. It was the headquarters for Lord Cornwallis, who described it as "the most considerable house in town." The front part of the house is the original building. Today the house contains a collection of 18th-century furnishings. A three-story kitchen dates from an earlier period, when it was part of the jail. The gardens are magnificent.

LODGING

C. W. WORTH HOUSE
412 S. Third St., Wilmington, NC 28401
800-340-8559, 910-762-8562;
www.worthhouse.com
The Queen Anne–style home dates from 1893 and is near the historic district and the waterfront. Seven guest rooms.

GRAYSTONE INN
100 S. Third St., Wilmington, NC 28401
888-763-4773, 910-763-2000;
www.graystoneinn.com
This historic B&B dates from 1906. The hand-carved staircase is stunning. Nine guest rooms.

ROSEHILL INN B&B
114 S. Third St., Wilmington, NC 28401
800-825-0250, 910-815-0250;
www.rosehill.com
The neoclassical revival home dates from 1848. Six guest rooms.

THE VERANDAS
202 Nun St., Wilmington, NC 28401
910-251-2212; www.verandas.com
This Italianate mansion has four verandas and a cupola. Eight guest rooms.

INFORMATION

CAPE FEAR COAST CONVENTION & VISITORS BUREAU
24 N. Third St., Wilmington, NC 28401
800-222-4757, 910-341-4030

CURRIE

Currie, the site of historic Moore's Creek Bridge, lies about 15 miles northwest of Wilmington, via US 421 and NC 210.

HISTORICAL SITES *and* MUSEUMS

Moore's Creek National Battlefield (910-283-5591; www.nps.gov/mocr), 40 Patriots Hall Dr., Currie, NC 28435. Open daily. In February 1776 Governor Josiah Martin recruited Loyalists in a plan to combine them with British troops coming by sea and vanquish the Patriots. Many of the Loyalists were Scots Highlanders who had pledged their allegiance to the Crown when they emigrated to the Cape Fear Valley. Now they gathered at Cross Creek (near modern Fayetteville) and prepared to march toward Wilmington. But Colonel Richard Caswell of the militia and Colonel James Moore of the First North Carolina Continentals decided to intercept them on their way to the coast. Colonel Alexander Lillington and his men arrived at Moore's Creek before the Loyalists did and built earthworks along the east side of the creek.

The next day Caswell arrived and established more earthworks on the west side. When the Loyalists arrived, they found that the Patriots had taken away planks from the bridge and greased the stringers. The Scottish Highlanders made a charge across the remains of the bridge to the sounds of bagpipes, drums, and the cry "King George and broadswords." But the Patriots met them with two cannon, called "Old Mother Covington and her daughter." The Patriots were victorious in minutes and also captured 850 Loyalists and much of their equipment after the battle. The British learned that it was not easy to squash the rebellion of the southern colonies.

> ✳ Mary Slocumb dreamed that her husband, Ezekiel, was wounded in battle. So she rode her horse for 60 miles during the night and got to Moore's Creek Bridge as the battle was ending. She found her husband safe and then nursed wounded Patriots before riding home.

The only original sites are the bridge and part of the Old Negro Head Point Road. Earthworks were reconstructed in the 1930s. There is an audio-visual presentation in the visitor center. Original weapons on display include a broadsword, a Highland pistol, a Brown Bess musket, and a swivel gun. There are trails to walk, with markers along the way. The History Trail includes markers for Negro Head Point Road, the Battle of Moore's Creek Bridge, the Patriot Monument honoring those who fought here, and the Heroic Women's Monument for those who provided support for their husbands in the battle.

The Tarheel Trail takes visitors through the cypress swamp.

INFORMATION

PENDER COUNTY
Box 177, 108 S. Cowan St., Burgaw, NC 28425
888-576-4556

THE PIEDMONT

The Piedmont in North Carolina is as much as 150 miles wide, marked by rolling hills and red clay soil. It stretches from the fall line at the edge of the Tidewater region to the Blue Ridge Mountains, gradually rising from as low as 30 to as high as 1,500 feet above sea level. Originally forested, this land was gradually cleared for farms as colonial settlers moved inland above the fall line, and its abundant water power led to the establishment of towns and cities. Eventually the cities—Raleigh, Durham, Greensboro, Winston-Salem, Charlotte—became the major industrial, financial, and cultural centers of the state.

Planned as the North Carolina state capital, Raleigh is named for Sir Walter Raleigh. William Christmas laid out the city in 1792 on land purchased to create a permanent capital for the state. The first statehouse was completed in 1794 but burned in 1831. Now part of the Research Triangle with Durham and Chapel Hill, a powerful linkage of high-tech industries and universities, Raleigh shares in their prosperity.

HISTORICAL SITES *and* MUSEUMS

Joel Lane House (919-833-3431; www.joellane.org), 728 W. Hargett St. Open Mar. 1 to mid-Dec, Tue.–Sat. The restored plantation manor house dates from 1760 and figured prominently as a meeting site for the founders of the city. It is thought to be the oldest building in Wake County. The house is furnished with 18th-century pieces, and the grounds include a garden designed in the colonial manner.

Mordecai Historic Park (919-857-4364; www.raleighnc.gov/mordecai), 1 Mimosa St. Open Tue.–Sun. The park has a number of buildings, including several from the colonial and Revolutionary period. The 1785 Mordecai House was the plantation of Henry Lane. His father, Joel Lane, owned the land where Raleigh was founded in 1792. Henry Lane's daughter Margaret married Moses Mordecai, and they lived in the north end of the present house. A Chippendale secretary in the library is thought to be where Joel Lane signed the deeds of the land for Raleigh.

A gambrel-roof house dates from ca. 1795 and was the birthplace of President Andrew Johnson in 1808. This house was moved from the corner of Fayetteville and Morgan Streets.

LODGING

THE OAKWOOD INN
411 N. Bloodworth St., Raleigh, NC 27604
800-267-9712, 919-832-9712;
www.oakwoodinnbb.com
This historic B&B dates from 1871. It has antique furnishings and six guest rooms.

RESTAURANTS

SECOND EMPIRE RESTAURANT AND TAVERN
330 Hillsborough St.
919-829-3663; www.second-empire.com
The restaurant occupies the restored Dodd-Hinsdale House, built in Second Empire Victorian style for Mayor William Dodd in 1871 and later bought by Colonel John Hinsdale, who married Ellen Devereaux, a descendant of Raleigh's founder, Joel Lane. The restaurant has an ornate formal dining room above with gourmet cuisine and an informal tavern below with lighter fare. Both are open for dinner.

INFORMATION

GREATER RALEIGH CONVENTION & VISITORS BUREAU
421 Fayetteville St. Mall, Raleigh, NC 27602
800-849-8499, 919-834-5900

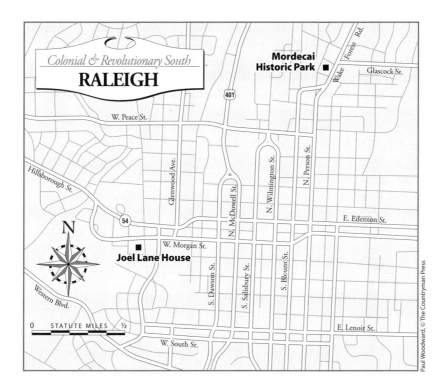

Colonial & Revolutionary South
RALEIGH

Mordecai Historic Park

Joel Lane House

Paul Woodward. © The Countryman Press

CHARLOTTE

Visitors to Charlotte now will be struck by the forest of towers—that is, bank buildings—each vying to be taller than the rest, just as cathedrals did in the Middle Ages. At night their lights brighten the whole area, but Charlotte is not all modern and glossy. At a lower level, some remnants of the city's interesting past have been preserved. Charlotte is now the largest city in North Carolina and the banking center for much of the South, matching the Research Triangle as an important urban area in the state.

As explorer John Lawson wandered through the Piedmont region during the early 1700s, he remarked that the Catawba Indians lived in the "finest part of Carolina," whereas the English had settled in the less desirable coastal sections. By 1740 settlers were traveling by covered wagon along the Great Wagon Road from Philadelphia and Maryland to the Piedmont. Thomas Spratt and his wife stopped where the center of Charlotte is now, worn out from the trip, and claimed it was "a gude place" to settle. Thomas Polk chose to build his home along the Indian Trading Path, now Tryon Street.

In 1762 the county was named Mecklenburg, to honor King George III's young bride, a princess of Mecklenburg-Strelitz in Germany. The village of Charlotte, named for the same young woman, was incorporated in 1768. By 1774

Hezekiah Alexander had completed his house on the hill, near those of a number of Scotch-Irish, French Huguenot, and German Lutheran immigrants.

As the Revolution approached, the citizens of Charlotte raised the cry of freedom and are said to have signed their own Mecklenburg Declaration of Independence on May 20, 1775. (The original document was said to be lost in a fire, and there is some question about its authenticity.)

HISTORICAL SITES *and* MUSEUMS

Declaration or no, there is no doubt about the patriotic sentiments of the residents. In 1780, some 150 local militiamen in buckskin, led by Colonel William Davie, fought the "Battle of the Bees" against Tarleton's dragoons, who outnumbered them with 2,000 men at the **McIntyre Farm** (704-336-3854; www.parkand rec.com), 5801 McIntyre Rd. Eventually the Patriots had to retreat before superior force. Cornwallis occupied Charlotte but found he was constantly badgered by the feisty militiamen, and left saying that Charlotte was "a veritable nest of hornets."

The **Hezekiah Alexander Homesite / Charlotte Museum of History** (704-568-1774; www.charlottemuseum.org), 3500 Shamrock Dr. Open daily. This

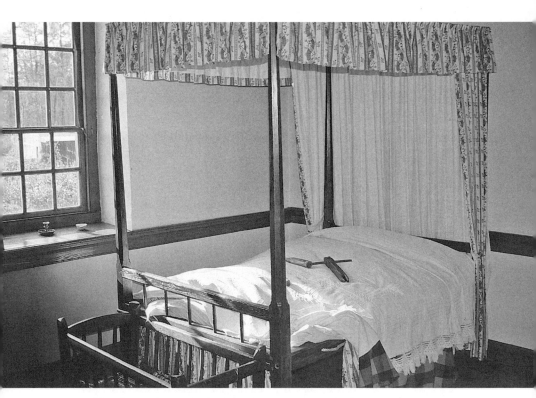

Bedchamber at the Hezekiah Alexander Homesite in Charlotte

is the oldest building still standing in Mecklenburg County. Dating from 1774, it is called the "Rock House." Hezekiah Alexander was said to be one of the signers of the 1775 Mecklenburg Declaration of Independence. He was a delegate to the Fifth Provincial Congress and helped draft the North Carolina Constitution and Bill of Rights.

A blacksmith by trade, Alexander lived with his wife and 10 children in the house,

> It is said that in 1799 Conrad Reed made the first documented discovery of gold in the country. In 1836 the U.S. government established a mint in Charlotte. But when gold was found in California, the focus turned to the West.

which is furnished with period pieces. Behind the house is a cabin with a large fireplace, herbs drying overhead, a "curfew" (a pottery piece used to cover coals at night), candle molds, and, behind the door, a set of stilts for children. The family stored their dairy products and food in a springhouse on the property to keep them from spoiling. Some say that it also held arms for Patriots.

LODGING

BALLANTYNE RESORT
10000 Ballantyne Commons Pkwy., Charlotte, NC 28277
866-248-4824, 704-248-4000;
www.ballantyneresort.com
This hotel has the feeling of Old World. There are 212 guest rooms.

DUKE MANSION
400 Hermitage Rd., Charlotte, NC 28207
888-202-1009, 704-714-4400;
www.dukemansion.org
This historic home dates from 1915. Twenty guest rooms.

VANLANDINGHAM ESTATE
2010 The Plaza, Charlotte, NC 28205
888-524-2020, 704-334-8909;
www.vanlandinghamestate.com
This B&B is in a quiet residential area and set back from the road. Nine guest rooms.

EVENTS

January: Twelfth Night: A Scots-Irish Holiday Celebration, 704-568-1774

INFORMATION

VISIT CHARLOTTE
500 S. College St., Charlotte, NC 28202
800-231-4636, 704-331-2700

GREENSBORO

Guilford County was founded in 1771 and Greensboro in 1808. The city was named after Revolutionary War hero General Nathanael Greene, who led the American forces at the Battle of Guilford Courthouse here in 1781.

HISTORIC SITES *and* MUSEUMS

Guilford Courthouse National Military Park (336-288-1776; www.nps .gov/guco), 2332 New Garden Rd., Greensboro, NC 27410. Open daily. The park contains more than 200 acres and 28 monuments of soldiers, statesman, and patriots of the American Revolution. On March 15, 1781, the Battle of Guilford

Courthouse took place here, a culmination of the British attempt to subdue the Carolinas. Lord Cornwallis fought against Nathanael Greene and held the field at the end of the battle. However, he had severe losses—more than a quarter of his army— and did not vanquish the Americans.

Greene had harassed British forces for several months in small engagements and chose this site for a direct confrontation. He deployed his 4,400-man army in three battle lines west of the Guilford Courthouse and did not suffer such heavy losses as the British. Afterward, Cornwallis took his troops back to Wilmington to recover and regroup before bringing his southern campaign north into Virginia. The battle is considered to have changed the course of the war, leading to American victory at Yorktown seven months later.

The visitor center sits midway between what were the American first and second battle lines. It offers a live-action film, an animated battle map program, and various displays. The General Nathanael Greene statue stands at the middle of the American second battle line. Francis H. Packer, a student of sculptor Augustus Saint-Gaudens, designed the statue.

Visitors can take an auto tour to see the sites of the first, second, and third American lines that were crucial to Greene's strategy. A tall granite shaft with the inscription "Regulars, Greene's 3rd Line" marks the spot of Greene's Continentals. The Cavalry Monument is a granite shaft to commemorate the charge of the American cavalry under Colonel William Washington during the fighting along the third line. The Hooper-Penn Monument marks the graves of William Hooper and John Penn. They were both signers of the Declaration of Independence.

Tannenbaum Historic Park (336-545-5315; www.march1781.org), 2200 New Garden Rd. Open Mar. 1 to mid-Dec, Tue.–Sun. Originally this 7-acre park was an 18th-century farmstead. The site includes two log cabins and a British hospital dating from 1778.

Greensboro Historical Museum (336-373-2043; www.greensborohistory.org), 130 Summit Ave. Open Tue.–Sun. The museum offers maps, weapons, and correspondence from General Greene to George Washington. There are also artifacts from the Battle of Guilford Courthouse.

EVENTS

March: Reenactment of the Battle of Guilford Courthouse, 336-288-1776
November: Colonial Fair, 336-545-5315

BURLINGTON

Not far from Greensboro, Burlington was the site of the Battle of Alamance on May 16, 1771.

HISTORICAL SITES *and* MUSEUMS
Alamance Battleground State Historic Site (336-227-4785; www.alamance

battleground.nchistoricsites.org), 5803 NC 62 South, Burlington, NC 27215. Open Mon.–Sat. Royal Governor William Tryon led the North Carolina militia against a group of western farmers. The "Regulators" protested excessive fees, inadequate representation in the assembly, and the practices of some corrupt officials. This battle suppressed and scattered the Regulators, ending their revolt. There is a visitor center and a number of markers and monuments on the grounds.

EVENTS

May: 18th-Century Live-in & Militia Muster, Alamance Battleground Site, 336-227-4785

WINSTON-SALEM

Winston-Salem was founded in 1753 after some Moravians from Pennsylvania bought land in the Piedmont. They built Bethabara, which means "House of Passage," and which became a trading and crafts center. Old Salem, the residential town, was consolidated with a newer and expanding Winston in 1913.

Historic Bethabara Park (336-924-8191; www.bethabarapark.org), 2147 Bethabara Rd., Winston-Salem, NC 27101. Open Apr. 1 to Nov. 30, Tue.–Sun. Fifteen Moravian men left Bethlehem, Pennsylvania, in 1753 and settled on a site selected earlier in the year by Moravian bishop August Spangenberg, which he called Die Wachau, or Wachovia. (Lord John Carteret subsequently bought the tract.) Bethabara, as it was called, became the first Moravian settlement in North Carolina. During the first 20 years the settlers built over 75 buildings.

During the French and Indian War Bethabara and its two forts were defensive centers for settlers in the region and a supply depot for the Catawba allies of the British. During the Revolutionary War, British prisoners captured at Kings Mountain in October 1780 were housed there. After the Battle of Cowpens, early in 1781, General Cornwallis marched his troops through town.

The park has a wealth of properties, including the 1788 Gemeinhaus (church), which was also a meeting place called a Saal, a school and minister's house. This is the only German colonial church that has living quarters for the minister adjacent. This Gemeinhaus replaced an original log structure built somewhere on the Bethabara grounds in 1756. Its location was decided by lot, with a number of solutions placed in a hat and the one chosen thought to be the Lord's decision. For example, "The Savior approves that the Gemeinsaal in Bethabara should be built along the street in Stach's garden," according to Moravian records.

Although both Moravians and non-Moravians worked on the building, the Moravians were paid 9 shillings and the non-Moravian 8 shillings; room and board was included. Stone came from a farm south of town, and yellow poplar shingles left from the building of a distillery across the street were used on the roof.

The minister's parlor was the front room, and the bedroom, kitchen, and Saal

A cabin in Historic Bethabara Park, in Winston-Salem

were on the same floor. The bedroom upstairs was for visiting church workers. Non-Moravians stayed in the tavern.

Moravians came to the Saal to hear scripture, hymns, and prayer as many as three times a day, often held in conjunction with a meal. They sat in choirs divided by age, gender, and marital status—women on the right and men on the left.

In 1755 Brother Aust went ahead of the group of single brothers and married couples coming from Pennsylvania. They played on their trumpets the hymn "Peace and Health and Every Good Be with You" as they approached the settlement. The residents trumpeted back to them as they welcomed Brother Aust the potter. Gottfried Aust made lead-glazed earthenware pottery, which was used by the local residents as well as settlers in the surrounding area. His pottery was located inside the walls of the palisade fort during the French and Indian War.

When Aust moved to Salem in 1771 the pottery went with him. Rudolph Christ started a pottery again in Bethabara, followed by Gottlob Krause, an apprentice of Aust's in Salem. Krause worked in the house

> Moravians held "love feasts," which included a sweetened "love" bread and cider to drink. The cabinet in the dining room stored the mugs, linens, and baskets.

of Johannes Schaub, then with John Buttner, and his son Joseph ran the pottery there. Today it is known as the **1782 Potter's House.**

The **1803 Herman Buttner House** was home for the family of the distiller and brewer Herman Buttner and was also a distribution point for the beer. Although the original distillery was built in 1778 and burned in 1802, a new distillery was detached and perhaps located next to the Buttner House.

Head for the visitor center for more information and brochures of the walking trails. Then walk across the street to the **French and Indian War Fort**

The Gemeinhaus in Bethabara Park

(reconstructed) and the archaeological site. Also visit the gardens and foundations of the original settlement. Interpreters in costume explain the history of the place.

Old Salem (888-653-7253, 336-721-7300; www.oldsalem.org), Old Salem Rd. Open daily except closed Mon. in Jan. and Feb. This is a restoration of the town as it stood in 1766. Originally the Moravians came from Bohemia and Moravia (in what is now the Czech Republic) but were persecuted there. When their leader, Jan Hus, was burned at the stake in 1415, they dispersed or went underground. A group that had found refuge in Saxon Germany settled missionaries in Bethlehem, Pennsylvania, in 1741, and then another group continued the journey to North Carolina.

Begin your tour at the **Old Salem Visitor Center** at 600 South Main St. to get a map and learn more about the town. Then head across the bridge to the **Frank L. Horton Museum Center.** In 1965 Frank Horton and his mother, Theo Taliaferro, founded the **Museum of Early Southern Decorative Arts** (888-348-4833, 336-721-7300), which has collected furnishings dating from 1640 to 1820. Visitors can now see 24 period rooms; don't miss the 1640 cupboard from Tidewater Virginia, or the silver pieces dating from 1711.

Also, in the Horton Museum Center you can visit the **Old Salem Children's Museum**. Children are offered the chance to dress up in Moravian costume and pretend to work at a joiner's bench, make a box with dovetails, or cook over an open fire in a model of the Miksch House (see below). They can also play with toys of the period and enjoy "touch boxes," as well as attend puppet shows and special classes.

The **Old Salem Toy Museum** includes more than 1,200 antique European and American toys. Moravian children played with toys, some of which are here; the doll collection has some from the 17th century. Don't miss the puppets, teddy bears, and doll houses. The Humpty Dumpty Circus is magical.

Follow your map to visit houses along the street. We visited the **J. Blum Shop**, where we saw a Moravian star with 26 points; we have one on our Christmas tree. You can also enjoy hopscotch games, sewing cards, Miss Poppet, and an early American doll kit, to name a few items in the shop.

The **Single Brothers House**, a half-timbered brick building, dates from 1769. Men and boys lived and worked here; today artisans are at work in craft rooms. You'll probably see the cooper's shop with tools of the era, stock for barrels, and a supply of hoops. The tailor's shop made clothing under the eye of the church; it had to conform to modest norms rather than be frivolous. The tinsmiths made kitchen utensils from black iron and also from tinned iron, which was sheet iron with a tinned surface. Weavers primarily produced linen and cotton fabrics. Thread was spun in the homes, dyed, and then brought to the weaver.

The oldest tobacco shop in the country is the **Miksch House**, which dates from 1771. It was home to Mathew Miksch and his wife, Henrietta. Wares inside include twists of chewing tobacco that have been sweetened with honey. As you wander around you may see a woman adding dye made from nuts, onion skins,

The Single Brothers House in Old Salem

or flowers to a boiling kettle. Perhaps someone will be dipping candles or roasting a pig. Mathew Miksch had a store selling candles, tobacco, ginger cakes, snuff, and garden seed. There are two spinning wheels in his house. Miksch cured tobacco and said that to sneeze made you healthy.

George Washington stayed in the **Salem Tavern** in 1791 and remarked that he enjoyed the music played for him that night. Today visitors can have a meal there; call 919-748-8585 for reservations.

LODGING

THE AUGUSTUS ZEVELY INN
803 S. Main St., Winston-Salem, NC 27101
800-928-9299, 336-748-9299;
www.winston-salem-inn.com
This B&B is in a building that dates from 1844, when it was a doctor's office and home. Thirteen guest rooms.

HENRY F. SHAFFNER HOUSE
150 S. Marshall St., Winston-Salem, NC 27101
800-952-2256, 336-777-0052;
www.shaffnerhouse.com

This 1907 house was home to Henry F. Shaffner, whose parents were Moravian. He founded the Wachovia Loan and Trust Company. There are four dining rooms. On Mon.–Fri. from 5 to 7 you can enjoy "Wine after Work." Houseguests may also make a reservation for dinner. Nine guest rooms.

RESTAURANTS

SALEM TAVERN
736 Main St.
336-748-8585
Have a meal in the Moravian-style dining rooms with costumed staff to serve you.

EVENTS

September: Apple Festival, Bethabara Park, 336-924-8191
December: Old Salem Christmas, 888-653-7253

INFORMATION

WINSTON-SALEM VISITOR CENTER
200 Brookstown Ave., Winston-Salem, NC 27101
866-728-4200, 336-728-4200

Current Information

TRAVEL & TOURISM DIVISION
301 N. Wilmington St.
Raleigh, NC 27601
800-VISIT-NC (847-4862) outside Raleigh
919-733-4171 in Raleigh; www.visitnc.com

South Carolina

Historical Introduction
to the
South Carolina Colony

During the 16th century a number of explorers ventured into the region that was to become South Carolina. Giovanni da Verrazano's exploration of the Carolina coast in 1524 intrigued both the French and the Spanish, each looking to establish claims to land in continental North America. Four years earlier Lucas Vázquez de Ayllón, a government official in Hispaniola, had landed on the coast and then left with a number of Indians to use as slaves. He returned in 1526 to found a settlement, possibly on the Waccamaw River near Georgetown, but the colony was abandoned after nine months of bad weather, disease, internal conflict, and Ayllón's death. In further exploration, Hernando de Soto crossed the Savannah River and passed through the region in 1540 to the Blue Ridge Mountains and then turned westward to the Mississippi.

The French were not far behind. Gaspard de Coligny, a prominent Huguenot and admiral of France, sent an expedition led by Jean Ribaut in 1562 to find suitable land north of the Spanish settlements. Ribaut discovered the harbor on Parris Island, which the Spaniard Ayllón had earlier named Santa Elena. Ribaut renamed it Port Royal and claimed it for France, erecting a stone post carved with the arms of the king. He built a four-bastioned fort and called it Charlesfort, after France's Charles IX, then departed for more supplies and colonists. The twenty-six men left behind planted no crops and depended upon friendly Indians for food. After Albert de la Pierra, the man put in charge, marooned one of their number, La Chère, as punishment, the others rescued La Chère and murdered Pierra. When their food ran out they decided to abandon the site and sail back to France.

These failures did not deter either the French or the Spanish from further attempts at settlement on the southern coast. Admiral Coligny sponsored another

Overleaf: St. Michael's Church in Charleston

The map shows:

TENN.

NORTH CAROLINA

Colonial & Revolutionary South
SOUTH CAROLINA

Cowpens National Battlefield

Kings Mountain National Military Park

Inman • York
Pickens • Greenville • Spartanburg
Walhalla • Lando
Clemson • Union
85 • Belton • Whitmire • Chester • Lancaster
Laurens • Great Falls • Cheraw
Greenwood • Newberry • Winnsboro • Bennettsville
26 • 77 • Camden • Bishopville • Hartsville • Dillon
Saluda • Florence • Mullins
Edgefield • Batesburg-Leesville • Columbia • Sumter • 95 • Lake City • Loris
20 • Aiken • Wagener • St. Matthews • Manning • Hemingway • Myrtle Beach
Wagener • Orangeburg • Kingstree
New Ellenton • Denmark • Holly Hill • St. Stephen • ■ Georgetown
St. George • 26 • Moncks Corner
Allendale • Summerville • McCellanville
Hampton • Walterboro • Jacksonboro • ■ Charleston
Estill • Yemassee
Ridgeland • ■ Beaufort
Hilton Head Island

N

GEORGIA

ATLANTIC OCEAN

0 STATUTE MILES 50

group that sailed up the St. John's River in northern Florida to build Fort Caroline in 1565, the same year that Pedro Menéndez de Avilés established a base at St. Augustine. The Spanish had returned to Santa Elena in 1564 to destroy the remnants of Charlesfort and remove the French marker, and Menéndez arrived in 1566 to build Fort San Felipe nearby. Indians decimated this settlement ten years later, but the Spaniards returned, only to leave again to reinforce St. Augustine after Sir Francis Drake burned that settlement in 1586.

For a number of reasons, both Spain and France failed to establish settlements that lasted. The Spanish did not deal fairly with the Indians, who had been friendly at first. Religious wars in France sapped needed support for colonization. Military competition for control of territory preoccupied many of the founders, especially Menéndez and Ribaut. And most significantly, the colonists themselves did not focus on planting crops, or learning how to fish and hunt effectively, or husbanding their limited resources. Like failed English colonies farther north, these infant settlements remained too dependent upon the unpredictable arrival of relief ships.

First Settlement at Charles Town

After this flurry of activity, the coast of the future South Carolina remained largely undisturbed by Europeans for seven decades. Then the English came to center stage as founders of the first successful settlement, Charles Town. Britain had failed

For one of the most ill-conceived voyages imaginable, the Charlesfort colonists built a boat, caulked it with moss, and made sails from shirts and sheets. They had no knowledge of navigation and no instruments, and packed guns in the boat but not enough food for a long voyage against prevailing westerlies in the North Atlantic. After eating leather shoes and jackets they turned to cannibalism, picking one of the group by casting lots. The twice unlucky La Chère lost the lottery and was consumed. The survivors were picked up by an English ship.

to sustain Roanoke in North Carolina but had proved more fortunate with Jamestown, Virginia, in 1607, as well as with later colonies farther north along the Atlantic seaboard. It had also occupied two key Spanish islands in the Caribbean— Barbados and Jamaica. The missing ingredient for successful colonization was substantial investment over a period of years, and that appeared shortly after the Restoration.

In 1663 King Charles II rewarded eight prominent men who had helped him regain the crown, naming them lords proprietor of Carolina at their request. The group included important noblemen: George Monck, Duke of Albemarle; Anthony Ashley Cooper, Earl of Shaftesbury; Edward Hyde, Earl of Clarendon and lord chancellor; William, Earl of Craven; Lord John Berkeley; Sir William Berkeley, former and future governor of Virginia; Sir George Carteret; and Sir John Colleton. Their generous land grant (as increased two years later) stretched from what is now the Virginia border to well south of the Georgia-Florida state line. In 1669 the proprietors set up Fundamental Constitutions to govern their holdings. Drafted by the Earl of Shaftesbury and his secretary, John Locke (later famous as a political philosopher), they contained a strange mix of feudal and modern principles of governance. On the one hand they created an aristocracy based on land, complete with the collection of quitrents (annual fees) from tenants; on the other, they provided significant legal rights—trial by jury and freedom from double jeopardy—as well as freedom of religion.

SOUTH CAROLINA *Time Line*

1526	1562	1566	1587
Lucas Vázquez de Ayllón leads an expedition and establishes short-lived settlement (possibly on the Waccamaw River)	Jean Ribaut settles a small contingent of French Huguenots at Port Royal on Parris Island	Pedro Menéndez de Avilés establishes a Spanish settlement at Santa Elena (Parris Island)	The Spanish abandon Santa Elena and return to St. Augustine

The latter provision, clearly unusual in a century wracked by religious wars and insistent on conformity, eventually proved useful in attracting settlers. But at the outset of their efforts to create settlements and thereby reap some profit from their investment, the proprietors had little success in recruiting either at home or in other American colonies, apart from the Virginians who drifted south into the Albermarle. Finally a connection with Barbados began to arouse some interest in the southern region of Carolina. Established sugar plantations had taken up most of the land in

> Hilton wrote a pamphlet entitled *A Relation of a Discovery* in which he praised the abundance and variety of wildlife and timber in Carolina. In addition, "The ayr is clear and sweet, the countrey very pleasant and delightful. And we could wish that all they that want a happy settlement of our English nation were well transported thither."

Barbados, and newcomers began to look elsewhere. Captain William Hilton of Massachusetts had explored the Cape Fear River area for New Englanders. By 1663, now on Barbados, he realized the need for more land and religious freedom than was available there. At the behest of promoters, he sailed for the Carolina coast, this time exploring Port Royal Sound as well as returning to the Cape Fear River. In 1666 Robert Sandford also explored a coast filled with rivers and islands that must have been attractive to mariners, and both men reported their enthusiastic reactions back to England.

By 1669 the Earl of Shaftesbury, Lord Ashley, had taken charge of the project, and to finance its start the proprietors agreed to contribute 500 pounds sterling each and 200 more annually for four years. A fleet of three small ships—two frigates and a sloop—left England in August 1669 with ninety-two passengers on board, heading for Barbados to pick up more colonists. Only one, the *Carolina,* survived and reached Port Royal the following March. The saga of this fleet's mishaps was a cautionary tale, demonstrating again how easily plans went awry in 17th-century seafaring. The sloop *Albermarle* reached Barbados but sank there in a gale, to be replaced by a chartered sloop, the *Three Brothers.* When the three ships got under way again to Carolina, a more severe storm scattered them over a wide

1663	**1669**	**1670**	**1680**
Charles II grants the region of Carolina to eight lords proprietor	The lords proprietor approve the Fundamental Constitutions of Carolina	The English establish the first permanent settlement at Charles Town (Albemarle Point)	Charles Town is moved to Oyster Point; French Huguenots arrive from England

expanse of ocean—the frigate *Port Royal* aground in the Bahamas, the *Carolina* blown to Bermuda, and the *Three Brothers* driven all the way to Virginia. The *Carolina* finally reached Kiawah (near Charleston) in April 1670, where the Indian chief invited the weary colonists to settle in his territory. After sailing to investigate their original destination, Port Royal, which they thought entirely too close to the Spanish, they settled in May at Albemarle Point on a river they named the Ashley, and the *Three Brothers* straggled in later that month. Lord Ashley informed the colonists that "the Town you are now planted on we have named and you are to call Charles Town."

Early Troubles and Trade

From the outset the Charles Town colonists worried about attacks from Spaniards and allied Indians. They needed to keep watch and also build more defenses, which left them little time to plant crops. Luckily, Henry Woodward, a naval surgeon and adventurer, had stayed ashore at Port Royal to learn Indian languages when Captain Robert Sandford returned to England from his exploration in 1666. Woodward became a pioneer of English expansion in the lower South, traded with the Indians, and developed a friendship with them. They returned his friendship with current news, so he heard about an impending attack in August 1670, just a few months after the colonists had arrived. With the help of local Indians, they mounted a successful defense of Charles Town, and the Spaniards returned to St. Augustine.

By 1671 relationships with the Indians had deteriorated, and Woodward changed allegiance from the coastal Indians to the Westo Indians, who conducted raids against the Spanish missions in Georgia. These Indians provided the settlement with a buffer zone against both Spanish and French invaders, as well as wider opportunities for trade.

Although the colonists had set out with plenty of food, two of three ships had been lost with most of their provisions. Governor Sayle wrote that "Wee have been put to purchase our maintenance from the Indians, and that in such small parcels as we could hardly get another supply before the former was gone." Apart from their understandable preoccupation with defense, a more funda-

---

SOUTH CAROLINA *Time Line*

1700	1706	1713	1715	1719
A hurricane strikes Charles Town	The Church of England becomes the state church	Separation of North and South Carolina begins	War with Yemassee Indians breaks out	South Carolina becomes a royal colony

"WITHOUT *having any* FORMAL STREETS"

 In 1672 the Spanish sent a soldier from St. Augustine to spy on Charles Town. His report, relayed to the Spanish governor, provides the best early description of the settlement:

"The place where they have the village built is a wooded village consisting of dwelling houses without having any formal streets although he could count about ninety houses, some higher than others apparently according to the means of each individual. And in this same tract they have their fields of maize, pumpkins, cow-peas, peas and in each house their trellises for grape vines of different sorts. And also a great quantity of sweet potatoes and some fig trees. . . . Inside of this fortification there are some lodgings and others of the same sort outside of it which, as he was informed, were built at first when they began to settle for fear of the Indians. . . . ships and frigates of good burden could enter [the harbor] because he saw an outrigger with yards which was about to sail for the island of Barbados whence they receive what they need in the way of food and other necessities."

mental problem was lack of experience in growing crops. As noted by Thomas Newe, a later emigrant, the first colonists "were most of them tradesmen, poor and wholly ignorant of husbandry . . . their whole business was to clear a little ground to get Bread for their Familyes." The first year was tough because ice nipped the crops, and for several more years drought and crop failure persisted, until the good harvest of 1674. Before that year food sometimes had to be rationed, and many colonists built up debts to the proprietors for food and other supplies advanced on credit.

Captain Joseph West became governor in 1674 and was tireless in developing the early colony, clearing land, building houses, and establishing defense palisades. The proprietors looked for profits from their substantial investments, and those depended upon wide settlement of land with the payment of quitrents and mar-

1739
Slaves on Stono River plantations rebel

1760
Treaty ends the Cherokee War and reopens the upcountry for settlement

1776
British repulsed at Battle of Sullivan's Island

1780
British occupy Charles Town after long siege; Patriots routed at battle of Camden; Loyalists routed at Kings Mountain

ketable exports. They had unrealistic visions of getting products that never developed in early Carolina—silk, wine, olive oil—from their own colonies rather than Europe. Gradually some exports, especially lumber and excess cattle, began to trickle out of the colony.

When the essential Henry Woodward risked traveling alone into the heart of Westo territory and came back with a treaty in 1674, Indian trade increased, especially in deerskins, furs, and Indian slaves sent to the West Indies. It had been common practice for Indians to enslave captives from other tribes in frequent wars, and the possibility of selling them for profit to English traders increased the reward. The Barbadian immigrants, who came from a culture of black slavery on the plantations, became heavily engaged in Indian slave trading, and some of the Indians were kept to work the land. The proprietors did not countenance Indian slave trading because they thought it would provoke troubles, and so took charge of all Indian trade in 1677 for seven years. Yet only in the 1690s, as rice and indigo became the staple export crops, did plantations turn to importing black slaves for their labor.

A New Charles Town

By 1680 the colony had moved the town site to Oyster Point at the junction of the Ashley and Cooper Rivers, a strategic location where a second Charles Town developed. In 1682 Thomas Ash, special agent to the king, wrote "... The town is regularly laid out into large and capacious streets, which to Buildings is a great Ornament and Beauty. In it they have reserved convenient places for Building of a Church, town House, and other publick Structures, an Artillery Ground for the Exercise of their Militia, and Wharfs for the Convenience of their Trade and Shipping."

The proprietors had established religious tolerance to promote needed immigration, and its effect became evident as non-Anglican sects developed during the 1680s and 1690s. French Huguenots arrived in 1680 and gave a boost to the economy with their skills as artisans and farmers. Colonists continued to trade with the Indians and export skins, barrel staves, pitch, tar, beef, and lumber. By the 1690s rice grown in lowland plantations along the tidal rivers had become a profitable cash crop. In 1692 Thomas Newe complained of inflation, reporting high prices—such as milk at two cents a quart and beef at four cents a pound—but the settlement prospered.

SOUTH CAROLINA *Time Line*

1781	1782	1783	1788	1790
British defeated at Battle of Cowpens	British evacuate Charles Town	Charles Town is renamed Charleston	South Carolina becomes a state	The capital moves from Charleston to Columbia

Continued immigration brought with it increasing conflict between Anglicans and Dissenters (Nonconformists) of other Protestant denominations. At its center were the original "Goose Creek men"—settlers from Barbados who clustered around Goose Creek north of Charles Town—and the influx of succeeding Barbadians, dedicated Anglicans who resented the competition of newcomers for the Indian trade and worked for the establishment of a state religion. By 1702 the Anglican population (42 percent) was outnumbered by various dissenting sects (58 percent) and feared losing control of the colony. When Governor Nathaniel Johnson called an emergency session of the assembly without allowing time for the Upcountry Dissenters to get there, the Anglicans carried the day and passed the Religious Act of 1704. It established the Church of England as the sole religion, barred Dissenters from assembly membership, and provided taxes for the support of the church.

Appalled Dissenters appealed to England, and the House of Lords overturned the act, but in 1706 a milder version that allowed them political rights held, and the colony had an established church. This change did much to reinforce the already disparate interests of Tidewater and upcountry factions, a division that remained through much of the century. Later waves of immigration, and increased importation of African slaves, increased both the population and the prosperity of the colony. Immigrants arrived to settle nine townships inland from Charles Town during the 1730s. Germans, Swiss, Scots, French, and Welsh joined the original Englishmen, Barbadians, and Huguenots.

Further Afflictions

The Spanish in St. Augustine continued to harass Charles Town, smallpox killed a large number of colonists between 1697 and 1699, and yellow fever and an earthquake added their toll. Yellow fever killed 160 persons in 1699 and was followed by a hurricane that flooded the town in 1700. Far more damaging was the disruption of alliances and trade with powerful Indian tribes. The Yemassees, moving into southern South Carolina from Georgia, became disturbed by plans for new settlements at Port Royal and Beaufort and continuing abuses by Indian traders. They massacred about ninety settlers at Pocotaligo (near Beaufort) in the spring of 1715 and were soon joined by many other tribes, including the powerful Creeks, in a concerted attempt to drive the English out. Settlers on the frontiers fled to Charles Town, and the colony solicited help from every hand, including other colonies and the proprietors. Nothing proved adequate until a risky alliance with the Cherokees drove the Yemassees southward and the Creeks west into Georgia by 1718. The war left devastation, with the frontiers depopulated and the colony deeply in debt.

Pirates had operated sporadically on a Carolina coast loaded with islands and creeks, but many more arrived as they were driven out of the West Indies. By 1718 they had become a serious threat to the economy as they snatched valuable cargoes going in and out of Charles Town harbor. In a dramatic incident the previous year, "Blackbeard" (Edward Teach), the most notorious of this breed, had taken a ship with some of the most prominent citizens in town on board and held them for ransom.

In the spring of 1718 he returned to blockade the harbor for a week with four ships and 300 men. Also on board was Stede Bonnet, a well-to-do Barbados landowner who had a penchant for pirating; Blackbeard had effectively commandeered his ship, the *Revenge*. A week later Blackbeard's flagship was stranded and lost at Beaufort Inlet, along with a smaller sloop. Blackbeard fled northward, while Bonnet regained control of his *Revenge,* renamed her *Royal James,* and resumed taking a heavy toll on South Carolina shipping. In response, Governor Robert Johnson commissioned Colonel William Rhett to hunt him down. After a five-hour battle at the mouth of the Cape Fear River in October, Bonnet was captured, tried, and was hanged on December 10, 1718. Forty-nine other pirates were hanged in Charles Town in November and December of that year. Thereafter an armed vessel hovered in the harbor and another cruised off the coast, putting an end to buccaneering in and around Charles Town.

In the same year the proprietors created the final disruption—this time political—of this troubled era. The colonists were already disturbed by the proprietors' maladministration and inability to solve Indian trade problems and angry at their refusal to help suppress the Yemassee Indians. Some of these problems occurred because the original proprietors had been replaced by heirs with little knowledge of the colony or interest in it beyond profit. After years of neglect and indifference, these later proprietors began a policy of direct interference, attacking popular laws passed by the assembly, reducing its powers of appointment, adding restrictions to their own land policies, limiting the colony's collection of import duties, and retiring paper currency. In a response to such political blunders—a lesson that Parliament would have to relearn decades later in the run-up to the Revolution—the assembly revolted without shedding blood. On December 10, 1719, it transformed itself into a provincial assembly to take charge of the colony, appointed James Moore Jr. as provisional governor, and requested the Crown to replace the proprietors' rule. After some confusion and delay in England, the Privy Council assumed temporary control and appointed Francis Nicholson, an experienced colonial governor, as South Carolina's first royal governor.

The Ascendancy of Charles Town

The assembly's action in 1719 precipitated a process not completed until North Carolina also became a royal colony ten years later. Even before the division of Carolina, the two regions followed different lines of development that lasted through the century. Geography along the coastal plains created many of these differences. Having few accessible ports along the upper half of its coast, the north remained largely agricultural, and scattered towns along rivers did not quickly grow or develop into cities. The south, on the other hand, with a smaller land mass and one major port in Charles Town, became a virtual city-state, both the center of trade and the core of surrounding plantations on tidal rivers. Ancillary towns in the region like Georgetown and Camden had their own independent structures but remained in the orbit of Charles Town through a variety of connections.

The development of two key crops—rice and indigo—in the 1690s laid the foundation for the later prosperity of lowland planters. They had markets with ready demand in northern colonies, Europe, and the West Indies for rice, and in Britain for indigo, where it replaced imports from more costly foreign sources. As planters became rich, sometimes very quickly after the multiple troubles at the beginning of the 18th century subsided, they built substantial homes and had the leisure to enjoy life to the fullest. They used their capital to expand and enhance their rice and indigo plantations. Rice cultivation became a science, with the construction of dikes and gates to control flooding. Indigo, a plant that looks like asparagus and provided blue dye for textiles in England, was cultivated on higher ground behind the rice fields.

These crops required extensive land and intensive labor, and those men with the largest tracts and greatest number of slaves stood to profit most. The Indian slavery that had dominated the plantations in the 17th century gave way to imported slaves from Africa. In 1708 the number of Africans in South Carolina (4,100) was in balance with the whites (4,080), but by 1724 the number of black slaves, estimated at 32,000, far outnumbered the white population of 14,000. The imbalance continued to grow, as by 1740 merchants were importing about 2,500 slaves a year to sell to planters. Apprehension that the imbalance might lead to slave revolts was justified by insurrections on the Stono River plantations as early as 1739, yet slavery was built into both the economy and a system of government based on property. To qualify for election to the assembly during this era, a man had to own 500 acres and ten slaves, or other property worth 1,000 pounds sterling, and those requirements increased throughout much of the century.

The merchants in Charles Town shared in the prosperity of the planters through marketing their exports, supplying their imports, and often managing their finances. Not bereft of slaves or land but needing neither in order to amass profits from trade in the busiest seaport in the South, they too became wealthy. Merchants and planters shared economic interests in commodities that benefited both, and they had a common interest in building a city that provided culture, entertainment, and luxury. As each group prospered in the 18th century, the merchants acquired country houses and the planters town mansions, cementing their shared interests. Among these interests were control of the political process and enjoyment of urban pleasures.

This conjunction of interests produced what has sometimes been called the "golden age" of Charles Town, shared by a self-made aristocracy that would have been labeled "nouveau riche" in later eras. It began in the 1740s and lasted at least until the Revolution, perhaps longer. But it is important to remember that such opulence applied only to a small segment of the population, even in the city. It was not shared by a very small middle class, tradesmen, artisans, or slaves. And outside of the lowlands in the Upcountry, waves of immigrants on the frontiers had little or no share in its pleasures. That split in conditions would come to haunt the colony as a whole in the run-up to the Revolution and the bitter aftermath of bloody confrontations between Patriots and Loyalists during the closing years of the war.

Seeds of Revolution

To some observers, South Carolina's active discontent with British policy and vigorous leadership of the movement toward revolution between 1765 and 1775 seem anomalous. Both Tidewater planters and Charles Town merchants had strong economic ties with Britain. They had established the Church of England as the official religion in 1706 and asked for a royal governor in 1719. Yet the fiery leaders demanding independence arose within this context of wealthy aristocrats.

Christopher Gadsden, both a merchant and a planter, denounced every intrusion of Parliament in the business of the colony and organized the Sons of Liberty among tradesmen and mechanics in Charles Town. William Henry Drayton and Henry Middleton, both planters (whose family estates along the Ashley River are now prime attractions for visitors), joined Gadsden in arousing the colony to rebellion. Henry Laurens, also a wealthy planter and merchant, represented the more moderate majority of aristocrats who resisted the duties imposed by the Stamp Act and Townshend Acts but deplored mob action—especially a rash of tar-and-feathering in the later years—and acceded only reluctantly to a total break with the Crown.

Sentiment in the Upcountry was another matter. A variety of settlers—Germans, Swiss, Scots, English, many Scotch-Irish, some French Huguenots—began to fill in the Piedmont before midcentury. Some were indentured servants who had served their term in the Tidewater and migrated to the Upcountry for land of their own. Others came down the Great Wagon Road from Pennsylvania through Virginia and North Carolina. The Cherokee War, largely coterminous with the French and Indian War, disrupted settlement of the Upcountry from the mid 1750s to 1761. Settlers in the Upcountry who had suffered raids from Cherokees angered by unfair treatment from unscrupulous traders blamed Charles Town apathy for their troubles. Like the Indians, they found the response of the capital inept, in spite of Governor James Glen's efforts to treat the Cherokee nation fairly and restore good trading practices. The blunders of his successor, Governor William Lyttleton, led to full-scale war for two years, and the burn-and-destroy tactics used by expeditions of British regulars exacerbated Indian hatred and retaliation on white settlers. The flow of new settlers moving down the Great Wagon Road increased greatly afterward, but the war had sharply etched the differences between the two regions.

Unlike the settlers in the North Carolina backcountry, who rebelled against unwarranted intrusions of Tidewater officials into their affairs, those in South Carolina felt totally neglected, and they resented the plutocracy in Charles Town. They had no law enforcement to ward off bands of thieves, no courts closer than Charles Town, no designated counties to send representatives to the assembly. So when the Tidewater Patriots began fomenting rebellion against the Crown, the upland settlers were largely unimpressed. In 1775 Drayton and William Tennent, a popular preacher, journeyed inland to convert Upcountry settlers to the cause and encountered either apathy or opposition. Before long the colony's first battle of the Revolution broke out at Ninety Six in November, with Tories facing the militia in this region of divided loyalties. Although the battle was a standoff with few casualties, this conflict augured a bloody civil war among settlers that erupted after British forces occupied Charles Town in 1780.

War Comes to Charles Town

Shortly after the outbreak of hostilities, the British had tried to capture the key city but failed. Their original plan called for establishing a base on the Cape Fear River in North Carolina. To accomplish this, General Clinton's troops would sail from Boston, rendezvous with a fleet and Lord Cornwallis's regulars, and attack from the sea while Highland Scots Tories marched on Wilmington. The Tories did not wait and were defeated at Moore's Creek Bridge. When Clinton and Cornwallis arrived months later, they diverted their attention to Charles Town and planned a double-pronged attack on June 28, 1776. An amphibious force positioned on Long Island (now the Isle of Palms) would wade across to Sullivan's Island at low tide to attack the hastily constructed palmetto fort by land while the fleet sailed around to its vulnerable side to bombard it from the sea. Like many good plans, it failed in execution. The water proved too deep for the troops to wade through, part of the fleet went aground directly in the fort's line of fire, and the palmetto walls absorbed the cannonballs rather than flying apart. Colonel William Moultrie's small force of defenders lost only 12 men killed with 25 wounded, while the British attackers suffered 115 killed with 65 wounded. Charles Town would remain free until the British returned nearly four years later.

The Southern Campaign

Northerners are sometimes surprised to learn that thirty-five Revolutionary War battles occurred in South Carolina—more than in any other colony, some claim, especially if smaller engagements count. But no one doubts how important the war-torn colony became during the latter stages of the Revolution in impeding the British southern campaign led by Lord Cornwallis. Based on the half-truth that the South contained many Loyalist subjects just waiting to join British regulars in retaking territory for the Crown, the campaign began in Savannah in January 1779, swept irregularly through both Carolinas, and ended in the final confrontation at Yorktown, Virginia, in October 1781.

British expectations of massive support from Loyalists never materialized, though there was enough of it to create a guerrilla civil war in the South Carolina Piedmont. Early in the campaign large British forces overwhelmed the defending

KEY *Revolutionary War Dates in South Carolina*

November 19–21, 1775: First siege of Fort Ninety Six. The Council of Safety orders Major Andrew Williamson to recapture the gunpowder and ammunition taken earlier by Loyalists. A larger force of Loyalists gathers and lays siege to his makeshift fort. The first land battle of the American Revolution in South Carolina ends in a truce.

June 28, 1776: Battle of Sullivan's Island. Patriot forces led by Colonel William Moultrie defend a hastily constructed palmetto-log fort on Sullivan's Island. They repel Sir Henry Clinton's forces arriving by land and sea and claim a major American victory.

May 12, 1780: Siege of Charleston ends. General Clinton's forces accept the surrender of General Benjamin Lincoln's defenders and take more than 5,000 American prisoners, paroling the militiamen. British occupation of the city begins.

August 16, 1780: Battle of Camden. General Horatio Gates meets British forces at night near Camden. His forces are routed by Lord Charles Cornwallis and disperse into North Carolina.

October 7, 1780: At the Battle of Kings Mountain, militia forces from the Carolinas, Tennessee, and Georgia defeat Loyalists led by Major Patrick Ferguson, annihilating his forces and killing Ferguson.

January 17, 1781: Battle of Cowpens. General Daniel Morgan outmaneuvers Banastre Tarleton, drives the British from the field, and takes many prisoners.

March 15, 1781: The Battle of Guilford Courthouse in North Carolina, though a costly victory for the British, clears the way for American general Nathanael Greene to resume operations in South Carolina.

May 22–June 19, 1781: Second siege of Ninety Six. General Greene conducts an unsuccessful siege of Loyalists defending a strong fort and withdraws.

September 9, 1781: The last major battle on South Carolina soil, at Eutaw Springs, ends with General Greene holding the field.

December 14, 1782: British troops, with many Tories and their slaves, evacuate Charles Town.

Americans, but their numbers later declined through harrying attacks by General Nathanael Greene, who took command in December 1780, and notable South Carolina patriot generals like Francis Marion, Andrew Pickens, and Thomas Sumter. Adopting a strategy close to guerrilla warfare, these forces harried parts of the British army in engagements designed to slow its progress and reduce its strength. After moving into North Carolina, Greene led Cornwallis to lengthen his supply lines and wear out his troops in a long chase. He finally chose to fight a major battle at Guilford Courthouse. Even in that case, he withdrew after inflicting heavy casualties on the British and returned to South Carolina to attack their remaining strongholds. Cornwallis limped back to Wilmington to recover, then marched quickly into Virginia for the final stage of the campaign.

Of course it is easy for historians to spot mistakes in retrospect, yet blunders on both sides contributed to the twenty-month length of a campaign that ended in failure. As a British move on Charles Town became imminent in early 1780, General Benjamin Lincoln expected an attack from the sea and focused on defenses around the harbor. Then overwhelming British forces (11,000 compared to 6,000 defenders) attacked from both sea and land. General Clinton captured Fort Johnson at the harbor entrance, while Cornwallis landed south of the city, circled around to cross the Ashley River upstream, then moved down the peninsula. City officials persuaded Lincoln to stay and mount a defense rather than move his troops to another location, then insisted on surrender to keep a bombardment from destroying the city. Like Cornwallis later at Yorktown, Lincoln was trapped at the end of a peninsula and had to surrender more than 5,000 men in May. Then the British made two mistakes that diminished their chances of widespread Loyalist support. The first occurred just after the fall of Charles Town, at the Battle of Waxhaws, when a daring and aggressive young officer committed an atrocity that made him infamous throughout the colonies: Colonel Banastre Tarleton's cavalry slaughtered a Virginia regiment led by Colonel Abraham Buford after it had signaled surrender with a white flag.

The second mistake was Clinton's. Before leaving Cornwallis in charge of the campaign and sailing away, he changed the terms of the parole granted to the militiamen captured at Charles Town. They were first allowed to return home by prom-

---

FRANCIS MARION, *the Swamp Fox*

One of the legendary figures of the time was the "Swamp Fox," South Carolina's Francis Marion. He had a tendency to appear mysteriously at just the right time, strike, and then disappear into the swamps. He was in the palmetto-log fort on Sullivan's Island when the British attacked in 1776 and fired the last cannon shot of the battle. He and his men were active in destroying boats on the Santee River to prevent Lord Cornwallis's movements. He rescued American prisoners at Great Savannah. He was there at Blue Savannah on the Little Pee Dee River when, with a much smaller force, he got the better of 250 Loyalist militia. Near Georgetown Marion attacked and captured supplies, horses, and Loyalist civilians. Colonel Banastre Tarleton tried to run down Marion but was led on a seven-hour chase. Tarleton gave up and told his men, "Come, my boys! Let us go back, and we will find the Gamecock [General Thomas Sumter, another guerrilla leader]. But as for this damned old fox, the devil himself could not catch him!" The "damned old fox" turned into "Swamp Fox."

THE *Fighting* QUAKER

Who was the American military leader second in importance only to George Washington during the war? Clearly it was Nathanael Greene, a fighting Quaker from Rhode Island. He first worked with Washington during the siege of Boston, and they became lifelong friends. Greene took charge of Boston after the British evacuated and Washington moved south. In 1776 he took command of Long Island, then moved to defend the shores of New Jersey and fought in the battles at Trenton and Princeton. In 1777 he led his men at Brandywine and Germantown. Washington and Greene were the only Continental generals who served during the entire War for Independence.

Greene took command of the Grand Army of the Southern Department of the United States in December 1780. He had only about 2,500 men, and their morale was low because they were on starvation rations. Throughout the hard winter campaign in North Carolina, Greene shared their hardships. He became the most able of Washington's officers as he moved from one battle to the next. He was very effective throughout the South, where he learned the local geography and made well-chosen contingency plans. In the "War of the Posts" in South Carolina he attacked the British circle of outer and inner posts protecting Charles Town. He captured all but one of them and took 3,500 prisoners. His guiding rationale was persistence: "We fight, get beat, rise, and fight again."

ising not to bear arms against Britain; now they were told to join the fight against their American neighbors or risk being hanged as traitors. And the same kind of haughty disregard for colonials that had annoyed Colonel George Washington as a colonial officer during the French and Indian War kept popping up. Before his defeat at Kings Mountain, British major Patrick Ferguson actually rallied the opposing "Overmountain men"—frontier settlers from the west—by threatening to cross the mountains, hang their leaders, and destroy their settlements. As it turned out, it was the Overmountain men who destroyed Ferguson and his Loyalists. And perhaps the most important mistake by Cornwallis was letting General Greene wage a war of attrition on his forces, wearing them down in numbers, health, and fighting effectiveness before they reached Virginia.

The most crucial phase of the southern campaign occurred in South Carolina during the five months between August 1780 and January 1781, when three major battles turned into routs. This sequence began on August 16 at Camden, where Lord Cornwallis had established a fortified supply depot for operations throughout the Piedmont. He knew about the approach of the American army from the north and set out to meet it; a surprise night encounter of forces proved disastrous for American General Horatio Gates, a man who had been widely revered for winning the Battle of Saratoga. After firing a few shots, both the American and British armies separated and regrouped for a morning engagement. Apart from seasoned Continental troops in the Maryland and Delaware regiments commanded by Baron Johann de Kalb, Gates had only green militia recruits from Virginia and North Carolina, and his men were exhausted from long marches on meager rations, and weakened with diarrhea brought on by half-cooked food. When the militiamen received the onslaught of disciplined British regulars, several thousand of them turned and ran, leaving the fighting to de Kalb's regiments, who were finally overwhelmed after fierce stands. De Kalb later died of his multiple wounds, while Gates fled all the way to Hillsborough, North Carolina, some 180 miles to the north. In disgrace, he was relieved of overall command after the battle and eventually replaced by General Greene.

The rout was soon reversed at Kings Mountain and again at Cowpens—both battlefields hard against the North Carolina border, barely twenty-five miles apart. Although neither battle involved the full force of the British or American army, together they marked and confirmed a turning point in the southern campaign.

On October 7, 1780, less than two months after the total American defeat at Camden, Loyalists trained and led by Major Patrick Ferguson, an able and respected British officer (in 1776 he had developed a breech-loading rifle for infantry use), met a collection of militias formed by men from across the Appalachians. Ferguson, ordered by Cornwallis to clear the countryside of those harassing his left flank, had taunted and threatened to destroy the settlements of these Patriots unless they desisted. That goaded the Overmountain men, as they were called, to meet in what is now eastern Tennessee and gather forces to confront Ferguson. When Ferguson discovered that he was outnumbered, he tried to join other British forces not far away in Charlotte, North Carolina, but realized he would not make it and positioned his Loyalists on the open, flat top of Kings Mountain. The Patriots reached the mountain, swarmed up the forested slopes that provided cover, picked off the exposed Loyalist officers, as well as Ferguson himself, with their accurate rifles, and took 700 prisoners.

Three months later Cowpens carried the demonstration of British vulnerability one step further, to the elite British Legion, composed of cavalry and light infantry and led by Colonel Banastre Tarleton. Aggressive and sometimes vicious,

Looking back on the southern campaign, British general Henry Clinton wrote that the Battle of Kings Mountain "unhappily proved the first link in a chain of evils that followed each other in regular succession until they at last ended in the total loss of America." The British had mounted the southern campaign with the expectation that large numbers of Loyalists in the southern colonies would flock to join them. This battle symbolically deflated those hopes by demonstrating that sufficiently angered Patriots could collect even more men and defeat very well trained and disciplined Loyalists.

Tarleton was infamous for refusing to give quarter to surrendering troops and for laying waste to the Carolina countryside, though few doubted his competence as a commander. Cornwallis ordered Tarleton to attack the half of Greene's army commanded by General Daniel Morgan, a farmer and fighter from backcountry Virginia who had played an important role in the victory at Saratoga. Tarleton and Morgan met on the morning of January 17, 1781, at Cowpens, where Morgan's forces were waiting with their backs to the Broad River. Though untrained in military science, Morgan was an intuitive leader and master tactician. His battle plan provided minimal exposure for the green militiamen, relied on the experienced and proven Continental regiments to stand fast, and employed the cavalry in a classic maneuver that sealed his victory. As the complex battle evolved, Tarleton's infantry ran and his cavalry refused to attack. In the rout his losses included 100 officers and men killed, 200 wounded, and some 600 taken prisoner.

Defeat at Cowpens did not end the southern campaign, which continued to a Pyrrhic victory for the British at the Battle of Guilford Courthouse two months later, but it increased the attrition of British regular forces that led to the campaign's ultimate failure.

Aftermath

After the British left Charles Town, its citizens tried to resume their normal lives as best they could, although many of the opportunities that made the city prosper had disappeared with independence. Planters could no longer sell their indigo crops to Britain, and rice also needed some replacement markets. As Eli Whitney perfected the cotton gin, setting off a crop revolution throughout the South, many turned to the single crop that would reestablish prosperity and eventually ruin the productivity of their land. Merchants who had suffered most by the nonimportation agreements in effect before and during the war also sought new business arrangements. Although there was lingering resentment of Loyalists, even former firebrands like Christopher Gadsden opposed confiscation of Loyalist plantations. And, in recognition of its severed ties with Britain, Charles Town became Charleston in 1783.

Resentments lasted longer and died harder in the Upcountry. Like New Jersey in the North, the Piedmont of South Carolina had been torn apart by conflicting loyalties for many years, and both colonies harbored more Loyalists than many of their neighbors. The end of the war did not bring the end of retribution for atrocities from both sides, and lynch law was not uncommon for several years. Perhaps more important for the future of the state, regional factions again resumed, pitting the interests and attitudes of the upland residents against those in the Tidewater. Although the Upcountry did not have representation equal to the Tidewater in the assembly, its legislators managed to pass a bill that would move the capital from Charleston to Columbia in 1786. The site chosen was a plantation in the middle of the Piedmont where rivers and trails used for trade joined. Since the new capitol and the town around it had to be built from scratch, it was not used until the legislature met there in 1790. While support for ratifying the U.S. Constitution became strong in coastal areas, opposition predominated in the Piedmont. The imbalance of voting power in a special convention called to consider adoption carried the day, and the Constitution was ratified in 1788. The convention did, however, insist on retaining the power to amend the Constitution and keep "every power not relinquished" by states, perhaps prefiguring South Carolina's lead role in seceding from the union in 1860.

Regions *to* Explore

CHARLES TOWN / CHARLESTON
GEORGETOWN
BEAUFORT
PIEDMONT BATTLEFIELDS

CHARLES TOWN

E nglish settlers sailed from Barbados in 1670 to settle on Old Towne Creek. The lords proprietor in London had paid for the trip to try to spread to America the financial success of the sugar plantations in Barbados. The Kiawah, a local Indian tribe, told the settlers that the Albemarle Point peninsula would secure their defense against enemies who came by water. This defense helped the settlers to survive, as did the mix of indentured servants who worked hard farming and trading.

HISTORICAL SITES *and* MUSEUMS
Today you can visit **Charles Towne Landing** (843-852-4200; www.southcarolinaparks.com), 1500 Old Towne Rd., Charleston, SC 29407. Open daily. The site, dating from 1670, is located on the west bank of the Ashley River, a state park with 663 acres of hands-on history.

We first visited in the 1970s after the park opened for South Carolina's tricentennial celebration. Later it closed for a $19 million renovation and reopened in 2006, better than ever, to share the story of this original site. Work remains ongoing, with archaeological digs and historical research providing new information.

The new visitors center features 12 rooms of interactive exhibits. You can see how settlers, slaves, traders, and Indians contributed to this area. We entered to find kids swarming around a "digital dig," where they could see instant results. Kids are also turned on by displays such as "Make Ready to Sail," with sounds of the sea and a model of the *Carolina,* which navigated by the stars. You can try your

The Adventure *under construction at Charles Towne Landing*

hand at feeding a family, or helping to build a house with logs, bricks, branches, mud, and palmetto leaves.

The "Trading Game" from 1672 involves those with little hard money who needed to trade such items as animal hides, corn, cattle, guns, slaves, olives, peas, and timber. There's a display on the archaelogical process with ticklers like: How do we know where to dig? Can we start digging? How do we know what we've got? How do we share what we've learned? What does it take to be an archaeologist?

The "Settlers' Life" area is a reconstructed 17th-century village complete with carpenter shop, print shop, and smithy. You can dip your own candles from a pot of wax or print colonial documents in the print shop. The crop garden grows rice, indigo, cotton, sugarcane, and other crops in season. Students who visit are encouraged to help in the planting or harvesting, depending upon the season.

Historian Walter Edgar writes in *South Carolina: A History:* "There were no gentleman adventurers here, as there were in James town, lollygagging about looking for gold and planting tobacco in the streets. Whatever human faults the Barbadians may have had, no one could accuse them of being impractical."

The Indians of Coastal Carolina area displays tools and other items used by Indians in their daily lives. One of the most popular attractions is the Pirate Program, in which students read the pirate's rules for life on board ship during the 16th and 17th centuries. You can also watch a "black powder" demonstration of a swivel gun, blunderbuss, pistol, and musket.

On the riverfront, the *Adventure,* a replica of a 17th-century trading vessel, is 53 feet long and 14 feet wide. She sails with a crew of eight. This vessel replaces another replica built in 1970 and serves to demonstrate the key role of shipping in the area.

The 664-acre park includes marshland, ponds, a creek, woods, gardens, and a number of exhibits. You can explore it on the history trail, the gardens trail, and the animal forest trail. The animal forest contains red and gray foxes, alligators, wood storks, and snowy egrets.

CHARLESTON

Although the city did not change its name from Charles Town to Charleston until the end of the Revolutionary War, it did stay put on its new site from 1680 onward. One of the nicest things about the "new" city on the peninsula between the Ashley and Cooper Rivers—is its low rather than high-rise profile. Church steeples are still taller than surrounding buildings, and it is a lot easier to imagine oneself living during colonial times without skyscrapers around to break the illusion.

Beyond this, the city fairly exudes Old World ambience that is not contrived, just a pattern of living and building that has not changed much in centuries. It even reemerges after disasters like the hurricane of 1989. To appreciate it, you must wander the streets aimlessly and peek into piazzas and gardens behind iron fences and gates. Among other things, you'll see marvelous flowers in full bloom, fountains, statues, and perhaps a small barking dog to scare off intruders.

In spite of its tranquil appearance, Charleston has suffered not only hurricanes, but disastrous fires as well. The 1752 hurricane took out 500 houses, and it was followed by equally destructive hurricanes in 1885, 1893, and 1989. The fire of 1698 destroyed 50 houses, and 300 houses were lost in the conflagration of 1740. The town has also been shaken by earthquakes and by enemy shelling during wars. But it has survived them all and still retains an extraordinary atmosphere of grace and beauty.

If you haven't visited Charleston before, you might want to start at the **Charleston Visitors Center**, 375 Meeting St. (800-868-8118, 800-774-0006, or 843-8534-8000; www.charleston

As you walk around you will notice "earthquake bolts"—iron circles with a bolt and nut protruding from the center. An iron rod extends through the building to give it protection and stability. They were first installed in buildings after the 1886 earthquake.

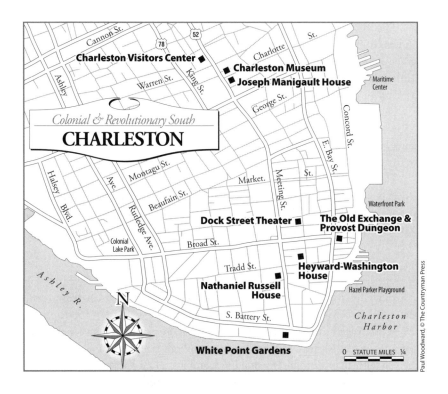

The map shows:

Cannon St.
Charleston Visitors Center ◆
Charlotte St.
Charleston Museum ■
Joseph Manigault House ■
Maritime Center
Ashley
Warren St.
King St.
George St.
Concord St.

Colonial & Revolutionary South
CHARLESTON

Halsey
Montagu St.
St.
E. Bay St.
Ave.
Market.
Meeting St.
Beaufain St.
Rutledge Ave.
Blvd.
Waterfront Park
Dock Street Theater ■
The Old Exchange & Provost Dungeon ■
Colonial Lake Park
Broad St.
Tradd St.
Heyward-Washington House ■
Nathaniel Russell House ■
Hazel Parker Playground
N
S. Battery St.
Ashley R.
Charleston Harbor
White Point Gardens ■
0   STATUTE MILES   ¼

Paul Woodward, © The Countryman Press

cvb.com). There you can see *Forever Charleston,* a multimedia show encapsulating the history of the city, and pick up scads of current information on special events throughout the city and surrounding countryside. This stop will be especially helpful if you are interested in arranging boat tours, architectural walking tours, or attending performances at the remodeled **Dock Street Theatre**, 135 Church St. (843-965-4032), first built in 1736. The **Festival of Houses and Gardens** also arranges tours of some private homes, gardens, and plantations in the spring, as well as special events. Call the Historic Charleston Foundation, 51 Meeting St., for more information and schedules (843-722-3405).

HISTORICAL SITES *and* MUSEUMS

Many of the fine historic houses of Charleston are of post-Revolutionary antebellum vintage, but one with a particularly interesting heritage belongs to the colonial era. Colonel Daniel Heyward bought the **Heyward-Washington House** (843-722-2996; www.charlestonmuseum.org), 87 Church St., at auction in 1770 after submitting the highest bid of 5,500 pounds. Open daily. He took down the existing structure and built a three-story house from Charleston gray brick. As a wealthy entrepreneur, Heyward owned many plantations where he grew rice and cotton. Since it was not easy to import cloth during the Revolution, he also developed a cotton factory to make fabric for his slaves' clothing.

The cuisine in Charleston offers a treat for the senses. A sample of recipes:

She-Crab Soup

1 tbsp butter
¼ pint cream (whipped)
½ tsp Worcestershire sauce
4 tbsp dry sherry
2 cups white crab meat and crab eggs (just crab meat is fine if you can't find eggs)

1 quart milk
few drops onion juice
1 tsp flour
½ tsp salt

Melt butter in top of double boiler and blend with flour until smooth. Add the milk gradually, stirring constantly. To this add crab meat and eggs and all seasonings except sherry. Cook slowly over hot water for 20 minutes. To serve, place one tablespoon of warmed sherry in individual soup bowls, then add soup and top with whipped cream. Sprinkle with paprika or finely chopped parsley. Secret: If unable to obtain crab eggs, crumble yolk of hard-boiled eggs in bottom of soup plates. *Serves 4–6.*

Benne (Sesame) Seed Wafers

Legend is that among descendants of slaves along the coast near Charleston, benne is a good-luck plant for those who eat it. It was originally brought in by the slaves from West Africa to this coastal region.

2 cups brown sugar
1 cup plain flour
1 tsp vanilla
¼ tsp salt

1 stick butter (¼ pound),
 or ¾ cup cooking oil
1 egg, beaten
½ tsp baking powder
¾ cup toasted benne seeds

Cream the butter and sugar, add beaten egg, then add flour sifted with salt and baking powder. Add vanilla and benne seed. Drop by teaspoon or less on greased cookie sheet. Bake in moderate oven at 325 degrees. Cook quickly. Allow to cool one minute before removing from pan. This makes a transparent wafer. *Yield: about 100.*

Frogmore Stew

This seasoned seafood boil serves a crowd.

salt
seafood seasonings
½ pound shrimp per person
1 stalk celery per person, chopped and
 tied in cheesecloth

¼ pound smoked sausage per
 person, cut in 2-inch pieces
2 ears corn per person

Bring a large amount of water to boil. There should be twice the volume of ingredients. Add ¾ cup salt per gallon of water. Add the celery and seafood seasoning. Add sausage to the pot and boil for 7 minutes. Add corn and continue to boil for 7 more minutes. Add shrimp and cook for 4 minutes. Do not overcook. Drain in a colander and serve in a large bowl or tub. Traditionally, the stew is spilled out onto a newspaper-lined table.

His son, Thomas Heyward Jr., read law at the Middle Temple of the Inns of Court in London and was admitted to the English bar in 1770 and the South Carolina bar in 1771. In company with James Parsons, Charles Cotesworth Pinckney, and Alexander Harvey Jr., Heyward defended Dr. John Haley, accused of murdering Peter DeLancey. The two men had fought a duel, and DeLancey, a royalist, was killed. When he was not quite 30 years old, Heyward became a signer of the Declaration of Independence.

Slaves were an important part of the labor force in the city. The municipal slave badge system required masters to buy badges for their slaves. The price of each depended on the degree of skill required for the slave's task.

In 1780 Charleston surrendered to the British and Thomas Heyward was sent into exile in St. Augustine with 28 other Revolutionary leaders. He was released in 1781. Heyward rented the house to the city of Charleston for the residency of President George Washington in 1791. Washington wrote that the citizens of Charleston were "wealthy-gay- & hospitable."

The house is filled with 18th-century furniture made in Charleston. A "library case," which looks like a very long china cabinet, measures about 15 feet. A "triple chest" unique to the area has handles on each end for ease of transport.

The dining room has a collection of china, an English mirror, 17th-century Dutch landscapes, portraits of Mr. and Mrs. Daniel Heyward, a mahogany cellarette for wine, a sugar box for a cone-shaped lump of sugar, and a fly catcher baited with honey. Upstairs, Heyward's own bed is in the green bedchamber. Most of the beds had movable headboards that could be raised during the summer to hold up mosquito netting.

George Washington entertained his guests in the drawing room. Today it contains a 1686 French spinet, a marble-top table, a settee and side chair belonging to Drayton Hall, and an English mirror with a gold peacock on it. Thomas Elfe, a cabinetmaker, made the mantel, and the fretwork resembles the style of Thomas Chippendale.

The **Charleston Museum** (843-722-2996; www.charlestonmuseum.org), 360 Meeting St. Open daily. It was founded in 1773 and may be the oldest museum in the country. Here you will find a fine collection of furniture made in the city, including the "rice" bed, which represents an important early industry in Charleston. Much of the furniture in the collection can be seen in the two properties owned by the museum: the Heyward-Washington House (see above) and the Joseph Manigault House (see below).

Besides its changing exhibits, the museum also displays part of its collections, such as Charleston silver, low-country textiles including costumes, quilts, and needlework, plus ceramics, Egyptian artifacts, and more. Don't miss the collection of Mark Catesby, who documented 57 new species of birds in South Carolina alone on a trip to America in the 1720s.

The **Joseph Manigault House** (843-722-2996; www.charlestonmuseum.org), 350 Meeting St. Open daily. This 1803 house was designed by architect Gabriel Manigault for his brother Joseph. Their ancestors had fled the religious persecution in France after Louis XIV revoked the Edict of Nantes in 1685.

The brothers' father, Pierre, had two brandy distilleries in Charleston. Gabriel became a rich merchant trading in the West Indies, importing rum, sugar, and wine and exporting rice, naval stores, and lumber. Gabriel's son Peter had a long political career, serving 16 years in the Commons House of the Assembly. He led the Commons in opposition to the Stamp Act in 1765. The neoclassical style of the house is also called Federal. The house has high ceilings, many windows, and two-story porches. American, English, and French furnishings are from the Charleston Museum's collections. Cabinetmaker Robert Walker began crafting furniture in 1790, and three of his pieces are in the house: a secretary with bookcase, a clothespress with original paper label, and a sideboard with his signature in ink.

The **Nathaniel Russell House** (843-724-8481; www.historiccharleston.org), 40 E. Bay St. Open daily. Nathaniel Russell built his Federal-style town house in 1808. Inside, the plasterwork ornamentation is elaborate, and some rooms are geometrically shaped. The free-flying staircase is graceful.

The **Battery,** lined with beautiful homes, is the best place for a pleasant stroll along the waterfront. Cannons stand in the park, as reminders of some of the devastating bombardments of the past. **White Point Gardens** got its name from the white oyster shells once tossed all over the point. The Ashley and Cooper Rivers meet here, and you can look out at Fort Sumter straight ahead.

While you're in this vicinity, don't miss a stop at the **Old Exchange and Provost Dungeon** (888-763-0448, 843-727-2165; www.oldexchange.com), 122 E. Bay at Broad. It was the site of much Revolutionary War history, including the election of delegates to the First Continental Congress in 1774 and the imprisonment of signers of the Declaration of Independence and other Patriots during the British occupation of 1780. Open daily.

The building was used to store goods such as rice, indigo, cotton, and other staples waiting to be shipped or delivered. In 1780, after a siege of 42 days, Charles Town fell to the British. General Cornwallis had a provost, or jailer, set up shop in the cellar of the Royal Exchange. Citizens were arrested, seized from their homes, and taken to the cellar. It was used as a dungeon for two years before the British evacuated the city in 1782.

Fort Moultrie (843-883-3123; www.nps.gov/fomo) 1214 W. Middle St., Sullivan's Island, SC. Open daily. On June 28, 1776, the defenders of the fort, commanded by Colonel William Moultrie,

A visiting New England clergyman described Nathaniel Russell at age 80 as "Like Moses . . . a merchant of great wealth & greater benevolence, of high character and standing . . . his recollections were prompt; his utterance easy & his manners & conversation interesting."

earned the first American victory in battle over combined British naval and land forces. At that time a crude, hastily constructed palmetto log fort was located on the shore of Sullivan's Island near the northeastern entrance to Charleston harbor. Although outnumbered, colonial militia managed to withstand bombardment by the British navy and attack by British regulars. Incoming shells were absorbed by the sponginess of the log-and-sand defenses. The visitor center offers exhibits on the fort from 1776 to 1947. Don't miss the 20-minute orientation film.

Even if you are focused on the colonial era, it's almost impossible to separate Charleston's major fort sites from their later role in the Civil War. Like Fort Moultrie, **Fort Johnson,** on James Island near the southwestern entrance to the harbor, played a role in both the Revolution and the Civil War; it fell to General Clinton in his successful 1780 attack on the city. Confederate forces fired the first shot of the War Between the States at **Fort Sumter,** named for a native hero of the Revolutionary War. **Castle Pinckney** was built on another island in the harbor; it once housed Union prisoners of war from the First Battle of Bull Run, and is now a national monument.

Three historic properties lie just outside Charleston on SC 61:

Drayton Hall (843-769-2600; www.draytonhall.org), 3380 Ashley River Rd., Charleston, SC 29414. Open daily. The house was built from 1738 to 1742 and remains an outstanding example of colonial architecture. Seven generations of the Drayton family lived in the house after John Drayton bought the land next to his family home, Magnolia Gardens.

Its Georgian-Palladian style is symmetrical and beautiful, now restored and open without furnishings. It may be easier to focus on the patterns in frieze and ceiling without the distraction of furniture. The Great Hall has a shell and fruit swag over the fireplace, and the ceiling is handsome, with a medallion in the center decorated with stars, flowers, and leaves.

The drawing room has a 17th-century freehand sculpted ceiling; a sham door was placed in the room for symmetry. Look for the doorjamb in the bedchamber where the family still comes to mark the heights of their children and dogs on the frame. A sign warns "Don't paint this panel."

Nearby is **Magnolia Plantation and Gardens** (800-3673517, 843-571-1266; www.magnoliaplantation.com), 3550 Ashley River Rd., Charleston, SC 29414. Open daily. The gardens were originally planned in the 1680s by the Drayton family. Taylor Drayton Nelson is the descendant of the original owners, and he was our guide through the oldest major garden in the country. You can wander through 50 wonderful acres, including a horticultural maze. We were captivated by the bronze crane statues—they are a symbol of longevity.

The first Drayton came from Barbados about 1671 and settled in a home called Magnolia. After its destruction, a second plantation house was built a few yards away on the site of the present house. This one was burned also, by General Sherman's men. The Reverend John Grimke Drayton, rector of St. Andrew's Episcopal Church, had his summer house taken apart, brought to Magnolia on

Drayton Hall, just outside Charleston, dates to ca. 1740

the river, and placed on the existing ground-floor walls. The home was occupied by Draytons until 1976. Visitors can tour the upper floor, which houses a gallery of local artists plus an outstanding collection of ornithological paintings collected by the owner.

John Grimke Drayton brought 250 varieties of azalea to the area, and the garden also features 900 varieties of camellias. The gardens include a waterfowl refuge and the Audubon swamp boardwalk. The Audubon swamp garden is new and offers thousands of plant and animal species within 60 acres of blackwater cypress and tupelo swamp. You may see nesting herons and egrets, otters, turtles, and alligators. John J. Audubon visited here to find waterfowl specimens for his paintings.

Middleton Place (800-782-3608, 843-556-6020; www.middletonplace.org),

---

Don't miss seeing the joggling board on the grounds. A long, flexible plank supported from below only near the ends, the joggling board magnifies the small movements of persons sitting on it, especially near the center, moving up and down, or "joggling." Such boards are regaining popularity in South Carolina and elsewhere. According to legend, there are no unmarried daughters in homes that had a joggling board. Grandfather proposed to grandmother there, military strategies were worked out there, and children gravitated to them like bees to honey.

4300 Ashley River Rd., Charleston, SC 29414. Open daily. Middleton was home to Henry Middleton, president of the First Continental Congress. His son, Arthur Middleton, was a signer of the Declaration of Independence. One wing survived of the original 1755 house; Union troops burned the rest during the Civil War. Inside, portraits of family members hang on the walls.

The dining room contains a graceful 1771 silver epergne for fruit, nuts, and candy; Lafayette and Andrew Jackson had dinner at the table. Upstairs there is a cowhide and brass trunk lined in camphor wood that was buried during the Civil War to keep precious things safe. The nursery contains a domino game, dolls, a desk, and a Noah's ark.

Extensive terraced gardens bloom with azaleas, camellias, magnolias, crepe myrtle, and roses at various times during the year. The plantation stable yards offer docents in costume who work as blacksmiths, potters, carpenters, and weavers. You'll see plenty of horses, mules, hogs, cows, sheep, goats, and guinea hens there.

The gardens at Middleton Place, outside Charleston

LODGING

ANSONBOROUGH INN
21 Hasell St., Charleston, SC 29401
800-522-2073, 843-723-1655;
www.ansonboroughinn.com
Once a 1900 stationer's warehouse, it has a three-story atrium. An extensive art collection and antiques decorate the inn, which has 37 guest rooms.

CHARLESTON PLACE HOTEL
205 Meeting St., Charleston, SC 29401
800-611-5545, 843-722-4900;
www.charlestonplacehotel.com
Located in the historic district, the hotel offers 18th-century charm with 21st-century comforts, including 430 guest rooms.

FRANCIS MARION HOTEL
387 King St., Charleston, SC 29401
877-756-2122, 843-722-0600;
www.francismarioncharleston.com
Dating from 1924, the hotel has been restored. It has 227 guest rooms.

THE INN AT MIDDLETON PLACE
4290 Ashley River Rd., Charleston, SC
843-556-0500; www.theinnatmiddle
tonplace.com
Located next to Middleton Gardens, the inn has views of the Ashley River. Rooms have wood-burning fireplaces. A recipient of the American Institute of Architects highest award, the elegantly modern inn has 53 guest rooms.

JOHN RUTLEDGE HOUSE INN
116 Broad St., Charleston, SC 29401
800-476-9741, 843-723-7999;
www.johnrutledgehouseinn.com
John Rutledge was one of the 55 signers of the U.S. Constitution. His home dates from 1763. The inn has 19 guest rooms.

KINGS COURTYARD INN
198 King St., Charleston, SC 29401
800-845-6119, 843-723-7000;
www.charminginns.com
Located in the historic district, the inn has 41 guest rooms surrounding two inner courtyards.

THE MILLS HOUSE HOTEL
115 Meeting St., Charleston, SC 29401
800-874-9600, 843-577-2400;
www.millshouse.com
The hotel is a reconstruction of the original Mills House and has 214 guest rooms.

WOODLANDS RESORT & INN
125 Parsons Rd., Summerville, SC 29483
800-774-9999, 843-875-2600;
www.woodlandsinn.com
The 1906 revival home is set within a 42-acre estate. Rooms are decorated with a West Indies flavor. Eighteen guest rooms.

RESTAURANTS

CAROLINA'S
10 Exchange St.
843-724-3800; www.carolinas
restaurant.com
The building dates to Revolutionary days and over the years has housed a cotton exchange, a bagging factory, and a sailors' tavern. It now offers a contemporary approach to classic low-country cuisine.

MAGNOLIA'S
185 East Bay St.
843-577-7771; www.magnolias-
blossom-cypress.com
The 1783 building was once the Customs House. Southern low-country dishes are on the menu.

MIDDLETON PLACE RESTAURANT
4300 Ashley River Rd.
800-782-3608, 843-556-6020;
www.middletonplace.org
Low-country cuisine is offered here in the oldest landscaped gardens in the country.

OAK STEAKHOUSE
17 Broad St.
843-722-4200; www.oaksteakhouse
restaurant.com
This Italian steakhouse is in an 1850s landmark building. The cuisine is enhanced by a stellar wine collection.

POOGAN'S PORCH
72 Queen St.
843-577-2337;
www.poogansporch.com
Low-country cuisine is on the menu.
Poogan was a dog who lounged on the
porch for years.

TRISTAN
55 S. Market St.
843-534-2155; www.tristandining.com
The restaurant is in the historic district.

EVENTS

Mid-March to mid-April: Festival of
Houses and Gardens tour, 800-868-8118
September: Candlelight Tour of Homes
and Gardens, 800-868-8118
November: Middleton Place's annual
Plantation Days; craftsmen demonstrate
18th- and 19th-century crafts, 800-782-
3608

INFORMATION

CHARLESTON VISITORS CENTER
375 Meeting St., Charleston, SC 29402
800-868-8118, 843-853-8000;
www.charlestoncvb.com

GEORGETOWN

The Spanish in 1526 tried to settle where Georgetown now stands but abandoned the site after they became disease ridden. John and Edward Perrie received the land from the lords proprietor of the Carolinas in 1705. John, a wealthy and prominent resident of the Leeward Islands, made an arrangement with John Mott to take goods and slaves for a settlement in South Carolina on the brigantine *Success*. He was to remain for ten years and share half the profits. Mott arrived in April and settled a plantation on the site that is now the Georgetown Historic District. By 1737 the area was filled with more than fifty homes.

HISTORICAL SITES *and* MUSEUMS

Prince George Winyah Church (843-546-4358; www.pgwinah.org), 300 Broad St. at Highmarket St., Georgetown, SC 29442, dates from 1735. Open daily. The first church in the parish was located at Brown's Ferry, then relocated here after merging with another church. Pews were sold in 1753 to raise money, and import duties collected in Georgetown helped finance the building. A number of colonial residents and Revolutionary War veterans are buried in the cemetery.

Rice was a major crop in Georgetown from its earliest days. Visitors can explore the **Rice Museum** (843-546-7423; www.ricemuseum.org), 633 Front St., to learn the history of rice culture from 1700 onward. Open Mon.–Sat. Maps, dioramas, and artifacts provide the story. Take the time to stroll in **Lafayette Park**, which winds around the Rice Museum.

The **Harold Kaminski House** (888-233-0383, 843-546-7706; www.cityof

The Prince George Winyah Church in Georgetown

georgetownsc.com), 600 Front St., overlooks the Sampit River. Open Mon.–Sat. This 1769 town house contains antiques, including a magnificent mahogany Chippendale-design banquet table that extends across the room. Many of the pieces were passed down through the Kaminski family; look in the library for the walnut slope-lid desk made by Thomas Elfe, a Charleston cabinetmaker.

South of Georgetown stands **Hopsewee Plantation** (843-546-7891; www.hopsewee.com), 494 Hopsewee Rd. Open Mon.–Fri. Thomas Lynch Sr. built the house in 1740, and his son, Thomas Jr., followed him in politics. Because Thomas Lynch Sr. had suffered a stroke and could not sign the Declaration of Independence, there was a space left for his name; Thomas Jr. did, however, sign. They were the only father-son team at the Continental Congress. Thomas Sr. died before the year was out. Thomas Jr. perished along with his wife in 1779 when their ship was lost at sea. This typical low-country rice plantation house has four rooms around a center hall on each floor. The foundation is tabby and the walls are sturdy black cypress.

LODGING

LITCHFIELD PLANTATION
Kings River Rd., Pawleys Island, SC 29585
800-869-1410, 843-237-9121
Litchfield Plantation is one of the oldest rice plantations on the Waccamaw River. The mansion dates from 1740. The estate offers 38 guest rooms, in several buildings.

BEAUFORT

The first inhabitants in Beaufort, over 4,000 years ago, were Indians. The 16th and 17th centuries saw a succession of explorers and settlers on what is now Parris Island. By 1514 a Spanish sea captain, Pedro de Salaza, landed, to be followed by Jean Ribaut with French Huguenots in 1562, who named their settlement Port Royal. After they had abandoned it, English privateers and pirates followed. In 1566 the Spanish returned to found the town of Santa Elena, which served as the Spanish capital of America until 1573. Archaeological excavation of these various layers and closely associated sites is in process now.

In 1670 an English colony intended for Port Royal thought it too close to threatening Spaniards and decided to settle Charles Town farther north. Their choice was wise, since Stuart Town, settled by a group of Scots in 1685, was annihilated by the Spanish a year later. Finally, in 1711, the British proclaimed that the town of Beaufort be established, and a new batch of settlers put up homes of tabby and clapboard.

Later houses built in the "Beaufort style" combined elements from Georgian, colonial, Greek revival, and semitropical Spanish styles. The typical Beaufort house was erected on a large lot, sometimes with a formal garden, and placed to take advantage of the prevailing southwesterly breeze. Unlike Savannah and Charleston homes, they were not built next to each other on small lots.

Beaufort houses sit high on brick or tabby foundations and offer cool comfort from their two-story piazzas. The houses are usually T-shaped, with inset chimneys and central hallways leading to an elegant stairway at the rear. Sometimes there is a Palladian window on the landing. Ornamental woodwork includes paneling, wainscoting, mantels, and cornices. Mantels ranged from marble to Delft tile to decoration in the Adam style. Plaster ceiling medallions and cornices were added at a later date; ceiling heights were generous, from 14 to 18 feet.

> ✴ Tabby is an early building material made from burning oyster shells, which produces lime. Mixing it with sand and shells produced the concrete you will see in many foundations.

HISTORICAL SITES *and* MUSEUMS

The **John Mark Verdier House** (843-379-6335; www.historic-beaufort.org), 801 Bay St., Beaufort, SC 29902. Open Mon.–Sat. This Federal-style house, built by a prominent merchant in 1790, stands on a raised tabby foundation and is five bays wide with a double portico. The fanlight over the door is semi-elliptical. Inside, each room reflects Adam-style decoration. The reception parlor and the dining room have beautifully carved mantels.

On March 18, 1825, the Marquis de Lafayette arrived for a visit in Beaufort. Because he had been delayed during festivities on Edisto Island, the people of Beaufort had gone home to bed. Word of his arrival spread, and the citizens sprinted to welcome him as he entered Verdier House.

After this high point of hospitality for an elegant house, its fortunes declined. During the Civil War, Union forces occupied it as headquarters. Then it became variously a fish market, ice house, law office, telephone office, and barber shop. After further deterioration precipitated by the Great Depression, the house was condemned, then saved by local citizens for dedication as a memorial to soldiers who had died in World War II.

The **Beaufort Arsenal Museum** (843-379-3331; www.historic-beaufort.org), 713 Craven St., was built in 1795 on the site of the first courthouse in Beaufort and rebuilt in 1852. Open Mon.–Sat. The building has Gothic windows and looks like a fortress. In April 1775 the Beaufort Volunteer Artillery was organized here. Two brass trophy guns taken from the British in 1779 were removed by Union solders in 1861 but finally returned to Beaufort after 1880. Inside the arsenal visitors see a collection of local memorabilia, including Indian pottery, swords, guns, and plantation crafts.

St. Helena's Episcopal Church (843-522-1712; www.sthelenas1712.org), 501 Church St. Open Tue.–Sat. One of the oldest functioning churches in the United States, St. Helen's was built in 1724 with ballast bricks brought from England. The church has a small steeple that replaced the old one. The altar silver was

Verdier House in Beaufort

given by Captain John Bull in 1734 to memorialize his wife, who was killed by the Yemassee Indians.

Colonel John Barnwell, who died in 1724 after becoming famous leading raids against the Tuscarora Indians, is buried in the churchyard here. So is a local physician, Dr. Perry, who asked his friends to bury him along with a loaf of bread, a jug of water, and an ax, just in case he awoke and decided to storm his way out. During the Civil War, graveyard slabs were removed and used as operating tables by the Federal troops stationed here.

The **Old Point** area contains many fine homes and gardens that are privately owned. Films including *The Great Santini* and *The Big Chill* were shot here. "Tidalholm" was built by Edgar Fripp in 1856 as a summer home. During the Civil War his brother, James Fripp, owned the house. He returned after the war to find that it was being sold for taxes by the U.S. Tax Commission. Tears rolled down his face when he realized that he could not bid on the house. A Frenchman bought the house, walked over to Fripp, kissed him on both cheeks, gave him the deed, and returned to France. Apart from special tours, the house is not open to the public.

LODGING

RHETT HOUSE INN
1009 Craven St., Beaufort, SC 29902
843-524-9030;
www.rhetthouseinn.com
The 1820 plantation house is furnished with English and American antiques. Seventeen guest rooms.

INFORMATION

GREATER BEAUFORT CHAMBER OF COMMERCE
1106 Carteret St., Beaufort, SC 29902
800-638-3525, 843-524-3163;
www.beaufortsc.org

PIEDMONT BATTLEFIELDS

The historical battlefields of Camden, Kings Mountain, and Cowpens, all in the north-central part of the state, trace the changing fortunes of the British and the American revolutionary forces in the South leading into the climactic final year of fighting. Also in the Piedmont is Ninety Six, site of one of the most dramatic sieges of the Revolution.

CAMDEN REVOLUTIONARY WAR SITE

Camden is the oldest inland town in South Carolina. In 1730 King George II ordered the establishment of eleven townships in South Carolina. James St. Julien, a surveyor, was named by the Royal Council in 1733 to design the town of Fredricksburg below the present site of Camden. However, the land was mostly in the Wateree swamp, and people did not want the lots. This township disappeared.

In 1750 Quakers from Ireland, led by Samuel Wyly, settled the area. Joseph Kershaw came in 1758 from England via Charles Town and built his store on Pine Tree Hill. This was the junction of Indian trails, and the river was a good place for trading and shipping supplies. In 1768 the name was changed to Camden to honor Lord Camden (Charles Pratt), who worked hard for colonial rights.

In 1780 Major General Henry Clinton sent troops to capture Charles Town, then planned to secure three towns as a protective outer circle—Camden, Ninety Six, and Augusta, on the Georgia border. Lord Charles Cornwallis led the army to Camden. The town was then the main supply post for all British operations in Upcountry South Carolina. A stockade wall and a series of six strong forts protected the town.

On August 15, 1780, the British and the Americans both planned a surprise night march and dawn attack on each other. The opposing forces were surprised to meet eight miles north of Camden. In early light Lord Cornwallis easily defeated General Horatio Gates, whose green and exhausted militias scattered under the fire of disciplined British regulars. Baron Johann de Kalb, a German-born French citizen and a general in the Continental Army, stood his ground and fought courageously but died of his many wounds three days after the battle. Gates fled 180 miles north to Hillsborough in three days, utterly destroying the reputation he had won at Saratoga.

Eight months later, after the Battle of Guilford Courthouse in North Carolina, General Nathanael Greene brought the remnants of the Continental Army scattered at Camden back into South Carolina to attack British outposts. Near Camden, forces under the able leadership of Lord Francis Rawdon surprised and defeated the Americans at the Battle of Hobkirk's Hill on April 25, 1781. But heavy losses suffered that day, as well as weakened British control of other outposts, led

Rawdon to evacuate Camden and return to Charleston. Today Hobkirk's Hill is an attractive residential area for Camden, with no traces of the battle.

HISTORICAL SITES *and* MUSEUMS

Historic Camden Revolutionary War Site (803-432-9841; www.historic-camden.org), 222 Broad St., Camden, SC 29020. Open Tue.–Sun. This site includes parts of colonial and Revolutionary Camden, several restored and refurnished period houses like the 1789 Craven House, reconstructions of military fortifications, and Patriot Joseph Kershaw's mansion.

We watched a slide presentation (soon to be DVD) on historic Camden. The scenes take you from the early forests and Indian attacks through Pine Tree Hill in the 1750s, Joseph Kershaw's store, and Charles Pratt's role as Lord Camden in 1768. When Cornwallis took possession of Camden, he had his headquarters in the **Kershaw-Cornwallis House**. Eventually the British forces left and Kershaw returned from the exile imposed on Patriot leaders by Cornwallis.

Although the original house burned, the reconstruction is now complete. A square spinet-style pianoforte and other furnishings were given or loaned to the

The Kershaw-Cornwallis House in Camden

house. The family lived in the house until 1805. You'll see a collection of Josiah Wedgwood plates in the "sea leaf" pattern. Kids can try on clothing in one of the rooms. Ghosts include a man in a red vest, another drinking wine, and a headless man. An exhibit on natural fabric dyes includes the use of nettle, Queen Anne's lace, butcher's broom, goldenrod, and juniper. After a visit, a fifth grader wrote: "Thank you Joseph."

LODGING

GREENLEAF INN OF CAMDEN
220 Wall St., Camden, SC 29020
803-425-1806; www.greenleafinnofcamden.com
The inn is located in the historic district and is in two houses, the
Joshua Reynolds House and the McLean House. Ten guest rooms.

KINGS MOUNTAIN NATIONAL MILITARY PARK

On the North Carolina border about forty miles west of Charlotte, the little town of Blacksburg is the site of one of the most crucial battles of the Revolutionary War, one in which virtually all the combatants were American colonials—Loyalists or Patriots.

HISTORICAL SITES *and* MUSEUMS

Kings Mountain National Military Park (864-936-7921; www.nps.gov/kimo), 2625 Park Rd., Blacksburg, SC 29702. Open daily. A Patriot victory on October 7, 1780, at Kings Mountain was a turning point in the fate of the southern campaign and the American Revolution as a whole. Like the Battle of Saratoga in 1777, it weakened a major British effort to control a large group of the colonies. General Henry Clinton judged that the defeat at Kings Mountain "unhappily proved the first link in a chain of evils that followed each other in regular succession until they at last ended in the total loss of America."

It may seem odd that a quickly resolved conflict between a thousand Loyalists and about the same number of Patriot "Overmountain" men could rank in importance with major confrontations between large armies. But it came at a crucial time in Cornwallis's campaign to subdue the Carolinas on his way to win the major objective, Virginia. Just eight weeks after his overwhelming victory at Camden, it stalled his momentum.

British major Patrick Ferguson, in charge of protecting Cornwallis's left flank, led 1,100 American Loyalist militiamen he had carefully trained. With a mission to eliminate harassing raids from so-called Overmountain men—settlers from over the Appalachians—he threatened them: If they did not desist in their efforts against the Crown, he would "hang their leaders and lay their country waste with fire and sword." Angered by the threat, the Overmountain men gathered and made their plans to strike first. Ferguson, learning of their approach, realized that he

The Overmountain Victory National Historic Trail was begun in 1975 by local citizens, many of them descendants of those who fought for freedom. This trail follows the route of the assembling Patriot army that defeated a Loyalist army at the Battle of Kings Mountain. It covers 220 miles from Abingdon, Virginia, through eastern Tennessee, over the mountains of North Carolina, across the Piedmont of North and South Carolina, to the Kings Mountain National Military Park.

could not reach Cornwallis at Charlotte and took a stand with his Loyalists on the flat summit of Kings Mountain, an open hill surrounded by wooded slopes.

The Overmountain men were without formal military training or recognized social standing—Ferguson called them "mongrels"—but they fought with courage and determination. These hardy backwoodsmen moved Indian-style behind trees and rocks, then fired at the enemy with hunting rifles that often far exceeded the range of their opponents' weapons. This battle was the only one where the Patriots used long rifles as their primary weapons. After Ferguson was shot and killed, the Loyalists were surrounded and either killed or captured, with 700 taken prisoner.

Begin exploring Kings Mountain at the visitor center with an excellent orientation film. As always, the rangers are very helpful and passionate about the site. We walked with a ranger around the 1.5-mile Battlefield Trail, where we saw the battlefield from both Loyalists' and Patriots' perspectives. Ferguson is honored by a granite memorial as a distinguished officer of the 71st Regiment, Highland Light Infantry. His grave is marked with a cairn.

COWPENS NATIONAL BATTLEFIELD

About twenty-five miles due west of the Kings Mountain battlefield is another historic Revolutionary War site, now located in the little town of Chesnee, where one of the most stunning American victories of the war was won.

HISTORICAL SITES *and* MUSEUMS

Cowpens National Battlefield (864-461-2828; www.nps.gov/cowp), Highways 110 and 11, Chesnee, SC 29341. Open daily. The Battle of Cowpens on January 17, 1781, confirmed the Patriot victory at Kings Mountain. General Greene had split the Continental Army, leaving half of it in the hands of General Daniel Morgan, to divide Lord Cornwallis's attention. Cornwallis also divided his forces, leaving command of one segment to Colonel Banastre Tarleton. The opposing leaders who met at Cowpens had quite different characters.

Morgan, a Virginian, was a self-made man, an explorer and a settler, a team-

You can tour the Cowpens battlefield on foot.

ster by trade. He had experience fighting Indians, and he led men in battle with courage. He took command of Greene's light troops in 1780. He had fought with distinction at Quebec in 1775 and at Saratoga in 1777. His army included Andrew Pickens, militia commander; John Eager Howard, Continental commander; and William Washington, cavalry commander and a distant cousin of George Washington.

Tarleton was ruthless and fearless, disliked by his fellow officers, and called "Bloody Tarleton" and "Butcher." After the battle of Charleston Tarleton had moved through the Carolina countryside burning, looting homes, and killing citizens. In May 1780 at the Battle of Waxhaws—Patriots called it the Waxhaw massacre—Tarleton's troops had given no quarter to the surrendering Americans. At Cowpens, Tarleton's army consisted of his mounted Loyalist Legion and regular British forces.

On the advice of his militia leaders, Morgan chose a battle site on a slight rise with a river at their backs and waited for Tarleton. Morgan placed green militia in the front line, instructing them to fire two or three shots, then retire behind the second line of seasoned Continental soldiers and reform. The more mobile cavalry formed the third line. As the battle began, the militiamen were quite effective in killing and wounding Tarleton's officers, then reformed behind the second line.

When that line also began to move back, Tarleton's infantry sensed a rout and broke ranks in pursuit. At the opportune moment, Morgan ordered the line to turn and fire at the charging infantry, which they did with great effect. In a classic military maneuver called double envelopment, Morgan ordered the militia to attack the British left flank while the cavalry circled to attack the rear of the right flank. Meanwhile, in the confusion, Tarleton's cavalry refused to attack and his dragoons finally fled.

The unsophisticated backcountry general had outmaneuvered the experienced and dashing colonel. Tarleton lost 100 killed, including 10 officers, plus 200 wounded, and 600 taken prisoner, decimating his army.

This was the second successive defeat for the British forces under General Cornwallis.

The visitor center has on display a 3-pounder cannon and other weapons of the Revolutionary War period. A fiber-optic map display details the southern campaign and the battle tactics used by Daniel Morgan at Cowpens. *Daybreak at the Cowpens* is a presentation on the events of the battle shown every hour.

You can walk a 1.3-mile trail and read wayside exhibits, see the historic Green River Road that was the center line of the battle, or drive the 3.8-mile one-way road around the battlefield.

NINETY SIX

About sixty miles west of what is now the state capital of Columbia, Ninety Six began life as a frontier settlement in the early 1700s and was named for its distance from the Cherokee village of Keowee. The town was headquarters for Indian trade and later became a Loyalist stronghold and was fortified by the British. It still contains ruins of the settlement and fort.

HISTORICAL SITES *and* MUSEUMS
Ninety Six National Historic Site (864-543-4068; www.pns.gov/nisi), SC 248, Ninety-Six, SC 29666. Open daily. In November 1775 the first land battle in the South was fought here between attacking Loyalists and a defending Patriot militia. After three days of inconclusive siege, a truce ended the first confrontation of many between Loyalists and Patriots in the Upcountry of South Carolina.

British major Patrick Ferguson had gathered an army of 4,000 Loyalists here by the summer of 1780 before he moved on to a disastrous defeat and death at Kings Mountain. His replacement was New York lieutenant colonel John Harris Cruger, who was in command as the longest siege of the war began in the late spring and early summer of 1781. Gen-

Banastre Tarleton was renowned as a leader of dragoons—mounted infantrymen who rode into battle, then dismounted and fought as infantry.

> If "Cowpens" seems an odd name for a major battlefield, there's a reason for it. Upcountry stock raisers wintered their cattle in the vales around Thicketty Mountain. Some say the ground was squatters' ground, others that it belonged to Hannah, and yet others that Hiram Saunder, a wealthy Loyalist, owned it and lived nearby. "Hannah's Cowpens" stuck among the locals.

eral Nathanael Greene sent his soldiers to dig a trench 70 yards from the fort, then one 400 yards back after they had been shot out of the first attempt. Greene also had the support of Colonel Tadeusz Kościuszko, a brilliant Polish military engineer who dug a trench with the intent to blast a hole in the walls of an almost impregnable star-shaped fort. Colonel Henry Lee also arrived to build an additional trench for artillery fire against the stockade fort that supplemented the star fort.

Loyalists resisted all these efforts but worried about their lack of water inside the forts. Although Patriot fire arrows caused damage and the siege had cut off the Tory water supply, a charge on June 18 failed. Ever mindful of preserving his forces, Greene withdrew as Lord Rawdon was marching an army from Charleston to relieve Ninety Six.

The visitor center has a museum with displays and an orientation video. Archaeological work has recovered traces of the star fort and the attacker's trenches, and the stockade fort has been reconstructed. You can also walk interpretive historic and nature trails on the property.

Current Information

DIVISION OF PARKS, RECREATION AND TOURISM
1205 Pendleton St.
Inquiry Division, Box 71
Columbia, SC 29201-0071
866-224-9339, 803-734 1700
www.discoversouthcarolina.com

Georgia

Historical Introduction
to the
Georgia Colony

The last of the original thirteen British colonies to be established, Georgia predated most of them in exploration and settlement by the Spanish and French. The maze of rivers, sounds, and islands along the coastline stretching from modern Charleston, South Carolina, to Jacksonville, Florida, attracted Europeans long before it fell under the control of separate colonies. In 1523 Spain's Lucas Vázquez de Ayllón sent two ships to find a site for a colony along this coast. Three years later Ayllón led a party of 600 men, women, and children from Hispaniola to found the colony of San Miguel de Gualdape. He probably established it on the Waccamaw River, though the exact location remains uncertain. Vasquez died of malaria within a month, and the colonists returned to Hispaniola. Spain's Hernando de Soto brought an armed force into Georgia from Florida searching for gold in 1540. Richard Hakluyt published an account of de Soto's travels, with the lengthy title beginning *Virginia richly valued by the description of the main land of Florida, her next neighbor . . .*

The French made the next move to claim this land. Jean Ribaut (or Ribault) left France in 1562, arrived in St. Augustine, and then sailed north along the Georgia coastal islands, giving French names to them. He landed at Port Royal (already named Santa Elena by the Spanish) and settled the colony of Charlesfort, which was abandoned after Ribaut sailed back to France for supplies. The site was soon reoccupied by a Spanish colony and later became the intended destination for the British settlers of Charles Town. Meanwhile the competition between France and Spain continued elsewhere. René de Laudonnière, a participant in Ribaut's first expedition, returned in 1564 and brought colonists to

Fort Frederica

settle on the "great river." They built Fort Caroline near the mouth of the St. Johns River at what is now Jacksonville, Florida.

Spain was quick to respond. King Philip II dispatched Pedro Menéndez de Avilés to capture the fort and establish Spanish control of the coastal region. He succeeded in 1565, both capturing Fort Caroline and defending the Spanish colony of St. Augustine that he had established as a base. (This complex story of attack and counterattack, a hurricane and a slaughter, is told in the Florida chapter.) The net result for the Georgia coast was a chain of Spanish missions. The first, established by Jesuits, appeared on St. Simons and Jekyll Islands as well as the adjacent

GEORGIA *Time Line*

1540	**1566**	**1580s**	**1721**
Hernando de Soto leads an armed force into what is now Georgia to find gold	The Spanish lay claim to Cumberland Island, calling it San Pedro	Franciscans establish a chain of missions along the Georgia coast	Colonel John Barnwell builds Fort King George at the mouth of the Altamaha River to protect British interests in South Carolina

mainland by 1566. The Spanish pattern of using presidios (frontier forts) and missions to provide order and both educate the Indians and convert them to Christianity evolved. It worked along the Georgia coast for more than a century and became particularly effective after the Franciscans replaced the Jesuits in 1573. But after the founding of Charles Town by the English in 1670, Spanish influence among the Indians gradually decreased as English traders moved into their territory.

Unlike the Spanish soldiers and friars, the English operated with very little supervision or effective control, and the trade in Indian slaves (captured prisoners of war) became an important part of the British colony's economy. Waning Spanish influence among the Indians, confirmed by an unsuccessful attack by British and Indians on the major mission on St. Catherines Island and Yemassee raids into Spanish Florida, led to the recall of all missions north of the St. Marys River. Nevertheless, the strong Spanish presence nearby made the British to the north nervous, and they were determined to create a buffer between them and their rivals. In 1720 Colonel John Barnwell ("Tuscarora Jack") went to London to present the case for a fort on the mouth of the Altamaha River. It would serve to discourage the French from expanding eastward from the interior and to ward off Spanish incursions northward.

Colonel Barnwell formed the Independent Company and sailed for Charles Town. In 1721, near present-day Darien on the Altamaha River, Fort King George rose as a palisaded earthen fort with blockhouse. This became the southern outpost for the British in the New World but did not last long. Barnwell and his men lived there for seven years, enduring deprivation, disease, and stormy winters. In 1726 a fire wiped out the barracks and damaged the blockhouse. The next year the troops abandoned the fort and moved to Port Royal, in South Carolina. Later, Scots Highlanders lived for a time at the fort while they were building Darien in 1736.

The First British Settlement in Georgia

James Oglethorpe was born in England in 1696, prepared for a military career, and received his commission at age sixteen. He was appointed to the Queen's Guard and later became an aide-de-camp to Prince Eugene of Savoy. On his return to

1733	**1734**	**1735**	**1736**
James Oglethorpe leads 116 colonists to Yamacraw Bluff to found Savannah and the colony of Georgia, by royal charter	Salzburger Protestants settle Ebenezer on Ebenezer Creek above Savannah	Scots Highlanders found Darien	Oglethorpe establishes Fort Frederica on St. Simons Island, at the site of an earlier Spanish mission, and Augusta at the head of navigation on the Savannah River

Among colonies in America, Georgia stands out as the work of one leader—a man not only in the background as founder, but also active on the scene. Unlike William Penn or Lord Baltimore, James Oglethorpe proposed the colonial charter, led the first shipload of emigrants, chose the site and laid out the first settlement, ran all its affairs during the crucial early years, organized the growth of the colony, defended its frontiers as a military leader, and retired to England only after actively leading the colony for ten years.

England, Oglethorpe entered Parliament, where he defended the rights of colonists and led an investigation into the deplorable conditions in prisons. With twenty other prominent men, he proposed a charter for a new colony, Georgia, and it was signed by the king in 1732. According to the good intentions of these trustees, the new colony would serve many purposes—providing useful employment for those released from debtors' prisons, settling and defending land in the buffer zone between British and Spanish colonial outposts, producing goods for import into England, and furnishing opportunities for missionary work among Indians.

Founders of colonies in the 17th century often had great difficulty in recruiting settlers in spite of glowing descriptions of a new and abundant life in America. This time the trustees had no difficulty raising money to finance their philanthropic enterprise, and generous conditions—free passage to America and tools, supplies, and food for a year—produced a flood of applicants. Oglethorpe had decided to hand-select the 116 men and women to sail on the *Anne*. In the rigorous process, the original intention to recruit those who had been thrown into prison for debt became subordinate, and the few debtors selected had to obtain permission from creditors. In the longer term, of the 5,000 who sailed for Georgia by 1750, only 2,000 came on charity, and it is estimated that no more than 650 of those might have been released debtors.

On February 12, 1733, the shipload of settlers reached the bluff on the Savannah River that would be their home. They were surprised at the warm welcome

GEORGIA *Time Line*

1737
Noble Jones, one of the original colonists to arrive with Oglethorpe, builds Wormsloe plantation

1741
Major William Horton establishes a plantation on Jekyll Island

1742
The Battle of Bloody Marsh on St. Simons Island ends the struggle with Spain for control of Georgia lands

1747
Mary Musgrove and Creek Indian warriors march into Savannah

> In October 1732 the settlers assembled on the galley *Anne* and went down below decks into crowded conditions. They sailed from London on November 17. Oglethorpe, who celebrated his thirty-sixth birthday during the long voyage, was an active leader. He visited the passengers belowdeck and paid attention to their needs. He also required all adult males to assemble on deck every day for military drills, since part of their obligation on land would be to protect the settlement. When passengers didn't get along, Oglethorpe gave each of them a pint of rum and told them to drink and be friends—a novel approach for a man who later banned rum from the colony.

provided by a nearby Yamacraw Indian tribe, who came in procession bearing gifts of friendship. Chief Tomochichi gave Oglethorpe a buffalo skin painted with the head of an eagle. The eagle symbolized swiftness and the buffalo strength, but in addition the soft feathers of the eagle signified love and the skin of the buffalo meant warmth and protection. John Musgrove and his wife, Mary—her mother was an Indian, her father an English trader—also arrived, and she interpreted for the English. Born in 1700, the daughter of a Creek princess, Mary had remained with her mother's tribe for ten years until she moved to South Carolina and lived with the English. She was familiar with the customs of both the Creek nation and the English settlers and so was invaluable to Oglethorpe in 1733 and succeeding years. The Musgroves had a trading post on Yamacraw Bluff near the site of Savannah.

The settlers went right to work clearing land for the town, building the fort and palisade, and preparing the ground for planting. The future city was carefully planned from the outset. Colonel William Bull had helped Oglethorpe pick the site, and the two laid out Savannah in four squares with connecting streets. The squares were originally planned to serve as military training grounds as well as grazing places for cattle. Each freeholder had his own lot in town for a house, a garden plot just outside, and a tract in the country for farming. While building proceeded, good relations with local Indians continued, and chiefs of the powerful Lower

| **1752** | **1771** | **1776** | **1778** | **1779** |
| New England Puritans move from South Carolina to settle Midway | Oglethorpe lays out Brunswick | Battle of the Rice Boats in Savannah | The British take and occupy Savannah | The British take Augusta; French and American siege of Savannah fails |

Creeks visited Oglethorpe, who treated them generously with gifts. During the heat of the first summer, as many as sixty settlers became ill and twenty-six died of a fever. Some help came from a doctor who arrived with an unexpected group of Jewish settlers from London; his treatments alleviated the fever—and Oglethorpe had banned rum as the probable cause. Finally it was realized that the water from shallow wells caused the sickness, and a deep well was dug to restore health to the settlement.

In spite of a good start, a number of problems arose in the colony's first decade. Among them was internal dissension, partly created by a lack of firm governing structure to manage the daily affairs of the settlers. Tradesmen and artisans with no knowledge of law served as magistrates and constables, annoying their peers. The trustees had also mandated experiments in producing highly valued commodities like wine, olives, and especially silk, while some of the sandy soil was not even good for growing needed food. The original ideal of building Georgia as a land of small yeoman farmers faltered when many of them could not support their families. These internal problems did not deter additional immigrants, and more settlers began to occupy surrounding areas. Religious groups not anticipated by the trustees arrived, including German-speaking Lutherans from Salzburg and Moravians.

After his second trip back to England to consult the trustees, Oglethorpe returned in 1738 with strong edicts. Running out of funds with no substantial exports to offset expenses, the trustees ordered many cutbacks and confirmed four original bans, some of which had been loosely enforced: no rum or strong spirits, no slaves, no large land grants, and no transfer of land to anyone but a male heir who could bear arms in case of need. Since Savannah was on the border with South Carolina, it had been relatively easy to circumvent the ban on rum. Even though some Georgians began "renting" slaves from South Carolina, this ban struck at the heart of their economic activity and especially angered them. While the Scots settlers in Darien and the Lutherans in Ebenezer spoke out strongly against slavery, many householders felt they could not work the land effectively without slaves and envied the prosperity of neighboring plantations in South Carolina. In response to the new edicts for strict enforcement, they sent

---

GEORGIA *Time Line*

1781	1782	1782	1791
Americans besiege and retake Augusta	General Anthony Wayne captures provisions for British Savannah in January; the British evacuate the city in July	Savannah becomes the capital of Georgia	George Washington reaches Savannah by ship on a ceremonial visit

a petition to the trustees, who turned it down, and Oglethorpe threatened to abandon the colony if it introduced slavery.

The succeeding decade would weaken the trustees' resistance to slavery in Georgia. Many of those promoting it moved to South Carolina, where they continued to agitate, and the rationale for Parliament's continuing to pour money into a debt-ridden colony waned after Oglethorpe's defeat of the invading Spanish armada at St. Simons Island in 1742. By 1750, when pastors Whitfield, Bolzius, and Habersham asked for the introduction of slavery on a limited basis, the trustees relented. Two years later they surrendered their charter, and the restrictions disappeared as Georgia became a royal colony.

Rapid Expansion for Defense

Concerned to create defenses that would make the buffer zone for Savannah a reality, Oglethorpe selected strategic sites on waterways. He founded Augusta in 1736 as a fort, one of many established for defense against the Spanish in this and succeeding years. It had long been a center for Indians, and during colonial days it continued to thrive as a trading center. Its location at the head of navigation on the Savannah River enticed traders with ties to Charles Town merchants, who could ship goods all the way by water.

Oglethorpe also focused efforts on the coast and the Sea Islands. Darien was settled in 1735 by Scots Highlanders escaping religious persecution and poverty; the next year Oglethorpe encouraged them to protect his new settlement established nearby at the mouth of the Altamaha River. He had placed a group of

The early Methodist leader John Wesley, then a zealous young Anglican cleric observed to be a stickler for doctrine and ritual, arrived in 1736. Failing to find Indians interested in conversion, he turned his attention to pastoral duties and singled out Sophia Hopkey as the object of his affections. When she refused to be courted and married another man, he refused to administer communion to her on technical grounds. An enormous uproar ensued, leading to a call for a grand jury by her uncle, a magistrate, and indictment. Wesley demanded an immediate trial, and when none was forthcoming he announced publicly that he would leave and did, reaching South Carolina. He was succeeded by George Whitfield, another preacher destined to become famous in religious history.

families on St. Simons Island, where they established Fort Frederica. First they built the fort, designed as the main defense along the water route, then replaced their palmetto huts with houses.

The War of Jenkins' Ear began in 1739 after Robert Jenkins, a British smuggler, lost an ear in a fracas with the Spanish off the Florida coast. Parliament construed this as an insult to British honor and used it as an excuse to wage war against the Spanish, which was their aim. By the late spring of 1740 Oglethorpe had gathered 900 troops and 1,100 Indians for an attack against the nearly impregnable fort at St. Augustine by land and sea, but it failed when the amphibious force could not get by Spanish galleys at the harbor entrance. A following siege proved equally ineffective, and the expedition, now racked with disease, retreated.

In 1742 the Spanish moved against Georgia with a much larger force of 50 ships, 1,000 seamen, and 1,800 soldiers gathered in Havana and commanded by Governor Manuel de Montiano of Florida. Oglethorpe's defenders were heavily outnumbered. For two weeks in July, small engagements and ambushes occurred on St. Simons Island. At one point Oglethorpe led a charge that caused a contingent of the much larger force to retreat; at another, remembered as the Battle of Bloody Marsh, the Scots Highlanders surprised resting Spanish troops and killed or captured two hundred. Oglethorpe's final weapon was misinformation provided to the Spanish through a counterspy. Disheartened by small defeats and the growing fear of hurricanes, the Spanish expedition sailed home, removing the colony's last threat from the south.

Conflict with Royal Governors

In 1752 Oglethorpe and the trustees surrendered their charter to the Crown by its original terms, and a new royal governor, Captain John Reynolds, arrived in 1754. A Royal Navy man accustomed to autocratic command, Reynolds was unsuited by training and temperament to his new post. He was unpopular at the outset because he seemed incapable of taking advice, and he soon alienated members of the assembly. He was removed and replaced by Lieutenant Governor Henry Ellis, a highly educated man who established good relations with all the politicians his predecessor had offended. After three years Ellis left and was succeeded by James Wright, a strong and respected governor who stayed until the Revolution forced him to leave. Born in South Carolina and educated in England, Wright arranged treaties to end Indian troubles, acquired great expanses of land from the Indians, encouraged rice plantations worked by slaves in the lowlands, and promoted population growth. He became the largest planter in his own right, eventually owning eleven plantations and more than 600 slaves.

Wright's problems, unlike those of some royal governors in other colonies, were often less of his own making than the result of external circumstances. In the decade preceding the Revolution, he remained committed to the welfare of the colony and dedicated to the Crown, a balancing act increasingly difficult to maintain. To be sure, he made a political mistake by forcing the legislature to accept part of the Stamp Act, making Georgia the only colony to do so. The sons of Loyalists formed the Sons of Liberty, and some even joined a group of South Carolinians in marching on Savannah to prevent the use of stamps. The Townshend Acts were even more troubling to commercial interests, yet Georgia never joined the nonimportation response endorsed by other colonies before the duties were repealed. Even in the summer of 1774, after Parliament had imposed the so-called Intolerable Acts on Boston, rallies by Patriots were counterbalanced by those of Loyalists. No delegates were sent to the First Continental Congress. Georgians had divided sympathies in the years preceding the Revolution, a split that lasted until the Second Continental Congress in 1775.

Serious trouble began in January of that year when Patriots convened a provincial congress to meet concurrently with the legislative assembly. In spite of inadequate representation from all the parishes, it selected three representatives to the Second Continental Congress and passed the action along to the assembly. Then total disarray set in. Governor Wright adjourned the assembly before it could vote. The three representatives, Archibald Bulloch, Noble W. Jones, and John Houston, all from Savannah (Christ Church parish), refused to go because the assembly had not approved them as delegates from the colony as a whole. Enraged Patriots in the Midway/Sunbury region (St. John's parish) first negotiated for annexation to South Carolina, and when that failed selected Dr. Lyman Hall to replace the Savannah representatives. Hall did attended the Second Continental Congress and brought both money and rice for the relief of Massachusetts, but he did not vote because he represented only a single parish rather than the whole colony.

When news of Lexington and Concord reached Savannah on May 10, things got worse. Noble Jones and Joseph Habersham—sons of staunch Loyalists close to Governor Wright—and others broke into the royal powder magazine and made off with 500 pounds of its contents. In an aftermath reminiscent of the Boston Tea Party and the burning of the *Gaspee* in Providence, everyone knew who did it but no one told. In June Patriots spiked guns in Savannah to prevent a salute for the king's birthday, and stole shot and guns from a warehouse. By the time the Second Provincial Congress convened on July 4, effective royal authority had almost disappeared. Many of the affairs of the colony were managed by that congress and its appointed committee of safety, which raised a battalion of Continental troops. The arrival of British warships off Tybee Island in early 1776 precipitated the finale of royal government. Major Joseph Habersham arrested Wright, who later broke his parole, eluded his guards, and escaped to the HMS *Scarborough*.

The Revolutionary War in Georgia

At the same time Georgia's first battle erupted on the river. Eleven boats loaded with rice to be sent to markets were blocked by the British, who wanted the cargo for military provisions. From the king's ship, Governor Wright sent a letter to the rebelling citizens, asking them to provide the fleet with rice and offering to work for their full pardon in London. It was ignored. The so-called Battle of the Rice Boats ensued when local inhabitants were ordered to remove rudders, sails, and rigging so the boats could not be moved; British troops had already boarded them the night before. The boats were anchored out of range of the Savannah battery at the head of an island, so the Patriots sent a fire ship among them that burned three or four. The British escaped with the rest downstream through a back channel on the other side of the island. During the action, Patriots tried to board the British ships, and one was set on fire and run aground, forcing the soldiers on board to slog through rice fields to escape.

Although the British had outwitted the defenders and gotten their rice, the battle had one positive effect for the Patriots. It highlighted the disorganization they had been in for more than half a year, with unclear lines of authority between the provincial congress, committee of safety, and various local groups. When the fall of Savannah seemed possible, the provincial congress retired to Augusta and developed a simple temporary constitution to govern Georgia. In thirteen paragraphs it created a one-house legislature, a president, and a council of safety, leaving the court structure intact. When it took effect on May 1, 1776, Archibald Bulloch became the first president, and after he died Button Gwinnett replaced him. Georgia was then committed to separation from the Crown.

No other major battles occurred on Georgia soil during the first three years of the Revolution, but internal conflict spread. Some families were divided in their stands as Tory or Patriot, and vicious guerrilla warfare raged throughout the backcountry. From 1775 onward many Tories moved across the border to St. Augustine in Florida, which had been under British control since the Peace of Paris in 1763. Florida Rangers crept into Georgia to kill settlers and their families and destroy their farms, and the retaliation of Patriots was sometimes equally brutal. On the recommendation of the Continental Congress, Georgians and South Carolinians mounted expeditions to capture St. Augustine and stop the raids. The first attempt, led by General Charles Lee in 1776, destroyed some settlements on the St. Johns River but got no farther. President Button Gwinnett led the next expedition, in 1777, but was persuaded to relinquish command at Sunbury to Colonel Samuel Elbert, who also stalled at the St. Johns. In 1778 a third attempt with militia from South Carolina and Georgia, a naval unit, and Continental troops under General Robert Howe of North Carolina faltered at the St. Marys River when, lacking supplies and afflicted by fever, its various components could not agree on what might be accomplished.

By 1778 the British considered the South to be the main center of opportunity to end the war and began the southern campaign in Georgia. From that point onward, both sides sought control of two strategic sites, Savannah and Augusta. British ships sailed from New York and unloaded men under Lieutenant Colonel Archibald Campbell at Tybee Island at the mouth of the Savannah River. General Augustine Prevost brought another group north from Florida. At the end of December, British forces led through the swamps surprised General Robert Howe's defenders and easily took Savannah in a rout that killed or captured 550 of Howe's men. In August 1779 French admiral d'Estaing arrived with twenty-two ships and 4,000 French soldiers to besiege Savannah with the support of General Benjamin Lincoln, who brought 1,500 South Carolina troops. In early September the combined force attacked in one of the bloodiest battles of the war. They were repulsed with the loss of 1,100 men killed or wounded. Governor Wright had returned before the attack to restore royal government, and the British remained in control of the city until the summer of 1782.

Augusta and its surrounding area proved difficult for either side to hold for long. The British had taken the city early in 1779 but pulled back toward Savannah when expected Loyalist support failed to materialize. Patriots surprised a group of 800 Tories at Kettle Creek and scattered them. This victory was offset when North Carolina general John Ashe, leading 2,300 men, was surprised by British regulars between Briar Creek and the Savannah River and defeated with heavy losses. Patriot Whigs set up not one but two competing governments in Augusta

> Button Gwinnett was born in England in 1735. He arrived in Savannah and started a store, but then bought land on St. Catherines Island, where he became a farmer. Gwinnett sold the plantation and by 1774 became committed to the Patriot cause after Parliament passed the Intolerable Acts. He attended the Second Continental Congress in Philadelphia in 1776, signed the Declaration of Independence, and helped develop the permanent state constitution of 1777. Insulted by Lachlan McIntosh, a bitter rival, Gwinnett challenged him to a duel and died of wounds he received.

during the summer of 1779, but Loyalists regained control of the city again after the fall of Charles Town the following spring. In the fall of 1780 Elijah Clarke led the Overmountain men of South Carolina in an attack on Augusta but was repulsed after Loyalist reinforcements arrived. A more powerful force including Clarke's men, South Carolina militia under General Andrew Pickens, and "Lighthorse Harry" Lee's legion besieged Augusta in May of 1781 and finally obtained its surrender. The seesaw of more than two years was over.

As was the case in New York City, the British remained in Savannah after Lord Cornwallis surrendered at Yorktown. But when General Anthony Wayne became Continental commander in Georgia in January 1782, he seized provisions meant for Savannah and drove British troops back toward the city. By May of 1782 Governor Wright was told that British forces were needed elsewhere and that the city would be evacuated. The terms laid down for Loyalists by John Martin, free Georgia's first governor, were generous. Savannah's citizens could also leave with the British troops, and about 2,000 who had supported the king did settle their affairs and leave, along with 5,000 slaves. Some who took the oath of allegiance to the United States stayed and were forgiven. Others, including Loyalist leaders and those who had committed crimes, were not forgiven, and their property was confiscated, with the money used to reward the officers who had worked hard for freedom, including generals Wayne and Nathanael Greene.

Regions *to* Explore

AUGUSTA
SAVANNAH
FORTS ALONG THE COAST SOUTH OF SAVANNAH
JEKYLL ISLAND

AUGUSTA

Founded in 1736, three years after Savannah, Augusta is the second-oldest city in Georgia. It was established as part of Oglethorpe's plan of military defenses at key locations in Georgia. Located on the South Carolina border, at the head of navigation on the Savannah River, it had been frequented by Indians and rapidly became a trading center for agents of Charles Town merchants. As a border town with ready access to the interior, Augusta prospered. (See the Historical Introduction for more details on Augusta's role in the Revolutionary War.)

WASHINGTON and the CREEKS

As Georgia's population began expanding again after the Revolution, the pressure for Indian land increased, and the Lower Creeks signed a number of treaties ceding land for settlement by whites. Most of these were not recognized by Upper Creek chief Alexander McGillivray, a shrewd and duplicitous leader born of a Scottish father and Creek mother of mixed blood. Since the prospect of war with the Creeks had loomed throughout the late 1780s, President Washington invited McGillivray to New York in 1790 for negotiations that led to a public federal treaty ceding some Indian land and another, secret, one conferring benefits on Creeks and paying McGillivray an annual stipend as an agent of the United States with the rank of brigadier general. (At the same time he was also receiving pay from Spanish Florida as superintendent general of the Creek nation.) The federal treaty did not resolve Georgia's problems with the Creeks, some of which originated in McGillivray's unwillingness to deal with a state that had confiscated his Tory father's plantations after the war. And there was uneasiness about questions of federal or state jurisdiction over ceded Indian lands. In May of 1791 President Washington chose to pay Georgia a ceremonial visit, reaching Savannah by ship. In response to the mayor's welcome, Washington obliquely recognized Georgia's difficulties with the Creeks: "While the virtuous conduct of your citizens, whose patriotism braved all hardships of the late war, engaged my esteem, the distresses peculiar to the State of Georgia, after the peace, excited my deepest regret."

HISTORICAL SITES and MUSEUMS

Augusta Museum of History (706-722-8454), 560 Reynolds St. Open Tue.–Sun. The history of Augusta and the area is presented in the exhibit Augusta's Story.

The **Monument to Georgia's Signers of the Declaration of Independence** stands on Greene Street between Fourth and Fifth Streets. Button Gwinnett is honored there; he is buried in Savannah.

St. Paul's Episcopal Church (706-724-2485), 605 Reynolds St. Open daily. Although the congregation was founded in 1750, the building was destroyed in the Revolution. The next building was erected in 1819 but also burned; the present church dates from 1919. A signer of the U.S. Constitution, Colonel William Few Jr., is buried in the cemetery.

Site of Fort Augusta, 605 Reynolds St. The site lies between St. Paul's Church and the river and is marked by a Celtic cross. A marker commemorates George Washington's visit here in 1791. The fort dated from 1736. A 1730s cannon stands near the cross.

SAVANNAH

James Oglethorpe asked King George II to grant him a charter to land in between the Carolinas and Florida. With strong support from prominent men, he wanted to settle released debtors and the working poor in a colony that would also export crops Britain wanted and serve as a buffer against the Spanish in Florida. Oglethorpe founded Savannah in February 1733 with 116 settlers on a bluff above the river. They were welcomed by the Yamacraw Indians, whose chief, Tomochichi, pledged friendship and goodwill toward the newcomers. He kept that pledge and was buried in Savannah at his own request. (See the Historical Introduction for more details about the charter and settlement.)

Savannah may be the first planned city in the country. Oglethorpe designed and laid out the streets in grids that included public squares and parks. They were used as places to conduct business, hold town meetings, graze cattle, and train militias.

In 1744 Francis Moore, in his *Voyage to Georgia Begun in the Year 1735,* wrote about Savannah's squares: "The use of this is, in case a War should happen that the Villages without may have Places in the Town, to bring their Cattle and Families into for Refuge, and to that Purpose there is a Square left in every Ward, big enough

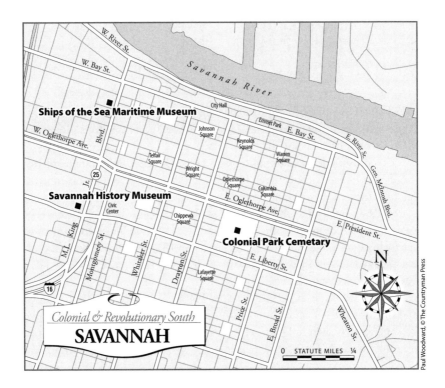

Mary Musgove (originally named Coosaponakeesa), a Creek-English inter-preter, became a key figure for James Oglethorpe because she was able to negotiate with the Indians in the area. Born of a Scottish trader father and a Creek mother, she learned the ways of her father's people, among whom she was baptized into the Church of England and given the name Mary. She opened a trading post with her husband, John Musgrove, at Yamacraw Bluff and was there when Oglethorpe arrived.

Oglethorpe and Mary negotiated the land treaties that led to the founding of Savannah in 1733. Creek warriors fought on the British side in wars, and even after Oglethorpe left Georgia Mary continued to work with the British. She established another trading post at Mount Venture on the Altamaha River that also served as a buffer against the Spanish.

for the Out-wards to encamp in." Today, Savannah has twenty-two squares, and all are lush with greenery, blooming flowers, and live oaks. Some of them have statues and fountains, with ironwork scrolled around them, others benches and paths for a quiet rest.

Another feature that marks Savannah is the prominent use of ironwork. Scrolled patterns enliven balconies, stair railings, doors, and the facades of buildings. Visitors continue to look for iron griffins as foot scrapers, iron dolphins as water-spouts, and iron storks as newel posts. Much of the first ironwork in the city arrived from England after the fire of 1796, when people were rebuilding their homes. Again, after the fire of 1820 William Jay encouraged builders to use iron for floor joists, rafters, shutters, and sash frames. Decorative ironwork was very much in vogue at that time; later it dwindled in popularity and now is highly prized.

During the Revolution, the British occupied Savannah from 1778 until July 1782. (For details see the Historical Introduction.)

HISTORICAL SITES *and* MUSEUMS

Visitors to Savannah can choose to look around on their own, perhaps with the official guidebook, *Sojourn in Savannah,* in hand, or take a Gray Line tour for an overall view.

The **Colonial Park Cemetery** (912-651-6843), 201 E. Oglethorpe Ave., on the east side of Abercorn Street, opened around 1750. A tabby sidewalk runs through the cemetery under lovely old trees providing shade on a hot day. Some inscriptions on tombstones are almost illegible, but plaques are provided so visitors can read about those buried here. Some famous Georgians interred at the cemetery include Button Gwinnett, a signer of the Declaration of Independence, Archibald Bulloch, James Habersham, Hugh McCall, and Edward Green Malbone.

The **Savannah History Museum** (912-238-1779; www.chsgeorgia.org), 303 Martin Luther King Jr. Blvd. Open daily. This museum is in the old Central of

Savannah's squares offer plenty of greenery.

Georgia Railway passenger shed. In 1984 the Great Savannah Exposition opened here. The Coastal Heritage Society operates the museum, which houses a wide variety of artifacts and collections. The oldest pieces on display date from the earliest inhabitants, including a spear point from ca. 1500 BC and another from ca. 8000 BC. Indian "poker chips" date from 1450 AD. Models wearing uniforms include a private from the 71st (Highlander) Regiment of Foot, and you'll see a 1760 Hessian flintlock pistol. Visitors can start with a film, *Savannah the Survivor,* for orientation.

The **Ships of the Sea Maritime Museum** (912-232-1511; www.ships ofthesea.org), 41 Martin Luther King Jr. Blvd. Open daily. The museum has a fine collection of scrimshaw (etching and carving done on whalebone), including an ostrich egg with the ship "Prince of Wales" on it. An unusual pirate figurehead looks both handsome and fearsome. The shell collection includes a green turban snail that was decorated and given to Queen Victoria and Prince Albert for the opening of Crystal Palace in 1851. Ship models are housed on each floor, including a 6th-century BC Greek trireme (the most effective warship of the ancient world), a 16th-century Mediterranean galley (the primary fighting ship of the Renaissance), the *Anne* (the galley that brought colonists to Georgia), the *Bonhomme Richard* (John Paul Jones's flagship during the Revolution), HMS *Victory* (Admiral Horatio Nelson's flagship at the Battle of Trafalgar), the *Flying Cloud* (record-breaking American clipper ship), the *Charles W. Morgan* (last of the American whaling ships, now at Mystic Seaport in Connecticut), four ships named *Savannah,* and many others in this excellent model collection.

Wormsloe State Historic Site (912-353-3023; www.wormsloe.org), 7601 Skidaway Rd. Open daily. Noble Jones, an English physician and carpenter, was one of Georgia's first settlers. He arrived with his wife, son, and daughter on the *Anne* with James Oglethorpe in 1733. In 1736 Jones received a lease on 500 acres on the Isle of Hope. In 1756 the Jones family received Wormsloe by royal grant, and it remained the only Savannah plantation in the possession of its original family, until 1974. At that time the site, with its tabby ruins of the house, was given to the Georgia Heritage Trust.

Noble Jones's fortified home was enclosed with 8-foot-high walls to protect it from either Spanish or Indian attack. Each corner had bastions where muskets could fire on anyone approaching. At the west wall there may have been a well dating from 1737. A double-hearth brick chimney stood on the western wall. The house was large for the area, with one and a half stories and five rooms.

Today visitors will find an avenue of live oaks leading to the tabby ruins of Wormsloe. There's a film on the founding, and artifacts from the excavations are on display. The "Colonial Life Area" is a living history section, which offers interpreters in period dress working as the early settlers did.

LODGING

BALLASTONE INN
14 E. Oglethorpe Ave., Savannah, GA 31401
912-236-1484; www.ballastone.com
This is a restored 1835 town house in the historic district. It was the first B&B in Savannah. Sixteen guest rooms.

EAST BAY INN BED & BREAKFAST
225 E. Bay St., Savannah, GA 31401
912-238-1225; www.eastbayinn.com
The inn is located in a restored 1853 warehouse with Georgian decor and 28 guest rooms.

FOLEY HOUSE INN
14 W. Hull St., Savannah, GA 31401
912-232-6622; www.foleyinn.com
The inn is furnished with period antiques, and there are two private garden courtyards. Seventeen guest rooms.

THE GASTONIAN
220 E. Gaston St., Savannah, GA 31401
912-232-2869; www.gastonian.com

The Gastonian is in connected 1868 houses, and there is a landscaped garden. Seventeen guest rooms.

HAMILTON-TURNER INN
330 Abercorn St., Savannah, GA 31401
923-232-1833; www.hamilton-turnerinn.com
The inn is in a Second French Empire–style mansion. Seventeen guest rooms.

KEHOE HOUSE
123 Habersham St., Savannah, GA 31401
912-232-1020; www.kehoehouse.com
The inn is in a restored 1892 Victorian mansion. Thirteen guest rooms.

MANSION ON FORSYTH PARK
700 Drayton St., Savannah, GA 31401
912-238-5158; www.mansion onforsythpark.com
This hotel also has a culinary school, art gallery, and a spa. There are 126 guest rooms.

OLDE HARBOUR INN
508 E. Factors Walk, Savannah, GA
31401
912-234-4100;
www.oldeharbousinn.com
The inn offers suites with living room and
kitchen, most of them overlooking the
water. Twenty-four guest rooms.

RESTAURANTS

BELFORD'S
315 W. St. Julian St.
912-233-2626
Casual dining in City Market specializing in
seafood and steaks.

BOAR'S HEAD GRILL
1 N. Lincoln St.
912-651-9660
Casual riverfront dining specializing in
steaks, Maine lobster, and local seafood.

THE CRAB SHACK
Chimney Creek on Tybee Island
912-786-9857
Seafood served low-country style.

45 SOUTH RESTAURANT
20 E. Broad St.
912-233-1881
Regional specialties including a tasting
menu.

MRS. WILKES DINING ROOM
107 W. Jones St.
912-232-5997 or 8970
A family-style restaurant serving regional
specialties for lunch.

THE OLDE PINK HOUSE
23 Abercorn St.
912-232-4286
This historic restaurant serves southern
cuisine for dinner.

PIRATES' HOUSE
20 E. Broad St.
912-233-5757
It opened in 1753 as an inn for seafarers.
Lunch, dinner, and Sunday brunch.

EVENTS

March: Tour of Homes and Gardens,
912-234-8054
May: Scottish Games Festival, 912-232-
3945
May: War of Jenkins' Ear reenactment at
Wormsloe Historic Site, 912-353-3023
December: Holiday Tour of Homes,
912-236-8362

INFORMATION

**SAVANNAH VISITOR INFORMATION
CENTER**
301 Martin Luther King Blvd.
Savannah, GA 31402
912-944-0455, 912-651-6662, 877-728-
2662; www.savannahvisit.com

FORTS ALONG THE
COAST SOUTH OF SAVANNAH

The coastal low country of Georgia resembles the Tidewater regions of the Carolinas in many respects, but here the long stretches of unbroken narrow sand spit are replaced by a string of more substantial barrier islands. This change to more intricate systems of tidal rivers, creeks, inlets, coves, and salt marshes begins in Charleston and characterizes the coastline all the way to Jacksonville. Early explorers and settlers prized this coast for easy access to and from the open Atlantic, while modern snowbirds flock to its major islands—Hilton Head, Tybee, Skidaway, St. Simons, Jekyll, Amelia—seeking refuge from northern winters.

FORT MORRIS AT MIDWAY

Settlement of the Midway district in Georgia, located between Savannah and Darien, is a paradigm of the American mobility that eventually swallowed all the land from coast to coast. Pilgrims from Dorset, England, settled first in Dorchester, Massachusetts, in the 17th century; then a part of that group splintered off to Dorchester, South Carolina; and in 1752 most of that settlement moved to the Midway region, founding towns named Dorchester and Midway. Congregationalists to the core in their daily lives, the settlers were both industrious in developing rice and indigo plantations and leaders among the impatient Patriots of St. John's parish pushing for independence from Britain.

A short drive east, on the other side of Interstate 95, is the town of Sunbury, which has all but disappeared. The town was founded in the 1750s and became an important port, second only to Savannah in volume. Its location was perfect for defending the coastline of Georgia. Among signers of the Declaration of Independence who lived in the town were Lyman Hall and Button Gwinnett. The Fort Morris site is here.

HISTORICAL SITES and MUSEUMS
Fort Morris State Historic Site (912-884-5999; www.gastateparks.org/info/ ftmorris/), Islands Hwy. and Fort Morris Rd., Midway, GA. Open Tue.–Sun. In 1776 the Continental Congress commissioned Fort Morris, built to protect the port of Sunbury. In an attack by the British in 1778, Lieutenant Colonel Lewis Fuser and his men surrounded the fort. Then he and Colonel John McIntosh inside the fort exchanged letters, including the last from McIntosh that read: "Come and take it!" Fuser, whose move was meant only to be diversionary, decided to withdraw. However, the British returned after Savannah fell later that year, in December. They surrounded the fort again and bombarded it until the Americans surrendered.

The visitor center offers an audiovisual program as well as the history of the town before the Revolutionary War. There's a diorama of Fort Morris and displays of colonial artifacts. A blacksmith shop has demonstrations. A walking trail and a nature trail are also on site.

Midway Museum (912-884-5837), US 17. Open Tue.–Sat. The museum, housed in an 18th-century raised-cottage-style building, claims to be Georgia's only colonial museum. Displays include documents from the early 18th century. Next door stands **Midway Church**, which was founded in 1752. Although the original church was destroyed in the Revolution, the replica dates from 1792.

FORT KING GEORGE AT DARIEN

In January 1736, 177 Scots Highlanders from the Inverness region arrived on the *Prince of Wales* to settle Darien. From the outset they were intended as a military force by the colony's trustees and James Oglethorpe, who had recruited them.

HISTORICAL SITES and MUSEUMS

Fort King George (912-437-4770; www.gastateparks.org) is on the east edge of town, east of US 17 on Fort King George Dr. (Box 711), Darien, GA 31305. Open daily except Mon. This fort was built in 1721 as the southernmost outpost of the British Empire in North America and was named for King George I of Britain.

Fort King George was a triangular European field fortification typical of the period. A moat shielded two sides, and the north branch of the Altamaha River the third. The blockhouse was the main defense structure. It had three stories: a powder, ammunition, and supply magazine on the lower level, a gun room with cannon ports in the walls on the second level, and a lookout post in a gun room on the third floor. Enemy soldiers and Indians may have been deterred by a log palisade in the moat.

The fort has been rebuilt on its foundation. Researchers found old records and drawings that enabled them to reconstruct the blockhouse to original specifications, using the same building material of cypress. Visitors can view a slide presentation to orient themselves and then walk through the exhibits in the museum. Interpreters wear hand-sewn clothing that looks like the garments people wore in the 1700s.

Men who lived here had to put up with heat, insects, sometimes hostile Indians, and the Spanish. During the 18th century this part of the country was not healthy because it was impossible to keep food fresh in the heat. Salt meat rotted, fresh rations frequently weren't available, and dietary knowledge was rudimentary, so many of the men died of scurvy. Remains of British soldiers still lie in graves adjoining the fort, in one of the oldest British military cemeteries in the country.

The fort was abandoned in 1732, but a group of Scots Highlanders lived there in 1736 while they established the settlement of Darien. They were in the area when needed during the Battle of Bloody Marsh on St. Simons Island in 1742.

On the grounds you'll also see the tabby-and-brick ruins of a sawmill from a later era; after the turn of the century, timber was floated down the Oconee, Ocmulgee, Ohoopee, and Altamaha Rivers to the sawmill. The museum has a collection of pieces from the Guale Indi-

> Just as in South Carolina, tabby was often the building material of choice in early Georgia. The concrete resulting from mixing the tabby with sand and shells can be seen in the foundations of many 17th- and 18th-century buildings throughout the state.

ans. There are also pieces of swords from the nearby Spanish mission. Displays explore the history of the area from prehistoric times through the Indian, Spanish, and English periods.

EVENTS

March: Scottish Heritage Day, 912-437-4770

INFORMATION

DARIEN-MCINTOSH COUNTY CHAMBER OF COMMERCE
105 Fort King George Dr., Box 149
Darien, GA 31305

FORT FREDERICA ON ST. SIMONS ISLAND

Not far away there are more islands to explore, But first you can stop in Brunswick, to see the shrimp fleet at the foot of Gloucester Street. Victorian houses line some of the streets near the courthouse. Drive out Glynn Avenue to Overlook Park for a fine view of the "Marshes of Glynn," immortalized during the 1870s by Georgia poet Sidney Lanier.

St. Simons Island, accessible by causeway from Brunswick, is filled with lush green foliage, blooming plants, and live oaks. Retreat Plantation, now the Sea Island Golf Course, houses the ruins of a slave hospital on its grounds, as well as a fishing pier.

HISTORICAL SITES *and* MUSEUMS

The **Bloody Marsh Battle Site** (912-638-3639; www.nps.gov/fofr), Demere Rd., St. Simons Island, GA 31522. Open daily. On July 7, 1742, the Spanish, on their way to attack Fort Frederica, were defeated here by British troops. Lieutenants Patrick Sutherland and Charles MacKay were considered the heroes of this battle and received recognition both in England and in America.

One account told by British survivors in later years holds that the Spanish thought the fighting had stopped, put their arms in a pile, and sat down to have some refreshment. At this a Highland bonnet emerged from the woods, which was the signal for the British to open fire into the Spanish contingent. A battle ensued, and the Spanish were repulsed. Among other skirmishes with Oglethorpe's defenders, this was the turning point in the Spanish aggression into Georgia. The Spanish force left St. Simons and headed back to Florida.

Another important site on St. Simons is **Christ Church** (912-638-8683; www.christchurchfrederica.org), 6329 Frederica Rd. Open daily. John

 A plaque at Bloody Marsh reads:
"We are resolved not to suffer defeat—we will rather die like Leonidas and his Spartans—if we can but protect Georgia and Carolina and the rest of the Americans from desolation."
—OGLETHORPE

> Documented gossip tells that Mrs. Hawkins was a veritable shrew, mean and a troublemaker, whose temperament may be deduced from the fact that she beat her servant, broke a bottle over a constable's head, and threatened John Wesley with a pistol, biting him in the wrist when he attempted to disarm her.

and Charles Wesley held services here under oak trees in 1736. Families of early settlers are buried in the churchyard. The first church on the site was built in 1820 but was destroyed during the Civil War. In 1884 Anson G. P. Dodge rebuilt the church. One of the windows, depicting the confession of Christ by St. Peter at Caesarea Philippi, was designed in Germany in 1899.

Eugenia Price, Georgia author of *The Beloved Invader*, is buried in the cemetery. She described the church in her book, and some of the characters also lie there.

Fort Frederica (912-638-3639; www.nps.gov/fofr), Frederica Rd. Open daily. This fort was developed by General Oglethorpe in 1736 and named after Frederick, the king's only son. At the time, it was the most expensive fort the British had built in North America. Ruins of the magazine still stand on the waterfront. The fort's guns were trained on the water, and enemy ships were unlikely to pass without being noticed.

Oglethorpe had a wall built completely around the entire town to protect its citizens. Broad Street divided the town in halves. The first settlers included 44 men, who were mostly craftsmen, and 72 women and children. Each family had a lot for building and 50 acres in the country for crops.

A visitor in 1745 wrote, "Frederica is defended by a pretty strong Fort of Tappy, which has several 18 Pounders mounted on a Ravelin in its Front, and commands the River both upwards and downwards; and is surrounded by a quadrangular Rampart, with 4 bastions, of Earth well stockaded and turfed, and a palisadoed Ditch."

Walk out on the grounds to read plaques beside the foundations of some of the buildings. The first houses were palmetto huts, replaced by structures of wood, tabby, and brick. The house on the left side of Broad directly behind the magazine was a double house, shared by two families. Dr. Thomas Hawkins and his wife, Beatre, lived on one side. He was the regimental surgeon and town physician and apothecary, as well as an officer of the court. Samuel and Susanna Davison lived on the other side. He was a tavern keeper, town constable, and ship inspector.

Hawkins incurred Oglethorpe's wrath by breaking the rule of not shooting on Sunday; he lost his post as first bailiff. The Davisons were well liked in town. John Caldwell, a candlemaker, lived across Broad Street in a three-story house. The Musgrove House was located back from the water near the town gate. Mary Musgrove was the daughter of a Scottish Indian trader and a Creek princess, niece of a Creek chief. She was very helpful to Oglethorpe in gaining respect from the Indians and also acted as an interpreter. (See Historical Introduction for more details about her role in the colony.)

The demise of Fort Frederica came with peace. Oglethorpe left for England in 1743, and the Highland regiment was disbanded in 1749. Shopkeepers could not continue with few customers, and soon the town became one of "houses without inhabitants, barracks without soldiers, guns without carriages, and streets overgrown with weeds."

INFORMATION

ST. SIMONS ISLAND VISITORS CENTER
530 Beachview Dr., St. Simons Island, GA 31522
800-933-2627

JEKYLL ISLAND

Jekyll Island, just south of St. Simons and accessible from the mainland by causeway, is one of the smaller Sea Islands protecting the coast of Georgia. Early residents included the Guale Indians, who called the island Ospo. During the 15th century, European explorers came seeking gold. Spanish missionaries arrived in the 16th and 17th centuries and founded Santiago de Ocone, a mission. Oglethorpe sailed by the island in 1734 and named it for his friend, Sir Joseph Jekyll.

HISTORICAL SITES and MUSEUMS

Horton House (912-635-2119, administrative office), 375 Riverview Dr., Jekyll Island, GA 31527. This ruin is part of the Jekyll Island Historic District. Major William Horton, one of Oglethorpe's officers, created a plantation on the island. The buildings were destroyed by the Spanish after the Battle of Bloody Marsh in 1742, but Horton rebuilt by 1746. Today the Horton House is in ruins, but it remains as one of the most significant tabby ruins in Georgia.

After his death the island belonged to several owners before Christophe Poulain du Bignon bought it in 1800. He raised sea-island cotton there until his death in 1825. In 1858 the slave ship *Wanderer* brought the last group of slaves to the island. The du Bignons were in trouble for bringing in slaves and eventually lost the island.

One of the du Bignon descendants, John Eugene du Bignon, bought a parcel of land on the island. He and his brother-in-law, Newton Finney, evolved the plan of selling Jekyll Island to a New York club as a private hunting retreat. As a member of the Union Club in New York, Finney had entrée to some of the most powerful men in the city. By 1885 du Bignon owned the entire island and sold it to the Jekyll Island Club. The Club House was finished in 1887 in Queen Anne architecture, with towers and wraparound porches. In 1901 an annex was built; a dining room was added in 1917 and a swimming pool a few years later. More

The remains of Major William Horton's house on Jekyll Island

recently, a ballroom was added to accommodate conferences, but the architectural impression of the original structure and surrounding cottages remains dominant through a large and pleasant campus.

LODGING

JEKYLL ISLAND CLUB HOTEL
371 Riverview Dr., Jekyll Island, GA 31527
800-535-9547 or 912-635-2600
www.jekyllclub.com
A restored hotel from the Gilded Age with cottages and a total of 157 guest rooms.

INFORMATION

JEKYLL ISLAND HISTORY CENTER AND NATIONAL HISTORIC LANDMARK DISTRICT
100 Stable Dr., Jekyll Island, GA 31527
877-4-Jekyll or 912-635-4036

JEKYLL ISLAND CONVENTION & VISITORS BUREAU
1 Beachview Dr., Jekyll Island, GA 31527
912-635-4157

Current Information

GEORGIA DEPARTMENT OF ECONOMIC DEVELOPMENT—TOURISM
75 Fifth St. NW, Suite 1200
Atlanta, GA 30308
800-847-4842, 404-962-4000
www.georgia.org

Florida

Historical Introduction
to the
Florida Colony

T he Spanish control of the New World that began with the four voyages of Columbus and spread throughout the Caribbean, Mexico, and South America reached Florida near the beginning of the 16th century. Ponce de León arrived near the future site of St. Augustine in April 1513 and named it La Florida. His statues stand tall in several parts of the city today. He was looking for the mythical Fountain of Youth and thought he had found it here, but claiming Florida for Spain became his most important accomplishment. In 1521 he landed on the southwestern coast near Charlotte Harbor or Cape Coral with 200 settlers but was soon driven out by attacks from Calusa Indians. Wounded by a poisoned arrow, he died in Havana. In any case, his claim for Spain set the stage for centuries of conflict with the French and the English, who also struggled to control North America.

Juan Ponce de León was born in 1474 in Tervas de San Campos in the province of Valladolid. As a young man he fought against the Moors under Ferdinand and Isabella. In 1493 he volunteered to sail with Columbus on his second voyage, and in 1506 he went to Puerto Rico with 100 soldiers to found a fortified capital. He became governor of Puerto Rico in 1509. The king gave him a grant to explore new territory, and he started on his quest to find the Fountain of Youth.

Ponce de León, Pánfilo de Narváez, and Hernando de Soto had explored Pensacola Bay during the first half of the 16th century, so it is not surprising that an attempt at settlement there preceded the founding of St. Augustine. In Veracruz, Mexico, Tristán de Luna y

Overleaf: The Oldest Schoolhouse, St. Augustine

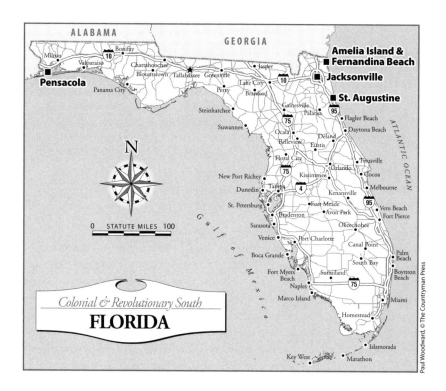

Paul Woodward, © The Countryman Press

Colonial & Revolutionary South
FLORIDA

Arellano organized a large expedition to plant a self-sustaining colony and reached Pensacola in August of 1559. A month later a hurricane destroyed all but three of the eleven ships and many of their supplies. With the help of some relief ships, the survivors struggled for two years to establish the colony, finally abandoning it in 1561. Four years later St. Augustine was founded, while Pensacola was not successfully resettled until 1698.

St. Augustine

Pedro Menéndez de Avilés established St. Augustine in September 1565. He had been commissioned by King Philip II to lead a group of settlers to Florida and landed at a place he named San Augustin. His focus was to establish fortified sites that would protect Spanish fleets, and St. Augustine was in a good position to provide defense against pirate attacks for Spanish galleons. A mission, Nombre de Dios (Name of God), was founded on the site of his landing; it was the first in a group of missions established on the southeastern coast. As the center of Spanish power in Florida, St. Augustine suffered many attacks and was left in ashes a number of times, but it survived as the first permanent settlement in North America.

Menéndez's second task became ridding the coast of the French Huguenot settlements promoted by Admiral Gaspard de Coligny and led by Jean Ribaut, which the Spaniard performed with savage efficiency. Ribaut had explored the "River of

> ✳ Captain General Pedro Menéndez de Avilés was born in 1519 in Avilés, Spain. His father died young, and Pedro ran away from his foster home to go to sea at age fourteen. He became an officer in the Spanish navy and rose to command of a fleet of ships. The king of Spain sent him to fight pirates off the Spanish coast in 1549, and a decade later he became the general of the Armada of the Spanish Crown. He was the captain of the Fleet of the Indies, with a brief interlude in prison for disobeying commands at sea. He paid a fine of 1,000 ducats and was reinstated by King Philip, who sent him to chart the coastline of Florida and start a colony.

May" (St. Johns) in 1562, and one of his companions in that venture, René de Laudonnière, returned two years later to build Fort Caroline near the mouth of the river. Ribaut returned in 1565 with a fleet of seven ships, colonists, and supplies to reinforce the fort. Aware of each other's presence, the Frenchman and the Spaniard both hastened to strike first. Ribaut sailed to attack Menéndez while the Spaniard's men were building the first fort at San Augustin, but a hurricane drove his ships farther south and beached and demolished them. Meanwhile Menéndez, realizing that Fort Caroline had been depleted of defenders, attacked and killed everyone except the few who claimed to be Catholics. He also dispatched patrols to capture the French survivors on the beach, including Ribaut, and then methodically killed them. The area where the shipwrecked French met their end is named *Matanzas*—slaughter.

Before the end of the 16th century, English privateers and pirates began to harass St. Augustine. They were drawn to the area because Spanish treasure fleets loaded with silver and gold rode the Gulf Stream through the Straits of Florida. In the 1570s Francis Drake, an enterprising Devon seaman, operated as a successful privateer against Spanish ships and ports in the Caribbean. In 1577 Queen Elizabeth I chose Drake to lead a secret expedition against the Spanish colonies on the Pacific coast of America. That led him to become the first Englishman to circumnavigate the world, for which he was knighted by Elizabeth when he returned

FLORIDA *Time Line*

1513	1559	1564	1565
Ponce de León arrives near the site of St. Augustine and claims Florida for Spain	Spanish expedition attempts to establish colony at Pensacola but is thwarted by hurricane; two years later colony is abandoned	French Huguenots found a colony at Fort Caroline on the St. Johns River	Pedro Menéndez de Avilés establishes St. Augustine, slaughters the survivors of the French expedition against it, and takes Fort Caroline

in 1580. Five years later she commissioned him to lead a fleet against Spanish settlements in the Caribbean. In 1586 Drake descended on St. Augustine with twenty-five ships and 2,300 men to capture the fort and burn the city.

A pirate raid in 1668 and the establishment of the English settlement of Charles Town two years later convinced Queen Regent Mariana of Spain to support building an impregnable stone fort in St. Augustine. This one would replace the nine wooden forts that had proved inadequate in past battles. By 1672 the massive fort we see, Castillo de San Marcos, was in the process of construction. Its first phase was completed in 1695, but like all forts that survive, it was modified and strengthened as its defenders prepared for new attacks. Foundations were set below high-tide level of the ocean. Rafts brought hand-hewn blocks of coquina from quarries on Anastasia Island.

Sir Francis Drake was born in Devon, England, around the year 1540 and became an admiral and explorer. He inherited strong Protestant convictions from his father, and his fighting against the Spanish became a matter of conscience. In 1567 he was on board the first English slaving voyage and continued to be active in the slave trade between the Spanish colonies in the West Indies and Africa. A number of the ships were attacked by the Spanish, and Drake developed a lifelong hostility toward them. His greatest feat after his circumnavigation was an important role in defeating the Spanish Armada in 1588.

In 1702 the British governor of Carolina, James Moore, invaded by land and sea, took the town, and then surrounded the fort for a siege that lasted two months. During the siege 1,200 residents and 300 soldiers stayed within the walls of the Castillo, which simply absorbed the cannonballs fired at them rather than shattering. When Spanish warships arrived to blockade the harbor, Moore burned his eight ships rather than have them captured and marched north after setting the town on fire.

Left with a town in ashes again when they emerged, as it had been after earlier attacks, the residents were prompted to action. They built walls and redoubts

1569	1586	1668	1672
Spanish build watchtower at Matanzas inlet	Sir Francis Drake attacks and burns St. Augustine	English pirates sack St. Augustine	Construction of Castillo de San Marcos begins in St. Augustine

Coquina, a whitish lime-stone, is an amalgam of millions of years' deposit of small seashells bonded together by their lime content, sand, and water.

around the entire perimeter so that all of St. Augustine was guarded, with the fort as the keystone of defense. It too was improved, with vaulted ceilings replacing wooden roofs, higher walls, and more guns around the entire fort. In 1725 another Carolina English commander, Colonel William Palmer, set forth and arrived at the gates of St. Augustine. He could not get in but did steal cattle and made friends with Indians who formerly had supported the Spanish. As a consequence of such raids, in 1738 the Spanish established a post called Gracia Real de Santa Teresa de Mose, or Fort Mose, just above St. Augustine to strengthen defenses in the northern approaches to the city. Fort Mose soon became a refuge for slaves escaping from the Carolinas.

The British nearby gradually became stronger and more of a threat. In 1740 General James Oglethorpe led a combined force from Georgia and South Carolina to attack St. Augustine by land and sea. When the British gunboats could not get past the galleys guarding the harbor entrance, and frontal attack was thwarted, Oglethorpe began a blockade and siege. As before, English guns failed to breech the walls of the Castillo, and Governor Manuel de Montiano successfully evaded the blockade by sending a shallow-draft vessel down to the Matanzas inlet. When relief provisions from Havana got through to the fort, Oglethorpe and his force ended the twenty-seven-day siege and departed.

Alternating Control by England and Spain

In the aftermath of the worldwide Seven Years War (in North America, the French and Indian War), the British received Florida in the first Treaty of Paris (1763) because they held the ace card in negotiations—control of Havana in the midst of the Spanish West Indies. Spain ceded Florida to England in exchange for Cuba and the Philippines. The British divided Florida into two colonies, East Florida and West Florida, with St. Augustine and Pensacola as capitals, respectively. With the radical change of government, almost all the Spanish residents repaired to

FLORIDA *Time Line*

1702	1740	1742	1763	1783
Carolina Governor James Moore besieges and burns St. Augustine but does not take the Castillo	Georgia founder James Oglethorpe besieges but fails to take St. Augustine	Spanish complete Fort Matanzas	First Treaty of Paris cedes Florida to England in exchange for Cuba	Spain regains Florida by the Second Treaty of Paris

Cuba, just as Cubans would flock to south Florida for similar reasons two centuries later.

In St. Augustine the British renamed the Castillo Fort St. Mark and brought it back into repair as the American Revolution approached. The threat of attacks increased when the Florida Rangers made raids over the border into Georgia, and a number of Patriot expeditions set out to take the fort but failed. (See Historical Introduction to Georgia for details.) British rule lasted for

> ✳ A laconic history might read "The French visited, the Spanish developed, the English named, and the Americans tamed." Apart from the oversimplification, it points to a confusing past as countries grabbed and then relinquished this land.

twenty years, and the merchants turned the city into a commercial seaport. Meanwhile, the Spanish succeeded where the Americans had failed to make incursions into Florida. After Spain, following the lead of France, declared war on England in 1779, Bernardo de Gálvez, governor of Spanish Louisiana, moved through West Florida, capturing Mobile and finally Pensacola after two months of fighting.

In 1783, the second Treaty of Paris, formally ending the Revolution, gave Florida back to Spain. This time there was little shift in population, since many of the British stayed and few of the Spanish who had gone to Cuba returned. Spain controlled Florida until 1821, against the wishes of many early settlers, then ceded it to the United States.

SEMINOLES *Move In*

✳ Like the French, Spanish, and English who took turns as new arrivals on Florida terrain, the Seminole Indians were relative newcomers. Earlier the Calusa and Timucuan Indians had lived on the land, but they were virtually wiped out by the combined effects of diseases introduced by Europeans and the wars between the French, Spanish, and English. As British colonists began to spread through Georgia land, groups of Creeks migrated south into depopulated northeastern Florida and became known as Seminoles, a derivative of the Spanish word cimarron, meaning "wild and untamed." By 1740, not long after James Oglethorpe had arrived to settle Savannah, the earliest recorded Seminole town, Alachua, had developed in north Florida. During the Revolution Seminole warriors joined British regulars and Florida rangers in raids on Georgia plantations; their own settlements were not attacked or burned. After the war those settlements expanded, and the Seminoles, unlike the Creeks to the north, became more powerful because they were insulated from loss of land to white settlers under both British and Spanish rule. Their battle against American expansionism was delayed well into the 19th century, when the first of three Seminole wars erupted in 1816.

Regions *to* Explore

NORTHEASTERN COAST
PANHANDLE

NORTHEASTERN COAST

The coastal region north of Jacksonville and the St. Johns River marks a geographical transition between Georgia's maze of Sea Islands and the long, narrow barrier islands that characterize the rest of Florida's Atlantic coast. Historically it was also a border region between English and Spanish dominions on North America's east coast.

AMELIA ISLAND / FERNANDINA BEACH

Amelia Island is the northernmost barrier island on Florida's Atlantic coast. The Spanish established an early mission here, which the British destroyed in 1702. In 1735 James Oglethorpe occupied the island and named it for the daughter of Britain's King George II, but it was returned to the Spanish in 1748. Amelia Island is the only territory in the country to have been under eight flags altogether, five of them within the period covered by this book: France (1562), Spain (1565), Great Britain (1763), Spain again (1783), and the Republic of Florida (1812). The last was characterized by a series of short-lived occupations by American and Spanish soldiers, adventurers, and rebel groups until Spain sold Florida to the United States in 1819; Florida became a U.S. territory in 1821. Throughout this era two American presidents, Madison and Monroe, were secretly or openly involved because Fernandina, on the border between loosely held Spanish territory and American Georgia, had become a haven for smugglers and pirates.

Don't miss the statue on the street of Copper Jack Aury, who lived from 1790 to 1830. The plaque says that he was the "bloodthirstiest, black-heartedest" pirate anywhere. He got his name from his fiery red beard. Jack died in 1830 "on the *Wagon*," which was the name of a schooner—he fell off.

The **Amelia Island Museum of History** (904-261-7378; www.amelia museum.org), 233 S. Third St., Fernandina Beach. Open daily. The museum is in Nassau County's former jailhouse. You can learn about the early history of the island and how the flags of eight nations flew over the harbor. The museum has prints of early French colonist and artist Jacques Le Moyne, who captured on canvas the Indians of the area. Digs have taken place at the 1683 Spanish-era Dorian Mission, and some of the pottery and other artifacts are on display.

Maria Mattair Fernandez watched the unusual history of Fernandina unfold from the days when it was controlled by the British, through Spanish occupation, until Florida became the 27th state in 1845. Maria watched English colonists leave the harbor after Florida was returned to Spain in 1783. She married Domingo Fernandez, a Spanish gunboat captain, on her 16th birthday. Two months later it became apparent that France had declared war on Spain, so the island was completely evacuated; everything was burned so that the French would not get it. Later Maria and Domingo returned, rebuilt, and added more land to their holdings. She watched while a group of Americans tried to win the land for the United States under the Patriots' flag in 1812, then, in an increasingly wild series of events, as a Scottish soldier of fortune briefly held sway under the Green Cross of Florida in 1817, and once again as two Americans—one a former Pennsylvania congressman—and a French pirate interceded, the latter under a Mexican rebel flag. The town had been laid out in 1811 and named for King Ferdinand VII of Spain. After Maria Fernandez died in 1846, her land became part of the foundation for the town of Fernandina Beach.

LODGING

AMELIA ISLAND PLANTATION

SR A1A, Box 3000, Fernandina Beach, FL 32035
888-261-6161; www.aipfl.com
This waterfront inn is landscaped with large trees and plants. There are 650 guest rooms, and villas are also available.

ELIZABETH POINTE LODGE

FL A1A, 98 S. Fletcher Ave., Fernandina Beach, FL 32034
800-772-3359, 904-277-4851;
www.elizabethpointelodge.com
This New England–style inn is decorated with a nautical theme. Enjoy the rocking chairs on the porch. Twenty-five guest rooms.

INFORMATION

AMELIA ISLAND TOURIST DEVELOPMENT COUNCIL

102 Center St., Amelia Island, FL 32034
800-226-3542; www.ameliaisland.org

AMELIA ISLAND CHAMBER OF COMMERCE

Gateway Blvd., Amelia Island, FL 32034
866-576-7050, 904-261-3248;
www.islandchamber.com

JACKSONVILLE

European settlement of the area began in 1564 when French Huguenots founded a colony on the St. Johns River and called it Fort Caroline. However, the Spanish, asserting a prior claim to the territory, annihilated the French outpost the following year. Nearly a century later, in 1763, Spain traded Florida to England for Cuba. After the King's Road reaching south from Savannah was completed, another settlement sprang up on the St. Johns River, but development was delayed by further changes. In 1783 the second Treaty of Paris proclaimed that Florida would again be Spanish. Jacksonville did not get its present name (honoring Andrew Jackson) until after 1821, when Florida became a territory of the United States.

HISTORICAL SITES *and* MUSEUMS

Fort Caroline (9904-641-7155; www.nps.gov), 12713 Fort Caroline Rd. Open daily. France was eager to stake a permanent claim in America, and the site chosen was near the mouth of the St. Johns River, which the French called the River of May. In April 1564 Admiral Gaspard de Coligny sent René de Goulaine de Laudonnière, who had been with Jean Ribaut on an earlier expedition to the area, with three ships and about 300 colonists to found La Caroline, named after French king Charles IX. A fort was in progress, but by the following year relationships with the Indians had soured, supplies had run out, and the colonists were about to leave when Ribaut arrived with supplies and hundreds more soldiers and settlers.

The French were still not out of trouble, however, as they soon faced a Spanish naval attack led by General Pedro Menéndez de Avilés. The French foiled the initial attack, whereupon the daring Ribaut, leaving Laudonnière behind at Fort Caroline with a small force, sailed most of his troops south to attack St. Augustine in turn. A hurricane proved his undoing, however, stranding and wrecking his fleet along the coast. Menéndez, learning of Ribaut's misfortune, quickly sent an army back north, overland, which attacked the poorly defended French fort and massacred 140 settlers. Only Laudonnière and a small group escaped. Ribaut and his shipwrecked and now defenseless survivors were soon rounded up and put to the sword by the Spanish. Fort Caroline was burned, then rebuilt, but abandoned in 1569.

Although the exact site of the fort is not known, the exhibit was planned on the basis of 16th-century sketches by Jacques Le Moyne. Take a look at the exhibits in the visitor center for your orientation, then walk down to the water for a fine view. Walk along the shore, following placards with sketches and explanation, to the replica fort with its flag flying.

The visitor center also has exhibits that tell the story of the St. Johns River estuary. Salt and freshwater meet and create a rich environment that may be among the most productive in the world. The tidal range of 5½ feet every six hours provides a rich habitat for all sorts of life.

You can walk or drive from the Fort Caroline visitor center to the Spanish Pond area. There the landscape is freshwater wetland with characteristic vegetation and wildlife. It may have been the site where Spanish soldiers camped the night before they attacked Fort Caroline in 1565.

The Timucuan Ecological and Historic Preserve exhibits are located at the Fort Caroline visitor center, and the preserve is a large area surrounding Fort Caroline. The Timucuan Indians collected shellfish, fished, hunted, and planted maize, squash, and beans. They lived in circular houses with conical palm-thatched roofs. When the French began to settle here, the Timucuans shared food and helped them build a village and a fort. French colonist Jacques Le Moyne sketched Timucuan ceremonies and customs. A replica of the stone column erected by Jean Ribaut stands on St. Johns Bluff.

Kingsley Plantation (904-251-3537) is part of the Timucuan Ecological and Historic Preserve. Zephaniah Kingsley arrived at Fort George Island in 1814. He brought his wife, Anna Madgigine Jai, whom he originally bought as a slave, and their three children. She was freed by Kingsley and received her own land at that time.

The plantation produced sea-island cotton, citrus fruit, sugarcane, and corn. Kingsley bought more property and eventually owned more than 32,000 acres on four plantations. The plantation house may date to 1798. It has a two-story central area with four square corner rooms. The kitchen house is in a separate building, designed to keep any fire from spreading to the main house. The garden has cotton growing. Although only ruins of 23 slave cabins remain, one of the cabins has been restored.

ST. AUGUSTINE

St. Augustine is the main destination for those interested in colonial sites in Florida, both for its long history and its well-preserved fortifications, unique for U.S. cities. **Old Town Trolley Tours of St. Augustine,** (904-829-3800), 167 San Marco Ave., offers on-and-off trolleys so visitors can stop and look at a site in detail, then climb aboard again to continue the tour. Our host advised us to ride completely around the trolley route once to catch a glimpse of sites we might want to visit later. We did and then returned to learn more.

HISTORICAL SITES *and* MUSEUMS
The trolley passed the 1808 city gates and the 200-plus-year-old **Oldest Wooden Schoolhouse** (800-OLD-SCHL, 904-824-0192; www.oldestwoodenschoolhouse .com), 14 St. George St. Inside, models depict the members of the last class in 1864 with their teacher. Look on the wall for a 1931 photo of the same members attending a reunion. Displays include 1872 Rules for Teachers (they couldn't do much and still remain in their posts), a letter beginning "Dear Teacher," slate and chalk, a Sixth Reader, and a book of farm ballads.

Our tour continued along Avenida Menéndez to the **Bridge of Lions**, turning right at the statue of Ponce de León. The **Basilica-Cathedral of St. Augustine** (904-824-2806) dates from the 1790s. Across the street stands **Government House** (904-825-5033; www.historicstaugustine.com), 48 King St. Open daily. An exhibit demonstrates the process of archaeological excavation, which is ongoing in the city. Artifacts are displayed inside the museum and include a collection of incised pots from 1000 AD, bullets, buckles, pipe stems, stoneware, and more.

A "History Puzzle" asks visitors to match what people used with the items by moving the artifacts around. There's a rack of clothes from the 1700s to try on. One room displays a wall containing objects found in a trash pit from 1580, a well shaft containing trash from 1760, an oyster-shell footing from 1720, and a 1720 coquina wall.

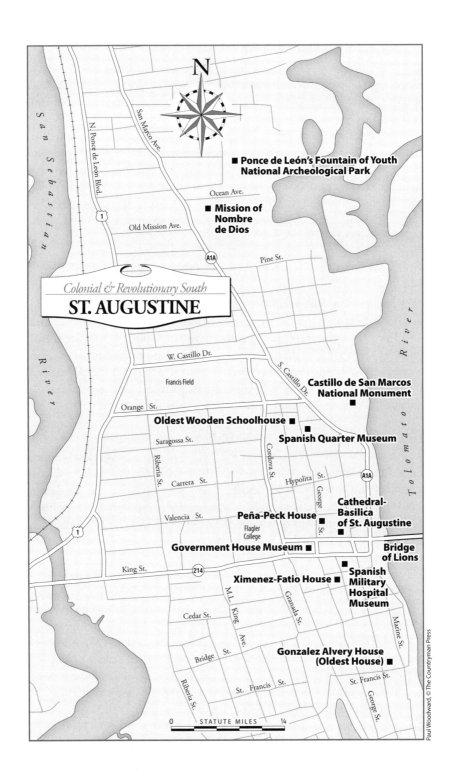

N

Ponce de León's Fountain of Youth
National Archeological Park

Ocean Ave.

Mission of
Nombre
de Dios

Old Mission Ave.

A1A   Pine St.

Colonial & Revolutionary South
ST. AUGUSTINE

W. Castillo Dr.

Francis Field

S. Castillo Dr.

Castillo de San Marcos
National Monument

Orange   St.

Oldest Wooden Schoolhouse ■

Saragossa St.

Spanish Quarter Museum ■

Riberia St.

Cordova St.

Carrera   St.

Hypolita   St.   A1A

Valencia   St.

Peña-Peck House ■

George St.

Cathedral-
Basilica
of St. Augustine

Flagler
College

Government House Museum ■

Bridge
of Lions

King St.   214

Ximenez-Fatio House ■

Spanish
Military
Hospital
Museum

Cedar St.

M.L. King Ave.

Granada St.

Marine St.

Bridge   St.

Gonzalez Alvery House
(Oldest House) ■

Riberia St.

St. Francis   St.

St. Francis St.

George St.

San Marco Ave.

N. Ponce de Leon Blvd.

San Sebastian River

Tolomato River

0   STATUTE MILES   ¼

Paul Woodward, © The Countryman Press

On guard at the Castillo de San Marcos in St. Augustine

The **Peña-Peck House** (904-829-5064; www.staugustinewomans-ex change.com/house), 143 St. George St., dates from the 1740s. Open Mon.–Sat. It was built of native coquina stone. Royal treasurer Juan Esteban de Pena lived here, and Dr. Seth Peck bought the house in 1834. Peck family furnishings are from the 18th century.

The **Gonzalez-Alvarez House** (904-824-2872; www.oldesthouse.org), 14 St. Francis St., is also the home of the St. Augustine Historical Society. It is known as the "Oldest House," and someone has lived on the site since the early 1600s. Its first occupants were the family of Tomas Gonzalez, an artilleryman at the Castillo; its second owner, Major Joseph Peavett, was a retired English officer who lived there during the British period; its third owner was his widow, Mary, who remarried John Hudson, "a young Irish adventurer" noted as both a gambler and a spendthrift. They had to auction the house in 1790 to pay his debts. The house is mentioned in Eugenia Price's book *Maria,* which refers to Maria Peavett. Visitors will find the living room on the second story, a typical Spanish custom.

The **Castillo de San Marcos** (904-829-6506; www.nps.gov/casa), 1 S. Castillo Dr. The nation's oldest stone fort was in the process of construction by 1672 but was not in its final configuration until 1695. It is a hollow-centered square with bombproof storerooms around the edge and diamond-shaped bastions at each corner. There is only one way into the fort, through the triangular-shaped ravelin,

A portcullis is a grating designed to close the entrance of a fort. It may be rolled across the entrance or lowered from above.

complete with a portcullis. Pirates and Indians still harassed the settlers, and sometimes everyone huddled together inside the fort even before it was complete.

Inside the fort, a diorama explains the 1740 battle when General James Oglethorpe's British troops arrived from Fort Frederica in Georgia. The fort stood strong during a 27-day siege. There are soldiers' quarters set up for guard duty, a chapel for Indians to visit, and a prison. The storage rooms once contained gunpowder, ammunition, weapons, lumber, tools, and food. Walk up the stairs to the bastions for a view of Matanzas Bay and the cannon spread along the parapets.

Nombre de Dios (904-824-2809; www.missionandshrine.org), San Marco Ave., is the site where Pedro Menéndez de Avilés landed in 1565. It is also the site of the first mission and the Shrine of Our Lady of La Leche. Walk by the Father Lopez Statue, larger than life-size; the Great Cross, which is 208 feet tall; the Shrine of St. Francis; and the Mission Chapel.

The **Fountain of Youth** (800-356-8222, 904-829-3168; www.fountainof youthflorida.com), at 155 Magnolia Ave., is said to be the one found by Ponce de León in 1513. Today visitors are invited to have a drink from the spring. A diorama depicts Ponce de León being welcomed by the Indians. Walk around the grounds to see artifacts from the remains of Christian Indian burials and archaeological exhibits.

The **Spanish Quarter Museum**, in Old St. Augustine (904-825-6830; www.his toricstaugustine.com), 53 St. George St., is a colonial village brought alive by docents in costume who demonstrate their skills at weaving, blacksmithing, sailmaking, carpentry, cooking, and gardening. This living history museum will take visitors back to the 1740s when Spanish soldiers, settlers, and their families lived here.

Take a walk around the Spanish Quarter, beginning with the **Maria Triay House,** which dates from the Minorcan families who came to the New World during the late 18th century. Inside, visitors can explore the orientation center and look at artifacts found on the property.

Next door, the **Lorenzo Gomez House** is small and belonged to a foot soldier. Take a look at the shop inside, which was the place to buy goods or to barter them for work. Martin Martinez Gallegos lived with his family in the next house, which is larger than the Gomez house because Martinez was an artillery sergeant and earned more.

Mike Wells, who welcomed us, was in the blacksmith shop. He was the third-generation blacksmith in a family that has practiced the occupation for 200 years. He explained that blacksmith guilds required an apprentice to work for five years,

Blacksmith at the Spanish Quarter Museum, St. Augustine

then four as a journeyman. To become a master blacksmith he needed to produce a product judged worthy and to have worked in the trade for 20 years. Most master blacksmiths were 40 or 50 years old before achieving this status.

We watched a docent in the **Bernardo Gonzales House** explaining the process of spinning, dying yarn from natural growing plants, and finally weaving it into garments and household fabrics. In the next house, Geronimo de Hita y Salazar lived with his family; all children in the house were expected to work for the family. Today school groups can become involved in hands-on activities.

Antonio de Mesa built part of the next house around 1763; later Juan Sanchez added to the house to make it a two-story building. The home is furnished as it would have been for a St. Augustine family in comfortable circumstances during the period from 1821 to 1845.

The next house was really a duplex built by José Peso de Burgo, from Corsica, and Francisco Pellicer, from Minorca. De Burgo was a merchant and Pellicer a carpenter.

The **Spanish Military Hospital Museum** (800-597-7177; www.spanish militaryhospital.com), 3 Aviles St., depicts hospital life in 1791. Although the building dates from the 1760s during the British occupation, the Spanish returned in 1784 and made it a hospital. Each room tells a story of hospital life. When a patient was about to die he was placed in the mourning room. A bell rang when the patient arrived, and a priest sat with him until he died, administering last rites and taking a final confession. A candle was lit to guide the soul into heaven.

The Surgeon's Office contains instruments used in operations. They were performed without anesthetic. Each patient was taken to the ward room after surgery and given his own bed. Patients were bathed and shaved daily, unlike the soldiers out in the field. Medications were kept in the apothecary. Herbs were grown in the garden, dried, and then crumbled and used to make medications.

Ximenez-Fatio House (904-839-3575; www.ximenezfatiohouse.org), 20 Aviles St. This former merchant's house dates to 1783. It was operated as an inn during the Territorial period (1821–61) and has been restored to that era.

Fort Matanzas (904-471-0116; www.nps.gov/foma), 8635 Hwy. A1A South. This site south of St. Augustine near the shallow inlet of the Matanzas River has a bloody history. In September of 1565, when the Spanish general Pedro Menéndez de Avilés learned that a group of Frenchmen, survivors from the wrecked ships of Jean Ribaut, were stranded on the beach south of St. Augustine, unable to cross the inlet, Menéndez marched south with 70 soldiers, captured the Frenchmen, and began a methodical massacre of his political and religious enemies. (See Jacksonville section, above.) The Spanish took 10 Frenchmen at a time across the inlet and began marching them to St. Augustine as prisoners. Then, at a prearranged site, soldiers fell on them with sword and pike. Only 16 were spared, and two weeks later more Frenchmen met the same fate, with only 12 musicians and four Catholics surviving. The inlet was then called Matanzas, the Spanish word for slaughter.

Fort Matanzas, south of St. Augustine

A watchtower and a thatched hut were built at Matanzas in 1569. Six soldiers were stationed there, and when a ship appeared on the horizon they set off to warn St. Augustine.

A small fort was built in 1743, after Oglethorpe's attack, to protect St. Augustine against further incursions from the south by the British or by pirates. It stands 50 feet on each side, with a 30-foot tower. The men assigned to live there for a one-month tour of duty included an officer, four infantrymen, and two gunners. They could bring five guns to bear on the inlet, and loopholes in the south wall of the tower allowed them to fire their muskets from inside the fort.

The Treaty of Paris in 1763 awarded Britain Fort Matanzas, which was still important in defending St. Augustine. The British remained there through the American Revolution. The second Treaty of Paris in 1783 gave Florida back to Spain. In 1819 Florida became the property of the United States with the Adams-Onís Treaty. Fort Matanzas was taken over by the United States in 1821, but it was on the way to ruin. You can see a film on the fort and the history of the area in the visitor center.

Fort Mose (904-461-2033; www.floridastateparks.org), Saratoga Blvd. Although trafficking in African slaves was widespread throughout the New World colonies of Spain as well as those of Britain, Spanish Florida had somewhat more liberal policies that gave slaves certain rights, including liberation if they converted to Catholicism and agreed to serve in a militia to defend the colony. In addition, free blacks who had come with the Spanish colonists to work formed a community that welcomed fugitives, and the first group arrived at what would become Fort Mose as early as 1687.

As slavery increased rapidly in the early decades of the 18th century to provide labor for the booming plantations in the Carolinas and Virginia, the number of fugitives who reached the protection of St. Augustine grew. Many, like Francisco Menendez, risked their lives to escape. He was born in Africa, enslaved early in the century, made the journey to St. Augustine in 1724, and was granted freedom for conversion and military service. He rose to the rank of captain in the St. Augustine militia, and when Governor Montiano chartered the fortified settlement of Gracia Real de Santa Teresa de Mose—Fort Mose—in 1738, Menendez became its commander.

By that time more than 100 fugitives were on hand, and the town included 38 households, the first black community in America. The first fort was small, with a watchtower, guardhouse, and log walls reinforced with an earthen berm. A ditch outside slowed down invaders with its "prickly palmetto royal" plants.

In 1739 war was declared between Spain and Britain. As Oglethorpe approached with a large expedition in 1740, the inhabitants of Fort Mose were evacuated to St. Augustine. British troops camped at the abandoned fort, and Spanish soldiers, including the black militia, attacked and recaptured it.

With the first fort in ruins after the campaign, the defenders built a new fort and town to the northeast of the original site. There were 22 homes for black families. They lived there until 1763, when Florida was ceded to Britain by treaty. Not wanting to remain under the thumb of more restrictive British laws and policies on slavery, the blacks migrated to Cuba.

Today the area is an island in the saltwater marsh that harbors many birds, including eagles. A boardwalk takes you to the site of the fort. In the future there will be a visitor center and exhibits to tell the story of Fort Mose.

LODGING

CASA DE SOLANA BED & BREAKFAST
21 Aviles St., St. Augustine, FL 32084
888-796-0980, 904-824-3555;
www.casadesolana.com
This historic inn in the Old City is set in tropical gardens and a walled courtyard. Ten guest rooms.

CASA MONICA HOTEL
95 Cordova St., St. Augustine, FL 32084
800-648-1888, 904-827-1888;
www.casamonica.com
Dating from 1888, Casa Monica is the landmark hotel of the historic district. It has 138 guest rooms.

CEDAR HOUSE INN
79 Cedar St., St. Augustine, FL 32084
800-845-0012, 904-829-0079;
www.cedarhouseinn.com
This Victorian bed & breakfast inn is located in the historic district. Seven guest rooms.

KENWOOD INN
38 Marine St., St. Augustine, FL 32084
800-824-8151, 904-824-2116;
www.thekenwoodinn.com
This Victorian bed & breakfast in the historic district near the waterfront dates from 1865. It has fourteen guest rooms.

ST. FRANCIS INN
279 St. George St., St. Augustine, FL
32084
800-824-6062, 904-824-6068;
www.stfrancisinn.com
This bed & breakfast inn occupies a building constructed in 1791 of coquina limestone. It faces a courtyard and garden. Seventeen guest rooms.

RESTAURANTS

COLUMBIA RESTAURANT
98 St. George St.
800-227-1905
This Old World–style restaurant serves Spanish-Cuban cuisine.

NINETY-FIVE CORDOVA
95 Cordova St.
904-810-6810
Located in the Casa Monica Hotel. Salmon is a specialty.

OLD CITY HOUSE RESTAURANT
115 Cordova St.
904-826-0184
Located in the Spanish historic district. Ostrich is a specialty.

EVENTS

March: Spanish Nightwatch and Torchlight March, 904-825-1004
June: Drake's Raid, 904-829-9792
November: British Garrison Weekend at the Castillo de San Marcos, 904-829-6506
November–January: Nights of Lights (colonists placed a white candle in their windows), 800-653-2489

INFORMATION

ST. AUGUSTINE, PONTE VEDRA, AND THE BEACHES VISITORS AND CONVENTION BUREAU
88 Riberia St., Suite 400, St. Augustine, FL 32084
800-653-2489, 904-829-1711; www.getaway4florida.com

PANHANDLE

The term "panhandle," a homely cookware image for the narrow strip of coastal Florida between the Alabama boot-heel and the capital region surrounding Tallahassee, has stuck. Framed by the Gulf of Mexico to the south and Alabama and Georgia to the north, the Panhandle has a split personality. Along its shores it seems related to peninsular Florida, with once-deserted spectacular white-sand beaches sprouting condos and second homes at their edge, interspersed with harbors filled with both shrimp boats and pleasure craft. Inland, it seems more closely aligned with the Deep South, where there are fewer visitors in a diversified agricultural world once filled with little but cotton plantations. The western section contains a number of military bases as well as the city of Pensacola, which has deep roots in the colonial era and was a prize sought after during the Revolution. At the Panhandle's eastern edge stands the city of Tallahassee, a political and cultural center established as the state capital in 1824 at a midway point between St. Augustine and Pensacola, then the two major cities in Florida.

PENSACOLA

Six years before Pedro Menéndez de Avilés established a base at St. Augustine, Pensacola's shores saw the first attempt at major settlement. Several Spanish explorers had already visited the area, including Ponce de León as early as 1513. In 1559, the viceroy of New Spain, Luis de Velasco, dispatched veteran conquistador Tristán de Luna y Arellano with an armada of eleven ships to found a settlement. On board were 540 soldiers, more than 1,000 settlers and servants, 4 Dominican priests, and some Mexican Indians, as well as 240 horses, arms, tools, and food for eighty days. The armada anchored in Pensacola Bay on August 15 and sent out scouting parties. De Luna bided his time, but delay proved fateful. A hurricane struck on September 19, destroying all but three of the ships, many lives, and a substantial portion of their supplies that had not yet been brought ashore. After the illness and replacement of the governor, partial starvation, and incipient mutiny, the settlement was abandoned two years later. Just as a hurricane destroyed French attempts to colonize northeastern Florida, this one kept Pensacola from becoming the first permanent settlement in North America.

The Spanish did not return to the area for nearly four decades, but the bay's strategic location in the center of the Gulf of Mexico was too important to be ignored. They returned to found Pensacola in 1698, naming it for the Panzacola Indians. This time another Spanish explorer, Admiral Andres de Arriolla, brought both slaves and free persons of African descent who built Fort San Carlos de Austria. (A dig is in process under the supervision of the Archaeological Institute at the University of West Florida.)

The natural deepwater harbor with a barrier island to shield it provided protection for both military forces and shipping. By 1743 the first commercial export cargo sailed out with pine and pitch products, wooden masts, and other spars for sailing vessels. Fort San Miguel was built in 1752 and later enlarged by the British several times after they were ceded Florida by the Treaty of Paris in 1763. (Today the parade grounds on either side of the fort exist as Plaza Ferdinand and Seville Square.)

When Spain followed France's lead and declared war on England in 1779, the able and aggressive governor of Louisiana, Bernardo Gálvez y Gallardo, immediately began successful campaigns against Mississippi ports and moved eastward along the Gulf Coast. In 1781 Gálvez landed with his troops on Santa Rosa Island. When a hurricane struck, the Spanish took their ships out to sea to ride it out and then returned to Red Cliffs near Pensacola. Gálvez was lucky because the British guns on Red Cliffs could not be lowered enough to hit ships in front of them. Gálvez struck the Fort Half Moon powder magazine and then took prisoners.

To finish his campaign, Gálvez was clever in building a tunnel and moving his cannon through it to bombard Fort George at close range. The British general surrendered, and Gálvez allowed the soldiers to leave with their families and possessions. The Spanish had regained control of Florida.

HISTORICAL SITES *and* MUSEUMS

Historic Pensacola Village (850-595-5985; www.historicpensacola.org), 205 E. Zaragoza St. Open daily except Sun. The village of 10 museum buildings offers a glimpse into 450 years of life in Pensacola.

The **Charles Lavalle House**, 205 E. Church St., dates from 1805. It is an example of French Creole colonial architecture. Charles Lavalle and Marianna Bonifay built the house together. She was separated from her military husband and had six children to support, so she wanted to rent to new residents of Pensacola. Lavalle provided the labor on the house, and they owned it jointly. They continued to buy land, construct buildings, and then rent and sell them—a very profitable enterprise. The house is furnished with pieces from around the 1820s. We noted bowls under the table legs as a pest deterrent, also a rat trap. A hanging *panetière* (bread cupboard) was used to keep bread away from rodents. The floor cloth was made of sailcloth decorated in a diamond pattern. A phoebe lamp is pear shaped, with a pan for oil or grease and a spout for the wick to lie in. A four-poster bed stands in the bedroom. The armoire was made of cypress, and clothes were

The Lavalle House at Historic Pensacola Village

folded and placed on shelves. Outside, the well dates from 1770; it was made of ballast rock and local red sandstone.

Tivoli High House was once a dance hall and saloon. The Julee Cottage dates from 1805, when Julee Panton, a free woman of color, lived there. It is now a Black History Museum.

The **T. T. Wentworth Jr. Museum** (850-595-5985; www.historicpensacola.org), 330 S. Jefferson St., was once City Hall. It is filled with artifacts, photographs, and a hands-on discovery gallery for children. We were fascinated by the "An Anchor to the Past" exhibit on the 1559 *Luna* expedition. Artifacts include a cannonball, buckle, coins, arquebus balls, leather shoe soles, and glazed ceramics.

A Colonial Archaeological Trail (850-474-3015; www.stmichaelscemetery.org) traces evidence of forts and buildings between 1752 and 1821. During that time Spanish, British, and American soldiers lived there. The trail includes archaeology exhibits in the T. T. Wentworth Museum, an officers' room and kitchen, a commanding officer's compound, a well, the British Government House, a garrison kitchen, Fort George, and St. Michael's Cemetery.

LODGING

PENSACOLA VICTORIAN BED AND BREAKFAST
203 W. Gregory St., Pensacola, FL 32501
800-370-8354, 850-434-2818;
www.pensacolavictorian.com
The Queen Anne Victorian was once home to Captain William Hazard Northup. There are rockers on the porch. Four guest rooms.

RESTAURANTS

BONEFISH GRILL
5025 N. 12th Ave.
850-471-2324
Fish is a specialty, including Gulf grouper.

JACKSON'S
400 S. Palafox Place
850-469-9898
This historic downtown restaurant offers prime meats and seafood.

INFORMATION

PENSACOLA BAY AREA CONVENTION & VISITORS CENTER
1401 E. Gregory St., Pensacola, FL 32502
800-874-1234, 850-434-1234;
www.visitpensacola.com

Current Information

VISIT FLORIDA INC.
(Mailing: Box 1100)
126 W. Van Buren St.
Tallahassee, FL 32302-1100
888-735-2872; www.visitflorida.com

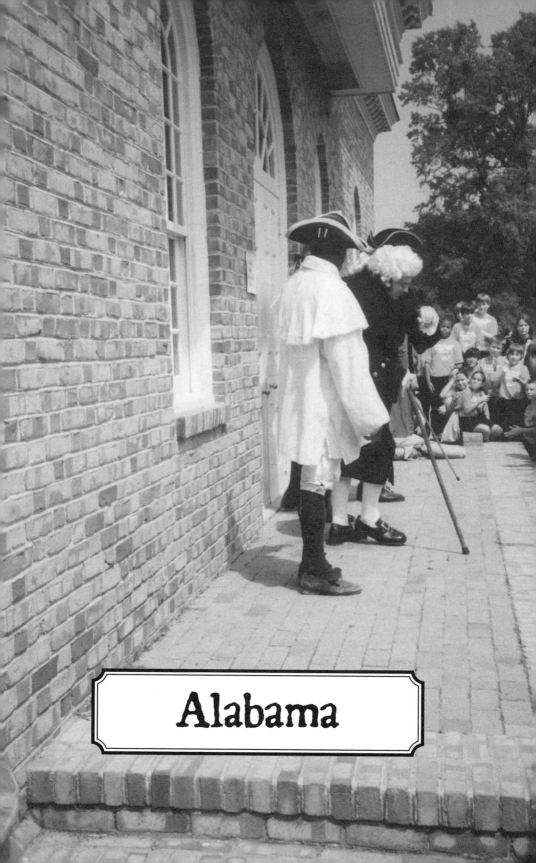

Alabama

Historical Introduction
to
Alabama

In the early 16th century, Spanish interest in southeastern North America was still driven by two elusive ambitions: discovering a water passage through the continent to the Orient, and finding more gold to increase their wealth. To pursue the first goal, the governor of Jamaica, Francisco de Garay, who had sailed on Columbus's second voyage, sent Alonso Álvarez de Pineda to explore rivers along the Gulf Coast. During a nine-month expedition Álvarez mapped 800 miles of shoreline. He found a large river, probably the Mississippi, and named it Bahia de Spiritu Santo. Some historians suggest that he also explored Mobile Bay. His report and map were sent to Governor Garay and then on to King Charles I of Spain. This information probably encouraged colonization along the Gulf Coast.

Hernando de Soto was also looking for an easy way to China, but his passion was finding gold. With the approval of Charles V, who had appointed him governor of Cuba, de Soto set out boldly with more than 600 men to explore the interior in May of 1539. Landing near Tampa Bay, he pushed northward through Florida, crossed Georgia to Savannah, and continued through South Carolina into the mountain territory of the Cherokees. In 1540 De Soto turned southward through Alabama and met Tuskaloosa, a powerful Choctaw chief, and exchanged gifts with him. But Tuskaloosa had apparently heard of the depredations of de Soto's men, and thousands of Indians attacked the expedition at the Indian town of Mabila (north of Mobile Bay). Dozens of Spaniards were killed or mortally wounded, but the Indian force was virtually annihilated in a long, bloody battle. Many committed suicide.

De Soto died of a fever on the shores of the Mississippi in what is now Arkansas in May 1542.

Overleaf: Reenactors at the American Village, Montevallo

After the failure of the Tristán de Luna y Arellano expedition to establish a permanent colony along the Gulf Coast of Florida in 1559–61, Spanish attempts to settle in the area of present-day Alabama stopped for nearly a century and a half. During that interval, Mississippian Indian groups began to coalesce into various tribes that would control Alabama terrain in the 17th and 18th centuries—Cherokees, Choctaws, Chickasaws, and especially Creeks. When the Le Moyne brothers arrived in 1702 to establish a French settlement on the Mobile River, they worked to create friendly relations with tribes in the Creek Confederacy and by 1717 had established Fort Toulouse at the junction of the Coosa and Tallapoosa Rivers near present-day Montgomery. Its purpose was both to promote trade with the Creeks and to buffer the colony from interference by British westward expansion from the Atlantic coast. Women were brought in from France to marry the colonists, and slavery was institutionalized by the French Code Noir. After Mobile moved downriver to the edge of Mobile Bay, where it became an important port, the colony grew and prospered throughout the first half of the century.

Then the French and Indian War began displacements that would put the city under a series of different flags until the War of 1812. In this game of European chess, the French lost the colony to Britain by the first Treaty of Paris in 1763. When Spain declared war on Britain late in the American Revolution, Louisiana governor Bernardo de Gálvez besieged and captured key forts on the Mississippi and ports along the Gulf Coast, including Mobile in 1780, and the second Treaty of Paris confirmed that possession three years later. When Spain became allied with Britain during the War of 1812, General James Wilkerson captured Mobile for the United States.

Farther inland, in the two decades between 1795 and 1814 the land that would constitute the bulk of Alabama saw a gradual incursion of settlers into Indian territory. At the outset, the Treaty of San Lorenzo had defined the boundary between Spanish and U.S. lands at the thirty-first parallel and declared the land north of it as belonging to the Indians who lived there. But white squatters began moving in as the boundary was being surveyed, and by 1800 an Alabama county had been carved out of what was then the undivided Mississippi Territory. Through the first decade of the 19th century, a series of treaties with Indians gradually carved out more land for white settlement, culminating in the Treaty of Fort Jackson in 1814 after Andrew Jackson's defeat of the warring Creeks at the Battle of Horseshoe Bend.

Regions *to* Explore

GULF COAST
CENTRAL ALABAMA

GULF COAST

Squeezed between the unbroken fine sand beaches of Mississippi and the Florida panhandle, Alabama's brief coastline might seem insignificant, but a single feature made it as important historically as any site of the Gulf Coast: Mobile Bay. At the head of this expansive, protected stretch of water lies one of the finest deepwater ports in the South and the gracious city that grew around it.

ALABAMA *Time Line*

1519	1540	1559
Alonzo Álvarez de Pineda of Spain explores Mobile Bay	Hernando de Soto expedition clashes with warriors of chief Tuskaloosa at the Indian town of Mabila between Mobile and Thomasville	Tristán de Luna y Arellano fails to establish a permanent Spanish colony on the Alabama-Florida coast

MOBILE

In 1702 French Canadian brothers Pierre Le Moyne, Sieur d'Iberville, and Jean Baptiste Le Moyne, Sieur de Bienville, founded a fortified village that became known as Mobile, from the Indian name Mabila. Fort Louis de la Louisiane, as it was then known, was on a bluff 27 miles up the Mobile River from Mobile Bay. In 1711, after floods and outbreaks of fever, the settlement was moved downriver to a site at the mouth of the Mobile River. Mobile was the capital of the French province of Louisiana until 1720, when the capital was moved to Biloxi. Two years later the capital was moved to New Orleans.

In 1721, some 100 slaves arrived on the *Africane*. In 1724 slavery was institutionalized in the Mobile area by the French Code Noir, which included the French West Indies as well as American colonies.

With the 1763 treaty ending the French and Indian War, Mobile became part of the British colony of West Florida. At the beginning of the American Revolution, the townspeople were Tories; they feared the Spanish and were bound to Britain by trade. When Spain entered the war against Britain, the activist Spanish governor of Louisiana, Bernardo de Gálvez, mounted a military expedition and seized the city from the British.

Throughout the tangled history of French, British, and Spanish attempts to dominate the Gulf Coast, Mobile remained a focal point. And that military history did not stop with statehood, because the strategic importance of Mobile Bay remained through the Civil War and into the wars of the 20th century.

> By 1704 "cassette girls," recruited from Catholic charitable organizations, had begun to arrive in Mobile. King Louis XIV agreed to pay for the dowries and transportation from France on the *Pélican* for 25 women to marry colonists. The women carried their belongings in little caskets, or cassettes. The first African slaves also arrived at this time. More cassette girls arrived in 1728.

1702
Le Moyne brothers, Iberville and Bienville, establish French settlement known as Mobile (from the Indian *Mabila*) and Fort Louis de la Louisiane, 27 miles upriver from present-day Mobile

1704
"Cassette girls" arrive to become wives of colonists

1711
Mobile colony moves south to the mouth of the Mobile River

HISTORICAL SITES *and* MUSEUMS

Fort Condé Museum (251-208-7569; www.museumofmobile.com), 150 S. Royal St., Mobile, AL 36602. Open daily. Cover your ears if you are nearby when the colonial-dressed soldier fires the cannon at Fort Condé. This replica 1720s French fort has a visitor center with interactive video highlights of attractions and events.

France, Britain, Spain, and the United States have flown their flags over this fort, called Fort Louis, Fort Condé, and Fort Charlotte at different times. The fort provided protection against Indians as well as against attacks by sea from rival powers. The first French fort was built with 14-inch-square cedar stakes that were pointed at the top. A new star-shaped brick fort arose inside the wooden stockade beginning in 1724. By 1740 the fort was finished and housed the naval cannon necessary for defense.

Remnants of three centuries of military history in Mobile are on display. Dioramas depict the construction of the fort by the French, occupation by the British, then siege and occupation by the Spanish.

LODGING

RADISSON ADMIRAL SEMMES HOTEL
251 Government St., Mobile, AL 36602
800-333-3333 or 251-432-8000;
www.radisson.com/mobileal
This downtown hotel dates from 1940. Oriental carpets in the lobby lead to an opulent stairway. There are 170 guest rooms.

RESTAURANTS

ORIGINAL OYSTER HOUSE
3733 Battleship Pkwy.
252-626-2188;
www.originaloysterhouse.com
Located on the Causeway overlooking Mobile Bay, this restaurant has specialized in seafood since 1985.

THE PILLARS
1757 Government St.
251-471-3411;
www.thepillarsmobile.com
Located downtown in a restored 1904 mansion, the Pillars is known for its fresh seafood, steak, and Maine lobster.

INFORMATION

MOBILE BAY CONVENTION & VISITORS BUREAU
One S. Water St., Mobile, AL 36602
800-566-2453 or 251-208-200;
www.mobilebay.org

ALABAMA *Time Line*

1717	**1720**	**1721**	**1724**
French from Mobile establish Fort Toulouse as an outpost for trade with Indians and barrier against British expansion	French Louisiana capital moves from Mobile west to Biloxi, then to New Orleans (1722)	*Africane* sails into Mobile harbor with cargo of over 100 slaves	French Code Noir institutionalizes slavery in Mobile area

Uniforms on display at the Museum of Mobile

1763
Treaty of Paris gives all of Florida, including Mobile, to Britain

1780
Spanish, led by Louisiana governor Gálvez, capture Mobile

1783
Spanish gain title to British West Florida, including Mobile, in second Treaty of Paris

1795
Treaty of San Lorenzo recognizes 31st parallel as southern border with Spanish West Florida

CENTRAL ALABAMA

In the 1540s Spanish conquistador Hernando de Soto led a small army across part of Alabama, leaving a legacy of brutality among the Indian peoples and presaging a long history of Indian troubles in the Southeast. When the French settled Mobile in the early 18th century, they established a fort and trading post near present-day Montgomery. Their presence in central Alabama fostered better relations with the Indians, promoted trade, and countered British influence in the area.

WETUMPKA

Twenty miles north of the capital city of Montgomery, Wetumpka, on the Coosa River, gets its name from a Creek word for the sound of the rapids here before the river was dammed.

HISTORICAL SITES and MUSEUMS

Fort Toulouse/Fort Jackson (334-567-3002; www.fttoulousejackson.org), 2521 Fort Toulouse Rd. (US 231), Wetumka, AL 36093. Open daily except Thanksgiving, Christmas, and New Year's Day. Located at the juncture of the Coosa and Tallapoosa Rivers, a major crossroads of Indian trade, Fort Toulouse was built in 1717, just 15 years after the French settled Mobile. Also called the Post of the Alabama for the surrounding tribe, it served as their major trading post. The fort was manned by a small garrison of French marines to provide a buffer against expansion by the British into Alabama. By the late 1740s one wall had washed away in a flood, and a new fort was built on adjoining land in 1751. This fort lasted until the end of the French and Indian War, when French territory passed into British hands. The newcomers were not welcomed by the Indians, so the fort was abandoned and fell into decay.

After winning the Battle of Horseshoe Bend on the Tallapoosa River against the warring faction of Creeks in 1814, General Andrew Jackson had a new fort

ALABAMA *Time Line*

1813	1814	1817	1819
American forces under General Wilkerson capture Mobile, and the Spanish depart	Andrew Jackson wins Creek War, builds new fort on site of Fort Toulouse, and signs treaty opening up half of present-day Alabama for white settlement	Congress creates Alabama Territory by dividing Mississippi Territory	Alabama joins the union as the twenty-second state

built on the site to serve as his base for southern operations during the latter stages of the War of 1812. Named for him, it also became the site for the treaty that opened up 20 million acres of Creek land—nearly half of Alabama—for white settlement in 1814.

On the site you will find a re-creation of the 1751 Fort Toulouse, the reconstructed 1814 Fort Jackson, and a visitor center and museum. Also on the grounds are a Mississippian Indian mound from ca. AD 1000, a nature trail with an arboretum, a picnic pavilion, a boat launch, and a campground.

EVENTS

April: French and Indian War Encampment
November: Alabama Frontier Days (a reenactment of life from 1700 to 1820)

MONTEVALLO

This town, located in the center of the state south of Birmingham, has seventy-three homes and buildings on the National Register of Historic Places. Twenty-eight of them are at the University of Montevallo. Of primary early historical interest, however, is the town's American Village, a nonprofit educational institute founded and sponsored by the state.

HISTORICAL SITES *and* MUSEUMS

The American Village (877-811-1776; www.americanvillage.org), Box 6, 3727 Hwy. 119, Montevallo, AL 35115. The campus of this educational center offers hands-on experience to visualize historic events of the past. Visitors are treated to face-to-face experience with the founders of our country, and the day we were there the campus was filled with school groups. Visitors are encouraged to step back in time and into the shoes of people who had choices to make and risks to take—and they did not know the end of the story. Costumed interpreters play their parts with vigor and quickly involve all children and adults as they move around the village.

Southern HOSPITALITY

We have a warm feeling toward the people of Montevallo, where we had car trouble while researching for this book. One after another, individuals went out of their way to help, finding us lodging when the town was full for spring commencement at the university, and recommending restaurants. The garage arranged for the needed part to be delivered early on a Saturday morning, and we were set to go by noon. Never underestimate the generosity of strangers while you are traveling!

We joined a group called "Massachusetts" and met first in front of the Court-house to experience the "Seeds of Revolution—1765–1775." "Hear ye, hear ye, hear the latest outrage of 1765—a new tax. The King is responsible for our mis-fortune. We have to purchase stamps for legal papers, marriage licenses (as if mar-riage was not taxing enough!). We Americans have no vote. Are you angry about the Stamp Act?" The students and adults chorused, "No taxation without repre-sentation!" "Down with George Grenville"—and they hanged his effigy.

On to the "Boston Tea Party" we went, and then to the Meetinghouse for "Spirit of Liberty—April 18, 1775." "General Gage's troops have left Boston . . . soldiers assembled . . . there were shots and screams . . . soldiers at Lexington and Concord. . . . It is war—Americans with Great Britain!"

We moved on to the Courthouse for "The Virginia Convention—May 16, 1776," then to the encampment for "Volley, Fire, and Battle Cry at Yorktown—1781." After lunch we walked to the Assembly Room in Washington Hall for "The Constitutional Convention—September 17, 1787." Some of the students were given parts to read, which they did with enthusiasm.

The park has a replica of the White House Oval Office, and Washington Hall is patterned after Mount Vernon.

Reenactors give a spirited performance at the American Village, Montevallo.

LODGING

MCKIBBON HOUSE
611 E. Boundary St., Montevallo, AL 35115
205-665-1275;
www.mckibbonhouse.com
This 1900 restored home is on the National Historic Registry. It retains the ambience of the Victorian era. Four guest rooms.

RAMSAY CONFERENCE CENTER AND LODGE
University of Montevallo
Station 6180, Montevallo, AL 35115
205-665-6280
The campus is attractive, with brick-paved walkways lined with water oaks and ginkgo trees. Rooms are for double-occupancy. Forty guest rooms.

RESTAURANTS

FOX VALLEY RESTAURANT
6745 Hwy. 17, Maylene, AL
205-664-8341
The restaurant specializes in seafood, including gulf red snapper "oscar." Don't miss the ice cream.

SAM & STELLAS
704 N. Boundary St., Montevallo, AL

EVENTS

February: George Washington Birthday Celebration, American Village, 877-811-1776
April: Patriots Weekend, American Village, 877-811-1776
July: Independence Day 1776, American Village, 877-811-1776

Current Information

ALABAMA BUREAU OF TOURISM & TRAVEL
401 Adams Ave., Box 4927
Montgomery, AL 36103
800-ALABAMA, 334-242-4169
www.800alabama.com/

Louisiana

Historical Introduction
to the
Louisiana Colony

Native Americans were the first inhabitants of Louisiana, dating back to around 3400 BC. Ceremonial mounds are reminders of early people who lived in farming groups. By the time Europeans arrived, the Caddo, Natchitoches, Yatasi, and Adai Indians lived in the northwestern section of the present state; the Houma, Choctaw, Acolapissa, and Taensa in east central Louisiana on or near the Mississippi River; the Chitimacha and Atakapa along the Gulf Coast. Further migrations in the second half of the 18th century brought in other tribes, including the Tunica-Biloxi and Coushatta.

Early European Explorers

European contact began in the 16th century with Spanish explorers. Hernando de Soto's expedition from 1539 to 1543 pushed through the southeastern region of the future United States and reached Louisiana in 1542, after de Soto had died of fever. Besides setting a precedent of brutal treatment of the native inhabitants, de Soto's men also brought diseases that devastated the Indians.

In 1682 a French explorer, René-Robert Cavelier, Sieur de La Salle, who had been based in Montreal, came down the Mississippi River, put up a cross at the mouth of the river, claimed the entire watershed of the great river system for France, and named it for King Louis XIV. To create a presence along the Gulf Coast, the French built forts at Biloxi in 1699 and upriver from Mobile Bay in 1702. The first permanent settlement in Louisiana grew at Natchitoches beginning in 1714. New Orleans dates from 1718, when Jean Baptiste Le Moyne, Sieur de Bienville, planted it between the Mississippi River and Lake Ponchartrain to guard the lower Mississippi from Spain and Great Britain. Strategically, the site that controlled two

---

The chapel at Acadian Village in Lafayette

water approaches to the city made sense, but with acute foresight an engineer advised against it, and damaging hurricanes in 1719 and 1721 confirmed his view (not to mention Katrina in our time). Nevertheless, New Orleans grew and became the capital of Louisiana in 1722.

Although Louisiana started as a Crown colony, it had become a proprietary colony under the control of Antoine Crozat, Marquis de Chatel, in 1712. The Company of the West, led by an emigrant Scot in France, John Law, gained control of the colony in 1717. Law established the French national bank and then proceeded to encourage more settlers through a plan that came to be known as

LOUISIANA *Time Line*

1541	**1682**	**1718**	**1762**
Hernando de Soto reaches the Mississippi River	René-Robert Cavalier, Sieur de La Salle, erects a cross at the mouth of the Mississippi River and claims its entire watershed for France	Jean Baptiste Le Moyne, Sieur de Bienville, founds New Orleans	France cedes Louisiana to Spain in the Treaty of Fontainebleau

the Mississippi Bubble. His promotion suggested quick riches in Louisiana and brought 7,000 immigrants to the colony in less than four years, including released prisoners, prostitutes, and indentured servants—more than the colonial government could cope with. The settlers were ill equipped to support themselves and stood in need of basic food and shelter. But they had no funds to sail back to Europe, and many starved or died of illness.

After the Natchez massacre at Fort Rosalie in 1729, and subsequent French retribution, Louisiana became a royal colony again in 1732 but suffered from neglect in the home country. For the next three decades there was little growth in population, food production, or trade, since there was little to export to foreign markets. In 1762 the French, fearing the loss of New France to Britain at the end of the French and Indian War, secretly ceded Louisiana to Spain instead in the Treaty of Fontaineableau.

The autocratic first Spanish governor, Antonio de Ulloa, did not arrive until 1766, three years after the first Treaty of Paris had confirmed Spanish rule in Louisiana. The inhabitants, who were mostly French, rebelled and expelled Ulloa in the fall of 1768 and continued to manage their own affairs for nine months, until General Alejandro O'Reilly arrived with a large naval and land force. An Irishman who had emigrated to Spain and risen to become a respected general in the army, O'Reilly took charge immediately, punished the ringleaders of the insurrection, pardoned the rest of the populace, and managed the colony with a firm but efficient hand. In little over a year, before he left for Spain, O'Reilly had set up many systems that remained in place throughout the Spanish era. French administrators continued to manage much of the business of the colony, and as a result of generous land policies, the population grew substantially, and many immigrants arrived as refugees.

The Acadians

The largest number of immigrants were Acadians, French Canadians originally from Poitou in western France. Early in the 17th century they had settled in the tidal marshlands of what is now Nova Scotia and spread to enclaves in present-day New Brunswick and Prince Edward Island. When the Peace of Utrecht in

1763	1764	1766	1768	1769
Treaty of Paris ends Seven Years War	Acadian immigrants arrive from Canada	Small Spanish force under Don Antonio de Ulloa arrives to take possession for Spain	Insurrection in New Orleans expels Ulloa and institutes home rule	General Alejandro O'Reilly arrives with large naval and land force to reinstitute Spanish rule in Louisiana

> ✺ Lieutenant Colonel John Winslow had summoned all the Acadian men and boys over ten years of age into the church at Grand Pré, on the Bay of Fundy, then locked the door. His journal gave the details: "Your lands and tenements, cattle of all kinds and livestock of all sorts are forfeited to the Crown with all your other effects saving your money and household goods and you yourselves [will] be removed from this Province. . . . The inhabitants, sadly and with great sorrow, abandoned their homes. The women, in great distress, carried their newborn or their youngest children in their arms. Others pulled carts with their household effects and crippled parents. It was a scene of confusion, despair and desolation."
>
> The men boarded ships on September 10, and a month later ships arrived to carry their families away, often to different places.

1713 gave their land to Britain, the Acadians had been guaranteed the right to maintain their French culture and religion, and especially not be forced to swear loyalty to the British Crown or bear arms against France. However, with the onset of the French and Indian War and the worsening of hostilities in 1755, Lieutenant Governor Charles Lawrence had revoked those privileges, ordered the Acadians deported, and confiscated their land, livestock, and homes. The expulsion was sudden and brutal.

Families were split up and forced to sail to English-speaking colonies along the Atlantic seaboard. Some of the colonies would not let them land, and so they sailed on. When the Acadians were allowed to land, they were often unwelcome, as some colonists did not want to assimilate French-speaking Catholics. Many of the Acadians died of exposure and starvation. Some ships sailed to England, others to France, and in both instances the Acadians endured extreme deprivation, as well as separation from their families and friends. The lucky ones eventually reached Spanish Louisiana, where Governor Ulloa welcomed them as settlers. They thought they would be reunited with their families, but this was not always the case. After Ulloa was removed, Governor O'Reilly gave them more choice in their settlements so that they might reunite.

LOUISIANA *Time Line*

1777	**1779**	**1793**	**1795**
Governor Bernardo de Gálvez begins supporting the American Revolution	Spain declares war on Britain, and Gálvez starts successful campaign to capture key British forts on the Mississippi and Gulf Coast	Pope Pius VI establishes the first Diocese of Louisiana	Treaty of San Lorenzo opens navigation of the Mississippi to Americans and gives them right to transship cargoes in New Orleans

Some Acadians remaining in Canada and those who had been resettled in Pennsylvania, Maryland, New York, Haiti, and France scrounged the money to flee to Louisiana. Settlements grew on both sides of the Mississippi, and families were reunited there. They continued some of their traditions in clothing, architecture, and food. Acadian cuisine, with Ceole, native American, and African influences, developed into a new "Cajun" style of cooking.

The American Revolution

During the American Revolution the Spanish in New Orleans tried to help the Patriots in the fight against Britain. Secret aid from Governor Gálvez began in 1777, reinforcing units in various colonies that needed gunpowder, arms, and other supplies.

> Joseph Beausoleil Broussard was revered as a leader of the Acadians and a patriot. He led one group of 193 Acadians to Louisiana, the New Acadia. (The Broussard brothers, Alexandre and Joseph, were both called Beausoleil, the name of their village in Nova Scotia.) They landed on February 28, 1765, and settled near present-day St. Martinville. Then French governor Charles Aubry named Beausoleil "Captain of the Militia and Commandant of the Acadians of the Attakapas."

In 1779 Spain, following the lead of France, declared war on Britain, and Gálvez immediately swung into action in an offensive campaign to remove British forts on the Mississippi and the Gulf Coast. In the next two years he captured Baton Rouge, Natchez, Biloxi, and, after carefully planned sieges, Mobile and Pensacola. Yet in 1800, after the war, secret negotiations in the home country resulted in a treaty that gave Louisiana back to France. And the shuttlecock of control in the territory was not over yet.

Louisiana Purchase

President Thomas Jefferson, despite his love for France, was not pleased with French actions in 1802 that undermined the interests of the United States. Napoleon Bonaparte had sent troops to Saint-Domingue (Haiti) to quell a slave rebellion and, it was feared, to use the island as a base for taking possession of New Orleans;

1800
Spain cedes Louisiana to Napoleonic France in secret, provisional Treaty of San Idelfonso

1802
King Carlos IV of Spain makes retrocession of Louisiana to France effective; Spain closes lower Mississippi River to American navigation and withdraws right of transshipment in port of New Orleans

1803
The United States purchases Louisiana from Napoleon

Bernardo de Gálvez y Madrid, Viscount of Galveston and Count of Gálvez, had an outstanding career as a successful military officer and popular governor in Spanish America. Born in a mountain town in Málaga, he attended the military academy in Avila and distinguished himself in campaigns in Europe and Spanish America. In 1777, at the age of thirty-one, he was appointed interim governor of Louisiana and proved of immense help to American independence by gaining control of British West Florida. Congress recognized his service; Galveston, Texas, is named after him as founder; and two parishes in Louisiana (East and West Feliciana) are named for his wife. After the Revolution he became governor of Cuba and eventually viceroy of New Spain.

also, American merchants could no longer avoid paying duty on goods warehoused in New Orleans waiting for transshipment. With free access to the Mississippi deemed essential, Robert Livingston, the U.S. minister in Paris, had been negotiating with the French foreign minister, Talleyrand, to buy New Orleans but had not been able to reach an agreement. Jefferson sent James Monroe to Paris to help, with instructions to demand cession of New Orleans and both East and West Florida. It did not turn out quite that way—instead evolving into an epochal deal that more than doubled the territory of the United States.

In 1803 Napoleon was in fact eager to sell Louisiana to the United States, as a result of complex geopolitical calculations. His enterprise in Haiti had failed, largely because yellow fever had taken a fearsome toll on the troops sent there, and he had no other base to prevent British occupation of New Orleans. As an inevitable conflict with Britain approached, Napoleon needed money to fight that war and perhaps was wary of levying heavy taxes in France to support it. He may have thought it better to sell New Orleans than have it wrested from him. For reasons that are not entirely clear, Napoleon insisted on selling the whole Louisiana Territory—a transaction that Livingston and Monroe were not authorized to pursue. Yet, after several rounds of negotiations, the price for the Louisiana Purchase was set at $15 million, and Livingston and Monroe risked coming back with far more than they needed to reopen the Mississippi.

The territory acquired was the largest ever added to the United States at one

LOUISIANA *Time Line*

1812
Louisiana becomes the 18th state and adopts its first constitution

1815
General Andrew Jackson defeats invading British force in the Battle of New Orleans

time, of inestimable benefit for the growth of the nation. In 1804 Louisiana was divided in two: the Territory of Louisiana, including land north of the thirty-third parallel, and the Territory of Orleans to its south. In 1812 the Territory of Orleans became the eighteenth state, Louisiana, with New Orleans as its capital. The final, dramatic act of the War of 1812 would take place at the doorstep to the city.

Regions *to* Explore

CENTRAL LOUISIANA
COASTAL LOUISIANA AND ACADIANA

CENTRAL LOUISIANA

Called the Crossroads Region for its many rivers and roads that developed from early trails, Central Louisiana is diagonally bisected by the Red River valley from northwest to southeast. Along the river, the earliest settlement at Natchitoches grew around a fort and colonial plantations on the Cane River, while a trading community at Alexandria started what developed into the region's largest city. Both cities are now surrounded by lakes and large sections of the Kisatchie National Forest.

NATCHITOCHES

The oldest permanent settlement in what became the Louisiana Purchase took place in Natchitoches, on the Red River. Louis Juchereau de St. Denis founded the French settlement in 1714. The colonists established trade with the Spanish in Texas and also provided security against Spanish forays into Louisiana. The town became an important crossroads as well as a river port. Cotton was a sure crop, and planters built plantations on the river and houses in town.

The Historic Landmark District stands on Cane River Lake and includes a thirty-three-block area. Creole-style cottages and Queen Anne and Victorian architecture make this area very attractive. There are more than a hundred historic homes and buildings, with several dating to the 18th century. The plantation district is on the banks of the Cane River. Colonial French and Spanish forts and an early American fort are also in the area.

HISTORICAL SITES *and* MUSEUMS
Fort St. Jean Baptiste State Historic Site (888-677-7853, 318-357-3101; www .lastateparks.com), 155 Rue Jefferson, Natchitoches, LA 71457. Open daily. A

group of Natchitoches Indians took French soldiers up the Red River, but they encountered a logjam and had to stop. They built two huts, and that was the beginning of the fort and the town.

The fort became a trading center useful to the Caddo Indians as well as the French and Spanish. In 1722 St. Denis became the commandant of the fort. After an attack by the Natchez Indians in 1731, the French built a stronger fort. French marines stayed there until 1762, when Louisiana was transferred to Spain. The Spanish continued to maintain the fort for a time, but it was eventually abandoned. A replica of the fort includes a warehouse, powder magazine, church, slave quarters, barracks, guardhouse, and bastions.

About 30 miles southeast of Natchitoches along Interstate 49 is the **Kate Chopin House** (318-379-2233), Cloutierville, LA. Open daily. The original resident was Alexis Cloutier, who built the home between 1805 and 1809. Oscar Chopin bought it in 1879 and lived there with his wife, Kate. She became a writer and published *The Awakening* in 1899. Her views anticipated those of the feminist movement of the 20th century.

INFORMATION

NATCHITOCHES CONVENTION & VISITORS BUREAU
781 Front St.
Natchitoches, LA 71457
800-259-1714 or 318-352-8072; www.natchitoches.net

COASTAL LOUISIANA AND ACADIANA

Why did the French who originally settled in Nova Scotia (which they called Acadie, or Acadia) end up in the bayous of Louisiana half a century later? The precipitating event was the war that was touched off in 1754 by Colonel George Washington at Fort Necessity in the backwoods of Pennsylvania and raged through the northern colonies and Canada, soon widening into a global conflict. In 1755, during the early stages of this conflict—the French and Indian War, as it was known in North America—the British lieutenant governor of Nova Scotia decided to forcibly deport all men who would not sign an oath of allegiance to King George II of England and bear arms against France, reversing what the French settlers had been verbally promised in 1730.

Thus began the Acadians' painful and long diaspora, which often separated men from their wives and children. It ended in Louisiana—for the luckier ones.

Acadia, Evangeline, and St. Landry parishes are in the heart of a region known as Acadiana, named for the French-speaking Acadians—Cajuns—who came here centuries ago. Today there are also French American families whose ancestors came from Europe to Louisiana with the first settlers in the early 1700s. Some French soldiers also fled here after Napoleon Bonaparte was exiled. German families came from the Midwest. Creoles arrived from Saint-Domingue, Haiti (now Santo Domingo in the Dominican Republic), which was once French. After the Louisiana Purchase, people arrived from many other European nations.

Musical Mélange

Reflecting this diversity, a rich mix of musical traditions now exists in the area. The old Louisiana French music, with the help of the German accordion, evolved into the traditional Cajun music. And if you've ever heard "zydeco," you won't forget it! It's a combination of the Louisiana French music with the African American blues and up-tempo Creole musical traditions. And by the 1950s, "Swamp Pop" had evolved from the blues, rock and roll, and Louisiana French. The music of Acadiana is one foot-tapping experience!

Don't miss visiting one of the restaurants where you can dance to Cajun music in between savoring great local cuisine. You'll hear the live band before you get in the door. You'll see people sitting at tables having café au lait. But most of them are there to dance—all ages, including grandmothers and granddaughters, grandfathers with toddlers, couples in their seventies, young people, black people and white people. One of us danced with a man who comes every Saturday morning—"just like going to church on Sunday."

When the Acadians were driven out of Nova Scotia in 1755, they left their instruments and had to recreate their rich musical heritage in Louisiana. More than 250 years later they still have that music, as alive as ever, and still evolving.

Food

Popular Cajun dishes include jambalaya, gumbo, boudin and smoked sausage, crawfish étouffée (crawfish tails, peppers, onions, and garlic), crawfish and andouille scramble, and eggplant pirogue Louis (eggplant, shrimp, crawfish, and crab, topped with sauce Louis).

LAFAYETTE

Cajun country surrounds Lafayette and spills over into the city as well. Acadian hospitality is reflected in the music, art, and food to be enjoyed. You will find a wide variety of activities, including cultural events, food, music, artists, great museums, and, at the right time of year, Mardi Gras.

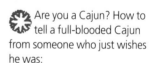 Are you a Cajun? How to tell a full-blooded Cajun from someone who just wishes he was:

1. Does your grandmother eat couche-couche for breakfast?
2. Does your grandmother step out on Saturday to cut a fine two-step?
3. If the doctor told you coffee causes cancer, would you rather take your chances than do without it?
4. Could you paddle a pirogue at a good clip down a stump-strewn stretch of bayou?
5. Do you hate to tell strangers you eat crawfish because it is considered inelegant and everybody knows that Cajuns eat crawfish?

Lafayette was first settled in 1763 as the exiled Acadians from Nova Scotia arrived. Many of them were given land in or near Lafayette on the Vermilion River. Jean Mouton gave some of his land to the Catholic congregation, and a church was blessed in 1821 in the name of St. John. Mouton also developed the town of Vermillionville. The name was changed to Lafayette to honor the Marquis de Lafayette.

HISTORICAL SITES *and* MUSEUMS

Acadian Cultural Center (337-232-0789; www.nps.gov/jela), 501 Fisher Rd. Open daily. The center is part of the Jean Lafitte National Historical Park and Preserve. The Acadian story begins with the first arrivals in North America of those who fled Poitou in France to escape religious wars, revolts, and epidemics. They settled on the Bay of Fundy in Canada in 1604, before the Pilgrims landed in Massachusetts and the Dutch in New York. In 1713 England acquired Acadia (Nova Scotia) under the Treaty of Utrecht. In 1755 the Acadians were expelled in a wrenching and violent deportation ordered by the lieutenant governor to rid the province of all French settlers.

You can witness this terrible event by watching a movie, *The Cajun Way: Echoes of Acadia.* The settlers had been guaranteed freedom of religion, language, and the right to refuse bearing arms against France. But that would change 25 years later. They had established a new life in Nova Scotia and lived there as farmers until an edict was proclaimed by Charles Lawrence for the king in 1755. Because they would not sign an oath of allegiance to England, they were to be deported, in an 18th-century example of ethnic cleansing. The British, in their own defense, contended that some Acadians had taken up arms against the English.

Using deceit and cunning, the British ordered all the men and boys over age 10 to assemble in the church at Grand-Pré. The doors were locked, and they were held prisoner until the ships arrived to transport them. The women and children gathered possessions and waited outside. Soldiers marched the men and boys to the ships, and then the women and children to other ships later. Families were split, never to meet again.

The Acadians were turned away from a number of British colonies along the East Coast. Eventually some landed in Louisiana, while others were sent back to France or England. Of the 10,000 exiled, more than half died.

The center has exhibits on Cajun music and dancing, as well as cooking demonstrations. Programs include talks by the rangers and ranger-guided boat tours of Bayou Vermillion.

Vermillionville (866-992-2968 or 337-233-4077; www.vermillionville.org), 300 Fisher Rd. Open daily. This living history museum interprets the life and culture of the Acadians from 1765 to 1890. Enter the museum and you will be immersed in the history and culture of those eras. A group of buildings provides settings to represent arts and crafts, music, dance, cuisine, and festivals. Spinning

Louisiana Seafood Gumbo
by Chef Patrick Mould

¼ cup oil
⅓ cup flour
1 cup chopped onion
½ cup chopped green pepper
½ cup chopped celery
2 tbsp minced garlic
1 14-ounce can diced tomato
1 tsp Cajun seasoning
1 tsp onion powder
1 tsp garlic powder

½ tsp dried thyme
4 cups water
3 cups chicken broth
2 bay leaves
½ tsp hot sauce
½ pound peeled shrimp
½ pound white crabmeat
12 shucked oysters
¼ cup chopped green onions
¼ cup minced parsley

In a medium size stockpot, heat oil, add flour, and cook until dark roux forms. Add half of onion, celery, and bell pepper, cook for 5 minutes. Stir in garlic, continue to cook for 5 minutes. Stir in diced tomato, Cajun seasoning, onion powder, garlic powder, dried thyme, and simmer for 10 minutes.

Stir in water, chicken broth, bay leaves, and hot sauce, bring to boil, lower fire to medium, and simmer for 45 minutes. Stir in shrimp and simmer for 5 minutes. Add oyster, crabmeat, and simmer for additional 5 minutes.

Stir in green onions and parsley. Serve with steamed rice. *Yields 4–6 servings.*

Fausse Pointe, at Vermillionville in Lafayette

The Alexandre Mouton House in Lafayette

and weaving take place in the Beau Bassin house. Look in Le Magasin for crafts such as boatbuilding, net and trap making, and decoy carving. In the schoolhouse the line "I will not speak French in school" dates back to the days when the law forbade the speaking of French.

The chapel is similar to 1760 churches. Armand Broussard, who brought 250 Acadians to Louisiana from their exile, lived at Fausse Pointe, a plantation house dating from 1790. He later became a Patriot in the American Revolution.

Acadian Village (337-981-2364; www.acadianvillage.org), 200 Greenleaf Dr. Open daily. The village interprets Acadian life in the 19th century. A project built during the 1970s on 10 acres of farmland belonging to the Lafayette Association for Retarded Citizens, the village was designed to encourage heritage tourism and provide revenue for the association and employment for developmentally disabled citizens.

The farmland has been transformed into a model of an early Acadian village typical of the region, complete with 11 buildings grouped around a pond and now shaded by large trees. Buildings include a chapel, general store, blacksmith shop, doctor's museum, art gallery, and half a dozen houses from various eras. Seven of the buildings, donated by descendants of the families who owned them, were moved from their original sites in pieces; the others are replicas of characteristic buildings. The oldest is the Aurelie Bernard House, built in 1800 with an addition in 1840.

Alexandre Mouton House (337-234-2208; www.lafayettemuseum@aol.com), 1122 Lafayette St. Jean Mouton is regarded as the founder of Lafayette. He built a small house in 1800 to be used as a "Sunday house" by his family when they came in town from their plantation to attend Mass. His son Alexandre married, moved into the Sunday house, and added three rooms. Alexandre became a U.S. senator, governor of Louisiana, and president of the Convention of Secession in 1860.

The house changed hands several times and in 1849 was purchased by Dr. W. G. Mills, who added the remaining rooms downstairs, the second and third floors, and the cupola. The house is also called the Lafayette Museum. Inside the main house the portraits give you a sense of the Mouton family.

The *Lady in Black* portrait has a history behind it. Young girls were often painted in white, and later another portrait was done in black. If the family did not want to pay for a second portrait, the artist simply painted a black dress over the white one. Look for the portrait of a lady smoking a pipe, who is said to be a relative of Zachary Taylor, twelfth president of the United States.

Upstairs there is a Mardi Gras room with sparkling costumes from 1934. The king and queen are named for Gabriel and Evangeline, diaspora victims immortalized in Henry Wadsworth Longfellow's poem *Evangeline*.

ST. MARTINVILLE

The town is a short drive southeast of Lafayette. Settlers arrived here in 1760 and bought land from the Attakapa Indians. When the Spanish administration began here in 1769, the town was a military post. Early Acadian settlers were later joined by titled Frenchmen who left France at the beginning of the revolution there.

HISTORICAL SITES *and* MUSEUMS

Henry Wadsworth Longfellow wrote about the sad story of two lovers, Evangeline and Gabriel, in his epic poem *Evangeline*. **The Evangeline Oak** stands at the end of Port St. Evangeline, and it is believed that the lovers met there. Gabriel arrived first and waited three years. Evangeline still had her wedding dress in her trunk when they found each other many years later. Gabriel had to tell her that he had married another.

The Acadian Memorial (337-394-2258; www.acadianmemorial.org), 121 S. New Market, St. Martinville, LA 70582. Open daily. This memorial honors the men, women, and children who were victims of the diaspora. Inside, the mural *The Arrival of the Acadians in Louisiana* extends the length of one wall. Listen to the audio to hear the words of some of the victims. A wall of names stands in bronze and granite. Outside there is an eternal flame and a replica of the deportation cross on the Bayou Teche.

The Evangeline Oak in St. Martinville

LODGING

AAAH! T'FRERE'S HOUSE BED & BREAKFAST
1905 Verot School Rd., Lafayette, LA 70508
800-984-9347 or 337-984-9347;
www.tfreres.com
Voted Best B&B in Acadiana. Eight guest rooms.

CHRETIEN POINT PLANTATION B&B
665 Chretien Point Rd., Sunset, LA 70584
800-880-7050 or 337-662-7050;
www.chretienpoint.com
Dating from 1831, the house is located on 20 secluded acres on the plantation. Five guest rooms.

COUNTRY FRENCH BED &BREAKFAST
616 General Mouton Ave., Lafayette, LA 70501
337-234-2866; www.countryfrench bedandbreakfast.com
This French chalet is surrounded by gardens with fountains and a courtyard. Two guest rooms.

MAISON DES AMIS
111 Washington St., Breaux Bridge, LA 70517
337-507-3399;
www.maisondesamis.com
The house is on the National Registry of Historic Homes and overlooks gardens and Bayou Teche. Four guest rooms.

RESTAURANTS

The cuisine in Lafayette includes both Cajun and Creole. The Acadians—or, dropping the initial *A*, "le Cadiens" or Cajuns—began to use spices from African Americans and American Indians. Cajun cooking was basically stewed meat and gravies with rice. Corn was added and also gumbo (made with okra and filé powder, from sassafras leaves).

Creole cuisine originated in New Orleans in the early 1700s. Creole comes from a mix of west European, African, Caribbean, and Native Indian. The Creoles also created zydeco music.

Some of the restaurants combine Cajun/Creole cooking with a dance hall. The combination of food and music is a winner.

BAILEY'S SEAFOOD & GRILL
5520-A Johnston St., Lafayette
337-988-6464
Specialties include gumbo, seafood stuffed speckled trout, and eggplant Acadiana.

BLUE DOG CAFÉ
1211 W. Pinhook Rd., Lafayette
337-237-0005
The walls contain artwork by George Rodrigue. Seafood, Cajun, Creole, and contemporary South cuisine are offered.

CAFE DES AMIS
140 E. Bridge St., Breaux Bridge
337-332-5273
An art gallery is in the building. The cuisine includes Cajun, Creole, and contemporary South.

CAFÉ VERMILIONVILLE
1304 W. Pinhook Rd., Lafayette
337-237-0100
Dating from 1818 and on the National Register, this is Lafayette's first inn. Known for its awards. The cuisine includes Cajun, Creole, and contemporary South.

CHARLEY G'S SEAFOOD GRILL
3809 Ambassador Caffery Pkwy., Lafayette
337-981-0108
The cuisine is contemporary south Louisiana.

FEZZO'S SEAFOOD, STEAKHOUSE & OYSTER BAR
109 Benoit Patin Rd., Scott
337-234-3536
Fezzo's offers Cajun, Creole, and family-style seafood.

MULATE'S
325 Mills Ave., Breaux Bridge
Live Cajun bands offer great dancing. The cuisine is family-style seafood and Cajun.

RANDOL'S RESTAURANT & CAJUN DANCEHALL
2320 Kaliste Saloom Rd., Lafayette
337-981-7080
"Two steppin', toe tappin', taste temptn." Seafood, steaks, and Cajun and Creole cuisine are offered.

EVENTS

April: Festival International, 337-232-8086
May: Breaux Bridge Crawfish Festival, 337-332-8500
October: Festivals Acadiens, 337-232-3737
December: A Cajun Christmas at Acadian Village, 337-981-2489

INFORMATION

LAFAYETTE CONVENTION & VISITORS COMMISSION
1400 NW Evangeline Thruway, Lafayette, LA 70501
337-232-3737;
www.lafayettetravel.com

Some residents say that the city of New Orleans began as a gleam in the eyes of an unscrupulous Scotsman. But before he perpetrated his outlandish scam, others with big ideas had arrived on the scene. A French explorer, René-Robert Cavelier, Sieur de La Salle, followed the Mississippi River south to find its mouth in 1682. He claimed for France all the fertile land drained by the Mississippi, from the Alleghenies to the Rockies. Unfortunately La Salle was murdered before he had the chance to create a settlement.

Pierre Le Moyne, Sieur d'Iberville, and his brother, Jean-Baptiste Le Moyne, Sieur de Bienville, established French settlements on the Gulf, in Mobile and at Ocean Springs and Biloxi. In 1699 Iberville entered the Mississippi on Mardi Gras ("Fat Tuesday," the feasting day before Ash Wednesday, which is the beginning of Lent, a fasting period). On March 3, when the explorers got to the mouth of the river, they toasted Mardi Gras. By 1718 Bienville had chosen the place for the settlement of Nouvelle Orléans, at a great bend in the Mississippi just south of the large, brackish Lake Pontchartrain.

Enter the Scotsman, John Law, a crafty financier and land speculator. In 1717 he had gotten the French Crown to grant a twenty-five-year charter for exploiting the Louisiana Territory. Law proceeded to spread the word that this

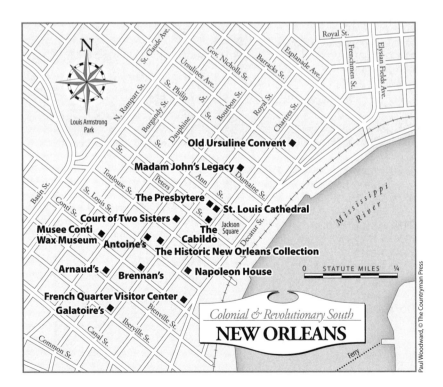

PIRATE *or* PATRIOT?

✳ Who was he? Where did he come from? Much of his life is a mystery, but some believe that Jean Laffite, or Lafitte, was born in southwestern France in 1780. He and his older brother, Pierre, traveled to the West Indies and then to Louisiana, probably as French privateers. They settled in New Orleans around 1802 and became agents for pirates.

The brothers were captured while smuggling, got lawyers, and then jumped bail. Major General Andrew Jackson accepted help from Jean Laffite before the Battle of New Orleans in 1815. President Madison gave a full pardon to those who helped win the American victory, so Jean and Pierre Laffite were considered Patriots.

part of the New World had a wealth of gold and silver. Instead, when people arrived they were astonished to find palmetto shacks, mosquito-infested swamps, and hostile Indians.

Those who believed Law did not have much choice but to grit their teeth and make the best of it. Among the emigrants recruited by Law and his successors were indigent men, petty criminals, and "correction girls" released from French prisons. These unlucky settlers lacked knowledge of farming and in general were unfit for the rigors of establishing a frontier colony. There is little documentation of exactly when this pattern of sweeping the slums and prisons to populate New Orleans stopped, since Law's company and its successor, the Company of the Indies, had immigration quotas to meet. Law's "Mississippi Bubble" of stock speculation finally burst in 1720, and many French investors lost fortunes. By 1731 New Orleans had become a Crown colony again.

In 1762 the colony became a Spanish possession, perhaps by mere chance: Some say that Louis XV of France lost the Louisiana Territory to his Bourbon cousin, Charles III of Spain, on a wager. In any case, at the end of the French and Indian War, France, besides losing Canada and its claims east of the Mississippi to Great Britain, was forced to give up to Spain its territory west of the Mississippi, as well as the city of New Orleans. It took four years for the news to reach New Orleans, and when the Spanish commissioner Don Antonio de Ulloa arrived to take charge, the local inhabitants were understandably bitter. They rebelled but had to relent when twenty-four Spanish warships and 2,000 troops arrived to quell the uprising.

During the American Revolution Spain sided with the Americans and in 1779 declared war on Great Britain; peace negotiations at the end of the war returned Florida to Spain. By 1801, however, with the rise of Napoleon Bonaparte in Europe, Spain lost the Louisiana Territory to France.

The Louisiana Purchase

Napoleon might have had visions of reviving France's North American empire, but military reverses and conflict with Britain drew his focus back to Europe. President Thomas Jefferson had sent Robert Livingston to Paris with an offer to buy New Orleans for $10 million, but to Livingston's astonishment, the French offered him the entire Louisiana Territory for $15 million. Livingston did not hesitate to exceed his commission, and when the Louisiana Purchase agreement was signed in the Cabildo in New Orleans in 1803, Louisiana now belonged to the United States, which had more than doubled its potential size overnight. Two years later, in 1805, New Orleans was incorporated as a city—but its history as a shuttlecock of warring powers was not quite over yet.

The Battle of New Orleans

In perhaps the most dramatic battle of the War of 1812, General Andrew Jackson, who had been busy fighting Creek Indians in the South and then expelling the British from Pensacola, rushed with his militia and volunteer troops to mount a defense of the city against a British invasion. Knowing he was greatly outnumbered and facing crack British troops, Jackson recruited all the help he could find, including the pirate Jean Laffite, free blacks, Creoles, and Choctaw Indians. (No one knew that the Treaty of Ghent ending the war had been negotiated since August and was already signed, on December 24.) Jackson tried to block approaches to New Orleans and stationed his troops so that they could repulse any British force sneaking into Lake Ponchartrain.

But the British got up to Bayou Bienvenue, near Chalmette. Jackson, trying to buy time to complete his defenses, struck first. With the help of riflemen from Tennessee and Kentucky as well as Choctaw warriors, he attacked the enemy camp at night. His force was repulsed after a fierce struggle, but the attack caused the British to wait until reinforcements arrived. When British General Edward Packenham finally attacked in force on January 8, 1815, he lost more than 2,000 men and was a casualty himself. The British decamped and turned their attention elsewhere on the Gulf.

Like the fate of the city through its history, the physical site of New Orleans is equally precarious—as Hurricane Katrina demonstrated. Sieur de Bienville chose the site between the waterways—against the advice of his engineer—because he wanted the city to control the Mississippi. Most

William Faulkner described the French Quarter in 1926: "Do you know our quarter, with its narrow streets, its old wrought-iron balconies and its southern European atmosphere? An atmosphere of richness and soft laughter, you know." Faulkner lived at 624 Pirate's Alley, John Dos Passos at 510 Esplanade Avenue, F. Scott Fitzgerald at 2900 Prytania Street. Gertrude Stein, Erskine Caldwell, Ernest Hemingway, and Tennessee Williams also lived in the city for a time.

of the city stands five feet below sea level, under the shadow of river dikes. The Mississippi winds along the city's southern edge, forming a crescent shape before it meets the Gulf of Mexico many miles downstream. Lake Pontchartrain, also connected to the Gulf, provides another watery barrier at the northern edge; bayous and swamps dot the outskirts, and many canals cut through the landscape. The heart of the city lies fan-shaped within the river crescent.

The French Quarter

Today visitors walking the streets of the French Quarter feel surrounded by the Old World, with its history and heritage to explore. The original colony was founded at the eastern edge of the crescent in the river. Two fires, in 1788 and 1794, wiped out most of the original buildings from the 18th century.

The original colonial settlement of New Orleans was known as Vieux Carré, or "old square." This is the heart of the city, historically and because of its vibrancy. Both famous and infamous characters have lived here, beginning with Jean Laffite, who had a building on Royal Street for his contraband. Because the quarter is on higher ground, Hurricane Katrina did not inflict permanent damage. There are many antiques shops, musical venues, historical sites, restaurants, and hotels to visit.

HISTORICAL SITES *and* MUSEUMS

The Louisiana State Museum (800-568-6968, 504-568-6968; http://lsm .crt.state.la.us) includes eight historic buildings in the French Quarter, among them the Cabildo, the Presbytere, 1850 House, the Old U.S. Mint, and Madame John's Legacy.

The Cabildo (800-568-6968, 504-524-9118; http://lsm.crt.state.la.us), 701 Chartres St. Open daily except Mon. The Louisiana Purchase transfer ceremony was held here. Exhibits trace Louisiana's history from early pre-exploration days through the Civil War. The building dates from 1795, and the American flag first flew from the balcony in 1803. French settlers used boats called pirogues, similar to native canoes, and there is one on display. A gun display includes a short gun with a large barrel known as a blunderbuss. On the second floor there is a death mask of Napoleon Bonaparte, made by his doctor.

The Presbytere (800-568-6968, 504-524-9118; http://lsm.crt.state.la.us), 751 Chartres St., Jackson Square. Dating from 1793 when it was an ecclesiastical house, the Presbytere became court chambers in 1813. Inside there is the Louisiana Portrait Gallery and a Mardi Gras exhibit. Changing exhibits explore Louisiana history.

Madame John's Legacy (800-568-6968, 504-524-9118; http://lsm.crt .state.la.us), 632 Dumaine St. Main house open daily except Mon. This National Historic Landmark dating to 1789 was built on a lot burned out by the fire of 1788 and luckily escaped the fire of 1795. Built by a French sea captain, this home is typical of Creole houses of that era, with a main two-story structure, a kitchen

The Cabildo in New Orleans

with cook's quarters, and a garçonnière (servant's quarters). The main house has living quarters and a broad gallery on the second floor.

The Historic New Orleans Collection (504-523-4662; www.hnoc.org), 533 Royal St. Open daily except Mon. This is a museum, research center, and publishing house dedicated to the history of New Orleans and Louisiana. It is housed in seven adjacent 18th- and 19th-century buildings. There are galleries, a house museum, and changing exhibits.

The **Merieult House**, 533 Royal St., dating from 1792, has 10 galleries on the second floor, offering displays from the beginning of New Orleans in 1718 to the 20th century. Transfer documents for the Louisiana Purchase are here, as well as rare maps and images of New Orleans.

The **Williams Research Center** (504-598-7171), at 410 Chartres St., houses a collection of materials on Louisiana and the Gulf South. The reading room is open to the public.

The **Ursuline Convent** (800-535-7786, 504-529-3040), 1112 Chartres St. Open Tue.–Sun. Ursuline nuns arrived from France in 1727. The convent, one

A quiet courtyard at the Historic New Orleans Collection

of the oldest in the Mississippi Valley, dates from 1750 and replaced another one on the same site dedicated in 1734. The nuns cared for orphans and the indigent in the city. Their school taught white, black, and Indian children. Since Katrina, the nuns have been rebuilding the soul of the people and giving hope.

St. Louis Cathedral (504-525-9585), 615 Père Antoine Alley. Open to visitors in between services. The first cathedral was lost during a hurricane in 1722 and the second consumed by fire in 1788. Don Almonester y Roxas built the present structure with the stipulation that the congregation pray for his soul.

Musée Conti Wax Museum (800-233-5405, 504-581-1993; www.get-waxed.com), 917 Conti St. Call for opening days. Life-size wax figures in costume tell the story of New Orleans, each in its own scene. The story begins in 1699. Henri de Tonti, La Salle's faithful lieutenant, searched for him without success, so he left a letter with the Bayougoula Choctaws and also gave the chief his Montreal blue coat. When Sieur d'Iberville later left on his own expedition, he knew that if he found the Indian with Tonti's letter and wearing Tonti's coat, then it was the Mississippi River.

"The Arrival of the Casket Girls—1752" depicts teenage Frenchwomen who volunteered to travel to New Orleans to marry. "As wards of the Crown, each was provided with a small casket (*cassette*) or trunk, containing two dresses, two petticoats, six headdresses, and sundries." The girls were the responsibility of the Ursuline nuns and lived at the convent until marriage.

Napoleon decided to sell all Louisiana to the Americans without consulting the French Assembly. The scene depicts him in his bath vehemently splashing as he tells his brothers Lucien and Joseph that he is selling it for $15 million.

"The Signing of the Louisiana Purchase" depicts Robert Livingston and James Monroe looking on as François Barbé-Marbois signs his name. Another scene shows Jean Laffite and Andrew Jackson planning the Battle New Orleans in Laffite's blacksmith shop.

Cities of the Dead

Mark Twain described New Orleans' cemeteries in *Life on the Mississippi* in 1883. "They bury their dead in vaults, above the ground. These vaults have a resemblance to houses—sometimes to temples; are built of marble, generally: are architecturally graceful and shapely; they face the walks and driveways of the cemetery; and when one moves through the midst of a thousand or so of them and sees their white roofs and gables stretching into the distance on every hand, the phrase 'city of the dead' has all at once a meaning to

> The cemeteries in New Orleans prompted one person to write, "You can tell a great deal about a community by the way they honor their dead, and without meeting any of the people of New Orleans yet, I can tell you I know I'm going to like them, for very few cities that I have visited throughout the world honor the dead as they do here in New Orleans."

him. . . . Fresh flowers, in vases of water, are to be seen at the portals of many of the vaults: placed there by the pious hands of bereaved parents, and children, husbands and wives, and renewed daily."

St. Louis Cemetery I was begun by the Spanish in 1789. **St. Louis Cemetery II** was consecrated in 1823 when the first cemetery was full, and **St. Louis Cemetery III** opened in 1854. (The cemeteries suffered some flooding after Katrina but no extensive damage.) Aboveground tombs were necessary because of the water table just a few feet down. Most of the tombs in the earlier cemetery were made of brick, then plastered and whitewashed. Facing stones were of marble or slate, which tended to warp and fall apart. When thicker blocks of marble were used on entire tombs the stone did not warp but often felt the effects of weather. Granite was introduced in 1830 and has stood the test of time and weather. Wrought-iron crosses stand on top of the earliest tombs. Cast iron was used for fences and gates around family areas.

> It is highly recommended to visit the cemeteries as part of a group or on a tour, because of some unsavory characters who may be lurking there. Two of our group left early to return to the hotel, and their purses were snatched. Tours are offered by Save Our Cemeteries, 888-721-7493; Gray Line, 800-535-7786; or Haunted History Tours, 888-644-6787.

Wall vaults enclose the cemetery grounds and were an economical use of space, as they were stacked in tiers. The most popular design was a rectangular box with an opening on the end. Those used for family burials had a pitched roof, with three or four vertical vaults. Pilasters at the four corners or the front made the tomb look like a temple.

J. N. B. de Pouilly came from France with pictures of the Père Lachaise cemetery in Paris. He designed tombs that looked like Greek temples.

During a cemetery tour we were told that the crypts were sealed for one year and one day, then the family bones were pushed to the back, the casket removed and burned, and a new casket could then be inserted. We were touched by some of the photographs of the deceased, the flower displays, and the obvious devotion of living family members for their dead.

Some say that the voodoo queen, Marie Laveau, who is buried in St. Louis I, can still cast a spell. Her tomb is easy to spot, with red Xs on it. Visitors are instructed to mark a large X with brick dust. Then rub your foot three times and make a wish, which should come true.

Chalmette Battlefield and National Cemetery (504-589-2133, 504-281-0510; www.nps.gov/jela/chalmettebattlefield.htm), off LA 46. Open daily. This site was badly damaged during Hurricane Katrina. When we visited in May 2007 it was not open. A visitor center and the cemetery have since opened. The Battle of New Orleans took place here on January 8, 1815. General Andrew Jackson and his men were victorious over the British.

LODGING

BIENVILLE HOUSE
320 Decatur St., New Orleans, LA
70130
800-535-9603, 504-529-2345;
www.bienvillehouse.com
Located close to the Convention Center.
Eighty guest rooms.

LE RICHELIEU
1234 Chartres St., New Orleans, LA
70116
800-535-9653, 504-529-2492;
www.lerichelieuhotel.com
The hotel is named for Cardinal Richelieu,
prime minister of Louis XIII; his portrait
hangs in the lobby. Seventy guest rooms.

HOTEL MAISON DE VILLE
727 Rue Toulouse, New Orleans, LA
70130
800-634-1600, 504-561-5858;
www.hotelmaisondeville.com
Dating from 1783, the hotel has a courtyard and cottages and an iron balcony.
Twenty-three guest rooms.

HOTEL MONTELEONE
214 Royal St., New Orleans, LA 70130
800-535-9595, 594-523-3341;
www.hotelmonteleone.com
This family-owned hotel dates back to
Antonio Monteleone, a nobleman from
Sicily who arrived here in 1870. It was one
of only three hotels in the country to
receive the Literary Landmark designation.
A number of writers have chosen to stay
here, including William Faulkner, Truman
Capote, and Eudora Welty. Six hundred
guest rooms.

MAISON DUPUY
1001 Rue Toulouse, New Orleans, LA
70112
800-535-9177, 504-586-8000;
www.maisondupuy.com
James Pitot built the first cotton press on
this site in 1802. Some rooms overlook the
courtyard and others the French Quarter.
Two hundred guest rooms.

RESTAURANTS

New Orleans is famous for its food, and
the variety starts with French, Creole, and
Cajun.

ANTOINE'S
713 St. Louis St.
504-581-4422
The restaurant dates from 1840, when
Antoine Alciatore arrived from Marseille,
France, and the same family still operates
it. Antoine learned under the great chefs in
France, and in New Orleans he created his
own special dishes. His son Jules created
oysters Rockefeller, a secret family recipe.

ARNAUD'S
813 Bienville St.
504-523-5433
The cuisine is classic French Creole. Signature dishes include Shrimp Arnaud. Don't
miss the Mardi Gras museum, with stunning dresses.

BRENNAN'S
417 Royal St.
504-525-9711
Breakfast at Brennan's is a well-known tra-
dition. Other meals include their French
Creole dishes.

COURT OF TWO SISTERS
613 Royal St.
504-522-7261
The cuisine is French Creole, and there is a
jazz brunch buffet daily in the courtyard.

GALATOIRE'S
209 Bourbon St.
504-525-2021
Jean Galatoire bought the 1830 home in
1905 and began his restaurant. Some of
the recipes were from his homeland, a
French village named Pau. When he
retired, his three nephews continued his
traditions, then their children and now
grandchildren operate the restaurant. Specialties include shrimp rémoulade.

Galatoire's Shrimp Rémoulade

¾ cup chopped celery
¼ cup red wine vinegar
¼ cup chopped scallions
2 tbsp Spanish hot paprika
½ cup chopped curly parsley
1tsp Worcestershire sauce
1 cup chopped yellow onion
½ cup salad oil
½ cup ketchup

4 dozen jumbo shrimp, peeled, boiled, chilled
½ cup tomato puree
1 small head iceberg lettuce, thin ribbons
½ cup Creole mustard or any coarse mustard
2 tbsp prepared horseradish, or to taste

Mince the celery, scallions, parsley, and onions in a food processor. Add the ketchup, tomato puree, Creole mustard, horseradish, red wine vinegar, paprika, and Worcestershire. Begin processing again and add the oil in a slow drizzle to emulsify. Stop when the dressing is smooth. Chill for 6 to 8 hours or overnight. Correct the seasoning with additional horseradish, if desired, after the ingredients have had the opportunity to marry. In a large mixing bowl, add the sauce to the shrimp and toss gently to coat. Divide the lettuce among 6 chilled salad plates. Divide the shrimp evenly atop the lettuce and serve. *Serves 6.*

The Napoleon House

NAPOLEON HOUSE
500 Chartres St.
504-524-9752
This is a European-style café. A specialty is the muffaletta sandwich for lunch. Mediterranean and southern French cuisine for dinner.

EVENTS

January: Anniversary of the Battle of New Orleans, with a military band and encampment including cooking and drilling, 504-281-0510

February or March: Mardi Gras, 800-810-3200
April: French Quarter Festival, 800-673-5725, 504-522-5730

INFORMATION

NEW ORLEANS TOURISM
365 Canal St., New Orleans, LA 70130
800-810-3200, 504-524-4784

Current Information

LOUISIANA DEPARTMENT OF TOURISM
P.O. Box 94291
Baton Rouge, LA 70804-9291
800-677-4082, 225-342-8119
www.louisianatravel.com

Mississippi

Historical Introduction
to
Mississippi

Mississippi's story, unlike that of other states bordering the Gulf of Mexico, is more often told by the influence of the great river that shares its name. The major permanent settlement during the colonial and Revolutionary eras evolved on high bluffs overlooking the river, some 150 miles from the sea, while settlements on the Gulf either languished or were abandoned. At least one group of Indians apparently made the same choice earlier, and Europeans who arrived called the settlement of Natchez by their name.

Archaeologists garnered knowledge of earlier inhabitants of the area from the mounds they left behind, which range from small humps to larger hills that can reach sixty feet in height. Some may have been used for signal towers, others for dwellings or even as islands in the floodplain for escape when the Mississippi rose. Archaeologists think the mounds served as ceremonial or religious centers. Excavations have uncovered artifacts from them, including stone implements, chipped flint, hoes, bowls, cups, nails, pipes, and beads.

Early European Explorers

Spanish conquistador Hernando de Soto had discovered the Mississippi River in 1541. After assembling a large, well-provisioned expedition in Havana, Cuba, he had landed on the Florida Gulf Coast and pushed through the present lands of Florida, Georgia, South Carolina, Alabama, Mississippi, and Arkansas looking for gold and for rivers that might cut through the continent to the Pacific and the riches of China. De Soto died on the banks of the Mississippi on May 21, 1542.

More than a century would pass before Europeans would again explore the

Overleaf: In the gardens at Monmouth Plantation

Paul Woodward, © The Countryman Press

great waterway cutting through the center of America. At the behest of those seeking to extend the power of France through the new continent, French explorers, priests, and trappers moved down from Canada, often by canoe, and eventually reached the Gulf of Mexico. In 1673 Governor Frontenac of New France appointed Father Jacques Marquette, a Jesuit missionary, and fur trapper Louis Jolliet to begin exploring the Mississippi River. They started their journey by navigating through Lake Michigan to Green Bay, then down the Fox and Wisconsin Rivers to the Mississippi.

The Illini (or Quapaw) Indians gave them a peace pipe, a calumet, to smoke with tribal leaders and then use on the journey. When they reached the Arkansas River in June 1673, Indians told them there were hostile tribes as well as the Spanish ahead, so they returned to Michigan. Father Louis Hennepin, a Belgian-born missionary, arrived in New France in

> ✳ More than a little mystery surrounds the fate of de Soto's body. According to some accounts, he had claimed to be an immortal, "Son of the Sun" to impress and manipulate the Indians. Soldiers in his party feared consequences if his death were discovered, so they buried him quickly at night. Later fearing that Indians might dig up his corpse, they did so themselves, again at night, weighted it to sink, and dropped it into the Mississippi.

Real estate scams are at least as old as early settlement of the New World. By 1717 John Law had begun promoting, with fraudulent claims, the French Mississippi Company, which became known as the Mississippi Bubble. Law indicated that immigrants would become rich and that the land he had was fertile. When the settlers arrived, they found those claims false but did not have enough money to return home, so many died.

1675. He joined La Salle's first expedition in 1678, and by 1683 his *Description de la Louisiane,* which contained a map of the Louisiana Territory, was published in France. A year earlier René-Robert Cavalier, Sieur de La Salle, had come down the river to its mouth and claimed the entire watershed for France.

Pierre Le Moyne, Sieur d'Iberville, a French Canadian sailor, soldier, and explorer, organized an expedition in France to substantiate La Salle's claim. He reached the Gulf Coast in 1699, explored several channels to the Mississippi, and built Fort Maurepas as the core of a settlement on Biloxi Bay. But the soil was unsuitable for crops, and the settlement did not prosper. Sieur de Sauvole, the man left in charge there, wrote, "In regard to the land, it is certainly unproductive. It is nothing but burning sand—our men have planted very often, and unprofitably." The men also suffered from the heat, disease, and dysentery, and the settlement was abandoned as French interests turned elsewhere.

As early as 1701 Sauvole sent scouts looking for a better site and found one 150 miles up the Mississippi on bluffs overlooking the river. Natchez Indians already lived there, however, and French intrusion into their land would wait for an incident to serve as an excuse. The Natchez provided it by murdering several French traders and looting a trading post on their land. In 1716 Jean Baptiste Le Moyne, Sieur de Bienville (Iberville's younger brother), led troops in a retaliatory raid, demanded execution of the offenders and restoration of goods, and even forced the Natchez to build Fort Rosalie for French occupation. Crops grew easily on the rich soil of this site, and settlers flocked in, with more than 750 living in the colony by 1729. That was the year the Natchez massacred the French garrison at Fort Rosalie.

MISSISSIPPI *Time Line*

1541	1673	1682	1699
Hernando De Soto reaches the Mississippi River	Father Jacques Marquette and Louis Jolliet explore the Mississippi River as far south as the Arkansas River	René-Robert Cavalier, Sieur de La Salle, reaches the mouth of the Mississippi River and claims the entire watershed for France	Pierre Le Moyne, Sieur d'Iberville, and his brother Jean Baptiste, Sieur de Bienville, explore the mouth of the Mississippi and build Fort Maurepas on Biloxi Bay

The Natchez Uprising

The French had continued ordering the Indians to serve them in various ways, and when they were asked to evacuate their own lands, resentment boiled over. The Natchez gathered support from neighboring tribes and determined to get rid of their oppressors. According to plan, they entered the fort as if they were going on a hunt. They brought poultry and corn to exchange for the guns and powder needed for their hunt. At the same moment, Indians inside the fort and many cabins attacked the settlers and killed between 200 and 300 and took 400 women and slaves captive as hostages. They then burned Fort Rosalie. For the next two years the French retaliated by methodically destroying Natchez villages. They eliminated the tribe, but the once-prosperous settlement did not revive for decades.

Four Decades of Rapid Change

By the Treaty of Paris in 1763 the English gained control of French territory east of the Mississippi River, while Spain took control of New Orleans and the territory west of the river. Many retired British soldiers, as well as new settlers, thrived in the Natchez area. But when the American Revolution broke out and France sided with the Americans, Spain also entered the war against Britain, and Governor Bernardo de Gálvez of Louisiana quickly captured Natchez and other river forts. The region reverted to Spanish control for most of two decades, even though the second Treaty of Paris granted it to the United States in 1783. But that grant was ambiguous, because the northern boundary of West Florida had been changed from the 31st parallel to 32 degrees, 28 minutes by the British in 1764, a year after the first Treaty of Paris, and the second treaty in 1783 did not define which border was legitimate. As a result, Spain, the United States, and Georgia all claimed the valuable strip of land stretching across the South from Georgia to the Mississippi River. In spite of the confusion, a Spanish policy of few restrictions and liberal land grants to American settlers and the Anglo-American population made the Spanish yoke light, and the Natchez district prospered again. Although the Treaty of San Lorenzo clarified the border and substantiated the U.S. claim, the Spanish delayed leaving. Not until 1798 did they evacuate their remaining troops and hand over the Mississippi Territory to full American control.

1716	1717	1729	1730	1763
Bienville forces the Natchez Indians to build Fort Rosalie for the French	John Law uses the French Mississippi Company as a scam to encourage settlers	Natchez Indians massacre French settlers at Fort Rosalie	The French retaliate and eventually destroy all Natchez settlements	Treaty of Paris cedes West Florida (including part of Mississippi) to England

A few years later President Jefferson made a bold move that guaranteed the future of Mississippi. With the Louisiana Purchase, signed in 1803, a land boom began and the river opened to navigation by Americans. Many settlers arrived along the Natchez Trace from Tennessee, a key link that had been made available by a treaty with Indians two years earlier, as well as overland from the southern Piedmont region. The War of 1812 and the related Creek War interrupted that growth. In September 1813 the Creek Indians massacred settlers at Fort Mims in the eastern part of the Mississippi Territory. General Andrew Jackson brought his Tennessee militia to deal with the Creeks and defeated them in the Battle of Horseshoe Bend on March 17, 1814. Mississippi would have to wait for almost four more years for statehood.

Regions *to* Explore

NATCHEZ
WOODVILLE

NATCHEZ

One of the oldest European settlements in the Mississippi Valley, Natchez had probably been continuously occupied by Indians since at least the eighth century. Of course the city is best known as an antebellum destination, loaded with some of the most impressive Mississippi plantations and many fine homes of merchants in town. Unless you are absolutely locked into the time period covered by this book, don't miss the wealth of other historic sites here. You can see them on a walking or driving tour, or take the Natchez trolley. Historic house tours of private homes are also available in the spring and the fall. Check with the Natchez Convention and Visitors Bureau for exact dates each year.

MISSISSIPPI *Time Line*

1779	**1795**	**1798**
Spain declares war on England; Bernardo de Gálvez, governor of Spanish Louisiana, captures Natchez	Treaty of San Lorenzo grants United States land north of the 31st parallel and rights of free navigation on the Mississippi River	Spain evacuates Natchez and other forts in Mississippi; Congress designates land north of the 31st parallel as Mississippi Territory

The younger brother of the Great Sun had the title of "Tattooed Serpent." He was a diplomat in negotiations with the French. Therefore the Great Sun did not become involved. When the Tattooed Serpent died, his wives and members of his retinue voluntarily allowed themselves to be strangled with bowstrings so they could accompany him and serve him.

Part of the problems with the French may have resulted from the death of the Tattooed Serpent in 1725 and the death of the Great Sun in 1728. His successor was young and inexperienced, and when the French made increasing demands on the Natchez, he was not able to proceed cautiously.

HISTORICAL SITES *and* MUSEUMS

Grand Village of the Natchez Indians (800-647-6724, 601-446-6502; www.mdah.state.ms.us), 400 Jefferson Davis Blvd. Open daily. Historians and archaeologists describe the Natchez Indians as a settled, agricultural people who lived within a stable social organization and followed their ancient religious traditions. Over the years they had dealings with individuals from both England and France and, other than the usual quarrels with neighbors, erupted in violence only when provoked.

They lived in family groups on farms, and trails connected the farms with mound centers. Planting and harvesting took precedence, and mound building stretched out over years. Tribal officials lived at the mound centers, which included a sacred temple building. The Natchez people would gather at the mounds for religious ceremonies.

The Natchez Indians remained in the area for a millennium, from 700 until they were hunted down and killed by the French between 1730 and 1732. Between 1682 and 1729 the Grand Village was their ceremonial center. Early French explorers, priests, and few others knew about the ceremonial mounds on the banks of St. Catherine Creek. In the beginning, relationships between the French and the Natchez were friendly, but by 1716 they had begun to worsen. In 1729 the Natchez massacred the French at Fort Rosalie, and the following year the French started

1801	**1803**	**1813**	**1817**
Indians allow development of Natchez Trace connecting Mississippi with Tennessee	The Louisiana Purchase opens the Mississippi River to American navigation	Indians massacre settlers in eastern Mississippi during Creek War	Congress splits Mississippi Territory; eastern part becomes Alabama Territory, the western part becomes the state of Mississippi

destroying Natchez villages. The survivors had to leave their homeland, and the tribe did not survive as an entity.

Take a walk around the Grand Village and you will see three platform mounds. We headed for the Great Sun's Mound, which rises up eight feet. This was the home of the Great Sun, who had inherited his position from his mother. The complex social organization of the Natchez was essentially matrilineal, a system whereby the family name and tribal standing came from the mother. Anyone who was related to the Great Sun was counted within the noble ranks, as opposed to the commoners. Men of the nobility married women from the commoners. The Great Sun did not pass his royal blood to his children, but the royal line came from his oldest sister. She had to marry a commoner, and her oldest son, the nephew of the Great Sun, was then the leader of the tribe. The uncle-nephew relationship was the key, rather than the father-son relationship.

The Temple Mound contains the bones of previous Suns. A perpetual fire burned in the inner sanctum. If the fire died, those tending to it were put to death. Nearby is the ceremonial plaza, dating from the early 1700s. A French siege trench there dates from 1730.

A reconstructed Natchez house and corn granary stands near the entrance. The museum in the visitor center offers displays on Fort Rosalie during the colonial period, as well as collections of eathenware and baskets.

LODGING

DUNLEITH
84 Homochitto St., Natchez, MS 39120
entered 800-433-2445, 601-446-8500;
www.dunleith.com
Dunleith is located on 40 acres of landscaped gardens and wooded bayous. Twenty-six guest rooms.

MONMOUTH PLANTATION
36 Melrose Ave., Natchez, MS 39120
800-828-4531, 601-442-5852;
www.monmouthplantation.com
This stunning home dates from 1818, and six more buildings just down the hill contain additional guest rooms and suites. The grounds are beautiful with gardens, ponds, fountains, oaks, and Spanish moss. Wisteria blooms, and there's even a gazebo. Monmouth Plantation also offers tours daily, as well as during plantation pilgrimages and other special events in Natchez. Thirty guest rooms.

NATCHEZ EOLA HOTEL
220 N. Pearl St., Natchez, MS 39120
866-445-3652, 601-445-6000;
www.eolahotel@natchezeola.com
The hotel dates from 1927 and is in the heart of downtown Natchez. There are 131 guest rooms.

NATCHEZ HISTORIC INN
201 N. Pearl St., Natchez, MS 39120
601-442-8848; www.natchez
historicinn.com
This B&B is in a building that dates from 1840 and contains a collection of both religious and secular works of art. Sixteen guest rooms.

RESTAURANTS

THE CARRIAGE HOUSE RESTAURANT
Stanton Hall
401 High St.
800-647-6742, 601-445-5151
Southern cuisine includes fried chicken, brisket of beef, and seafood.

Monmouth Plantation in Natchez

MONMOUTH PLANTATION
36 Melrose Ave.
800-828-4531, 601-442-5852
The Empire dining room offers a five-course dinner by candlelight.

KING'S TAVERN
619 Jefferson St.
601-446-8845
The restaurant is in a building that dates from 1789 or before. Specialties include prime rib, seafood, and pasta.

EVENTS

March: Natchez Pow Wow, Grand Village, 601-446-6502; www.mdah.state.ms.us

March–April and September–October: Natchez Spring and Fall Plantation Pilgrimage, 800-647-6742, 601-446-6631; www.natchezpilgrimage.com

INFORMATION

NATCHEZ CONVENTION & VISITORS BUREAU
211 Main St., Natchez, MS 39120
800-647-6724, 601-446-6345; www.visitnatchez.com

Crawfish Chowder from Monmouth Plantation

1 bunch green onions, chopped
4–5 slices hickory smoked bacon
¼ cup vegetable oil
1 large onion, ¼-inch diced
2 ribs celery, ¼-inch diced
1 bell pepper, ¼-inch diced
1 pint diced tomatoes with juice
1 pint crawfish stock (made from boiled shells)

3 large bay leaves
3 pounds peeled crawfish tails, cooked (may substitute shrimp)
1 cup heavy whipping cream
¼ cup flour
3 medium-size potatoes, peeled and diced
Cajun seasoning to taste

Cook bacon until crisp, remove bacon and discard oil. Add onions, celery, and bell pepper and cook for about 5 minutes. Add flour. Mixture will become soft and sticky. Add tomatoes, juice, and stock. Mix well. Add some of the seasoning mix and bay leaves. Bring to a boil, stirring frequently to avoid sticking. Add potatoes and cook until slightly firm. Add cream and return to boil. Then let simmer for about 5 minutes. Add crawfish tails, cook for 2 minutes, and remove from heat. Add chopped green onions. Season to taste. Serve in warmed soup plates with crusty bread.

WOODVILLE

The town of Woodville, the boyhood home of Jefferson Davis, is about 30 miles due south of Natchez on US 61.

HISTORICAL SITES and MUSEUMS

Rosemont Plantation 1810 (601-888-6809; www.rosemontplantation1810.com; mailing address: Box 814, MS 24, Woodville, MS 39669.) Open daily except Mon. In 1810 Samuel and Jane Davis settled here when their son, Jefferson Davis, was two years old. He later became a U.S. congressman from Mississippi, secretary of war under President Franklin Pierce, and the first and only president of the Confederacy. The home, the outbuildings, and grounds have been restored, and many of the original furnishings and paintings are in the house.

Look in the center hall to see the height marks for children from the 1890s. Girls and boys were measured in stocking feet. The portrait of Jefferson Davis is an oil copy of an 1849 likeness of him. The lithograph of President Davis in the parlor is a prized Davis family heirloom. Another likeness of Davis hangs in the dining room, along with an engraving of George and Martha Washington. The champagne glasses came from Davis's home, Beauvoir, on the Mississippi coast.

The NATCHEZ *Trace*

Buffalo roamed on the Old Natchez Trace when the Natchez, Chickasaw, and Choctaw Indians used it. The French mapped the trail in 1733. Farmers in the Ohio River Valley floated their crops down the rivers to Natchez or New Orleans on flatboats that were then broken up and sold for lumber; the only way for the farmers to get home was either riding or walking. The trace was the most direct route.

In 1801 an Indian treaty allowed the trace to be developed as a major road and mail route. By 1810 improvements had been made, and then inns cropped up along the way. Hazards included thieves, swamps, floods, disease-carrying insects, and unfriendly Indians. The need for the trace diminished as steamboats entered the scene and provided transportation on the Mississippi. The **Natchez Trace Parkway** (866.SEE.MISS; www.visitmississippi.org), 124 N. Jackson St., Kosciusko, MS 39090), following the old route, now stretches from the Mississippi River in Natchez northeast all the way to Nashville.

The National Park Service has a brochure listing the mileposts and points of interest. Phone 800-305-7417 or 662-680-4027. A drive along the trace is very pleasant, with views of large trees and skilled landscaping. Stop in one of the information centers, such as the one at milepost 8.7, to see an Old Trace exhibit detailing the wilderness road used by southeastern Indian tribes, American Indians, traders, soldiers, "Kaintucks," post riders, settlers, slaves, circuit-riding preachers, outlaws, and adventurers. At milepost 10.3 you will find Emerald Mound, which dates to around 1400. There is a trail to the top.

Mount Locust (800-305-7417, 662-680-4027; www.nps.gov/natr), Natchez Trace Parkway at milepost 15.6. Open daily. This 1780 inn is the only remaining inn, also called a "stand." Rangers are there to give talks on the inn as well as the Natchez Trace Parkway. Someday we would like to return and enjoy driving the entire trail, one of the gems of this region.

Mount Locust on the Natchez Trace

Rosemount Plantation in Woodville, the boyhood home of Jefferson Davis

Current Information

TRAVEL AND TOURISM INFORMATION
P.O. Box 849, Jackson, MS 39205
866-SEE-MISS (733-6477), 601-359-3297
www.visitmississippi.org

Tennessee

Historical Introduction
to
Tennessee

In 1540 conquistador Hernando de Soto is said to have led his mounted expedition, including Spanish aristocrats, and Indians to carry their gear, along the Hiwassee and Tennessee Rivers in the eastern part of what would become Tennessee. He was seeking gold but instead found a yellow-colored metal, copper. By the following year, after considerable wanderings and beleaguered by hostile Indians, de Soto and his men had reached the land of the Chickasaws in southwestern Tennessee. Possibly somewhere near present-day Memphis, de Soto crossed the Mississippi into Arkansas, where he would die the following year.

Well more than a century later, in 1673, Frenchmen from the north arrived at the Fourth Chickasaw Bluff. Louis Jolliet of Quebec, a fur trader, and Father Jacques Marquette, a Jesuit missionary, had traveled down the Mississippi River in birch-bark canoes, plagued by troublesome "musquitoes." But when the Frenchmen reached the Arkansas River, Indians warned them of the Spanish ahead, and they decided to turn back north.

Also in 1673 Abraham Wood, who owned a Virginia trading post, sent Englishmen James Needham, a planter, and Gabriel Arthur, an indentured servant, on a mission into the Appalachian backcountry. They traveled with eight Tomahitan Indians and arrived in "Overhill" lands to trade with the Indians there.

In 1682 Sieur de La Salle, having explored southward from Canada, claimed possession of the entire Mississippi River basin for Louis XIV. He envisioned a French empire stretching from the St. Lawrence River to the Gulf of Mexico. Fort Prudhomme was erected, possibly near the mouth of the Hatchie River on the Second Chickasaw Bluff, but did not last long. Martin Chartier deserted La Salle

Overleaf: An Indian family domestic scene at the Chucalissa Museum in Memphis

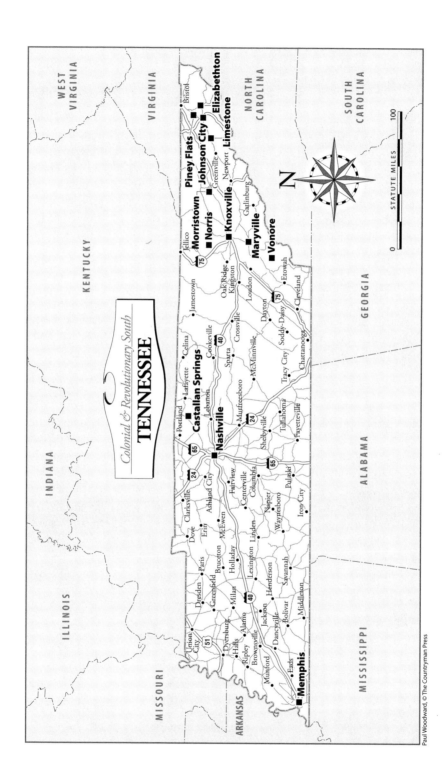

Colonial & Revolutionary South

TENNESSEE

WEST VIRGINIA

VIRGINIA

KENTUCKY

INDIANA

ILLINOIS

MISSOURI

ARKANSAS

MISSISSIPPI

ALABAMA

GEORGIA

NORTH CAROLINA

SOUTH CAROLINA

N

STATUTE MILES

0 · 100

Bristol

Piney Flats

Johnson City

Elizabethton

Limestone

Greenville

Newport

Morristown

Norris

Knoxville

Gatlinburg

Maryville

Vonore

Jellico

Oak Ridge

Kingston

Loudon

Etowah

Cleveland

Jamestown

Dayton

Soddy-Daisy

Crossville

Sparta

McMinnville

Tracy City

Chattanooga

Cookeville

Celina

Lafayette

Portland

Castallan Springs

Lebanon

Murfreesboro

Shelbyville

Tullahoma

Fayetteville

Nashville

Columbia

Pulaski

Iron City

Fairview

Centerville

Napier

Waynesboro

Ashland City

Clarksville

Dove

Erin

McEwen

Linden

Henderson

Savannah

Middleton

Paris

Greenfield

Bruceton

Holladay

Lexington

Jackson

Bolivar

Dresden

Milan

Alamo

Union City

Dyersburg

Halls

Ripley

Brownsville

Dancyville

Munford

Eads

Memphis

Paul Woodward, © The Countryman Press

and was befriended by the Shawnee in the lower Cumberland Valley. The Shawnee took him with them as they left the valley in 1692.

The Overhill Cherokees

Sir Alexander Cuming was a clever entrepreneur in South Carolina who managed to start a loan office to encourage men to mortgage their plantations to him. Then he became active in shipping from Charles Town. In 1730 he went into the wilderness and presented himself as an ambassador for King George II in the Cherokee town of Keowee. Next he crossed the mountains into the Overhill country and the Cherokee town of Great Tellico. He had left England to look for Cherokee royalty but, finding none, dubbed an important chief Emperor Moytoy of Tellico. The Indians listened to him and agreed to become subjects of King George II.

Cuming invited a group of Cherokees to travel to England with him. One of the braves was Attakullakulla, also called Little Carpenter, who later became a peacemaker between the English and the Cherokee. After a voyage on the *Fox,* they reached London, where they had dinner with the king. Articles of Agreement were written and signed. The Indians returned home, but Cuming did not, for he had swindled men in South Carolina and felt he would not be welcome.

Utopian Dreams

America has always attracted visionaries, and Tennessee was no exception. A German Jesuit from Saxony, Christian Gottlieb Priber, came to the Tennessee country in 1736, initially as a French agent. But quickly Priber began to put his own utopian plan for a new kind of colony into practice at Great Tellico. He used his books and writing to gather converts into his "Kingdom of Paradise." There the Cherokees and the white men would be equals, goods would be held by everyone, people would work for the common good, and women would be equal to men. The chief medicine man became emperor, and Priber was the secretary of state.

Priber sent a letter to the English governor in Charles Town, telling him that the English had better leave America because it belonged to the Indians. He signed it "Christian Priber, Prime Minister." The governor in Charles Town sent a man,

---

TENNESSEE *Time Line*

1541
Hernando de Soto crosses the Mississippi River, possibly near the Fourth Chickasaw Bluff (Memphis)

1682
René-Robert Cavelier, Sieur de La Salle, builds Fort Prudhomme at one of the Chickasaw bluffs; he proceeds downriver and claims the entire Mississippi basin for France

1730
Freelance English diplomat Alexander Cuming visits the Overhill Cherokee towns

unsuccessfully, to arrest Priber. Eventually Priber was captured by the Cherokees' enemies, the Creek, who turned him over to authorities in South Carolina. There he was imprisoned in Fort Frederica, where he died, along with his scheme of Paradise.

Fort Loudoun

At the outbreak of the French and Indian War in 1754, the Cherokee warriors, who were allied with the British, needed protection for their families against the raids of Indians allied with France. Fort Loudoun, at the junction of the Little Tennessee and Tellico Rivers, was built in 1756 by the South Carolina militia to provide that protection, with Captain Raymond Demere in charge of the garrison. Indians came with food, and twelve cannon also arrived, but arguments and dissension spoiled the spirit of cooperation first felt by both sides, and by late 1759 open hostilities broke out. The Cherokee laid siege to the fort, which they captured the following summer, after ambushing a British relief force. Soldiers from the garrison were allowed to depart, but Indians slaughtered many of them on the second day of their journey.

Sycamore Shoals

In 1775 a group of Cherokees and whites met at Sycamore Shoals on the Watauga River (at Elizabethton) and signed a treaty, whereby the Transylvania Company, headed by Richard Henderson of North Carolina, bought some 20 million acres from the Indians, for 10,000 pounds worth of money and goods. The massive land deal included the part of present-day Tennessee north of the Cumberland River and a large portion of present-day Kentucky. One Cherokee leader, Chief Dragging Canoe, opposed the treaty, but the other chiefs signed the deeds. Under British law such private purchases of land from Indians were illegal—and other Indian nations also claimed ownership of the land—but on the eve of the Revolution, authority was in doubt, and the question of legality was easy to ignore. Virginia nullified the purchase in 1776, as did North Carolina in 1783—in both cases after the settlements of Boonesborough had been established in Kentucky and Nashborough in Tennessee.

1736
Christian Priber, a German Jesuit, arrives in Great Tellico and plans to establish his utopian "Kingdom of Paradise"

1757
South Carolina militia build Fort Loudoun near Overhill Cherokee towns

1775
Richard Henderson creates the Transylvania Land Company, buys land from the Indians, then resells the Watauga Territory to settlers led by Charles Robertson

At Sycamore Shoals, Dragging Canoe spoke to Richard Henderson: "You have bought a fair land, but there is a cloud hanging over it. You will find its settlement dark and bloody."

In Cherokee practice, agreements were not binding on those who refused to consent to them, so in 1776 Dragging Canoe and his Cherokee friends, now known as the Chickamauga, attacked Fort Watauga at Sycamore Shoals. The Revolutionary War was now raging in the East, and the Chickamauga had cast their lot with British Loyalists. However, the pioneer defenders did not surrender, and the Indians left. Four years later, the fort became the staging area for a famed long march of Patriot backwoodsmen to Kings Mountain in South Carolina.

The Overmountain Men

The hardy settlers who lived in and beyond the Appalachians at this time, often making their own laws, were called Overmountain men. In 1780, as fighting in the Revolution had shifted to the South, British major Patrick Ferguson sent a messenger to notify all militia officers on the Watauga, Nolichucky, and Holston Rivers that they must stop opposing the royal government. If they did not, Ferguson would bring his men over the mountains, hang the leaders, and devastate the countryside.

This threat angered the independent, self-sufficient Overmountain men, and in late September militia members and volunteers alike congregated at Sycamore Shoals on the Watauga River. Forces under Colonel John Sevier were reinforced by those of Isaac Shelby and many others. After an arduous ten-day march to the southeast over high mountain passes and then through the Piedmont, the Overmountain men crossed the South Carolina border and camped at Cowpens (the site of a later major battle). Major Ferguson and his Loyalists had learned of their approach and took up positions on the minor rise of Kings Mountain to face them. That terrain was much easier than what the Overmountain men had just crossed, and they marched to Kings Mountain the next day, where they proceeded to attack Indian-style, moving from behind trees. Despite having to fight their way uphill

---

TENNESSEE *Time Line*

1781	**1785**	**1791**	**1796**
Cumberland settlers and Chickamauga Cherokees fight Battle of the Bluffs at Fort Nashborough, the site of modern Nashville	The Treaty of Hopewell establishes boundaries between the United States and the Cherokee nation; White's Fort built at site of Knoxville	William Blount, first and only governor of the new Southwest Territory, establishes headquarters at White's Fort, Knoxville	Tennessee admitted to the union as 16th state

---

against an entrenched enemy, an hour later the Overmountain men had virtually annihilated Ferguson's Loyalists, and Ferguson himself lay dead.

Fort Nashborough

After the Virginia legislature had nullified the Transylvania Company's holdings in territory that Virginia itself claimed, Richard Henderson was eager to pursue settlement of Tennessee lands. With Henderson's encouragement, James Robertson (whom Andrew Jackson called the Father of Tennessee) had traveled early in 1778 to the valley of the Cumberland and found the land heavily timbered and well drained by the river. He chose a site at French Lick and, the following fall, returned overland with a party of 200 men, while his partner, John Donelson, led the settlers' families in a flotilla of flatboats down the Tennessee River to the Ohio and up the Cumberland to join them. During this long and difficult voyage they had problems with rapids

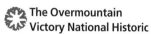 **The Overmountain Victory National Historic Trail** retraces the route of Patriot militia as they searched for the British. This trail is being developed through partnerships and ends at Kings Mountain National Military Park in South Carolina. Much of it is available to walkers today. For information contact the Superintendent, 2635 Park Rd., Blacksburg, SC 29702; 864-936-3477.

Inside the stockade at the Fort Loudoun State Historic Park in Vonore

The woodsmen from Tennessee used an Indian war-whoop as they charged into battle. They were called "the damned yelling boys."

and were attacked as they passed Chickamauga towns on the Tennessee; exhausted and depleted in numbers by casualties, some would not undertake the struggle against the current on the Cumberland.

Before the remaining boats reached French Lick, the Chickamauga, led by Dragging Canoe, attacked the fort on April 2, 1781, in what came to be known as the Battle of the Bluffs. First the Indians tricked and trapped Robertson and his men in an ambush outside the stockade. Mrs. Robertson could see the men's dire predicament and opened the gates and let out the dogs. These large dogs had been trained to attack Indians, and so they did. As the Indians scattered, Robertson and his men ran back to the fort. The day was won by dogs! The Chickamauga returned to attack the fort the next day, but it held.

The Chickamauga opposition led by Dragging Canoe had its roots not only in excessive and illegal grants of their hunting lands but also in broken treaties that had promised cessation of settlement in lands held by Indians. The Treaty of Hopewell, signed in 1785 in a town of that name in South Carolina, continued this disheartening pattern. It established boundaries between lands of the United States and those of the Cherokee and gave the right to the Indians to punish settlers who refused to leave hunting lands. Article 13 of the treaty proclaimed that "the hatchet shall be forever buried, and the peace given by the United States, and friendship re-established between said states on the one part, and all Cherokees on the other, shall be universal." As incursions on the Indians' lands continued and grew, the irony of the treaty's name became apparent to the Cherokees, who referred to it as "talking leaves" that could blow away when they no longer suited the settlers.

State of Franklin

The Watauga Association, a form of self-government, had been created by the settlers at Sycamore Shoals in 1772, when there was no other effective government. After the Revolutionary War ended, the association became involved in the formation of the state of Franklin. At that time, the counties in present-day eastern Tennessee were part of North Carolina, though North Carolina exercised no control and had even voted to give the counties to Congress to help pay their war bills. The settlers, feeling uncertain of their future, decided to declare their independence and petition Congress for statehood; they wanted to create the fourteenth state. Delegates met at Jonesborough, where they made a plan and drafted a constitution. The new "state" lasted only four years, until 1790, when opposition from North Carolina and then Indian attacks led the counties back to the protection of North Carolina. That state would soon cede the troublesome western lands to the federal government.

Southwest Territory

The Northwest Territory, established in 1787 and affirmed by Congress in 1789, was followed by the Southwest Territory a year later. Together the territories encompassed all U.S.-claimed land east of the Mississippi at the time. The Southwest Ordinance of 1790 established the Southwest Territory—equivalent in extent to present-day Tennessee—from the land ceded to the federal government by North Carolina. William Blount, an aggressive North Carolina land speculator who had acquired large tracts in Tennessee, was appointed territorial governor by President Washington. Blount presided at the first capital, Rocky Mount, and a year later moved the capital to White's Fort, renamed Knoxville in honor of Henry Knox. Statehood followed in 1796, when the population exceeded the required number.

Regions to Explore

EASTERN TENNESSEE
MIDDLE TENNESSEE
WESTERN TENNESSEE

EASTERN TENNESSEE

Near the southern end of the Appalachian Mountain range, this part of Tennessee includes the Blue Ridge, Great Smoky, Chilhowee, Unicoi, Iron, and Snowbird Mountains. The average elevation of the Blue Ridge is 5,000 feet. The region is noted for its tributaries, which join to form the Tennessee River. Throughout the region, northeast-to-southwest-oriented fertile valleys are separated by wooded ridges. The Great Valley is in the western area of the Tennessee Valley.

ELIZABETHTON

In 1772 settlers from North Carolina created the Watauga Association, perhaps the first independent government in the country. A bronze marker identifies the place beside the courthouse. The massive but legally dubious Transylvania Purchase was signed in Elizabethton in 1775.

HISTORICAL SITES *and* MUSEUMS
Sycamore Shoals State Historic Park (423-543-5808; www.sycamoreshoals.org), 1651 W. Elk Ave., Elizabethton, TN 37643. Open year-round. This interpretive site presents the first permanent American settlement outside the original 13

colonies. Sixteen families from North Carolina, fleeing over the mountains in the wake of the failed Regulator uprising in 1771, settled here, even though they knew they would be outside the protection of the colonies. By necessity they developed their own government, forming the Watauga Association in May 1772. This was the first "majority-rule" system of American democratic government. Settlers drafted the Articles of the Watauga Association and elected five men, called a court, to "govern and direct for the common good of all the people."

Additional pioneers from Virginia and North Carolina arrived, and trails connected Sycamore Shoals with Fort Robinson (1761), Fort Patrick Henry (1776), Sapling Grove (Bristol), Rocky Mount (Piney Flats), and settlements in northwestern North Carolina and South Carolina.

Richard Henderson led the Transylvania Company in its purchase of over 20 million acres for 2,000 pounds sterling and goods worth 8,000 pounds. It took weeks for 1,200 Indians to agree to the signing of the deed. They were opposed by Chief Dragging Canoe, but the other chiefs signed.

A reconstruction of Fort Watauga (the fort originally stood on the shores of the Watauga River) was based on archaeological and historical data.

The John & Landon Carter Mansion (423-543-6140), 1013 Broad St. Open May–Sep. by appointment at Sycamore Shoals State Historic Park. On land bought from the Cherokee, this house was begun in 1775 by John Carter and finished by his son Landon. John Carter was among the founders of the Watauga Association. Landon Carter fought in the Revolutionary War and was known as an Indian fighter. Don't miss the paintings over the mantel, probably done by family members around 1870. They depict scenery of the area. Much of the house is original, and three of the rooms still have the original wall finishes.

LODGING

DOE RIVER INN
217 Academy St., Elizabethton, TN 37643
423-543-1444, 423-292-2848;
www.doeriverinn.com
This Victorian home dates from 1894. Two guest rooms.

MEREDITH VALLEY CABINS
341 Sycamore Shoals Dr., Elizabethton, TN 37643
423-543-8603, 423-895-0036;
www.meredithvalleycabins.com
Three cabins, with kitchen facilities.

OLD MAIN MANOR BED & BREAKFAST
708 N. Main St., Elizabethton, TN 37643
423-542-8277;
www.oldmainmanor.com
Guest rooms have Old English charm, and some have balconies with a view of the garden. Four guest rooms, including one in the carriage house.

EVENTS

February: Fort Garrison Overmountain Men, 423-543-5808
May: Muster at Fort Watauga, 423-543-5808
September: Overmountain Victory Trail Celebration, 423-543-5808
December: Christmas Garrison at Fort Watauga, 423-543-5808

INFORMATION

ELIZABETHTON / CARTER COUNTY TOURISM ASSOCIATION
500 Veterans Memorial Pkwy., P.O. Box 190
Elizabethton, TN 37644
423-547-3850; www.tourelizabethton.com

PINEY FLATS

For a short time this was the site of the capital of the Southwest Territory. Piney Flats is about ten miles from Elizabethton, via Wautaga.

HISTORICAL SITES *and* MUSEUMS

Rocky Mount (888-538-1791; www.rockymountmuseum.com), 200 Hyder Hill Rd., Piney Flats, TN 37686. Open Mar. to mid-Dec., Tue.–Sat. William Cobb, one of the first settlers in the area, built his log home here in 1772. George Washington appointed William Blount as territorial governor of the Southwest Territory in 1790, and Rocky Mount was the capitol. Blount, as a guest in the house, wrote, "I am very well accommodated with a Room with glass Windows, Fireplace, Etc."

Interpreters in costume depict the Cobb family. They are involved in daily chores in the kitchen, barn, weaving cabin, and gardens. There are also farm animals. The visitor center offers views of life in 1790–92.

JOHNSON CITY

The original community started with the 18th-century St. John's Mill. Johnson City completes a triangle with Elizabethton and Piney Flats, with Watauga in the middle.

HISTORICAL SITES *and* MUSEUMS

Tipton-Haynes State Historic Site (423-926-3631; www.tipton-haynes.org), 2620 S. Roan St., Johnson City, TN 37601. Open Apr.–Nov., Mon.–Sat.; Dec.–Mar., Mon.–Fri. Colonel John Tipton, from Virginia, bought the land in 1784 and built his log home. He used stone in between the logs as well as mud chinking. Tipton was a member of the Territorial Assembly and a signer and framer of the first Tennessee Constitution.

The "battle" of Franklin took place on this land in 1788 when Colonel Tipton persuaded a North Carolina sheriff to seize some of Franklin governor John Sevier's property for back taxes. This brief and inconclusive siege of Tipton's house pitted supporters of Sevier against Tipton, who advocated a return to the jurisdiction of North Carolina. In 1839 the home was given to Landon Carter Haynes, who enlarged the house into clapboard buildings.

LODGING

HART HOUSE INN B&B
207 E. Holston Ave., Johnson City, TN
37601
888-915-7239, 423-926-3147
This 1910 Dutch colonial–style house has
antique furnishings. Three guest rooms.

JAM 'N JELLY INN
1310 Indian Ridge Rd., Johnson City, TN
37604
423-929-0039
This inn is a custom-built log cabin. Three
guest rooms.

INFORMATION

**JOHNSON CITY CHAMBER OF
COMMERCE / CONVENTION
AND VISITORS BUREAU**
603 E. Market St., Box 180, Johnson
City, TN 37605
800-852-3392, 423-461-8000

LIMESTONE

About twenty miles southwest of Johnson City is the birthplace of a true American legend, Davy Crockett.

HISTORICAL SITES *and* MUSEUMS

Davy Crockett's Birthplace State Park (423-257-2167; www.tnstateparks.com)
1245 Davy Crockett Park Rd., Limestone, TN 37681. Exhibits in the museum describe Davy Crockett in his roles as hunter, frontier politician, and hero who died at the Battle of the Alamo in 1836. There is a replica of a cabin similar to his birthplace in 1786.

MORRISTOWN

During the 1790s Rebecca and John Crockett moved farther west with their family to Morristown, where they built a tavern.

HISTORICAL SITES *and* MUSEUMS

The Crockett Tavern Museum (423-587-9900; www.discoveret.org/crockett),
2002 Morningside Dr., Morristown, TN 27814. Open May–Oct., Tue.–Sat. This log replica shows how the Crockett family lived and ran their tavern. In 1799 Davy left home after a fight at school when he was 12 and did not return for two and a half years.

INFORMATION

GREEN COUNTY TOURISM
115 Academy St., Greenville, TN 37743
423-638-4111

NORRIS

Not far north of Knoxville on Interstate 75 take exit 22 east and proceed about a mile on TN 61 to reach the campus of a major living-history museum devoted to frontier life in Tennessee.

HISTORICAL SITES *and* MUSEUMS

Museum of Appalachia (865-494-7680; www.museumofappalachia.com), 2819 Andersonville Hwy., Clinton, TN 37716. Open daily. The museum began as a single log building on 2 acres and now has 36 buildings, mostly authentic log structures moved from the mountains to a working farm and wooded hillside of 65 acres. John Rice Irwin's grandparents lived in the area, as well as ancestors dating from 1784. He began collecting household items that meant a lot to his grandparents, then attended auctions and bid on more pieces and buildings. Don't miss Uncle John's cabin, which was used in the CBS series *Young Dan'l Boone,* filmed here.

MARYVILLE

Maryville is about seventeen miles south of Knoxville via US 129.

HISTORICAL SITES *and* MUSEUMS

Sam Houston Schoolhouse (865-983-1550; www.geocities.com/samhouston schoolhouse), 3650 Old Sam Houston School Rd., Maryville, TN 37804. Open Feb.–Dec., Tue.–Sun. The log cabin was built as a schoolhouse in 1794, two years before Tennessee became a state. It is the oldest schoolhouse in the state. Sam Houston taught here when he was 18 years of age.

KNOXVILLE

Knoxville is the major city in the eastern part of the state and was Tennessee's first capital after statehood.

HISTORICAL SITES *and* MUSEUMS

James White's Fort (865-525-6514; www.whitesfort.org), 205 E. Hill Ave., Knoxville, TN 37902. Open daily. Settlers arrived in the area during the late 1700s. The founder of Knoxville, James White, arrived in 1785 from Iredell County, North Carolina. He had fought in the Revolution and was given a grant of 1,000 acres, which by 1800 he had increased to 128,000 acres through land speculation.

With his two eldest sons, White built a two-story log house with glazed windows and a chimney of dressed stone—an elegant structure by frontier standards. He planted his first crop, turnips, to tide his family of four girls and three boys

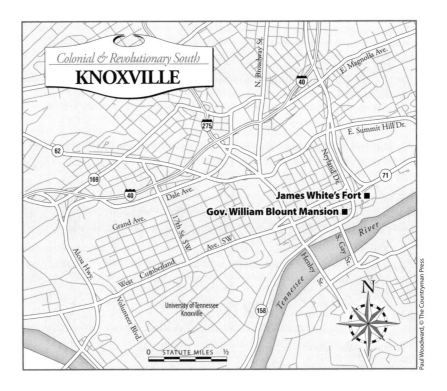

Colonial & Revolutionary South
KNOXVILLE

James White's Fort ■
Gov. William Blount Mansion ■

University of Tennessee
Knoxville

N

0   STATUTE MILES   ½

Paul Woodward, © The Countryman Press

over the winter. White was friendly with the Cherokees and negotiated their treaties. They came to his home to trade with him.

In following years White added a stockade fence to enclose the house and its outbuildings from predatory wild animals, including panthers, bears, and wildcats. In addition to his family, often 35 or 40 people slept within the compound, so he built several cabins and a kitchen. Horses, cattle, sheep, pigs, chickens, and goats lived in the courtyard, as well as more families.

In 1791 William Blount, governor of the Territory South of the River Ohio—the formal name of the Southwest Territory—asked White for part of his land to establish a future capital to be named for Henry Knox, Washington's secretary of war. Each of 64 half-acre lots cost $8, and a lottery was held to assign the lots among rich and poor alike. In 1796 Tennessee became the 16th state, with Knoxville as its capital.

When we visited, Robert McGinnis, dressed in frontier costume, invited us into the kitchen. A blazing fire warmed the room, and the table was set for refreshments. The house, just a few steps across the dog-trot, is the original structure twice moved and reconstructed; it is furnished for a family, with four beds upstairs, each covered with a quilt.

We walked over to the museum to see a fine arrowhead collection, which came from the Tennessee River near Gay Street when the river was dredged in the 1930s.

Some of the arrowheads date to around 2,000 BC. There's a carved wooden bust of Sequoyah, a Cherokee who created an alphabet for his people.

Also within the stockade, the guesthouse housed more than one family, with the boys sleeping up in the loft and the girls downstairs with the adults. The blacksmith shop made all the tools and hardware needed on the farm, such as hoes, plows, and horseshoes. The smokehouse preserved the hams, for which this part of the South is still famous.

James White lived in the fort until 1793 and then moved upriver to less confined quarters on a plantation. He was promoted to general in the War of 1812 and remained active in developing Knoxville until his death in 1821, donating more land for the Presbyterian Church and Blount College, predecessor of the University of Tennessee.

Blount Mansion (888-654-0016; www.blountmansion.org), 200 W. Hill Ave. Open Apr.–Dec., Mon.–Sat.; Jan.–Mar., Mon.–Fri. A few blocks from James White's fort, you can see how quickly frontier life began to undergo transformation. In 1792, just a year after Knoxville became the capital of the Southwest Territory, Governor William Blount began building his mansion on a bluff overlooking the Tennessee River. Representing North Carolina, he had served in the Continental Congress, later signed the Constitution, and was appointed governor of the Southwest Territory by George Washington in 1790.

He was also a land speculator with an interest in over a million acres at one time, and later a U.S. senator facing an impeachment proceeding that tested the separation of powers doctrine of the new Constitution. Although expelled from the Senate, he successfully resumed his political career in Tennessee.

Like many colonial homes, the mansion evolved over time with the addition of west and east wings. It was one of the first frame houses in Tennessee, and its oldest section was built with a hall leading to a main room and parlor, rather than room-to-room connections. The Cherokees called it the "House of Many Eyes" because of the many glass windows.

The main room in the oldest section is furnished with a canopy bed, a corner cupboard, dining table, and several chairs. A portrait of George Washington hangs over the fireplace. Blount wanted to bring high style to what was then "the West," so his daughter had a 1790 dulcimer piano. The family served tea with white sugar instead of sorghum (molasses or

The Blount Mansion has many stories to tell about those who lived or worked here, as well as guests. One involves Louis Philippe, future king of France (1830–48), who was staying overnight in Knoxville, perhaps at the Chisholm Tavern. He later wrote, "The Holstein [Holston] River, which flows below the town, is broad and beautiful. We bathed in it; the day was very hot." What he didn't write is a staple of local legend: He got into bed, then leaped up and ran down to the river naked to escape the bedbug-infested mattress.

honey), and the tea table was set with a sterling teapot, pitcher, bowl, and a cone of white sugar.

While he was a U.S. senator, Blount gave a friend a letter to take to another friend in Knoxville with the admonition to read and then burn it. However, the directions were ignored, and the letter was turned over to Blount's political enemies in Washington. Thomas Jefferson read it, and the House wanted to impeach Blount. But the Senate dismissed the charges, so the House could not carry out the impeachment of a senator. Nevertheless, Blount was expelled by his colleagues.

Ramsey House Plantation (865-546-0745; www.ramseyhouse.org), 2614 Thorngrove Pike. Open Tue.–Sun. In 1783 Francis Ramsey left the Shenandoah Valley at age 19 in pursuit of land. He had been invited by his maternal uncle, who settled on Big Limestone Creek, to live with him. Francis set out with his surveyor's chain and compass and his horse. He had a good education, could write well, and had studied surveying.

Like James White and William Blount, he wanted land, and he didn't waste any time. He obtained 500 acres in one area and 400 acres on Big and Little Limestone Creeks in 1783, hoping to make it his home. He was appointed county surveyor by the Washington County court. However, the Cherokee Indians were still hostile because his lands were also their hunting grounds. The Dumplin Creek Treaty signed in June of 1785 between the short-lived state of Franklin and some Cherokee chiefs was the basis for land claimed by Ramsey and other settlers, but that claim was overturned five months later in the Treaty of Hopewell.

Ramsey married Peggy Alexander and, a decade later, in 1797, built the first stone house in Knox County. It was designed by Thomas Hope, an Englishman from Charleston, South Carolina, who was influenced by Christopher Wren and Charles Bulfinch. Outside, walls of native pink marble and blue limestone created a facade of simple elegance. Inside, the restored house contains two Chippendale cushioned chairs that were given to Peggy and Francis as a wedding present from her father.

LODGING

MAPLE GROVE INN
8800 Westland Dr., Knoxville, TN 37923
800-645-0713, 865-690-9565;
www.maplegroveinn.com
Thomas Campbell McCaughan built the house in 1799. The original Georgian-style home was two rooms up and two rooms down, but it has since been expanded. The rooms are furnished with antiques. Eight guest rooms.

MAPLEHURST INN
800 W. Hill Ave., Knoxville, TN 37902
800-451-1562, 865-523-7773
The inn offers 18th-century charm with 21st-century amenities. It is located in the historic district and on the Tennessee River. Eleven guest rooms.

INFORMATION

KNOXVILLE TOURISM
301 S. Gay St., Knoxville, TN 37902
800-727-8045, 865-523-7263;
www.knoxville.org

VONORE

In 1979 the Tellico Dam changed the topographical outline of the valley. But two historical sites were left intact.

HISTORICAL SITES and MUSEUMS

Fort Loudoun State Historic Park (423-884-6217; www.fortloudon.com), 338 Fort Loudoun Rd., Vonore, TN 37885. Open daily. Fort Loudon was built in 1756 with William Gerald DeBrahm as the engineer. Captain Raymond Demere was the commander of the post, which was garrisoned by 90 British regulars and 120 South Carolina militiamen. He turned over the fort command to his brother Paul in 1757.

Now situated on 100 acres, Ramsey House Plantation has become a center for heritage gardening and agricultural crafts. Special programs include churning butter, making corn-husk dolls, herbal lore, and archaeology. The Heirloom Gardening program offers plants introduced to American gardens from 1600 to 1950.

It was the first planned British fort in the "Overhill" country. In late 1759 the Cherokee Indians, former British allies, began a siege of the fort, cutting off the supply line through the mountains. By August Paul Demere agreed to terms of surrender. Some 180 men and 60 women and children left the fort, and the next morning the Cherokee attacked and killed about 25, with the rest taken as slaves.

The William C. Watson Visitor Center has a slide presentation and displays of artifacts. The foundation of the Tellico Blockhouse is nearby. It dates from 1794, and several treaties were negotiated here. A trading post was adjacent to the blockhouse.

Sequoyah Birthplace Museum (423-884-6246; www.sequoyahmuseum.org), 576 Hwy. 360. Open daily. Sequoyah, the Cherokee who created a written language for his people, was born here in 1776. Visitors can hear Cherokee myths and learn about the history of the nation in the museum. One of the programs gives information on how to pronounce the Cherokee syllabary.

MIDDLE TENNESSEE

Middle Tennessee is bounded by the Cumberland Plateau on the east and the Tennessee River on the west. To the west of the Cumberland Plateau is the Highland Rim, which surrounds the Nashville basin. This basin has fertile farm country, and tobacco is grown there. The Natchez Trace was first an Indian trail and later a busy trading route connecting middle Tennessee with the town of Natchez, Mississippi. Now this route is a scenic and historic highway called the Natchez Trace Parkway.

CASTALIAN SPRINGS

Indians knew about the mineral spring here. Isaac Bledsoe arrived in the late 1770s, and the spring was called Bledsoe's Lick. He and his brother built Bledsoe's Fort overlooking the spring. Both men were killed by Indians, and their graves are marked with a monument.

HISTORICAL SITES and MUSEUMS

Cragfont (615-452-7070; www.cragfont.org), 200 Cragfont Rd., Castalian Springs, TN 37031. Open Apr. 15 to Oct. 31, Tue.–Sun. General James Winchester built his Georgian-style home in 1798 on a rocky bluff. Some of the Federal antiques inside belonged to the Winchester family. The ballroom on the second floor was the first in Tennessee. Guests included Andrew Jackson, Sam Houston, and the Marquis de Lafayette.

NASHVILLE

Nashville was founded in 1779 as James Robertson arrived with a group of men and livestock. A second group included women and children, and they came by boat from Kingsport in northeastern Tennessee by an incredibly long, circuitous, and difficult voyage down the Holston River to the Tennessee River, following its great semicircle all the way to the Ohio River, then up against the current on the Cumberland to French Lick. The settlers called their stockade Fort Nashborough after Francis Nash, who fought in the Revolutionary War. They drew up the Cumberland Compact, which was the first civil government in Middle Tennessee.

HISTORICAL SITES and MUSEUMS

Fort Nashborough (615-862-8400; www.nashville.gov/parks), 170 First Ave. N., Riverfront Park, Nashville, TN 37201. Open Tue.–Sun. Part of this 1780 log fort has been reconstructed on the riverfront. It looks like a little log cabin, and there are no furnishings inside.

Travellers Rest Plantation & Museum (866-832-8197, 615-832-8197; www.travellersrestplantation.org), 636 Farrell Pkwy. Open daily. John Overton, a lawyer and judge, built a small two-story home in 1799. He originally called it Golgotha because it was built on a Indian burial ground. Additions in the early 1800s enlarged the house to its present configuration. Overton and Andrew Jackson had lived together when both were young, and Overton later helped Jackson with his political campaigns.

Tennessee State Museum (800-407-4324; www.tnmuseum.org), Fifth and Deaderick Sts. Open Tue.–Sat. This sizable museum has collections that cover a

The Natchez Trace was an essential part of the developing trade pattern from Tennessee and Kentucky, where shipments of goods were floated down the tributaries and the Mississippi to New Orleans and there transshipped to their ultimate destinations. The Natchez Trace was the main route back home for the men who broke up their flatboats at the end of the voyage and either walked or rode home along the trace. That trade pattern, and the closure of the lower Mississippi to Americans just after the turn of the nineteenth century, were the major incentives for the Louisiana Purchase.

wide range of topics. Highlights include Davy Crockett's rifle, Daniel Boone's knife, and a reconstructed log cabin.

The Hermitage (615-889-2941; www.thehermitage.com), 4580 Rachel's Lane. Open daily. Begin your tour in the Andrew Jackson Visitor Center, where you can watch a 15-minute introductory film on Jackson and the Hermitage. The mansion dates from 1819 and has been expanded since. After a fire in 1834 the house was rebuilt in Greek-revival style. Six Corinthian columns stand in the front of the house.

Inside, some original furnishings belonged to the Jackson family. Andrew Jackson returned here after his second term as president. Six of the original wallpapers placed after the fire are still intact. Family portraits hang on the walls, and Jackson's swords and books are on display.

Outside, you can visit the garden, Jackson's tomb, and take a "Beyond the Mansion" tour, which includes information on slavery, farming, and nature. Paths are marked. You can also drive one-half mile to the Hermitage Church and the Tulip Grove mansion, to view from the outside.

The Hermitage also offers a wagon tour from April through October. The tour goes to the First Hermitage, where Jackson lived from 1804 to 1821, the site of the cotton gin and press, and to the field quarters and archaeological sites connected with slavery and farming.

LODGING

THE HERITAGE HOTEL
231 Sixth Ave. N., Nashville, TN 37219
888-888-9414, 615-244-3121; www
.theheritagehotel.com
Dating from 1910, this classic hotel had a total renovation in 2002. There are 123 guest rooms.

UNION STATION
1001 Broadway, Nashville, TN 37203
615-726-1001; www.unionstation
hotelnashville.com
The building was built as the train station in 1900. The atrium lobby has a barrel-vaulted ceiling with Tiffany-style skylight. There are 125 guest rooms.

WESTERN TENNESSEE

T he western fringe of Tennessee has always been valued for its access to the great river that serves as its boundary, and the region's development has been closely tied to the economic and military value of the Mississippi. From prehistoric Indian settlement to 19th-century plantations, the river provided a way to move people and goods, until the Civil War and Reconstruction brought a temporary decline in trade. The 20th century saw renewed prosperity, and Memphis became known as a center of music, from the blues to Elvis Presley, as well as for its tragic role in the assassination of Martin Luther King Jr.

MEMPHIS

The Chickasaw Indians lived in the area, giving their name to the four "Chickasaw bluff" highlands on the eastern side of the river. Memphis rose on the site of the southernmost, Fourth Chickasaw Bluff. Hernando de Soto may have crossed the Mississippi near here in 1541. More than a century later Frenchman René-Robert Cavalier, Sieur de La Salle, passed by on his way to the mouth of the Mississippi, and proclaimed that the region belonged to France. Memphis was planned on the Chickasaw bluff overlooking the Mississippi River by Andrew Jackson, James Winchester, and John Overton and named for the ancient city on another great river, the Nile.

An abandoned Indian settlement from the 15th century was discovered in the late 1930s when workers for the Tennessee Division of State Parks found part of the prehistoric village. It was excavated by archaeologists and partly reconstructed, complete with thatched huts, after World War II.

HISTORICAL SITES and MUSEUMS
Chucalissa Museum (901-785-3160; www.chucalissa.org), 1987 Indian Village Dr., Memphis, TN 38109. Open Tue.–Sun. In the Choctaw language, chucalissa means "abandoned house," and the archaeological excavations have unearthed part of the Mississippian village. To set it in context, the museum has displays that offer a window into Native American life. They begin with the Paleo Indian period (20,000–8000 BC), move through the Archaic period (8000–1500 BC), the Woodland period (1500 BC–900 AD), the Mississippian period (900–1600 AD), and end with the European Explorers period.

Part of the village has been reconstructed to show the last occupied period. The plaza, where people gathered for gossip and trade, games and ceremonies, stands in the center. Houses of dignitaries and craftsmen circle the plaza, and the temple and residence of the chief and priests are sited on a large mound.

A dugout canoe rests at the entrance to the village. Canoes were made from a

Dugout canoe with temple mound in background at the Chucalissa Museum in Memphis

single cypress log hollowed out by fire. They served as the principal mode of transportation on the river and its tributaries.

Walk into House No. 1 to see models of a mother with her pottery bowls around her. The father is playing with the baby. Gourds and corn hang from the roof. Bearskins and woven mats line the bench beds along the walls. House No. 2 demonstrates various crafts, and the Shaman's Hut portrays the medicine man's use of herbal cures.

Outside the village you can walk the Chickasaw Bluff Interpretive Trail for more than half a mile. On it you will see depressions called borrow sites, ravines, and the Mississippi River.

Mississippi River Museum (800-507-6507; www.mudisland.com/museum .asp), 125 N. Front St. Open Tue.–Sun. This museum offers the natural and cultural history of the lower Mississippi River. Visitors learn about settlement from Indians to European explorers to later pioneers. Exhibits explore the tools and modes of transport, weapons, and imports of all these groups, as well as river engineering, disaster, Civil War operations, and music.

LODGING

THE PEABODY HOTEL MEMPHIS
149 Union Ave., Memphis, TN 38103
800-42 DUCKS, 901-578-3700; www.peabodymemphis.com
The hotel is called the "South's Grand Hotel," and it has been newly renovated. Don't miss the Peabody Ducks marching through the lobby twice a day. There are 468 guest rooms.

Current Information

TENNESSEE DEPARTMENT OF TOURIST DEVELOPMENT
312 8th Ave. N., 25th floor
Nashville, TN 37243
800-462-8366, 615-741-2159; www.tnvacation.com

OX YOKE

FLAX HACKLE

SHOULDER YOKE

COLLAR

Kentucky

Historical Introduction
to
Kentucky

K entucky may not have the old history of the original thirteen colonies, but it is home to the oldest mountains in the country—the Appalachians. As they are now, long ago they were covered by forests, had natural bridges, and a stunning underground cave system. Prehistoric people inhabited the region and left burial remains and mounds.

Early Explorers

Exploration from colonies on the Atlantic seaboard was hindered by the Allegheny Mountains, but by the 1670s Father Jacques Marquette and Louis Jolliet had come down waterways from French Canada to explore part of the Mississippi River. In 1682 La Salle claimed the Mississippi River valley and its entire watershed for France. The first English explorers, James Needham and Gabriel Arthur, traveled across the Alleghenies in 1673.

By the time European explorers and pioneers arrived in what is now Kentucky, most of the state was not heavily inhabited by Indians but rather was used as a hunting ground by Cherokees and other tribes from the south and Shawnees from the north; it may have been a de facto buffer zone between Indian nations.

In 1750 the Loyal Land Company of Virginia sent out Dr. Thomas Walker (he was the guardian of a young man named Thomas Jefferson), who walked through a gap in the Appalachians and emerged in what is now Barbourville. Walker noted the existence of a "plain Indian Road." He named the passage Cumberland Gap and brought back information on the potential of this region. The gap would later become the major conduit for settlers coming into Kentucky.

Overleaf: A reenactor at Old Fort Harrod

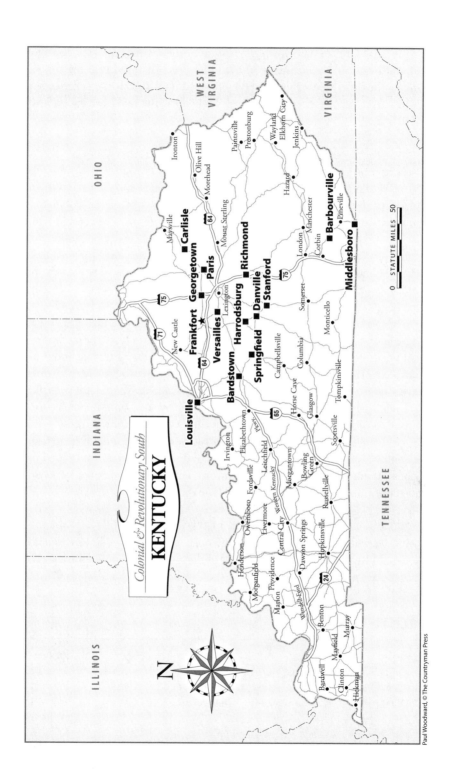

Colonial & Revolutionary South

KENTUCKY

ILLINOIS

INDIANA

OHIO

WEST VIRGINIA

VIRGINIA

TENNESSEE

Louisville

Frankfort
Georgetown
Carlisle
Paris
Versailles
Harrodsburg
Richmond
Danville
Stanford
Bardstown
Springfield
Middlesboro
Barbourville

Maysville
Ironton
Olive Hill
Morehead
Mount Sterling
Lexington
New Castle
Painesville
Prestonburg
Wayland
Elkhorn City
Jenkins
Hazard
Manchester
London
Corbin
Pineville
Somerset
Monticello
Campbellsville
Columbia
Horse Cave
Glasgow
Tompkinsville
Scottsville
Irvington
Elizabethtown
Leitchfield
Morgantown
Bowling Green
Russellville
Owensboro
Fordsville
Central City
Western Kentucky
Dawson Springs
Hopkinsville
Henderson
Evermore
Providence
Morganfield
Marion
Wendell-Ford
Mayfield
Benton
Murray
Bardwell
Clinton
Hickman

N

STATUTE MILES
0   50

Paul Woodward, © The Countryman Press

In 1751 Christopher Gist, a neighbor of Daniel Boone's, traveled down the Ohio River until he heard that hostile Indians were camped near his destination at the Falls of the Ohio, near present-day Louisville. He then changed his plan and crossed the mountains to reach his home in the Yadkin Valley of North Carolina.

French and Indian War

Reports from both Walker and Gist reached Robert Dinwiddie, governor of the Virginia colony, who in 1753 sent George Washington, accompanied by Gist, to investigate French activity in the Ohio country, as it was then called. Washington's mission was to deliver a letter ordering the French to depart. The young Virginian reported back that the French were holding on to their claims. Washington and Gist would return the following year with a detachment of Virginia militia, clash with a French patrol, and be defeated at Fort Necessity. The French and Indian War, and subsequently the globe-spanning Seven Years War, would erupt out of this struggle on the frontier.

In 1755 England sent General Edward Braddock to Virginia to mount an expedition to expel the French. Approaching French Fort Duquesne (at the present site of Pittsburgh) for an attack, Braddock's army was ambushed and badly mauled by French and Indians, and the general died of his wounds. Men involved in this unlucky expedition included Washington as aide-de-camp, Thomas Walker as commissary, Gist, a scout, Indian trader John Finley, and Daniel Boone, a wagon driver. All would play a role in the subsequent development of Kentucky.

Although the Treaty of Paris ending the war assigned the former French claims east of the Mississippi to the English, George III banned settlement beyond the Appalachians in 1763, reserving it for Indians. This did not stop explorers, including Finley, Boone, James Harrod, and Thomas Bullitt.

James Harrod

James Harrod, as well as the McAfee brothers, James, George, and Robert, explored the Ohio River valley and the meadows of the bluegrass region in north central Kentucky, a rolling plateau bounded by the Ohio to the north and west and a ring

---

KENTUCKY *Time Line*

1739	1750	1751	1763	1768
Indian guides lead Captain Charles de Longueuil, a French Canadian explorer, to Big Bone Lick	Thomas Walker explores Kentucky through the Cumberland Gap	Christopher Gist explores area along the Ohio River	France cedes vast area, including Kentucky, to Britain in the Treaty of Paris	Daniel Boone and John Finley begin exploring Kentucky during two-year hunting expedition

---

of hills to the south and east. There he found prehistoric bones and teeth on Big Bone Lick, a salt lick in Boone County that later fostered Thomas Jefferson's interest in paleontology. In 1774 Harrod and his men laid out a town on the south side of the branch of the Salt River beside a natural spring. Harrod's Town (later Harrodsburg), would eventually become the first permanent white settlement in this region west of the Allegheny Mountains.

According to one of many theories about the origin of the name "Kentucky," the Cherokee called the land *Ken-tah-the,* which meant "tomorrow," or "the land where we will live."

The site was abandoned that same year because of Indian hostilities (Lord Dunmore's War), but by the following year settlers were back and moved the town site west of Big Spring. They built a 264-foot-square fort with thick oak walls and three corner blockhouses, as well as seven cabins and a schoolhouse. Small stockades, or stations, were built in the vicinity of Fort Harrod. Families lived together for protection, and the fort was manned all the time by "forters."

Boone, Boonesborough, and Transylvania

An earlier attempt to settle the Kentucky country had been made in 1773 by Daniel Boone, William Russell, and a small group of families. Both Boone's and Russell's sons were caught by Indians and tortured and killed, and the group turned back. Boone had subsequently been involved in Indian fighting in Lord Dunmore's War, then served as an intermediary with the Overhill Cherokees in negotiating the massive, dubious land sale to Richard Henderson's Transylvania Company.

The Transylvania Company had devised a plan to hold a meeting with Cherokee chiefs in the spring of 1775. A long wagon train of goods to trade with the Indians crossed the mountains, with Boone on hand to lead the first settlers. Whites and Cherokee enjoyed feasting and bartering near Elizabethton in eastern Tennessee. The resulting Treaty of Sycamore Shoals was agreed upon in March of 1775. The Indians were to receive goods and sterling of 10,000 pounds, in return for a large tract of land including much of present-day Kentucky west and south

1774
James Harrod builds the first permanent settlement in Kentucky at Fort Harrod

1775
Daniel Boone builds the Wilderness Trail and establishes Fort Boonesborough; Richard Henderson creates the Transylvania Land Company, buys most of Kentucky from the Cherokees

1776
Harrodsburg settlers send George Rogers Clark and John Jones to ask Virginia's aid; Virginia declares Transylvania Land Company illegal and creates Kentucky County

of the Kentucky River to the Cumberland River. The "Path Deed" was a piece of land that connected western North Carolina with the Kentucky area through the Cumberland Gap.

It was Henderson who then hired Boone to blaze the famous Wilderness Road through the Cumberland Gap. When Boone and his axmen reached the site they had in mind on the Kentucky River (just south of present-day Lexington), they began building log huts they dubbed "Fort Boone." By the summer of 1775 there were twenty-six log cabins and four blockhouses arranged in a square 260 feet long and 180 feet wide.

The whole idea of Transylvania wasn't to everyone's liking. The Virginian George Rogers Clark, who had been a surveyor in Kentucky for the rival Ohio Company of Virginia, became a leader of the opposing faction. The Ohio Company also claimed a good part of Kentucky, based on a land grant from the British government. Clark asked that a conference take place in Harrodstown in June 1776 and was named a delegate to Williamsburg. By now the Revolutionary War was raging back east, and Clark was dispatched from the Virginia capital with 500 pounds of gunpowder to help Kentucky settlers protect themselves against Indians. On December 7, 1776, the County of Kentucky was proclaimed by Virginia, with Harrodstown named as the seat of government. This action, managed in the legislature by Thomas Jefferson, effectively nullified the largest part of Henderson's purchase, but he was given 200,000 acres in recompense. He then turned his attention to the Tennessee land north of the Cumberland River, until North Carolina reclaimed it and awarded him similar acreage as compensation.

During the Revolution, British outposts in the north and west armed and encouraged Indian allies to attack the frontier. In January 1778, while Boone and about thirty men were at Lower Blue Licks on a salt-making trip, they were captured by the Shawnees. They were taken to Chillicothe in Ohio, and then to the British outpost at Detroit. Chief Blackfish was so taken with Boone that he would not accept the British reward for him but instead adopted Boone and named him Sheltowee, or "Big Turtle."

When Boone realized that the Shawnee were making plans to attack Boonesborough in June, he escaped and returned to his settlement to warn them. When

---

KENTUCKY *Time Line*

1778	**1782**	**1792**	**1794**
Indians led by Shawnees unsuccessfully besiege Fort Boonesborough for 10 days	The last major battle of the American Revolution fought at Blue Licks, near Mount Olivet	Kentucky becomes the 15th state	General Anthony Wayne's victory at Fallen Timbers in Ohio ends Indian attacks in Kentucky

he arrived the settlers were at first very suspicious of him because his hair was plucked in the Indian style, and they thought he had sided with the enemy while a captive. Nevertheless he soon played a leading role again, and when Chief Blackfish reached the fort in early September with more than 400 warriors against about forty defenders, Boone used negotiations with the chief to stall for time, hoping for expected reinforcements. When talks broke down, a siege of ten days began. Heavy rains helped the defenders quell attempts to set their house roofs on fire. The Indians also tried to tunnel under the fortifications, and after a final assault, in which the Shawnees suffered many casualties, the attackers withdrew.

In the aftermath Boone was court-martialed for some of his previous stalling actions. Although the court cleared him of all charges, he left Boonesborough and later resettled elsewhere in Kentucky.

The Battle of Blue Licks

In 1782 British captain William Caldwell, leading a force of British rangers and Indians, and with the help of famous frontier scout Simon Girty, attacked Bryan Station near Lexington. Kentuckian settlers defended their frontier outpost, with men, women, and children fighting fiercely. As the British withdrew, quickly assembled Kentucky militia followed them to the Licking River.

Boone, one of the militia leaders, thought that the Kentuckians were being drawn into a trap and should wait for reinforcements, but Major Hugh McGary wanted to attack and did so. Boone was right; the Kentuckians were outnumbered almost two to one, and many were killed. Boone's son Israel was among those dead. But Caldwell and Girty knew more Kentucky militia were on the way, so they fled. The Battle of Blue Licks, with the Americans defeated, was the last battle with Indians in Kentucky.

Yet Indian troubles on the frontier were far from over, as the British, after the Revolution, continued to encourage Indian coalitions in the struggle for control of land north of the Ohio River and south of the Great Lakes. In 1790 and 1791 the Indian Western Lakes Confederacy had won victories that impelled President Washington to appoint General "Mad Anthony" Wayne to the command of an army that could reverse those losses. More than a decade after the Battle of Blue Licks, in 1794, Wayne moved north from Cincinnati to Maumee, Ohio, with 3,000 troops, almost evenly split between trained regulars and Kentucky militia. There he confronted and defeated a coalition of Miami, Delaware, and Shawnee warriors (including the famed Tecumseh) in the Battle of Fallen Timbers, fought on land that had been devastated by a tornado. It has sometimes been called the "last battle of the Revolution" because it snuffed out British efforts to use Indian coalitions as a bulwark against American westward expansion.

Reaching Statehood

With the Revolution over, the Kentuckians wanted to separate from Virginia and met for that purpose in 1784. By April 1792 a constitution was in place, and Kentucky became the fifteenth state. Its boundaries were extended in 1818 when Andrew Jackson negotiated with the Chickasaw Indians. It was called the Jackson Purchase and included 8,500 square miles of wilderness west of the Tennessee River.

Early settlers had begun growing tobacco, and by the 1790s Louisville factories were making cigars and pipe and chewing tobacco, as well as snuff. Even earlier, alcohol distilleries were producing cider and peach brandy from orchards, and bourbon and rye from corn. And by 1800 horses and racing were already popular, anticipating Kentucky's future role in breeding fine racehorses.

Regions *to* Explore

DANIEL BOONE COUNTRY
BLUEGRASS REGION
DERBY REGION

DANIEL BOONE COUNTRY

Daniel Boone led the way through the Cumberland Gap toward westward expansion. He has come down through the years as the epitome of the American frontiersman. He loved exploring and accepted the challenges of the wilderness for seventy of his eighty-six years. He was born to a Quaker family in Berks County, Pennsylvania, in 1734, moved to Yadkin Valley, North Carolina, in 1752, and continued developing his skill as a marksman and hunter.

After serving as a wagoner with General Edward Braddock's catastrophic expedition in 1755 against the French at Fort Duquesne, Boone returned home to North Carolina, married, and started a family, supporting himself as a "long hunter." His hunting trips would sometimes keep him away from home for months or even years at a time. In 1767 Boone ranged as far as Kentucky with his brother Squire Boone, but they were "ketched in a snowstorm" and did not continue. On a subsequent hunting trip to Kentucky, Boone lost all his pelts to Shawnee Indians, who warned him never to return.

> One of the basic needs of pioneers was salt. Expeditions searched for salt "licks," where wild animals went to lick the saline, brackish earth around mineral springs. Water was poured from buckets into a trough, then funneled into boiling kettles. They were placed on furnaces made of stone cemented with mud. About 840 gallons of water were necessary to make one bushel of salt. After every use the furnace had to be re-cemented—a tedious process.

Even after his abortive attempt in 1773 to lead settlers to the Kentucky country, when his son James was tortured and killed by Indians, Boone was not discouraged. Two years later, as revolution was brewing in the colonies, Boone and a group of thirty-one axmen were blazing a path through the Cumberland Gap, from Long Island of the Holston River (Kingsport, Tennessee) to Otter Creek in Kentucky. Called the Wilderness Trail, this primitive route opened the west to colonization. Near the end of their work, the group was attacked twice by Indians and lost several men. Boone kept going and reached the settlement site in April 1775. By the summer of 1775 four blockhouses and twenty-six log cabins were in place at "Fort Boone," which would become Boonesborough.

During the Revolution the Indians attacked Boonesborough as a special target several times. In September 1778 a force of 400 Indians besieged and set fire to the fort, but a heavy rainfall and the efforts of the women and children put out the flames. (See Historical Introduction for more details about the siege.)

After the Revolutionary War the fort went into decline and many of the settlers left. By 1810 only 68 people in eight houses remained. In 1987 an archaeological dig uncovered the remains of the 1775 fort and the town.

RICHMOND

Richmond, off Interstate 75 south of Lexington, is a farming, cattle ranching, and commercial center for the area. There are three historic districts from the 19th century. It is also home to Eastern Kentucky University.

HISTORICAL SITES *and* MUSEUMS

Fort Boonesborough State Park (800-255-PARK, 859-527-3131; www
.parks.ky.gov), 4375 Boonesborough Rd. Open Apr. 1 to Oct. 1, closed Mon.
and Tue. after Labor Day. Fort Boonesborough has been reconstructed as a working fort. It has cabins, blockhouses, and 18th-century-style furnishings. During the season interpreters demonstrate crafts and skills. The visitor center in a
blockhouse offers a film depicting the struggles at the fort.

White Hall State Historic Site (859-623-9178; www.richmond-ky.com),
White Hall State Shrine Rd. Open daily Apr. 1 to Labor Day; Wed.– Sun. Labor
Day to Oct. 31; Wed.– Fri., Nov.– Mar. The first section of the house, Clermont,
was built by Green Clay in 1798. His son was the emancipationist Cassius Mar-
cellus Clay, who added an Italianate addition to the house. White Hall has guides
in period costume to take visitors on tours.

BARBOURVILLE

Barbourville is located on the Wilderness Road in the Cumberland Valley. It was
one of the first settlements in southeastern Kentucky.

HISTORICAL SITES *and* MUSEUMS

Dr. Thomas Walker State Historic Site (606-546-4400; www.parks.ky.gov),
14929 KY 459. Open daily. The Loyal Land Company employed Dr. Thomas
Walker, a physician and surveyor, to lead the first expedition through the Cumberland Gap in 1750. He did not reach the open country beyond but reported
that the land he saw offered plentiful wildlife, dense woods, and rugged terrain.
One source claimed that he thought this land was not worth settling. A replica of
the cabin he built is on the grounds.

MIDDLESBORO

Cumberland Gap is located at the point where Virginia, Kentucky, and Tennessee
meet. The Wilderness Road through the gap became a funnel for America's first
westward movement. Historian Frederick Jackson Turner's description in 1893 is
both eloquent and classic: "Stand at Cumberland Gap and watch the progression
of civilization, marching single file—the buffalo following the trail to the salt
springs, the Indian, the fur-trader and hunter, the cattleraiser, the pioneer farmer—
and the frontier has passed by."

This 1,640-foot-high pass through the mountains became famous after Daniel
Boone led a group of hunters through it in 1769. North of the gap, the mountains were impassable for 400 miles. Like the passes through the much higher
Rockies a century later, the gap allowed settlers sealed off by the Appalachians to
move westward all the way to the Mississippi. By the end of the Revolution, 12,000

Reconstruction of Boonesborough at Fort Boonesborough State Park in Richmond

had crossed the gap, by 1792 perhaps 100,000, and by 1810 some 200,000 to 300,000 more. (No one was counting.)

HISTORICAL SITES *and* MUSEUMS

Cumberland Gap National Historical Park (606-248-2817; www.nps.gov/cuga), Box 1848. Open daily. There is a visitor center, plus an overlook and a number of strategically placed parking lots serving trailheads. We chose to take a hike beginning at the Thomas Walker parking lot. The grade is not difficult and the path well worn by thousands of predecessors, so the hike was more an exercise in comprehending history than a challenge. Along the way we imagined how those moving families and goods from safer coastal territory wondered what might be ahead on the other side of the gap. This journey whittled those who took the trail into the sturdy, self-reliant men and women who settled in the mountains of eastern Tennessee. They were the precursors of those who pushed all the way to the Pacific Ocean less than a century later.

BLUEGRASS REGION

The Bluegrass Region in north central Kentucky is a piedmont over extensive limestone deposits. Bluegrass country is known for its rolling hills, green pastures, stone walls, and white (or black) plank fences. The grass seeds itself every year, and little blue cornflowers appear in late May. This grass has special qualities because the limestone deposits underground give it more calcium and phosphorous. Horses reared here are known for their strength. There is money in raising thoroughbred horses, and estates take great care to maintain the quality and reputation of their stables. Racing, steeplechases, and horse shows are popular activities.

STANFORD

Stanford, located south of Harrodsburg and Danville, is known for the first circular racetrack in Kentucky, built in the late 1700s on William Whitley's land. This track was unique because it was made of clay instead of turf. Although the British raced in a clockwise direction, Whitley designed this track to race counterclockwise, perhaps as a response to anti-British sentiment at the time. It was known as Sportsman's Hill and attracted many prominent Kentuckians.

William Whitley, the son of Irish immigrants, became intrigued by stories of the promised land in Kentucky and set out with his brother-in-law, George Clark, in 1775. They established a station at Stanford. Whitley returned to Virginia to bring his wife, Esther, and their two daughters, Elizabeth and Isabella. Their journey lasted thirty-three days and was sometimes so arduous that possessions had to be unpacked from the horses and carried over the mountains.

Because for a time there had been few attacks on settlements by the Indians, the Whitleys chose to "settle out," as opposed to near a fort. They built a cabin and planted ten acres of corn to stake their claim to the land. Other travelers congregated at Whitley's station before venturing farther. The Whitleys kept track of Indian conflicts and sometimes asked the Kentucky militia for help.

Whitley wrote: "Many times in our travels we had to unpack and at times leave the family to find out a way to get on at times my wife would fall, horse and all and at other times, she and her children all in a file tied together for where one went all must go in that situation we were 33 days in the Wilderness in this unkind season of the year, had rain, hail and snow with the disadvantages of large Cane breaks to wade through we then landed at Whitleys Old Station."

HISTORICAL SITES and MUSEUMS
William Whitley House State Historic Site (606-355-2881; www.williamwhitleyhouse.com), 625 William Whitley Rd. Open daily Memorial Day to Labor Day; Tue.–Sun. mid-Mar. to day before Memorial Day and day after Labor Day to mid-Dec. The brick house dates from 1785, and the initials WW and EW are on the front and back. The Flemish bond pattern, where one brick was laid lengthwise and the next endwise, gave strength to the walls. Inside, the house has walnut and pine paneling, crown molding, and chair railings. There are S-shaped carvings over the fireplace, and the footers on

the stairs have eagle carving. Don't miss the secret chamber for hiding in case Indians attacked. The house was called "Guardian of Wilderness Road."

DANVILLE

Danville was long considered a place for settlers to stop after traveling on the Wilderness Road. It had a good water supply and rich soil. In 1783 the territory of Virginia, later Kentucky, became a district under the Virginia Legislature. The first district court was in Harrodsburg, then moved to Danville. Buildings rose, ten constitutional conventions were held, and by 1792 Kentucky became a state. Isaac Shelby was named the first governor. He had been a convention delegate as well as a Revolutionary War hero, helping to gather and lead the Overmountain men to their victory at Kings Mountain in South Carolina.

HISTORICAL SITES
and MUSEUMS
Constitution Square State Historic Site (859-239-7089; www.paprks.ky.gov), 134 Second St. The first state constitution was adopted here in 1792. A number of historic buildings (some replicas) include the 1785 log courthouse, the jail, a 1784 meetinghouse, a 1792 post office, and the 1785 Grayson's Tavern. A bronze statue depicting a statesman and a frontiersman stands in Governor's Circle.

The fireplace was the most important feature of a pioneer cabin. Besides providing heat it was the site of food preparation. Utensils, such as bread toasters, waffle irons, coffee roaster, kettles, and reflector ovens, were kept beside the fireplace. Kentuckian women did a lot of boiling in kettles over the open fire, but they also used other methods, including roasting, baking, and frying. Each household bought basic supplements such as salt, molasses, herbs, and spices. Food was stored in cold springs and brooks, root crops in cellars, meat and fish in salt brine, and some food was smoked.

HARRODSBURG

James Harrod explored the region in 1767 and 1773, then decided to establish a settlement. He collected thirty-two men from the Monongahela Valley in Pennsylvania and obtained dugout canoes for them. They traveled down the Monongahela and Ohio Rivers to the Kentucky River and on for another hundred miles to Harrod's Landing (about ten miles north of Harrodsburg). Then they walked overland to the beginning of the Salt River, where there was a natural spring. By June 1774 they were creating a town, which they named Harrodstown.

Just after the town was laid out, Governor Dunsmore of Virginia sent Daniel Boone to request Harrodstown men to fight with their Virginia regiments in a campaign against Shawnee and Mingo Indians, who refused to recognize a treaty

✳ The women of Fort Harrod had to be tough and resourceful. They assumed many roles, including cook, seamstress, nurse, weaver, spinner, shoemaker, gardener, teacher, and more. Sometimes they even made bullets or hoisted up a rifle.

Ann Coburn McDonald lost her first husband in an Indian attack and then married James Harrod. She opened a Latin school in her home in 1786. Her daughter, Margaret, became a wealthy heiress.

Ann Kennedy Wilson Poague Lindsay McGinty married and was widowed four times. She opened an "ordinary" to serve meals and persuaded the Lincoln County Court to run the Wilderness Road by her ordinary. Jane Coomes began the first school inside Fort Harrod and taught the pioneer children for nine years. She devised a version of the Old English hornbook from clapboard cut in the shape of a paddle. Berry juice and charcoal were used to draw the alphabet and the Lord's Prayer on the paddles.

that had deprived them of their land. The Indians were defeated at the Battle of Point Pleasant in West Virginia, on the eve of the Revolutionary War.

The settlers returned to Harrodstown and finished laying out the town. By September their families had arrived and a fort was under construction. Seven cabins, blockhouses, and a schoolhouse were built there.

HISTORICAL SITES *and* MUSEUMS

Old Fort Harrod State Park 859-734-3314; www.parks.ky.gov), 100 S. College St. Open year-round. The fort was reconstructed near the original site. Costumed craftspeople work on weaving, woodworking, basketry, and blacksmithing. They also tend gardens and the farm animals. You can visit settlers' cabins, the William Poague cabin, a schoolhouse, the Ann McGinty blockhouse, James Harrod blockhouse, George Rogers Clark blockhouse, and the James Harrod amphitheater. The Mansion Museum has Indian artifacts, paintings, displays, and documents. The Lincoln Marriage Temple includes the log cabin where Abraham Lincoln's parents, Thomas Lincoln and Nancy Hanks, were married in 1806. The cabin was moved from Beechland in Washington County.

Shaker Village of Pleasant Hill (800-734-8011, 859-734-5411; www.shakervillageky.org), 3501 Lexington Rd. Open daily. The United Society of Believers in Christ's Second Appearing were better known as the Shakers. The founder, Mother Ann Lee, arrived from England just after the American Revolution. Ann Lee came from Manchester, where she had been subjected to child labor, married, and given birth to four children who did not live long. She was intent on forgetting her miserable life and planning for security after death; she had visions in which Christ stressed celibacy and confession of sin. Although she was illiterate, Ann Lee became the leader of the society.

In 1805 Shakers arrived at a site above the Kentucky River where they estab-

Reconstruction of the stockade and blockhouse at Old Fort Harrod State Park in Harrodsburg

lished a community on Pleasant Hill. The community prospered throughout the century, but by 1910 celibacy had taken its toll, members of the community dwindled, the village closed, and the community reverted to a farming area. In 1961 a nonprofit group formed to preserve this unique example of the Shaker heritage. Thirty-four of the original buildings have been restored, and visitors can even stay overnight in some of them.

The Center Family Dwelling is a large three-story house, once home to over 100 Shakers. Two doors lead from this structure across the street to two doors in the Meeting House—men and women could file across without speaking to each other. They also worked and ate in silence

Inside the Center Family Dwelling, rooms are dormitory style, with the women on one side and the men on the other. Peg rails were for hanging clothing, and everything was kept neatly in its place. Chairs were also hung on wall pegs. Bags at the foot of each bed held herbs and spices, designed to ward off any intruding bugs.

Shaker furniture and artifacts are displayed in the house. Costumed interpreters demonstrate crafts and describe the Shaker way of life. Although the Shakers were celebate, orphaned children were brought into the village as a forerunner

The Center Family Dwelling at Pleasant Hill Shaker Village in Harrodsburg

of public orphanages. They stayed until the age of 18 and then had the choice of remaining within the community or leaving for the outer world.

The kitchen is set up as it had been and is painted "kitchen red," a popular color at the village. A beehive oven produced all the community's bread, usually baked in early morning before the heat of the day.

Upstairs, the Meeting Room was the only place where men and women could talk with each other freely, and apparently they enjoyed conversation about George Washington, the Indian Tecumseh, and other news of the day. They sang and smoked clay pipes up there.

Pleasant Hill craftsmen were busy working while we were there, and visitors are welcome to talk with them. Two men making brooms told us how long each broomcorn cluster needed to age before being fashioned into a broom. The cooper was making buckets and had samples of tubs, churns, barrels, and casks to show us. Men who made "dry" barrels could make ten a day, but far fewer, perhaps two a day, of those used to contain liquids. Good joiner work and seasoned wood are essential to make them watertight.

Elegant Shaker workmanship at Pleasant Hill Shaker Village

Shaker Lemon Pie

2 large lemons	4 eggs, well beaten
2 cups sugar	

Slice lemons as thin as paper, rind and all. Combine with sugar; mix well. Let stand 2 hours, or overnight, blending occasionally. Add beaten eggs to lemon mixture; mix well. Turn into 9-inch pie shell, arranging lemon slices evenly. Cover with top crust. Cut several slits near center. Bake at 450 degrees for 15 minutes. Reduce heat to 375 degrees and bake for about 20 minutes or until silver knife inserted near edge of pie comes out clean. Cool before serving.

COURTESY OF SHAKER VILLAGE OF PLEASANT HILL

LODGING

BEAUMONT INN
638 Beaumont Inn Dr., Harrodsburg, KY 40330
800-352-3992, 859-734-3381;
www.beaumontinn.com
The building dates from 1845, when it was a school for young ladies; later it housed Beaumont College, until 1916. The inn has been owned and operated by five generations of the same family and is listed on the National Register of Historic Places. Thirty-three guest rooms.

THE INN AT SHAKER VILLAGE
3501 Lexington Rd., Harrodsburg, KY 40330
800-734-5611 859-734-5411;
www.shakervillageky.org
You can sleep right in this early 19th-century farm village. The 81 guest rooms are furnished with Shaker reproductions.

RESTAURANTS

BEAUMONT INN DINING ROOM & OLD OWL TAVERN
638 Beaumont Inn Dr.
859-734-3381
Specialties include Filet Mignon Beaumont and the classic Beaumont dinner of "yellow-legged" fried chicken and Kentucky-cured country ham.

TRUSTEES' OFFICE DINING ROOM
The Inn at Shaker Village
3501 Lexington Rd.
859-734-5411
Specialties include the Shaker dish of the day, Shaker garden salad, and Shaker lemon pie

PARIS

Paris, just northeast of Lexington, was originally known as Hopewell when the town was established in 1789, but the name was changed in response to French involvement in the Revolutionary War. The county of Bourbon was so named after the Bourbons of France. Jacob Spears began a distillery here in 1790 and it was called Bourbon, named after the county.

HISTORICAL SITES *and* MUSEUMS
Duncan Tavern (859-987-1788; www.kentuckydar.org/duncantavern.htm), 323

High St. Open Apr. to mid-Dec., Thu.– Sat. Major Joseph Duncan built his stone house in 1788. It is three stories high and contains 20 rooms. The rooms are furnished with period pieces dating from 1790 to 1860. Daniel Boone was a visitor here. The genealogical library has a collection of pre-1820 materials. The garden is enhanced with the old Bourbon County Court House gate, with a spread eagle from Wales. The kitchen has an old batten door with a crude original carving of the name Aaron Burr.

The Anne Duncan House adjoins Duncan Tavern. After Major Duncan died, his wife was left with six small children. Although she tried to operate the inn, she subsequently leased it to John Porter in 1803 and built her home against the tavern wall. She raised her children there and saved for their education. Today the home exhibits early cabinetwork found in Kentucky. Period antiques furnish the house.

Cane Ridge Meeting House and Barton Warren Stone Museum (859-987-5350; www.caaneridge.com), 1655 Cane Ridge Rd. The Meeting House is open year-round; the Stone Museum is open Apr. to Oct. 31. The Meeting House dates from 1791 and was the site of the 1801 Great Revival and also the 1804 dissolution of the Springfield Presbytery. The Stone House has displays of early tools and documents.

GEORGETOWN

Georgetown is located just northwest of Lexington. Baptist minister Elijah Craig and some of his flock came to Royal Spring in 1784. The Virginia legislature named the town George Town in 1790 to honor George Washington.

HISTORICAL SITES *and* MUSEUMS
Georgetown & Scott County Museum and Royal Spring Park (502-863-6201; www.scottcountymuseum.org), 229 E. Main St. (Royal Spring: Main & Water Sts.) Open May 15 to Sep. 15. The museum tells the story of Georgetown with displays and a videotape presentation. McClelland's Fort was originally on the site.

CARLISLE

The Nicholas County seat, Carlisle is about thirty-five miles northeast of Lexington.

HISTORICAL SITES *and* MUSEUMS
Blue Licks Battlefield State Park (859-289-5507; www.parksky.gov), 10299 Maysville Rd. Open daily. (See more information in the Historical Introduction to this chapter.) This is the site of the last major battle of the Revolutionary War. A renovation has just taken place in the Pioneer Museum. There is a new diorama of the battle, a video, and many exhibits.

FRANKFORT

James Wilkinson bought property in Frankfort in 1786. The town, located not far west of modern Lexington, was named Frank's Ford after Stephen Frank, who was killed by Indians, but not before he laid out the town, naming one of the streets for himself. It has been the seat of government in Kentucky since 1792.

HISTORICAL SITES *and* MUSEUMS

Frankfort Cemetery (502-227-2403), 215 E. Main St. Daniel Boone and his wife, Rebecca, are buried here. Their remains were moved from Defiance, Missouri, their original burial site. The marker has marble relief carvings of Daniel fighting an Indian and with a slain deer. Rebecca Boone is seen milking a cow.

Liberty Hall Historic Site (888-516-5101, 502-227-2560; www.liberty hall.org), 218 Wilkinson St. Open Mar. 1 to mid-Dec. John Brown built this Georgian-style house, Liberty Hall, in 1796. He was one of the first senators from Kentucky. Some furnishings were Brown family pieces. Portraits hang in the house. Guests included Presidents James Monroe, Andrew Jackson, and Zachary Taylor, and the Marquis de Lafayette.

The gardens at Liberty Hall include a wide variety of plants arranged in linear form toward the river. Two devoted gardeners have been working in the garden for many years.

The Orlando Brown House, built by John Brown's younger son on the family estate, dates from 1835. Gideon Shryock, who designed the State Capitol, also designed this house. Many of the furnishings belonged to the Browns. The chandeliers burned whale oil in early days.

Kentucky Military History Museum (502-564-3265; www.history.ky .gov), 125 E. Main St. Open Tue.–Sun. Housed in the Old State Arsenal, the collection includes artifacts from frontier days, the Revolutionary War, through Desert Storm.

Thomas D. Clark Center for Kentucky History (502-564-1792; www .history.ky.gov), 100 W. Broadway. Open Tue.–Sun. The permanent display, "A Kentucky Journal," ranges from prehistoric times to today. A research library has genealogical records for tracing Kentucky ancestors.

VERSAILLES

Versailles, between Frankfort and Lexington, is the Woodford County seat.

HISTORICAL SITES *and* MUSEUMS

Jack Jouett House (859-873-7902; www.jackjouetthouse.org), 255 Craig's Creek Rd., Versailles, KY 40383. Open Apr.–Oct., Wed. and weekends. Captain Jack Jouett was dubbed the "Paul Revere of the South" after he rode 40 miles to warn

Virginia state legislators and Thomas Jefferson that the British were on their way. Jouett moved here after the war. The site includes a 1780s frontier stone cabin and a 1797 Federal brick cottage. They are furnished with period pieces.

Woodford County Historical Society Library & Museum (859-873-6786; www.woodfordkyhistory.org), 121 Rose Hill Ave. Open Tue.–Sat. The building was originally Big Spring Church. Exhibits include pieces from the 1700s. A genealogical library offers material from Woodford County families.

LODGING

HISTORIC ROSE HILL INN
233 Rose Hill, Versailles, KY 40383
859-873-5957; www.rosehillinn.com
The inn dates from 1823. Seven guest rooms.

> The "Gray Lady" is the ghost of Margaretta Brown's aunt, Mrs. Varick. Some say that she appears at the top of the stairs every now and then.

DERBY REGION

Named for the Kentucky Derby at Churchill Downs, the region south and east of Louisville is filled with traces of early settlement and sites related to the Revolutionary War and Abraham Lincoln.

BARDSTOWN

One of the oldest cities in Kentucky, Bardstown dates from the 1780s. John Fitch, who built the first working steamboat in the United States, lived here and died in 1798. There's a monument to him on the Courthouse Square. Distilling is the major industry in town; in fact, Bardstown calls itself the Bourbon Capital of the World.

HISTORICAL SITES *and* MUSEUMS
Oscar Getz Museum of Whiskey History & Bardstown Historical Museum (502-348-2999; www.whiskeymuseum.com), 114 N. 5th St. Open daily May–Oct.; rest of the year, Tue.–Sun. The collection has pieces from pre-colonial days through the 1960s. Don't miss the 60-gallon copper still dating from 1787.

SPRINGFIELD

While Springfield, Illinois, is closely identified with Abraham Lincoln, little Springfield, Kentucky, located west of Danville, has a similar attachment to Old Abe's father, Thomas Lincoln.

HISTORICAL SITES *and* MUSEUMS

Lincoln Homestead State Park (859-336-7461; www.parks.ky.gov), 5079 Lincoln Park Rd. Open daily May–Sep. The reproduction of the cabin that was the boyhood home of Abraham Lincoln's father, Thomas Lincoln, was built on the original site. He lived with his mother, Bersheba, and his brothers Mordecai and Josiah, and his sisters Mary and Nancy. Thomas Lincoln lived there until he was 25 years old. Some of the furniture was made by him. There are also replicas of a blacksmith shop and a woodworking shop.

> ✿ Carl Sandburg wrote of the wedding: "The groom was wearing his fancy new beaver hat, a new black suit, his new silk suspenders. The bride's outfit had in it linen and silk, perhaps a dash somewhere of the one-fourth yard of scarlet cloth Thomas had bought at Bleakley and Montgomery's."

The Francis Berry House is a two-story log home that was later moved from the Beechland section a mile away to the present location. It is the original cabin where Lincoln's mother, Nancy Hanks, lived during her courtship with Thomas Lincoln. They were married in 1806.

Mordecai Lincoln House (859-336-7461; www.parks.ky.gov), 5079 Lincoln Park Rd. Open daily, May–Sep. Mordecai Lincoln, uncle of President Lincoln, was the eldest son of Captain Abraham Lincoln and Bersheba Lincoln. He lived here with his wife, Mary Mudd Lincoln, and their five children.

LOUISVILLE

The Kentucky Derby is the centerpiece of Louisville every May. But horseracing is not the only focus of Louisville, the biggest city in Kentucky in a region rich in history. Captain Thomas Bullitt surveyed the land in 1773. Colonel George Rogers Clark arrived with 120 soldiers and 20 families in 1778. Thomas Jefferson signed the charter of the city in 1780. It was named Louisville after the French king Louis XVI, as a thank-you for the French help during the Revolution. Settlers built Fort Nelson by 1782. More settlers came, and the town became more commercial as the frontier moved west. Distilling bourbon whiskey was a major industry, and now it is said that Louisville manufactures more than half the bourbon sold around the world.

HISTORICAL SITES *and* MUSEUMS

Frazier International History Museum (866-886-7103, 502-753-5663; www.fraziermuseum.org), 829 W. Main St. Open daily. The collection encompasses 1,000 years of history and includes armor, arms, and many related artifacts. The Boone family Bible is here. Performances are given by costumed guides.

Historic Locust Grove (502-897-9845; www.locustgrove.org), 561 Blaken-baker Lane. Open daily. George Rogers Clark, the founder of Louisville, retired to this home and lived here for the last nine years of his life. The site has nine out-buildings, restored 18th-century style gardens, and a museum gallery. Don't miss the Hands-on History center where children can have a peek in a Revolutionary War soldier's trunk plus try on clothing of the period.

LODGING

THE BROWN
335 W. Broadway, Louisville, KY 40202
888-888-5252, 502-583-1234; www.brownhotel.com
Dating from 1923, the hotel has been restored and features European antiques. There are 299 guest rooms.

Current Information

DEPARTMENT OF TOURISM
500 Mero St., Frankfort, KY 40601
800-225-8747, 502-564-4930; www.kentuckytourism.com

Washington, D.C.

Historical Introduction
to
Washington, D.C.

T he Constitution of the United States called on Congress to establish a federal city as the new nation's capital, but from the outset its location was a political hot potato. No fewer than sixteen sites suggested by regional factions had been rejected by the whole body. Remaining contenders were New York City, the first temporary location of Congress and the federal administration; Philadelphia, site of the Continental Congresses; Baltimore; a mid-Pennsylvania site somewhere along the Susquehanna River; and a similarly undetermined spot on the Potomac.

By 1790, as Congress faced much more portentous issues—the staggering war debts of individual states and fragile credit abroad; dealing with the slave trade and skirting the larger question of slavery itself; avoiding involvement in the imminent conflict between European nations—the location of the permanent capital became a bargaining chip in satisfying competing interests. The mercantile interests of northern states, led by Alexander Hamilton of New York, wanted the new government to assume the Revolutionary War debts of states and thereby restore American credit abroad. The southern states, led by Thomas Jefferson of Virginia, opposed assumption of state debts and wanted the capital in a location near to slave-holding agricultural interests. Issues that could have broken up the new union—and did six decades later—were resolved successfully in what has been called the compromise of 1790.

Intensive bargaining for weeks on debt assumption and site selection culminated in an attractive piece of early American political lore. Thomas Jefferson hosted a dinner party in New York City on June 20, 1790, perhaps setting a precedent in how seemingly intractable positions might be reconciled to

---

The Jefferson Memorial reflected in the Tidal Basin

forestall paralysis in government. In such a private setting, eminent politicians could shed their public personas in ways that would have been impossible on the floor of Congress and reach toward compromise. At the end of the evening Jefferson, Madison, and Hamilton had agreed to accept the federal assumption of state debts in return for two stages in the location of the federal capital, a decade in Philadelphia followed by a permanent site on the Potomac. Each of the participants left with tasks of political persuasion, and both the Assumption Act and the Residency Act passed in July. The Residency Act of 1790 authorized a site not to exceed ten miles square on the east bank of the Potomac somewhere between the East Branch (now Anacostia River) and the Connogocheague Creek (now Conococheague), near Hagerstown.

Because the sponsors of the Residency Act wanted to prevent any resurgence of disputes in Congress about the site, they vested sole authority for its selection and subsequent construction in the president. It was a wise decision, though perhaps it might have been impossible with a less iconic figure in that office. George Washington chose a site at the junction of the Potomac and Anacostia Rivers and appointed commissioners to make preparations for the new government. The site had some problems, especially the mosquito-infested swampland along the rivers, but advantages as well. By an amendment in 1791 Washington was allowed to shift the location downstream and partially across the river to include Alexandria—where he owned property, and also close to Mount Vernon—with the provision that no federal buildings be erected on that side of the river.

Thus the prospective site included two adjacent port towns—Alexandria, Virginia, and Georgetown, Maryland, both important as shipping centers, first for tobacco and later wheat. Back in 1748 tobacco merchants and planters had petitioned the Virginia Assembly to establish a port town on the Potomac to promote their trade, creating Alexandria. Three years later the Maryland Assembly had followed suit to found George Town—just upriver from Alexandria on the opposite shore—created in part to develop inspection and shipment stations for tobacco. George Washington had long been interested in promoting navigation on the river as a way to develop interior lands, and he had helped found

WASHINGTON *Time Line*

1600	1748	1751	1790
Piscataway Indians live in the area	Virginia Assembly grants petition of tobacco merchants to found Alexandria	Maryland Assembly appoints commissioners to lay out George Town	The Residency Act of 1790 gives the president power to choose a site for the capital city; Philadelphia becomes the capital for ten years

the Potowmack Company in 1785. A predecessor of the Chesapeake and Ohio Company, it started building canals around unnavigable sections of the river, including Great Falls not far upstream from the new federal site, but ran out of funds.

Building the "City of Magnificent Intentions"

In this apt phrase coined in 1842, Charles Dickens caught the essence of grandiose plans for the new capital that had not been fully realized four decades later. Jefferson preferred starting with a village that would gradually grow, but Washington endorsed the much more expansive vision of chief architect Pierre-Charles L'Enfant, a military engineer who had served with Lafayette and Washington in the war. L'Enfant saw the site in 1791, then planned a large city with wide boulevards and open spaces similar to those in newer European capitals like St. Petersburg. Major Andrew Ellicott began the survey of the District of Columbia at the same time, assisted by the astronomical calculations of free African American Benjamin Banneker, a self-taught farmer who was regarded as a mathematical genius. L'Enfant's designs included monumental sculptures and fountains that would not be realized fully for another hundred years, after the McMillan Commission created the National Mall and Monuments.

Washington supervised the whole project directly during his presidency, urging the commissioners to complete negotiations with landowners and meeting with those who balked at giving up a large portion of their land without compensation. Washington also chose sites and architects for the President's Mansion and the Capitol. In 1792 James Hoban won a local competition with his architectural design for the President's Mansion, and Dr. William Thornton, an amateur who could not supervise construction, won another for the Capitol. Washington officiated as cornerstones were laid for both key buildings of official Washington in 1792 and 1793. Yet in an odd quirk of history, he was the only president not to live in the mansion, because it was not habitable before his second term ended in March 1797. His successor, John Adams, moved into the still unfinished President's Mansion in 1800.

1791
President George Washington selects a new permanent site on the Potomac and acquires 100 square miles of land from Maryland and Virginia. Major Pierre-Charles L'Enfant lays out plan for the city

1792
Washington lays cornerstone for President's Mansion; after disputes with commissioners, L'Enfant dismissed by Washington

1793
Washington lays cornerstone for the Capitol

Early Troubles

Through the 1790s George Washington bore the brunt of persistent difficulties in building parts of the large new city with reasonable speed, always fearful that those difficulties might induce Congress to change its mind about the site. At the outset L'Enfant's stubborn unwillingness to adjust or compromise his own evolving vision in any way brought him into direct conflict with the commissioners, who were more concerned with raising the money needed to start the public buildings. He failed to produce the engraved map needed for land auctions in the fall of 1791 and still had not done so during the winter of 1792, irritating both the commissioners and Washington. He further aroused their ire by demolishing part of a manor house being constructed by Commissioner Daniel Carroll's uncle, member of the prominent Maryland family and largest landholder in the District. L'Enfant did not want to see shoddy, uncontrolled construction marring the beautiful, broad avenues he envisioned, and his failure to provide an engraved map for the second auction in the fall threatened finances for the entire project. Washington reluctantly fired him.

Throughout the decade lack of money and the large scale of the enterprise continued to slow progress in building a city from scratch on unsettled land. The result was scattered clusters of buildings around active centers like the Capitol and the Navy Yard, with vast empty spaces between them. These problems were exacerbated by the actions of land speculators. When loans to build the President's Mansion and the Capitol were not forthcoming, the commissioners turned to James Greenleaf of Massachusetts for help. With Washington's approval, they sold him 3,000 lots at a reduced price, to be paid for in seven annual installments; in return, he would provide monthly loans for construction of the two key federal buildings. When Robert Morris, remembered as the financier of the Revolution, and James Nicholson joined Greenleaf under even more generous terms (no cash down), the syndicate was able to acquire more than a third of the land available in Washington, creating a real estate boom. They started constructing buildings along Pennsylvania Avenue, but as no buyers appeared for land, they fell behind on payments to the commissioners.

The bust followed with their bankruptcy in 1797, a landscape littered with

---

WASHINGTON *Time Line*

1800	1802	1814	1815	1846
The federal capital moves from Philadelphia to the incomplete new city	Congress grants the City of Washington its first municipal charter	English troops burn the capital during the War of 1812	Reconstruction of capital begins	District of Columbia land acquired from Virginia retroceded to that state

---

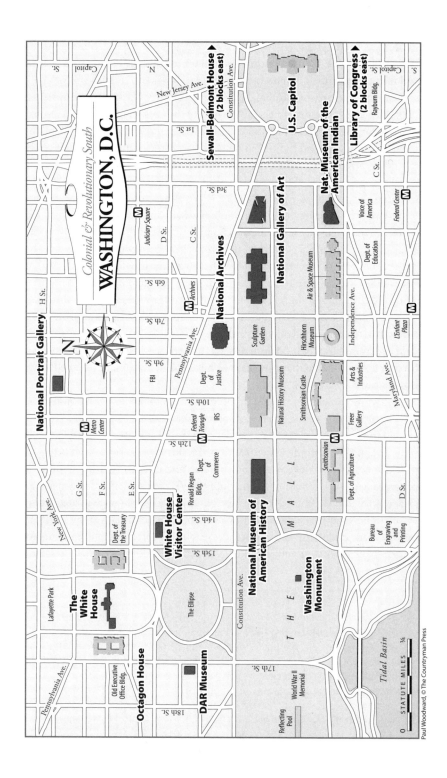

Colonial & Revolutionary South
WASHINGTON, D.C.

National Portrait Gallery

Sewall-Belmont House
(2 blocks east)

U.S. Capitol

Nat. Museum of the American Indian

Library of Congress
(2 blocks east)

National Archives

National Gallery of Art

White House Visitor Center

National Museum of American History

Washington Monument

The White House

Octagon House

DAR Museum

Metro Center

Federal Triangle

The Ellipse

Tidal Basin

Air & Space Museum

Sculpture Garden

Hirschhorn Museum

Natural History Museum

Smithsonian Castle

Arts & Industries

Freer Gallery

Dept. of Agriculture

Bureau of Engraving and Printing

World War II Memorial

Reflecting Pool

FBI

Dept. of Justice

IRS

Dept. of Commerce

Ronald Reagan Bldg.

Dept. of the Treasury

Old Executive Office Bldg.

Lafayette Park

Voice of America

Dept. of Education

Rayburn Bldg.

Federal Center

L'Enfant Plaza

Smithsonian

THE MALL

Constitution Ave.

Pennsylvania Ave.

New York Ave.

New Jersey Ave.

Constitution Ave.

Independence Ave.

Maryland Ave.

Pennsylvania Ave.

Capitol St.

Capitol St.

N.

S.

H St.

G St.

F St.

E St.

D St.

C St.

C St.

Judiciary Square

Archives

1st St.

3rd St.

6th St.

7th St.

9th St.

10th St.

12th St.

14th St.

15th St.

17th St.

18th St.

D St.

N

0   STATUTE MILES   ¼

Paul Woodward, © The Countryman Press

unfinished buildings, as well as stunted growth and a bad reputation for Washington. Since Congress had not provided money to build the President's Mansion and the Capitol, much of the work force had to be laid off. It consisted of a mix of European stonemasons, colonial workmen, some free blacks, and many slaves, both skilled and unskilled. (The 1800 census of the District of Columbia records 783 free Negroes and 3,244 slaves.) Unemployment drove many workmen out of town and impoverished those who remained with their families. By 1798 only ninety slaves remained as the core of the work force on the Capitol.

Yet in spite of delayed construction, the move from Philadelphia to Washington occurred on schedule in November 1800. When John and Abigail Adams moved into the mansion, they found it barely habitable, with many unfinished rooms, no main stairway, scarce firewood, and few conveniences; by her own report Abigail hung the family laundry in the unfinished ceremonial East Room. The state of the Capitol was comparable, with only its north wing finished. At that time the 131 federal employees who moved from Philadelphia had little room to work and difficulty in finding living quarters nearby. The substantial distances between three federal centers—the President's Mansion, the Capitol, and the Navy Yard—had to be traversed on tracks either windblown with dust or mired in mud, with tree stumps to avoid and deep ruts to trap carriage wheels. For those who had become accustomed to the amenities of Philadelphia, Washington seemed a raw frontier town.

Notwithstanding this rough start for the new capital, life in Washington gradually improved during the first decade of the 19th century. Neighborhoods grew around the widely separated Navy Yard, Capitol, and at a city center on Pennsylvania Avenue between the Capitol and the President's Mansion. Each began to provide necessary services, including churches and taverns, boardinghouses for congressmen, hotels for visitors, and a public market for residents. Craftsmen and professionals joined shipyard workers and government employees as residents, and small businesses appeared. Completion of a canal around the falls of the Potomac in 1802 made trade with the interior more feasible for merchants and encouraged entrepreneurs. Work on public buildings resumed at a slow pace when President

---

When the twenty-year extension of the African slave trade allowed by the Constitution expired in 1808, a domestic slave market came to flourish in both Washington and Alexandria, marring both the capital's reputation and the reality of life in the District of Columbia. The image was devastating for visitors from abroad, especially in undeveloped areas near the President's Mansion and on what would become the mall, and groups of slaves marching down Pennsylvania Avenue became a blot on the new federal capital. This market did not disappear until the retrocession of district land on the right bank of the Potomac to Virginia made the ban in the Compromise of 1850 possible.

Thomas Jefferson appointed Benjamin Latrobe, a distinguished architect, as the surveyor of public buildings in 1803 and he started on the Capitol. Residents objected to the very limited self-government Congress allowed them throughout the decade, and many civic problems remained unaddressed—lack of adequate education, care of the poor, and the seemingly always impassable roads to connect parts of the city.

Yet the population of the District of Columbia increased from 14,000 to 24,000 in the decade, including a higher proportion of free blacks to slaves. However, the War of 1812 put all these gains at risk again.

Washington Burns

When George Washington chose the site for the capital just below the head of navigation at the fall line on the Potomac, he thought it would be far enough upriver to deter attack from any enemy. The British fleet and army proved that assumption false in a dramatic amphibious operation on August 24, 1814, burning the Capitol, the President's Mansion, the Treasury, the War Department, and blowing up the Arsenal before they left, while defenders burned the Navy Yard with its ships and stores to keep them from enemy hands. In one quick raid, the British had destroyed the symbolic heart of America and the major buildings it had taken a decade to establish, before moving on to attack Baltimore, this time without success. The city had been forewarned for more than a year as Admiral Cockburn's fleet effectively blockaded the Chesapeake and made devastating raids ashore as far up the bay as Havre de Grace in May of 1813. That same July they had reached up the Potomac within sixty miles of Washington, creating an alarm that called out the militia and sent naval vessels from the shipyard downstream to intercept them. Before there was any confrontation the British had turned back, and the ships and militia came home.

There were further warnings in June of 1814, when landing parties from Cockburn's fleet came as close as twenty-two miles from Washington. When 4,500 British regular troops landed in the Patuxent River in mid-August, the militia was again called out to set up defenses where the main road crossed the Anacostia River at Bladensburg, and male citizens were urged to help build the earthworks. Meanwhile other citizens began to collect their possessions and flee westward, while government officials packed important documents and moved them out of town. In the early afternoon of August 24 the British reached Bladensburg and quickly overwhelmed the green defenders in half an hour, a rout later dubbed "the Bladensburg Races" by angry citizens. The invading troops reached the capital city by dusk and began their methodical destruction.

Rebuilding

When citizens returned to survey their devastated city, its future appeared uncertain. Yet those who had invested in property looked beyond the grim visual prospect and began to promote rebuilding quickly to make the return of government offices and Congress a practical possibility. How congressmen would react when they saw the blackened walls and wrecked interiors of public buildings was another matter, to be determined when they reconvened for a special session less than a month after the disaster. Almost immediately Philadelphia and Lancaster, Pennsylvania, proposed temporarily relocating the capital to their cities. After three weeks of debate and an offer of a half million dollars in loans to start rebuilding the public buildings, the House voted to stay. The Senate was slower, finally concurring more than three months later, the day before the news of General Andrew Jackson's victory at the Battle of New Orleans reached Washington.

Places *to* Explore

CAPITOL HILL
THE MALL
WHITE HOUSE AND BEYOND

CAPITOL HILL

The street plan of Washington, D.C. is divided into the compass quadrants—all street addresses are followed by a NW, NE, SW, or SE—and the focus of this plan, the symbolic center of the city, is the Capitol Building on Capitol Hill.

HISTORICAL SITES *and* MUSEUMS

U.S. Capitol (202-225-6827), Capitol Hill. Open Mon.–Sat. Timed entry passes are offered on a first-come, first-served basis, beginning at 9 AM Mon.–Sat. They are distributed at the kiosk at the corner of First St. and Maryland Ave. SW. Tours last an hour. For a gallery pass phone 202-224-3131 and ask to be connected to a legislator for your state.

President Washington had established competitions for the design of the Capitol and the President's Mansion, and winners were split between a gifted amateur and a professional architect. In this era of multiple, nonspecialized talents, Dr. William Thornton's design won the competition for the Capitol in 1793, eliciting the praise of both Washington and Jefferson. Supervision of construction details was given first to Stephen Hallet and George Hadfield, who tried to make design changes, then to James Hoban, winner of the competition for the design of the President's Mansion. Hoban had the north wing ready for the first session of

The U.S. Capitol

After British Rear Admiral Sir George Cockburn burned Havre de Grace in 1813, he sent a message to the President's Mansion that "he would make his bow" in President James Madison's drawing room. He skipped that formality as he torched the mansion a year later, but riding around Washington on his horse, he managed to keep his troops in line. Simultaneously arrogant and punctilious, according to firsthand reports of his conduct, he insisted on meticulous politeness to the ladies of Washington. Earlier Dolley Madison had packed up valuables in the house and found a wagon to transport them to the Bank of Maryland. While waiting for the president to return from the front lines, she cut out Gilbert Stewart's painting of George Washington from its frame to take with her when she had to flee before her husband arrived.

Congress in the building in November 1800, but further work was assigned to famous professional architects. Benjamin Latrobe completed both north and south wings by 1813 and returned to oversee repairs after the British burned the building in 1814. He was succeeded by Charles Bulfinch, who redesigned the center and the dome and completed restoration.

The complicated architectural history of the Capitol continued through the 19th and 20th centuries with a number of expansions and restorations, including a new, bigger dome. The building is now 751 feet long and 350 feet wide with more than 500 rooms. You can't miss the statue of *Freedom* on the dome. Two marble wings house the Senate and House chambers. The center of the building is composed of the Rotunda, Statuary Hall, and the original Supreme Court and Senate chambers. (The Supreme Court is now housed in its own building, just across First Street NE.)

John Trumbull, an aide to George Washington, painted four of the historical paintings on the Rotunda walls. Did you know that this is a whispering dome? There are a number of places where you can stand and hear people talking from across the Rotunda, which must be inconvenient at times for congressmen.

Library of Congress (202-707-8000; www.loc.gov), 10 First St. SE. Open Mon.–Sat. Two highly literate early presidents are responsible for establishing and promoting the Library of Congress. Before the capital moved to Washington in 1800, John Adams established the library and ordered 740 volumes and three maps from London. His successor, Thomas Jefferson, appointed the first librarian of Congress, established the library's rules and budget, and expanded its scope beyond law and history. Most important, after the burning of the Capitol building had destroyed the original collection of some 3,000 volumes, Jefferson sold his own wide-ranging collection of 6,487 volumes to reestablish the library in 1814. That new beginning redefined it as a national library, a role it continues to play today.

The library now occupies three buildings just southeast of the Capitol, appropriately named for Jefferson, Adams, and Madison. The Jefferson Building has stunning 19th-century architecture and decoration. It houses a permanent exhibit, "American Treasures of the Library of Congress," a collection of more than 200 objects. Rotating exhibits feature Memory (history), Reason (philosophy, law, science, and geography), and Imagination (fine arts, architecture, music, literature, and sports). Halls and reading rooms contain sculpture, paintings, and murals. Look up to see the stained glass in the top of the Great Hall.

Sewall-Belmont House and Museum (202-546-1210, 202-546-3989; www.sewallbelmont.org), 144 Constitution Ave. NE. Open Tue.–Sat. The building dates from around 1800. In 1814 parts of it were burned by the British. Since 1929 the house has been the headquarters of the National Women's Party, and it serves as a museum of American women's political lives. It is thought that Albert Gallatin, secretary of the treasury under Thomas Jefferson, worked on details of the Louisiana Purchase in the house.

THE MALL

The nation's town common, the Mall stretches nearly two miles between the U.S. Capitol in the east and the Lincoln Memorial in the west, with the Washington Monument rising majestically in the middle. Between the Washington Monument and the Capitol, the north and south sides of the Mall are lined with the incomparable—and free—museums of the Smithsonian Institution.

HISTORICAL SITES *and* MUSEUMS

National Museum of American History (202-633-1000; www.american history.si.edu), 14th St. and Constitution Ave. NW. The museum has been under renovation and is scheduled to reopen in the fall of 2008. A new gallery showcasing the Star-Spangled Banner will be in place when the museum reopens. On September 14, 1814, Major George Armistead hoisted the flag over Fort McHenry, and Francis Scott Key wrote his poem, then set the words to music. Mary Pickersgill had made the flag and was paid $405.90 for her work. Armistead was given the flag when he left the military. It passed down through the family and eventually was given to the Smithsonian. As a symbol of our country the flag will continue to be preserved in a specially designed gallery.

A permanent exhibition, "The Price of Freedom: Americans at War," examines the defining role of wars in American history,

Did you know that in 1873 "snippings" of the Star-Spangled Banner were given away as souvenirs to friends and those who had been of service to the nation? Some of the snippings were sent to the museum, but the fifteenth star has never been found.

from the French and Indian War to the present. Highlights include a flintlock pistol given to George Washington by the British general Edward Braddock. When Braddock died on the road after the Battle of Monongahela in 1755 George Washington took over command. Washington's sword and scabbard were last used by him when he reviewed troops during the Whiskey Rebellion in 1794. One of the few Revolutionary War uniforms still left is that of Brigadier General Peter Gansevoort. His troops held Fort Stanwix (in present-day Rome, New York) during the siege led by British general Barry St. Leger in 1777—a defense that contributed to the American victory at Saratoga. The author Herman Melville was Gansevoort's grandson.

Another exhibit, "The American Presidency: A Glorious Burden," was in place on our last visit. It brings back memories of past presidents, no matter when you grew up, and films shown continuously bring their characters and decisions, as well as momentous events, back to life. The exhibit's display of personal possessions begins with George Washington, who used a brass reflector candelabrum when he wrote his farewell address to the nation. In it he warned us against the danger of excessive partisanship and factionalism—a prophetic message that grew out of his experience during the tumultuous 1790s and is still acutely relevant today.

The "Within These Walls" exhibit is large—a 2½-story timber-frame house dating from the 1760s. The house and the exhibition around it tell the stories of five families who lived in the house north of Boston. It represents the lives of ordinary people who have helped determine the course of American history.

Of related interest are 18th-century items in the museum's costume collection, including a silk damask dress made for Eliza Lucas Pinckney from material produced by her own silkworms in colonial South Carolina. A prominent and inventive plantation owner, she also introduced indigo as a cash crop, experimented with flax and hemp, and improved education for children and slaves. Two of her sons were active political leaders, Charles as a signer of the Constitution and Thomas as governor of South Carolina and later minister to Spain and Great Britain.

The exhibit "Jamestown, Quebec, Santa Fe: Three North American Beginnings" will open in 2009. This timely exhibit will feature the 400th anniversary of the founding of Jamestown, Virginia, in 1607. The French followed in 1608 in Quebec and the Spanish in 1609 in Santa Fe. You can trace their developments in the exhibit.

National Museum of the American Indian (202-633-1000; www.american indian.si.edu), 4th St. and Independence Ave. SW. Open daily. The museum was founded on the collection of the former Museum of the American Indian / Heye Foundation in New York City. George Gustav Heye collected thousands of native masterworks around the turn of the century. They include wood and stone carvings and masks from the Northwest Coast; painted and quilled hides, clothing, and feather bonnets from the North American plains; pottery and basketry from the southwestern United States; 18th-century artifacts from the Great Lakes area;

and artifacts from the Caribbean, Mexico, and Central and South America.

You will enter the Potomac atrium, which often offers music, dance, and cultural events. Highlight tours are available during the day. Four permanent exhibitions provide orientation to American Indian history, experience, and beliefs. "Our Universe" examines cosmology, creation, and a spiritual relationship with nature. "Our Peoples"

> ✳ Did you know that Thomas Jefferson wrote the Declaration of Independence in 1776 on a portable lap desk? (Not a laptop!) He had invented the desk and used it all his life.

tells the story of the last 500 years, with emphasis on the various impacts of European settlement and American expansion. "Return to a Native Place" focuses on the Algonquian peoples of the Chesapeake region, and "Our Lives" traces the survival of native communities into the 21st century. A film is presented in the Lelawi Theater on the vitality and diversity of Native American life. The "Window on Collections" is the place to see native-made dolls, beadwork, peace medals, and arrowheads.

National Archives (202-357-5000; www.archives.gov), Constitution Ave. NW between 7th and 9th Sts. Open daily. Reservations are suggested to avoid waiting to enter the building. The Rotunda for the Charters of Freedom features the Declaration of Independence, the Constitution, and the Bill of Rights.

The Public Vaults is a multimedia center beginning with a pathway through the "Record of America." These records change from year to year, but you may see George Washington's handwritten letters or Abraham Lincoln's wartime telegrams. There are five "vaults" from the pathway: "We the People"—records of family and citizenship; "To Form a More Perfect Union"—records of liberty and law; "Provide for the Common Defense"—records of war and diplomacy; "Promote the General Welfare"—records of frontiers; and "To Ourselves and Our Posterity"—keeping records for future generations. Electronic tools allow you to explore these topics. You may research your own family history, if you wish. Perhaps you will want to learn how to care for your family records. The William G. McGowan Theater offers documentary films.

National Portrait Gallery (202-633-1000; www.npg.si.edu), 8th and F Sts. NW. Open daily. This is one of the few Smithsonian museums not directly on the Mall. Located three blocks north of the National Archives, the National Portrait Gallery offers visitors the chance to see portraits from 225 years of history. You can learn about poets, presidents, visionaries and villains, actors and activists—all those who shaped our country's history and culture.

One of the favorite galleries is the Hall of Presidents. It is the largest collection of presidential portraits in the world, outside of the White House. The many images of the 42 presidents (43, if you count both of Grover Cleveland's unconsecutive terms) include Gilbert Stuart's "Lansdowne" portrait of George Washington.

The museum shares its historic Greek-revival building, one of the oldest in Washington, with the Smithsonian American Art Museum, also not to be missed. As the first federal art collection, it dates to 1829, before the Smithsonian was founded in 1846. One collection, "The American Colonies and the Emerging Nation," contains portraits by John Singleton Copley, Charles Willson Peale, and Gilbert Stuart.

Washington Monument (202-426-6841; www.nps.gov/archive/wamo/ monument), 15th St. at Madison Dr. (in the center of the Mall). Open daily. George Washington earned the title Father of His Country for his leadership during the fight for American independence. As president he set the example for the relationships between the three branches of government and started the new government on its way. In gratitude and respect the citizens erected a monument to him. Congress made the decision in 1783, but bureaucratic hurdles and the Civil War slowed progress for a century; the cornerstone was finally laid in 1848, and the monument was finished in 1885. Every state in the Union contributed stones for the interior stairway. Exterior marble came from Maryland and interior granite from Maine. The final design, one of many proposed, produced an elegantly simple obelisk 555 feet tall weighing more than 90,000 tons. Today an elevator, rather than the stairwell, gives access to the top observation area. Visitors need to reserve tickets in advance. You can go online at www.nps.gov one to two days in advance for your tickets. At the kiosk at the base of the monument they are free but run out early, and lines form by 7:30 AM. Some tickets are also available when the door opens at 8:30 AM. Entry starts at 9 AM and stops at 4:45 PM.

WHITE HOUSE AND BEYOND

T he White House is almost directly north of the Washington Monument; between them is the Ellipse, a large, grassy park just north of the Mall.

THE WHITE HOUSE

HISTORICAL SITES *and* MUSEUMS
The White House (202-456-2200; www.nps.gov/whho/), 1600 Pennsylvania Ave. NW. Open Tue.–Sat. Two key buildings in the new federal capital, the President's Mansion and the Capitol, preoccupied Pierre L'Enfant as he studied the land for appropriate sites. He wanted the Capitol on the highest rise and the President's Mansion on a lesser one as two focal points for the whole city. President Washington selected James Hoban, an Irish immigrant who had studied architecture in Dublin, as winner of the President's Mansion design competition in July of 1792 and laid the cornerstone in October. Hoban supervised the construction, and the building was partially finished and barely habitable when John and Abi-

The Washington Monument

gail Adams moved in during the fall of 1800, which was the target date for shifting the capital from Philadelphia to Washington. Every president except George Washington has called it home for his term in office.

Like the Capitol, the President's Mansion has a complicated architectural history, and what we see today is the result of many restorations and additions. The first mansion was burned by the British in 1814 and left a shell. Both Hoban and Benjamin Henry Latrobe supervised reconstruction. The south portico was added in 1824, the north portico in 1830, and the West and East Wings later in the 20th century as more space was needed. A major renovation was carried out after World War II.

Public tours take place Tue.–Sat., 7:30 AM to12:30 PM, for groups of 10 or more. Phone 202-224-3121, the Capitol switchboard, to reach your legislator and arrange a tour; call as long as six months before your visit, since tours often fill early. Arrive 15 minutes before the scheduled time at the Southeast Gate. A photo ID is necessary for those 15 years of age and older. Screening will take place, and some personal items are prohibited.

Visitors walk from room to room at their own pace. You will pass the Vermeil Room and the Library, then walk upstairs to the State floor and through the East, Green, Blue, and Red Rooms and the State dining rooms. Exit from the north portico lobby.

White House Visitor Center (202-208-1631), 1450 Pennsylvania Ave. NW. Open daily. The center has displays on many aspects of the White House, including architecture, furnishings, first families, and social events, plus a 30-minute video.

WEST OF THE WHITE HOUSE

Octagon House (202-638-3221; www.nps.gov/nr/travel/wash/dc), 1799 New York Ave. NW. Open Tue.–Sun. Dr. William Thornton, architect of the Capitol, designed the house, which was built between 1798 and 1800. Colonel John Tayloe owned the house and built it at the suggestion of George Washington. He offered his home to President and Mrs. Madison in 1814 as a temporary "Executive Mansion" after the White House was burned by the British. Madison signed the Treaty of Ghent in the circular room over the entrance to end the War of 1812. The house layout combines a circle, two rectangles, and a triangle. In 1899 the Octagon House became the home of the American Institute of Architects. Today it is owned by the American Architectural Foundation.

DAR Museum (202-628-1776; www.dar.org), 1776 D St. NW. Open Mon.–Sat. The museum offers 33 period rooms with early American furnishings, ceramics, silver, toys, and paintings. The first period room was the New Jersey Room, a 17th-century council chamber. Don't miss the New Hampshire attic containing toys and dolls. A recent acquisition is an 18th-century violin made by Benjamin Banks in Salisbury, England.

GEORGETOWN

Dumbarton House (202-337-2288; www.dumbartonhouse.org), 2715 Q St. NW. Open Tue.–Sat. Ninian Beall patented his property in 1703. Samuel Jackson bought some of the land and built a home in 1799 but went bankrupt before it was finished. Joseph Nourse bought it at public auction and lived there from

1804 to 1813. In 1813 Charles Carroll bought the house, and on August 24, 1814, he hosted Dolley Madison as she fled from the British invaders. The National Society of the Colonial Dames bought the house in 1928 and restored it. Today the house contains early American furnishings, paintings, silver, and ceramics.

SOUTH OF THE WHITE HOUSE

Jefferson Memorial (202-426-6841), Tidal Basin, south end of 15th St. SW. Open daily 24 hours. President Franklin Roosevelt laid the cornerstone in 1939, and the monument was dedicated in 1943, during the depth of World War II. Designed by John Russell Pope to reflect Jefferson's architectural tastes, the memorial is modeled after the Pantheon in Rome. The circular classical dome rises over 54 Ionic columns, and the 19-foot bronze statue of Jefferson inside looks across the Tidal Basin toward the White House. Passages from the Declaration of Independence and some of Jefferson's writings are inscribed in the rotunda.

LODGING

ADAM'S INN B&B
1746 Lanier Place NW
Washington DC 20009
800-578-6807, 202-745-3600;
www.adamsinn.com
A turn-of-the-century B&B one block from the Adams Morgan restaurant district. Twenty-six guest rooms.

THE HAY-ADAMS
One Lafayette Square NW
Washington DC 20006
800-424-5054, 202-638-6600;
www.hayadams.com
On Lafayette Square across from the White House, this luxury hotel was built in 1927 in Italian Renaissance style. Medici tapestry, gold leaf, and antique furnishings. There are 145 guest rooms.

HOTEL GEORGE
15 E St. NW
Washington DC 20001
800-576-8331, 202-347-4200;
www.hotelgeorge.com
This ultra-modern boutique hotel is located three blocks north of the Capitol, near Union Station. There are 139 guest rooms.

MORRISON-CLARK INN
1015 L St. NW
Washington DC 20001
800-332-7898, 202-898-1200;
www.morrisonclark.com
Within the hotel is an 1876 mansion. Some rooms have balconies overlooking a courtyard. Fifty-four guest rooms.

WILLARD INTERCONTINENTAL
1401 Pennsylvania Ave. NW
Washington DC 20004
800-827-1747, 202-628-9100;
www.washington.interconti.com
A short stroll from the White House, this landmark hotel has been restored to its Beaux Arts high style. There are 334 guest rooms.

RESTAURANTS

THE MONOCLE ON CAPITOL HILL
107 D St. NE
202-546-4488
Photographs of congressional members adorn the walls.

MORRISON-CLARK INN RESTAURANT
1015 L St. NW
202-898-1200
Contemporary American cuisine is served in the Victorian dining room.

OLD EBBITT GRILL
675 15th St. NW
202-347-4801
The establishment dates from 1856. They
also serve Sunday brunch.

Current Information

WASHINGTON, D.C., CONVENTION & TOURISM CORP.
901 7th St. NW, fourth floor
Washington, D.C. 20001
800-422-8644, 207-789-7000; www.washington.org

Resources

Colonial and Beyond

Bearor, Bob. *Leading by Example: Partisan Fighters & Leaders of New France, 1660-1760.* Westminster, MD: Heritage Books, 2003.

Billings, Warren M. *Colonial Virginia: A History.* White Plains, NY: KTO Press, 1986.

Boorstin, Daniel J. *The Americans: The Colonial Experience.* New York: Random House, 1958.

Calloway, Colin G. *The Scratch of a Pen: 1763 and the Transformation of North America.* New York: Oxford University Press, 2006.

Channing, Steven A. *Kentucky: A Bicentennial History.* New York: W. W. Norton, 1977.

Dykeman, Wilma. *Tennessee: A Bicentennial History.* New York: W. W. Norton, 1975.

Fischer, David Hackett. *Albion's Seed: Four British Folkways in America.* Oxford, UK, and New York: Oxford University Press, 1989.

Greene, Jack P. *Pursuits of Happiness: The Social Development of Early Modern British Colonies and the Formation of American Culture.* Chapel Hill: University of North Carolina Press, 1988.

Hamilton, Virginia Van der Veer. *Alabama: A Bicentennial History.* New York: W. W. Norton, 1977.

Hawke, David. *The Colonial Experience.* Indianapolis, New York, Kansas City: Bobbs-Merrill, 1966.

Jahoda, Gloria. *Florida: A Bicentennial History.* New York: W. W. Norton, 1976.

Kennedy, Roger G. *Rediscovering America: Journeys through Our Forgotten Past.* Boston: Houghton Mifflin, 1990.

Leder, Lawrence H. *America 1602–1789: Prelude to a Nation.* Minneapolis: Burgess Publishing, 1972.

Lefler, Hugh T. *Colonial North Carolina: A History.* New York: Charles Scribner's Sons, 1973.

Martin, Harold H. *Georgia: A Bicentennial History.* New York: W. W. Norton, 1977.

Middleton, Richard. *Colonial America: A History, 1607–1760.* Cambridge, MA, and Oxford, UK: Blackwell, 1992.

Powell, William S. *North Carolina: A Bicentennial History.* New York: W. W. Norton, 1977.

Reich, Jerome R. *Colonial America.* Englewood Cliffs, NJ: Prentice Hall, 1989.

Rubin, Louis D. *Virginia: A Bicentennial History.* New York: W. W. Norton, 1977.

Skates, John Ray. *Mississippi: A Bicentennial History.* New York: W. W. Norton, 1979.

Taylor, Joe Gray. *Louisiana: A Bicentennial History.* New York: W. W. Norton, 1976.

Wright, Louis B. *South Carolina: A Bicentennial History.* New York: W. W. Norton, 1976.

Revolutionary War

Bohrer, Melissa Lukeman. *Glory, Passion and Principle: The Story of Eight Remarkable Women at the Core of the American Revolution.* New York: Atria Press, 2003.

Ellis, Joseph J. *Founding Brothers: The Revolutionary Generation.* New York: Alfred A. Knopf, 2004.

Ferling, John. *A Leap in the Dark: The Struggle to Create the American Republic.* New York: Oxford University Press, 2003.

Kelly, C. Brian. *Best Little Stories from the American Revolution.* Nashville, TN: Cumberland House, 1999.

McCullough, David. *1776.* New York: Simon & Schuster, 2005.

Raphael, Ray. *A People's History of the American Revolution: How Common People Shaped the Fight for Independence.* New York: The New Press, 2001.

Wood, Gordon S. *Revolutionary Characters: What Made the Founders Different.* New York: The Penguin Press, 2006

Biography

Brady, Patricia. *Martha Washington: An American Life.* New York: Viking, 2005.

Chernow, Ron. *Alexander Hamilton.* New York: Penguin, 2004.

Ellis, Joseph J. *His Excellency George Washington.* New York: Alfred A. Knopf, 2004.

Grant, James. *John Adams: Party of One.* New York: Farrar, Straus, and Giroux, 2005.

Isaacson, Walter. *Benjamin Franklin: An American Life.* New York: Simon & Schuster, 2003.

Index

F